Library of
Davidson College

Persistent Patterns and Emergent Structures in a Waning Century

INTERNATIONAL STUDIES ASSOCIATION

New Dimensions in International Studies
Published in Cooperation with
the International Studies Association

PERSISTENT PATTERNS AND EMERGENT STRUCTURES IN A WANING CENTURY

Edited by
Margaret P. Karns

PRAEGER

PRAEGER SPECIAL STUDIES • PRAEGER SCIENTIFIC

New York • Westport, Connecticut • London

Library of Congress Cataloging-in-Publication Data
Main entry under title:

Persistent patterns and emergent structures in a
 waning century.

 (New dimensions in international studies)
 "Published in cooperation with the International
Studies Association."
 Bibliography: p.
 Includes index.
 1. International relations—Research—Addresses,
essays, lectures. I. Karns, Margaret P. II. International Studies Association. III. Series.
JX1291.P46 1986   327'.072   85-25590
ISBN 0-275-92011-9 (alk. paper)

Copyright © 1986 by Praeger Publishers

All rights reserved. No portion of this book may be
reproduced, by any process or technique, without the
express written consent of the publisher.

Library of Congress Catalog Card Number: 85-25590
ISBN: 0-275-92011-9

First published in 1986

Praeger Publishers, 521 Fifth Avenue, New York, NY 10175
A division of Greenwood Press, Inc.

Printed in the United States of America

The paper used in this book complies with the Permanent
Paper Standard issued by the National Information Standards
Organization (Z39.48-1984).

10 9 8 7 6 5 4 3 2 1

Foreword

At a time when change seems to be everywhere, it is all too easy to ignore the constancies that also mark global life. Change captures our attention because it is exciting intellectually and threatening emotionally, whereas constancy appears dull and repetitive. Yet, there can be no change without the continuities against which it is experienced, measured, and evaluated. Without persistent patterns to which individuals and collectivities are accustomed, there would be no way of recognizing the emergent structures that portend alteration in the conduct of world affairs.

Equally important, it is the tensions inherent in the conflict between old habits and the requirements of new structures that underlie most of the issues on the global agenda. Should old forms of diplomacy be employed to cope with new weapons of war? Can long-standing political structures manage the advent of unfamiliar shifts in the international economy? Can nation-states adequately meet the challenges of a mounting global interdependence, or are innovative political structures (for example, international regimes) needed to address such emergent issues as pollution, terrorism, and currency crises? These are but a few of the more salient questions embedded in the tensions between continuity and change.

Indeed, one could readily argue that these tensions are so persuasive and profound as to be elevated to the status of an organizing premise of any theory of world affairs one might use or evolve. Theories that are static, that treat actors as if their orientations and behavioral patterns are undifferentiated from the past, are bound to be increasingly obsolete as the pace of change feeds on itself in the waning twentieth century. At the same time, theories that ignore the pull of tradition and the compelling nature of habit are bound to be increasingly inappropriate, however rapid the pace of change may prove to be. So analysts have little choice but to come to terms with how they comprehend the interaction between persistent patterns and emergent structures and the resulting tensions between the forces of constancy and those pressing for transformation.

To confront these tensions in a conceptually imaginative and meaningful way is also to have a clear-cut notion of what one understands continuity and change to be. How much does a structure have to be different at time 2 from what it was at time 1 to be classified as a change? How long must deviations in a trend line be for enduring change to be discerned? Indeed, how does one know change when one sees it? These are not trivial questions, and they also point up the large extent to which the tensions between persistent patterns and emergent structures pose important methodological challenges as well as basic theoretical questions.

It is also noteworthy that the tensions between constancy and change in world affairs are one point at which the diverse approaches to the field converge. Empiricists who employ scientific methods cannot avoid efforts to trace the tensions any more than can realists who analyze them qualitatively as struggles for power, or Marxists whose dialectic methods are especially tuned to probe the clash of opposites.

In short, the unifying theme of this volume is important and highly relevant to the future of global life. The essays themselves amply demonstrate that it is a theme that can be creatively and usefully explored.

James N. Rosenau

Preface

This is the third volume in the Praeger series "New Dimensions in International Studies" published by special arrangement with the International Studies Association (ISA). Among the more than 200 panels at the 1985 ISA convention were 9 organized around the theme "Persistent Patterns and Emergent Structures in a Waning Century." My final task as program cochair, but solo editor, was to select the dozen papers that appear in this volume. I sought, in doing so, to retain the richness and diversity that marked those theme panels and the convention as a whole, while searching for a "persistent pattern and emergent structure" to link them together.

I would like to take this opportunity to acknowledge the contributions that James N. Rosenau, president of the ISA, and E. Miriam Steiner, cochair of the 1985 ISA program, made in the selection of the convention theme and the shaping of the panels. In addition, I am indebted to Janet Croon and David Deardoff for assistance with the index and to Sharon Underwood for help with the typing. Finally, I would like to thank the contributors for their willingness to meet a demanding schedule. The diversity of methodological approaches, foci, and ideological orientations contained herein represent the views of the individual authors and are not necessarily those of the editor or of the ISA.

Contents

Foreword
   James N. Rosenau   v

Preface   vii

Introduction
   Margaret P. Karns   1

PART I THE DEVELOPMENT OF INTERNATIONAL RELATIONS THEORY: "THE LONG ROAD"

1. Values and Paradigm Change: The Elusive Quest for International Relations Theory
   Richard W. Mansbach and Yale H. Ferguson   11

2. From Systems Physics to World Politics: Invitation to an Enterprise
   David Wilkinson and Arthur S. Iberall   35

PART II SOURCES AND PATTERNS OF CONFLICT AND VIOLENCE

3. The Structure of the International System and the Relationship Between the Frequency and Seriousness of War
   T. Clifton Morgan and Jack S. Levy   75

4. The Vietnam War and Generational Differences in Foreign Policy Attitudes
   Robert A. Wells   99

5. The War-Weariness Hypothesis: An Empirical Test
   Jack S. Levy and T. Clifton Morgan   126

6. Persisting Patterns of Repression and Rebellion: Foundations for a General Theory of Political Coercion
   Ted Robert Gurr   149

PART III BREAKING THE CYCLE

7   Nonviolent Alternatives in International Studies: Five Questions
     Glenn D. Paige   171

8   Folie à Deux: A Psychological Perspective on Soviet-American Relations
     Morton Deutsch   185

9   Arms Control, Disarmament, and Global Peace and Security
     Michael D. Intriligator and Dagobert L. Brito   197

PART IV CONCEPTUALIZING NONVIOLENCE PATTERNS: POPULATION, RESOURCES, AND ECONOMIC PERFORMANCE

10   Social Time and International Policy: Conceptualizing Global Population and Resource Issues
     John Gerard Ruggie   211

11   Using GLOBUS to Explore Alternative Taxation and Security Policies in the West
     Thomas R. Cusack and Barry B. Hughes   237

12   Multiple Thresholds and Fertility Declines in Third World Populations: Paths to Low Fertility by the Years 2000 and 2010
     Phillips Cutright and Herbert L. Smith   273

Index   303

About the Editor and Contributors

Introduction

Tensions between persistent patterns and emergent structures, between continuity and change, between established ways of interacting and challenges to them, can be discerned at all levels of global life. They touch individuals, small communities, nation-states, and international organizations. They stimulate the reexamination of existing theories and the development of new ones. Key tasks in the study of international politics are the identification of such patterns of change and continuity and analysis of their sources, scope, and future direction—tasks that require the specification of the time frame associated with those patterns.

The approaching end of a century invites both a look backward and a look ahead. How far have students of international politics come in their efforts to develop theories to explain both persistent phenomena and sources and processes of transformation? Closer to the middle of the century, Stanley Hoffmann (1961) described the "long road" to international relations theory. Does that "long road" still stretch unendingly ahead, or have key milestones been reached? And, for those seeking to apply the greater rigor and methodological sophistication of the "hard" sciences, what problems persist and what new structures loom on the horizon? For students of that most persistent of patterns, organized violence or war, what insights have the intensive studies employing both the methodologies and the insights of hard and soft sciences yielded? More importantly, what has been learned with respect to breaking such patterns to enable humankind to avert what all agree would be the certain self-destruction of nuclear holocaust? Finally, what "new" issues and problems loom on the horizon? Are they, in fact, "new" or rather persistent issues for which present circumstances lend new urgency or perspective?

The chapters have been clustered into four sections, the first dealing with the development of international relations theory, the second with patterns of conflict and violence, the third with ways of breaking such patterns, and the fourth with conceptualizations of nonviolence patterns in population, resource, and economic performance issues.

At first glance, it appears that few, if any, chapters deal explicitly with emergent structures, certainly none with international organizations or other such formal structures. It is worth noting in this connection that in the last decade, scholars of international organization themselves have concentrated on informal patterns of organization—transnational and transgovernmental networks and regimes—as means to cooperation, coordination, and management of global problems. As Keohane (1984) has noted, study of these processes does not require abandonment of the realist paradigm as much as changed definition of national interests. Hence, structures are not necessarily discrete, formal entities, but may well, in fact, be patterned, regularized processes of interaction.

THE DEVELOPMENT OF INTERNATIONAL RELATIONS THEORY

Students of world politics have regularly debated whether the field has made progress in the development of theory and the search for appropriate paradigms. A persistent pattern in the field itself, then, is the search for theory, a search traditionally infused with normative concerns.

Richard W. Mansbach and Yale H. Ferguson raise the question of whether, in fact, the discipline of international relations and the social sciences in general have made progress in the march down the "long road." Their response is rather pessimistic despite the admitted advances in data collection and methodology. The entwining of normative and empirical bases of research, they argue, leads to recurring debates involving recurring normative themes. Since dominant theories are more products of fashion and ideology than science, shifts in such theories result from a conjunction of change-inducing events, changing perceptions of issue linkages, and changing stakes.

David Wilkinson and Arthur S. Iberall's optimism with respect to the structures emerging from linkages between disciplines is striking by comparison with Mansbach and Ferguson's pessimism. They challenge our views of the relationship of "hard" science to the study of world politics by proposing the adoption not of scientific method and approach, but of basic paradigm. Arguing that physics is the science whose insights into fundamental principles of movement and change for all systems can be an appropriate grounding for the study of both politics and economics, Wilkinson and Iberall trace the linkages between key concepts and phenomena in the disciplines. They suggest that the answer to the question of why politics persists and appears to be a necessary phenomenon may lie in the physical requirements of all complex systems for command and control mechanisms. They propose the application not of the paradigm of solid-state physics but that of patterned processes, arguing that a system of states is not a structure but a pattern, as is the political "superstructure" within states. Indeed, Wilkinson and Iberall suggest that the "membranes" of students of world politics may be more "permeable" than those of other political scientists because of their lack of adequate paradigms and ongoing debates about the concept of the state.

SOURCES AND PATTERNS OF CONFLICT AND VIOLENCE

Violent conflict or war is the phenomenon most persistently studied by students of international relations beginning with Thucydides. The puzzles associated with the propensity of states to engage in costly violent conflict have not readily yielded to scrutiny by diverse methodologies. T. Clifton Morgan and Jack S. Levy test the hypothesis that the seriousness of war is inversely related to its frequency through two systemic-level variables: polarity and outlets for expansionist activity. Previous studies have suggested that both affect frequency and seriousness. After developing a series of alternative causal models, Morgan and Levy attempt to explain the relationship through partial correlation analysis, analysis of covariance, and multiple regression. In fact, the hypothesis is disconfirmed in spite of the consistent pattern of relationship—a result that emphasizes the multidimensional character of the seriousness variable and the importance of a variety of domestic-level variables. Their conclusions also underscore the lack of understanding of escalatory processes from small to large wars.

The chapter by Robert A. Wells turns to national-level data to examine the attitudes of the Vietnam generation toward the use of military force in the Third World. Assumptions about the lessons of U.S. involvement in Vietnam and studies of the breakdown of consensus on the nature of U.S. global interests and responsibilities would suggest a greater reluctance to use force in the generation for whom that involvement was a socializing event. However, a key question addressed by Wells is whether Vietnam was, in fact, such a socializing event. The results are surprising and raise doubts about the prospects for a new policy consensus inasmuch as reactions to Vietnam cut across generations. There is no negative reaction to the use of military force among the Vietnam generation; rather it is the post-Vietnam generation that is more isolationist and reluctant to undertake overseas commitments.

A different perspective on the question of generation and propensity to use force (or go to war) is presented in the chapter by Jack Levy and Clifton Morgan on war weariness. Noting that previous research has negated any systemic-level contagion, the authors test the hypothesis that at the national level states are less likely to enter new wars or to employ military force short of war in the wake of a war. Focusing on the great powers, they first conduct an aggregate analysis of war behavior of all great powers and then a disaggregated analysis of each power. Particularly important is their recognition of the possibilities of both positive and negative contagion, which, in fact, they find tend to cancel each other out to produce no distinctive pattern for the great powers either individually or collectively to engage in subsequent wars.

Violence, however, is clearly not confined to intrastate relations. Indeed, a casual observation of current events points to the spillover possibilities of domestic violence. In this context, Ted Robert Gurr develops a framework for integrating theories of "why states coerce" with those of "why people rebel" and with the interactions between the two, a subject largely ignored in most conflict analysis. The price of political order in the Third World is an increase in structures of repression and increased reliance on violent action to express opposition for reasons both domestic and international. Incorporating both rational and nonrational decision factors, Gurr notes the existence of a tendency toward equilibrium in the levels of coercion used by all groups contending for power. This leads to a "syndrome of coercion" in societies in which regimes must rely heavily on coercion to retain power and opponents (partisans) are also dependent on it to express their opposition. Most analysts have ignored the interactions between oppositions and regimes, which makes Gurr's theory particularly important. Internationally, the development of such patterns is reinforced by the spread of structures of repression facilitated by transnational communication networks and inspired by the example of a growing number of states that have experienced both revolution and have successfully practiced repression.

In the international organization literature, theories of functionalism and neofunctionalism posit patterns of spillover in habits of cooperation, and it is customary to note the tendency of IGOs to beget other IGOs. There is an inherent bias toward expanding patterns of order at the systemic level—a bias that is not necessarily widely shared beyond the subfield. Indeed, Gurr's conclusion with respect to the proliferation of disorder and repression at the national level in continuing domestic struggles for power clearly represents a contradictory tendency.

As Mansbach and Ferguson suggest, however, the study of international relations is guided by normative concerns. Hence, efforts to develop alternatives to violent conflict, to seek ways of breaking cycles or violence of potential violence, have long had a prominent place.

BREAKING THE CYCLE

In his essay, Glenn D. Paige raises the important question of the feasibility of a "nonkilling society," one in which there is an absence of violence and threats thereof, of preparations for killing, and of deprivation attributable to lethality. Although he does not present arguments to prove his points, Paige does suggest that the chief obstacle is the conviction that such a society is impossible. Like Gurr, he posits a relationship between the means chosen by opposing groups, those in power and out, the advantaged and the disadvantaged. Noting the responsiveness of many to nonviolent alternatives, he calls for the development of a theory for nonviolent global transformation.

The possibility of avoiding violent conflict and of reversing "malignant social processes" such as characterize U.S.–Soviet relations is the subject of Morton Deutsch's chapter drawn from his recently published book, *Distributive Justice: A Social Pyschological Perspective* (1985). The pathological social process that drives the arms race and the threat of nuclear war is a special form of competitive conflict. It is perpetuated by the internal needs of the parties, their tendencies to misjudgments and misperceptions, unwitting commitments that result from efforts to reduce dissonance, self-fulfilling prophecies, and the psychological satisfaction inherent in nuclear gamesmanship, Deutsch suggests. Reversing the process and averting nuclear holocaust are not implausible, however.

One means of breaking cycles of violence is through arms control and disarmament. Michael D. Intriligator and Dagobert L. Brito in their brief essay call attention to fundamental conceptual differences between the two and argue that a principal goal of arms control, in particular, is stability against the outbreak of war. In situations between the superpowers, this has meant mutual deterrence and the seemingly contradictory situation in which nuclear stockpiles are both insurance against the outbreak of war and the source of the problem of nuclear war. Arms control agreements under such conditions may permit increases in weapons levels in order to preserve stability. Hence, future arms control agendas should concentrate on areas of current or future instability, including the erosion of deterrence.

CONCEPTUALIZING NONVIOLENCE PATTERNS

While students of international politics have traditionally been preoccupied with patterns of violent conflict and the means of breaking such cycles, awareness has grown since the early 1970s especially of the importance of other issues: population, resources, economic well-being. Thus, within the discipline, the burgeoning structures of international political economy and ecopolitics attest to changing paradigms.

John Gerard Ruggie's chapter reminds us of the importance of the time frames on which theories are built and conclusions drawn.

Emphasizing how the dimension of time and differences in time frames affect both the definition of specific global population and resource problems as well as the criteria for policy responses, he provides a way of conceptualizing neatly both global resource and population issues. Ruggie's call for attention to the importance of the knowledge base on which informed foreign policy decisions are made reminds us of the prescriptive possibilities of the discipline.

The final two chapters represent efforts to build such knowledge bases. That by Thomas B. Cusack and Barry B. Hughes is a product of the GLOBUS project for modeling global economic structures. The authors suggest how government taxing and spending patterns affect economic performance and the future ability of governments to provide for the general welfare under different scenarios. The results are suggestive, although Cusack and Hughes emphasize that they are still in the early stages of model development, let alone analysis, and that the purpose of GLOBUS is theory building, not forecasting.

Lastly, Phillips Cutright and Herbert L. Smith explore the hypothesis that the use of different thresholds of social and economic development will permit better forecasts of future fertility levels in developing countries than do current models. Thus, they address the critical question of forecasting future demographic trends based on the social ingredients underlying fertility declines, most notably the attainment of two thresholds of life expectancy.

The tensions between the patterns of change and continuity in international politics are part of the fundamental dynamics of global interactions. Whatever shape those interactions take in the twenty-first century will be a consequence of phenomena deeply rooted in the present as well as those that emerge in the future. There will be those who will argue that the patterns of violent conflict have their roots in the nature of humans, or in human social interactions. Yet, Deutsch's chapter on malignant processes suggests room for optimism even while Wells's findings on the effects of Vietnam and Levy and Morgan's conclusions with respect to war weariness leave us pessimistic about the prospects for breaking persistent patterns. The difficulties of developing theories and paradigms to inform the study of international politics as well as the complexities of most phenomena, however, remind us that the "long road" still looms before us. Forecasting is a risky business even in the seemingly more predictable area of demographic trends. Analysts bring different normative concerns to their work and adopt different time frames as the bases of their conclusions, thus complicating the task of cumulating knowledge and reminding us that what is perceived as persistent pattern or emergent structure is a function of the different perspectives and time frames.

REFERENCES

Deutsch, Morton. 1985. *Distributive Justice: A Social Psychological Perspective.* New Haven, CT: Yale University Press.
Hoffmann, Stanley. 1961. "International Relations: The Long Road to Theory," *World Politics* 13 (April):3 pp. 346-77.
Keohane, Robert O. 1984. *After Hegemony: Cooperation and Discord in the World Political Economy.* Princeton, NJ: Princeton University Press.

I
The Development of International Relations Theory: "The Long Road"

1
Values and Paradigm Change: The Elusive Quest For International Relations Theory
Richard W. Mansbach and Yale H. Ferguson

It is difficult to find a major work on international relations that either does not urge that the discipline synthesize a new paradigm or does not itself offer such a paradigm.[1] Implicit in such works is the assumption that the "constellation of beliefs, values, techniques, and so on shared by the members"[2] of the international relations fraternity is undergoing change in the manner in which science, according to Thomas Kuhn, evolves, for example, that our basic understanding of the world around us is growing even as theoretical consensus breaks down.

Kuhn's analysis of the natural sciences suggests that when a discipline is confronted by significant and unanswerable anomalies, it ultimately enters a period of crisis during which an existing paradigm is replaced by another that can effectively overcome these anomalies. For Kuhn, understanding and knowledge proceed progressively; earlier paradigms become no more than historical curiosities to subsequent generations of scholars. "Why," asks Kuhn, "should the student of physics, for example, read the works of Newton, Faraday, Einstein, or Schrodinger, when everything he needs to know about these works is recapitulated in a far briefer, more precise, and more systematic form in a number of up-to-date textbooks?"[3] For a discipline in need of confidence that progress is indeed occurring, Kuhn's analysis provides a confidence-building rationale for apparent disarray. After all, "during a pre-paradigm period, when there is a multiplicity of competing schools, evidence of progress is very hard to find," and "during periods of revolution... doubts are repeatedly expressed about the very possibility of continued progress if one or another of the opposed paradigms is adopted."[4]

There is thus actually more at stake for those who claim that our discipline is a science than the outcome of methodological controversies. The claim to scientific status among scholars of international relations appears to be necessary for many of us to maintain a sense of intellectual and institutional well-being in the face of disciplinary adversity. To the extent that we can manage to keep up our faith in James Rosenau's assertion "that the same methods that unraveled the mysteries of atomic structure can reveal the dynamics of societal behavior,"[5] we may also continue to trust that progress is taking place despite the theoretical chaos around us.

Our intention is not to reopen the "science" versus "traditionalist" controversy,[6] but rather to suggest that there are sufficient differences between the evolution of theoretical change in the social sciences, including international relations, and Kuhn's version of the natural sciences that his analysis may not be applicable. If that is the case, our perception of progress may be illusory. In addition, we wish to describe briefly a most un-Kuhnian version of the way in which ideas emerge and compete in international relations.

THE SOURCE AND ROLE OF VALUES

Kuhn himself highlights the most significant difference between the natural and social sciences when he notes "the unparalleled insulation of mature scientific communities from the demands of the laity and of everyday life."[7]

> In this respect... the contrast between natural scientists and many social scientists proves instructive. The latter often tend, as the former almost never do, to defend their choice of a research problem... chiefly in terms of the social importance of achieving a solution.[8]

In other words, the work of the social scientist is generally infused by a commitment to serve the needs of the society of which he/she is a member.

The importance of Kuhn's observation was appreciated two decades before by E. H. Carr when he wrote:

> The science of international politics has... come into being in response to a popular demand. It has been created to serve a purpose.... At first sight, this pattern may appear illogical. Our first business, it will be said, is to collect, classify and analyse our facts and draw out inferences; and we shall then be ready to investigate the purpose to which our facts and our deductions can be put. The

processes of the human mind do not, however, appear to develop in this logical order.... Purpose, which should logically follow analysis, is required to give it both its initial impulse and its direction.[9]

Thus, the facts that scholars amass and the phenomena with which they preoccupy themselves are selections derived initially from a set of specific normative concerns. In proceeding in this fashion, they inevitably decide to ignore other facts and phenomena. If they choose to take cognizance of the latter at a future date, that choice reflects a shift in normative concerns rather than a paradigm change in the Kuhnian sense.[10] Carr sees this as a condition of the physical sciences as well, but notes correctly how much more difficult it is to isolate facts from values in social science:

> The purpose is not, as in the physical sciences, irrelevant to the investigation and separable from it: it is itself one of the facts. In theory, the distinction may no doubt still be drawn between the role of the investigator who establishes the facts and the role of the practitioner who considers the right course of action. In practice, one role shades imperceptibly into the other. Purpose and analysis become part and parcel of a single process.[11]

This synthesis of purpose and analysis is clearly in evidence in R. J. Rummel's autobiographical reflection, which could probably be echoed by many in our profession. "My lifelong superordinate goal," Rummel declares, "has been to eliminate war and social violence; only by understanding this goal's genesis and enveloping cognitive structure can Dimensionality of Nations Project (DON) research and my current reorientation be grasped. For to me science or quantitative research are not the aims, but tools to be pragmatically applied to doing something about war."[12] How different from this was the normative commitment of the German historian Heinrich Von Treitschke when he thundered that the "grandeur of history lies in the perpetual conflict of nations, and it is simply foolish to desire the suppression of their rivalry.[13] How well these contrasting admissions reveal the starkly different normative climates of the societies in which they were written!

In many ways, Jacob Bronowski's arguments against the "naturalistic fallacy" in the natural sciences are, if anything, even more germane to the social sciences. Bronowski suggests that normative consequences inhere in scientific discovery for at least three reasons.[14] The first is that discovery reveals that certain forms of conduct are "obviously ridiculous" and that one ought to tailor one's own actions so as not to be ridiculous. The second is that science informs us of our capabilities as human beings and "that it is right that we should practice those gifts." Finally, and most importantly for Bronowski, scientists must behave in certain ways in order to learn what is true, which is the object of their calling: "What is the good of talking about what is, when in fact you are told how to behave in order to discover what is true. "Ought" is dictated by "is" in the actual inquiry for knowledge. Knowledge cannot be gained unless you behave in certain ways."[15]

In large measure, theoretical debates among political scientists reflect different normative commitments that are indirectly revealed in competing claims over which actors should be studied, which level of analysis is most appropriate, which variables are critical, and which issues are most pressing. What is striking about these debates and what distinguishes them from debates in the natural sciences is that essentially the same arguments and emphases tend to recur over and over again through time, despite superficial changes in concepts and language. As we shall suggest, such debates recur because they revolve around enduring normative themes.[16] The key assertions of realism and idealism, for example, have been present in intellectual discourse about international relations at least since Thucydides.

Thucydides's *Melian Dialogue* and Thrasymachus's argument with Socrates in Plato's *Republic* are enduring reflections of the antimony between power and justice. Centuries of European political theorists served the roles of "realists" and "idealists." Machiavelli and those later known as Machiavellians consciously propounded their versions of realism in contrast to the so-called idealists of their time.[17] The old realist–idealist debate is currently manifested in debates among structural realists, neo-Marxists, and unrepentant neofunctionalists.

Although the normative elements in these debates are, perhaps, less evident in contemporary international relations discourse than in the past, owing to conscious efforts of social scientists to be "scientific" and "value-free," the debates are no less value-laden than their precursors. Dominant schools of thought in international relations are as much a part of the *Zeitgeist* of their age as are dominant theories of art and literature; all are part of the *ductus* of a culture.[18] Indeed, the contemporary devotion to science in international relations is a phenomenon that will always be associated with the late twentieth-century United States and the numerous symbols of its "modernity"—pragmatism, technology, nonrepresentational art, functional architecture, and so forth. All reflect a similar ethos, fully as much as did *The Trojan Women* of Euripides and Thucydides's *History*.[19]

Whatever the prospects, then, for applying the scientific method to studying political phenomena, political science will continue to develop more like one of the arts than one of the sciences unless or until political scientists can isolate themselves from the milieu whose problems they seek to address. This, we believe, is an impossible task and probably not one worth undertaking.

THE REALIST "PARADIGM"

Scholars of international relations who are content to view their discipline as evolving in a Kuhnian manner are wont to cite the fate of realism, which, they claim, once assumed the role of a paradigm but has had to give way in the face of persistent anomalies. It is certainly the case that in the years following World War II, realism came to dominate the field. It even had an "exemplar" in Hans J. Morgenthau's *Politics Among Nations* (1948); and, in general, textbooks from the 1940s to the end of the 1960s tended to share realist assumptions.[20] Realist theory, especially as articulated by Morgenthau, was at once elegant and parsimonious, but the theory did not achieve ascendancy simply because it was able to account for anomalies that its competitors had failed to explain. In fact, so-called idealist and Marxist theory can explain the outbreak of World War II quite as convincingly as can realism. Although the facts of history do not change, dominant interpretations do vary as those facts are viewed through changing normative lenses. And normative disputes of this ilk are anchored in genuine political and policy quarrels among practitioners seeking to cope with life and death issues; such disputes are not the stuff of ivory towers alone. In recent years, this phenomenon has been most clearly reflected in analyses of the Cold War, but it was equally characteristic of analyses of earlier wars as well.

Realists accused Western statesmen in the interwar period of having "deprecated" power in favor of legal and moral solutions to the problems of their time. In doing so, according to realists, idealists confused theory with practice and confounded scientific with normative analysis. Yet, for the most part, the supposedly offending statesmen were quite as aware of the balance of power as their realist critics but were as unable as are contemporary analysts to assess that balance in a manner that could provide clear policy guidelines. In addition, they were conscious of the role that balance-of-power politics had played in bringing about the conflagration of 1914. Furthermore, national power, as Morgenthau himself notes, includes such unmeasurable elements as "national character," "national morale," "the quality of diplomacy," and "the quality of government."[21] Diplomats' efforts to formulate policy sought to account for these several factors, yet realist criticisms come perilously near to focusing only on military factors. Ultimately, Morgenthau admits that the calculation of national power "is an ideal task and, hence, incapable of achievement,"[22] and this admission forces us to ask why realists think that they could have done better. Ironically, the factor that was least understood by interwar politicians was one for which realists cannot account: the motives and personality of Hitler, who refused to behave according to the dictates of balance of power. History revealed to the realists (and to many of the practitioners of that time as well) that the interwar statesmen should have acted differently. Unfortunately, theory that can provide answers only retrospectively is of limited value.

The victory of realism after World War II, then, supports the notion that theory in international relations evolves somewhat differently than does the almost dialectical manner in which Kuhn views paradigm change in the natural sciences.[23] Realism was not merely a product of "the recognition that nature has somehow violated the paradigm-induced expectations,"[24] but also represented a condemnation of earlier norms brought about by the revolutionary effects of the war. For Kuhn, a paradigm shift occurs not because the natural universe itself changes but because something about that universe is revealed for which the existing paradigm cannot account. In contrast, realism achieved ascendancy because the political universe itself changed after 1945. The occurrence of World War II served less to reveal anomalies in an existing paradigm than to provide normative justification for the claims of power thinkers who had been competing with "idealist" rivals for centuries. In the same way, World War I had previously provided normative justification for Wilsonians to assert the superiority of moral universalism over "narrow nationalists" and "balance-of-power" advocates, and the early years of the interwar period seemed to represent the final victory of the Gladstone-Cobden school over the adherents of Disraeli.

For their part, twentieth-century realists were not especially innovative theoretically; nor did they claim to be, as reflected in their repeated references to eighteenth-century European political practice and the ideas of Alexander Hamilton as sources of their wisdom.[25] It was not, then, that they could account for anomalies in an existing body of thought, but that they eloquently asserted the normative superiority of the national interest over universalism. The key to their victory lay less in the power of their assumptions than in the claim that their work was "empirical and pragmatic"[26] and that they could discern a "science of international politics."[27] For a number of reasons, this claim exercised a powerful attraction in the years after World War II; the soil was indeed fertile for what Morgenthau declared to be "another great debate."[28] Realism entailed a rejection of ideologies such as those that had legitimized the excesses of the previous years, as well as of those institutional and legal efforts to eliminate world conflict that had failed in the 1920s and 1930s. Moreover, realism meshed nicely with the United States' self-image at a time that the country had so clearly emerged as *primus inter pares* in the global system.[29]

U.S. science and economic productivity had won the war, and the atom bomb would secure the peace. Of course, pragmatism, positivism, faith in scientific advancement, and free enterprise themselves constituted an ideology, but one that appeared to be objective and rational. In this context, realism was especially attractive because it, too, appeared to offer an alternative to ideological and moralistic analysis. "Intellectually," declared Morgenthau, "the political realist maintains the autonomy of the political sphere, as the economist, the lawyer, the moralist maintain theirs,"[30] a claim that served the paradigmatic purpose of providing disciplinary boundaries and predicted the reductionist preferences of later scholars. Although, like Machiavelli, realists were accused of being amoral, like Machiavelli, they, in fact, provided a rather clear set of moral and prescriptive dicta that constituted the obligations of official decision makers seeking to serve the national interest. Indeed, one of the ironies of the realist triumph is that the realists were able to make a powerful moral case against their intellectual adversaries by asserting the value-free character of their theories, while simultaneously providing moral and prescriptive guidelines for a generation of scholars and statesmen.

Surveys have shown that Morgenthau is the political theorist whose ideas have been most familiar to U.S. policymakers.[31] Bernard Brodie writes of a "strong and rigid...professional tradition" among them, holding that the intrusion of moral considerations is "inherently mischievous, that is...likely to cause the warping of what otherwise would be trimly correct thinking about foreign affairs."[32] Richard J. Barnet summarizes this position:

> Those who run nations cannot be unselfish, generous, or even honest in the jungle world of international relations because such impulses are not reciprocated. To recognize external limits on discretion is to compromise the interests of the American people and of future generations for whom the statesman is supposed to act as trustee.

To the realist, he continues, "what was expedient also became right.... Neither God, law, world opinion, right reason, or any other outside standard was recognized as a limit on their own discretion, for that discretion, they convinced themselves, would be exercised in pursuit of the highest moral values."[33]

In justifying expediency, realism neatly reinforced the ideological tenet of "pragmatism" that has been central to U.S. culture and for policymakers who are the product of that culture. For instance, David Halberstam reports:

> In the early days of the [Kennedy] Administration [the word pragmatism] had been used so frequently that David Brinkley, writing the introduction of an early book of portraits of the Kennedy people, would dwell on that single word, and note that at an early Washington cocktail party a woman had gone around the room asking each of the hundred people there if he was a pragmatist.[34]

Pragmatism is an example of what might be termed "the attitude of ideology toward itself," advancing as it does the proposition that "practical" responses to the "real world" should take precedence over the dictates of ideology (other than pragmatism). In fact, pragmatism has regularly allowed decision makers to conceal from themselves the ideological premises behind their policies and, less often, to congratulate themselves on the "rightness" of their policies when the dictates of ideology and the demands of the "real world" have seemed to coincide. The concealing function of pragmatism has been enhanced by its links to the realist concept of the "national interest," purporting as it does to provide an "objective" standard for national policy. Of course, as numerous critics have pointed out, this supposed standard is so vague that its interpretation cannot help but involve a highly subjective judgment. Arnold Wolfers states:

> Political formulas such as 'national interest' may not mean the same thing to different people. They may not have any precise meaning at all. Thus, while appearing to offer guidance and a basis for broad consensus they may be permitting everyone to label whatever policy he favors with an attractive and possibly deceptive name.[35]

Realism thus provided the legerdemain through which the sow's ear of the pragmatist's expediency could be converted into the silk purse of the pursuit of the national interest.

The realist's association of the national interest concept with the "struggle for power," in turn, has reinforced yet another aspect of what Richard Barnet sees as part of the U.S. tradition, a phenomenon that he terms "bureaucratic machismo." He writes: "One of the first lessons a national security manager learns after a day in the bureaucratic climate of the Pentagon, State Department, White House, or CIA is that toughness is the most highly prized virtue." U.S. officials have customarily adopted a self-consciously "tough," "hard-nosed" brand of decision making and evidenced a profound distrust of policies favored by "soft-headed," "liberal" "idealists" and "intellectuals."[36]

Many intellectuals, too, were influenced by realism. Realism's apparent rejection of institutional and legal mechanisms and its assertion of the value-free nature of theory were instrumental in encouraging the behavioral and scientific revolutions in international politics. Morgenthau's assertion that realism "requires indeed a sharp distinction between the desirable and the possible"[37] was, especially in the 1960s, repeated by a generation of scholars who believed that it was possible to separate values from the study of political phenomena. For the most part, these scholars retained the assumptions of realism and, in retrospect, performed the task of "normal science" in the Kuhnian sense.[38] Their contributions were primarily methodological rather than theoretical and served to institutionalize and legitimize realism's key assumptions.

THE VICISSITUDES OF THEORY: THE DECLINE OF REALISM

The 1970s witnessed a concerted assault on the several realist assumptions—the centrality of the unitary state as actor, the autonomy of the international and domestic realms of politics, and the existence of the single issue of managing power—accompanied by an implicit "declaration of independence" from the doctrine.

Among the principal lines of attack were those that highlighted nonrational sources of decision makers' behavior,[39] the impact of situations on decision making,[40] the importance of bureaucratic politics and organizational behavior,[41] the significance of transnationalism and interdependence,[42] the role of nonstate actors,[43] and the influence of issues on behavior.[44] In a word, realism was no longer a "disciplinary matrix."[45]

None of the above phenomena identified by these scholars as detracting from realism was new, and none was in any sense "discovered" in the 1970s. For example, as regards nonrational sources of behavior, even as realism was in the ascendant the ideas of Freud were entering the discipline;[46] the evolution of the containment policy and the reorganization of the U.S. defense and foreign policy establishment were providing clear cases of the impact of situation and bureaucracies;[47] the integration of Western Europe was revealing some of the implications of interdependence and transnationalism;[48] the emergence of revolutionary and anticolonial movements and of multinational corporations reflected the potential roles of nonstate actors, while the appearance of a North–South axis, alongside an East–West axis, illustrated the role of issues.[49]

What had changed was the frame of reference of scholars and the ethos of the society in which they were working. Although many factors were involved in bringing about these changes, the decline in U.S. hegemony symbolized by Vietnam, the growing salience of nonmilitary problems with an economic or environmental basis, and growing fears of nuclear war encouraged scholarly criticisms that were grounded in an unarticulated criticism of realist norms.

The Vietnam debacle suggested that the elements of power were even more obscure than had been realized, that national power was contextual, and that military capabilities had limited utility. Successive energy crises highlighted the existence of fragile economic interdependence and the finite nature of key resources. Endemic stagflation in the West pointed to the central role of economics in national power, reinforced the growing sense of interdependence, and focused attention upon issues without any evident military dimension. In many ways, successive environmental traumas had the same effects. Finally, the demise of détente and the achievement of technomilitary breakthroughs unleashed dormant fears in the United States and Europe regarding the adequacy of nuclear deterrence as a formula for managing conflict.

These events promoted a shift in the nature of political vocabulary and dialogue. That altered vocabulary emphasized the linked fate of humanity as a whole, processes and interactions only partly controlled by national decision makers, and potential outcomes in which the differences between "winning" and "losing" were unclear. For the most part, these were precisely the concerns that had motivated political thinkers after 1919 and had shaped their vocabulary and dialogue.

Although a feedback loop of sorts is obviously involved, political dialogue is most accurately seen as a reflection, rather than a cause, of the normative temper of an era. It is the shift in that temper, rather than the appearance of anomalies, that seems to stimulate paradigm shifts in international relations. Such a shift occurs under conditions of rapid change and stressful events that generate an atmosphere of unpredictability and instability, a sense that somehow new and baleful forces are at work that will alter existing conditions in ways not as yet fully apprehended. In these circumstances, prior patterns of behavior and standard procedures no longer seem able to perform the tasks for which they were established or appear unsuited for new tasks that are identified.

Although the causal sequence remains unclear, such periods seem to be associated with the genesis of sharply different religious, scientific, social, and ideological concepts; qualitative technological changes; and major unanticipated events, especially wars and environmental disasters. Often these occur together, though not necessarily so. Fifth-century Greece was one such period. This era witnessed the development of tragedy by the Athenian poets, the philosophic relativism of the Sophists, the introduction of empirical diagnosis by Hippocrates of Cos, the development of mining at Mount Laurion (which provided precious metals for a monied economy), the earthquake and helot revolt in Sparta (464 B.C.), the plague in Athens (430 B.C.), and the Peloponnesian War. These developments provided the bases for Thucydides's view of the world. The late fifteenth through the early seventeenth century in Europe was another tumultuous period. A renewal of the plague; the rise of Protestantism; the ideas of Brahe, Galileo, and Kepler regarding the physical universe; the spread of movable type; the rifling of guns and the boring of cannons; and, finally, the Thirty Years' War—all combined to constitute a sharp break with the past and to usher in fundamental revisions of the normative order. Changes of such magnitude pointed to new issues in need of resolution and/or new opportunities to be exploited.

Intervening between changing conditions and revision of the normative order are perceptions of linkages among stakes at issue in the global arena and the hierarchy of issues on the global agenda.[50] Fears of value deprivation and/or identification of new opportunities for value satisfaction occur as old stakes disappear and new ones emerge. Although these processes are continuous, they are especially intense during periods of potential or actual shifts in the global status hierarchy when the enfeeblement of high-status actors encourages challenges to an existing distribution of stakes and the energizing of low-status actors spurs their ambition.[51] Thus, the dramatic increase in German industrial and military strength and significant medical advances in the second half of the nineteenth century, coupled with the relative decline of Great Britain and France, made available as stakes territories in Africa that previously had been seen as preempted or qualitatively inaccessible. Similarly, the decline of traditional trade unions in the West and the growing obsolescence of traditional industries at a time of recession and high unemployment in the 1980s have transformed into stakes many social and economic benefits that until recently were regarded as sacrosanct.

As new stakes become available for, and old ones removed from, contention, new issues emerge, old ones are redefined, and the salience of issues on the global agenda may shift dramatically. Changes in issue salience redirect attention toward the values that underlie the newly important issues and away from values that are associated with declining issues.[52] Accordingly, the value of prosperity, which had dominated the value hierarchy during the Great Depression, became a secondary concern with the outbreak of World War II and its aftermath, during which time physical security and freedom became principal preoccupations. As memories of the war receded in the 1960s and 1970s and the relative salience of key issues continued to change, values like peace, health, and human dignity assumed greater importance.

Changes in the global agenda of issues and in the value hierarchy invariably produce new normative emphases, which are reflected in what we have called the normative temper of an era. Normative shifts occur along several dimensions, often at the same time. Among the most important of these are mutability–immutability, optimism–pessimism, competitiveness–community, and elitism–nonelitism.

Mutability–immutability is the degree to which it is believed that human affairs and the conditions that shape them can or will be purposefully modified. In traditional cultures, the status quo in human affairs is accepted as inevitable and unchanging and the conditions in which humans find themselves are viewed as not subject to manipulation. Arguments that attribute behavior to the supernatural or to human nature commonly assume immutability. By contrast, modern Western science assumes almost unlimited mutability. The normative implication of a belief in immutability is that efforts to change the human condition are, at best, a waste of time and, at worst, dangerous and illusory. In any event, such efforts ought not to be made. Realism in its several versions tends to view political conditions as relatively immutable, whether owing to "human nature" (Morgenthau), "original sin" (Niebuhr), or system anarchy (Waltz). Although realists accept that alterations in the distribution of power continuously occur, they see a struggle for power as a permanent feature of international politics. Nowhere is this emphasis on immutability more succinctly expressed than in Morgenthau's observation that, "human nature, in which the laws of politics have their roots, has not changed since the classical philosophies of China, India, and Greece endeavored to discover these laws. Hence novelty is not necessarily a virtue in political theory, nor is old age a defect."[53]

This emphasis leads realists to criticize those who seek to reform prevailing conditions; such individuals are "divorced from the facts ...and informed by prejudice and wishful thinking," and the laws of politics, rooted as they are in human nature, are "impervious to our preferences."[54] In the United States and Europe, at least, such an emphasis found ready acceptance after World War II with the apparent failure of bold experiments like the League of Nations. Those who sought to make fundamental changes were dismissed as "idealists." Even Marxism-Leninism, with its putative belief in the march of history and the uplifting of humankind, seemed to have lost its vigor in Stalin's conservative empire. Since experimentation entailed an element of peril, "prudence" became the prescriptive hallmark of realism. The prudent leader understands the immutability of historical laws and eschews bold efforts to transform humankind or the global system.

Optimism-pessimism constitutes a second key normative dimension. Unlike mutability-immutability, which describes the degree to which it is believed that change can be engineered by human intervention, optimism-pessimism refers to the direction in which change is taking place, whether such change is the consequence of purposeful modification or not. More simply, it describes the answer given to the question, Are conditions likely to improve or not? Nevertheless, as the previous discussion of realism suggests, those who see conditions as relatively immutable are also likely to view change in a distinctly pessimistic light. After all, if the forces of change cannot be governed and directed, change itself is likely to be fickle, unpredictable, and ultimately dangerous. There are, of course, significant exceptions to this intellectual propensity. Classical Marxists, for example, view history itself as an engine of progress governed by laws of economic development that will in time improve the human condition. As Kenneth Waltz points out, even those who start from an assumption that human nature is relatively immutable can be divided into "optimists" and "pessimists."[55] There are obviously degrees of immutability that allow for varying assessments of the potential for change.

Overall, however, optimism is at least partly a function of belief in mutability. Natural and behavioral scientists and social reformers share a common acceptance of the possibility that conditions and behavior can be improved by the accumulation of knowledge and the application of that knowledge. (How clearly this emerges from the passages cited earlier from Bronowski!) The normative implication of such optimism is that it is the obligation of those with knowledge and insight to apply these for the benefit of humanity.[56] In the context of political life, liberalism tends to be associated with optimism and conservatism with pessimism.[57]

It is no coincidence that intellectual optimism and scientific advance are associated with eras and places in which the norms of a culture were also characterized by a wave of optimism—Renaissance Italy, late eighteenth-century France, Edwardian England, and pre-Depression United States. While pessimism encourages political conservatism and inertia, waves of optimism inspire great efforts to give history a push. Political revolutions, for example, generally occur in the context of growing optimism, or at least a belief that the improvement of conditions is probable once the weight of existing institutions is swept away. As the historian George Soule observed:

> When the people are in their most desperate and miserable condition, they are often least inclined to revolt, for then they are hopeless.... Only after their position is somewhat improved and they have sensed the possibility of change, do they revolt effectively against oppression and injustice. What touches off insurrection is hope, not lack of it, rising confidence, not bleak suffering.[58]

Wordsworth's description in book 12 of *Prelude* of his feelings at the time of the French Revolution captures perfectly the optimism of that era:[59] "Bliss was it in that dawn to be alive,/But to be young was very heaven!"

In the context of international relations theory, the ascendance of realism reflected in part a rejection of the prevailing optimism of the 1920s and early 1930s. Yet realism is not a doctrine of unrelieved gloom. Realists do see it as possible to ameliorate the effects of international conflict by the judicious management of power. Indeed, some neorealists, like Kenneth Waltz, can be regarded as cautiously optimistic.[60] As a whole, advocates of a scientific approach to the discipline in the 1960s, while retaining many of realism's critical assumptions, reflected an increasing optimism about the prospects for overcoming the most dangerous problems of international relations insofar as the methods of the natural sciences were to be applied to an understanding of them. However, growing fears about environmental, political, and economic trends in the early 1970s produced a renewal of pessimism that was perhaps most vividly reflected in Robert Heilbroner's *Inquiry into the Human Prospect*:

> At this final stage of our inquiry, with the full spectacle of the human prospect before us, the spirit quails and the will falters. We find ourselves pressed to the very limit of our personal capacities, not alone in summoning up the courage to look squarely at the dimensions of the impending predicament, but in finding words that can offer some plausible relief in a situation so bleak. There is now nowhere to turn other than to those private beliefs and disbeliefs that guide each of us through life.[61]

And this pessimism was a significant aspect of the revolt against realism and the reemergence of doubts regarding the ultimate prospects for a science of international relations.

A third normative variable that is central to international relations theory is that of *competitiveness–community*, that is, the degree to which welfare and/or deprivation is perceived in relative or absolute terms. Are evaluations of status and value satisfaction made in comparison with others, or are they made in terms of an absolute level that changes over time? The former emphasizes competition for scarce resources, and the latter linked fates and interdependence. When evaluation is made in relative terms, it implies that greater value satisfaction can be achieved only at the expense of others; changes in the absolute level of well-being matter less than the distribution of costs and benefits. Outcomes are viewed in zero-sum, rather than positive- or negative-sum, terms.

It is commonly argued that the emphasis on competition intensifies as perceptions of scarcity grow. This is not, however, necessarily the case. Highly competitive doctrines such as Adam Smith's version of capitalism or late nineteenth-century Social Darwinism became popular in exuberantly expansionist eras. In contrast, recent doctrines of interdependence and "limits to growth," which are at least in part based on perceptions of scarcity, emphasize the shared condition of humankind and the absolute nature of value enhancement and deprivation. Nor does there seem to be any necessary connection between competitiveness–community and optimism–pessimism, despite the common assertion that pessimism encourages competitive evaluations.

Realism, with its emphasis on national interest, clearly falls on the competitive end of the spectrum. Morgenthau's definition of international politics "as a continuing effort to maintain and to increase the power of one's own nation and to keep in check or reduce the power of other nations"[62] highlights the realist emphasis on the relative nature of status and security in the global system. Although there is an implication that a scarcity of political goods conditions the intensity of competition, it is the absence of central power and trust that is fundamental in the analysis. Efforts to equate the national interest with a global interest through international law and organization are dismissed as "legalistic-moralistic,"[63] "too wildly improbable,"[64] or, more generally, idealistic. Efforts to achieve justice must, in the realist vision, give way to the more basic search for security that can limit the prospect of relative loss with scant possibility for universal gain.[65]

In practice, emphasizing competitive elements in global politics necessitates undervaluing prospects for international, supranational, or transnational organization, whether formal or informal. Actors that are more powerful, wealthier, or more skillful should, it is implied, see to their own well-being and security before concerning themselves with some "abstract" global good unless it can somehow be shown that the two are identical.[66]

The devaluation of the norm of equality by those who emphasize competition tends as well to make them relatively elitist in their perceptions of global politics. This normative dimension entails perceptions of who ought to be involved in the making of decisions and the management of issues. Elitists emphasize that the possession of some attribute—wealth, power, skill, and so forth—renders some individuals or groups legitimate leaders (and others, followers).

Among international relations theorists, elitism takes the form of an assertion that certain actors in the global system are and ought to be responsible for significant outcomes that affect the system as a whole. An elitist emphasis can be manifested at different levels of analysis. At the system level, for instance, it may assume the form of claims that the discipline should limit its focus to "sovereign" entities and exclude nongovernmental and transnational interactions. In more extreme form, it may implicitly or explicitly entail the assertion that only the governments of "great powers" or "superpowers" matter and that the interests and aspirations of minor states can (and, by implication, ought to) be ignored except in unusual circumstances.

Realist admiration for the virtues of the eighteenth-century balance of power is elitist in this sense. Among contemporary scholars, Kenneth Waltz's unabashed preference for bipolarity is perhaps the clearest expression of the elitist norm.[67] Waltz believes that the world has remained fundamentally bipolar since 1945 and, more importantly, thinks this is a virtue. He argues persuasively that bipolarity ensures greater stability than any alternative structure and appears to restrict himself to empirical and prescriptive analysis. However, there is a clear, if unstated, normative position underlying the analysis. For both Waltz and realists in general, the avoidance of catastrophic war is the most important of values. In order to secure this, they are prepared to assume as irrational the value hierarchies of those for whom the risks of war might be preferable to the perpetuation of unbearable political, economic, and social conditions. They assume that the great powers are somehow more responsible than lesser powers, presumably because the former have so much more to lose than the latter. The poor or the weak might be tempted to behave rashly and promote instability in order to improve their status. Whether this argument takes the form of opposition to nuclear proliferation or praise for the ability of the balance of power to preserve the independence of major states, it is profoundly conservative and elitist. In effect, it is an international version of the argument that there should be a property or educational qualification for voting in democracies.[68]

The Wilsonian critique of balance-of-power politics was dismissed by realists as utopian because it did not sufficiently take account of the role of power in international relations. Yet, however "unscientific"

Woodrow Wilson's analysis of international politics was, what probably incensed realists most was his denunciation of the prevailing elitist ethic. It is not simply that Wilson denounced aristocratic rule within states, but also that he rejected a condominium of the great powers. His assertion of the rights of nationalities and ethnic minorities, along with his praise of democracy and the rights of small states, constituted a brief in favor of greater participation in global decision making. There is an irony in the fact that although Wilson was accused of being naive for advocating such participation, he effectively predicted what has become an elemental process in the global politics of the late twentieth century.

At a different level of analysis, elitism may also take the form of assertions that foreign policy should be left in the hands of small coteries of professional diplomats. The arguments are often made in the context of expressions of concern about the injurious impact of public opinion or shifting electoral majorities on the possibility of formulating consistent and farsighted foreign policy. Thus, Walter Lippmann saw the "devitalization of the governing power" as "the malady of democratic states,"[69] and Alexis de Tocqueville concluded that "a democracy can only with great difficulty regulate the details of an important undertaking, persevere in a fixed design, and work out its execution in spite of serious obstacles."[70] For their part, realists consistently lament the passing of the age of the professional diplomat and the onset of the era of mass politics. George Kennan believes that "a good deal of our trouble seems to have stemmed from the extent to which the executive has felt itself beholden to short-term trends of public opinion in the country and from ... the erratic and subjective nature of public reaction to foreign-policy questions";[71] and Morgenthau cites as one of his "four fundamental rules": "The government is the leader of public opinion, not its slave."[72] In sum, the elitist bias of realists is characteristic of their perception of all levels of analysis, just as Wilson's antielitist bent was present in his views of both internal and external political life.

Historically, most societies have been characterized by the presence of several normative strands simultaneously competing with one another. For this reason, theories of international relations that reflected one or another extreme have rarely monopolized scholarly discourse. For every self-professed Machiavellian, there has been an anti-Machiavellian; and Jeremy Bentham and Richard Cobden flourished alongside the nineteenth-century advocates of balance of power and imperialism. However, for reasons noted earlier, the normative temper of any era is likely to have distinctive emphases. Typically, if these are extreme in one period, a compensating shift will take place during the following period. These shifts are reflected in changing fashions in the social sciences, including international relations.

Such a shift has been underway since the early 1970s. In its postwar heyday, realism emphasized immutability, pessimism, competitiveness, and elitism. These emphases were at least partly the product of a global preoccupation with the value of security in the wake of World War II, and this preoccupation was manifested in the overriding salience of a single critical issue, the Cold War.[73] Having emerged from a catastrophic conflict that had been inflicted by the aggressive behavior of a small group of dissatisfied and expanionist actors, publics and governments were ready to embrace policies and theories that focused upon the prevention of war through strength.

By the 1970s, the salience of the Cold War issue had begun to recede, permitting renewed attention to be paid to a host of other global issues that had been "hidden" in the previous years. These issues involved disputes and concerns revolving around global resource allocation, the maintenance of postwar prosperity, and environmental decay.[74] Many were, of course, not new issues but issues that had been quietly managed after the war by international institutions and regimes that had been constructed largely by U.S. efforts. The growing prominence of these issues in the 1970s, however, was especially the product of a decline in the preoccupation with security in a military sense that accompanied the flowering of détente, along with an intensified sense of potential deprivation of other base values. In a more general sense, their prominence grew as the United States found itself increasingly less able to dominate unilaterally key international regimes like oil and money.

In this climate, realism and the norms it reflected seemed less relevant.[75] The decline in cold war anxieties was largely responsible for reducing, at least in the West, the belief in human immutability and competitiveness, and the emergence of power centers other than Washington and Moscow necessarily diluted the atmosphere of postwar elitism. There was, however, little change along the dimension of optimism–pessimism because even as acute anxieties concerning some survival issues eased, new anxieties about other survival issues increased.

Such change in the global agenda and shift in normative emphases were reflected in the breakdown of consensus about international relations theory and the proliferation of new approaches, frameworks, and theories that rejected some or all of the realist assumptions. There was a retreat from grand theory and an impulse to the investigation of specific issues and cases in inductive fashion. The nonmilitary nature of many issues encouraged the introduction of concepts and ideas from allied disciplines, especially economics, psychology, biology, and sociology; and this increased doubts about the disciplinary autonomy of political science. Although the heterogeneity and ecumenical nature of postrealist international relations scholarship makes it difficult to generalize, some of the key concepts have been "linkage," "interdependence," "regimes," "political economy," and "transnationalism."[76]

The shift in normative emphases that is reflected in postrealism is perhaps best seen in the work of Robert Keohane, who seeks explicitly to graft such concepts onto realist insights about power.[77] Among other reasons, Keohane is especially interesting because he has been a prolific writer during the 1970s and early 1980s, has been unusually self-conscious regarding the evolution of his ideas, and has openly discussed the normative content of those ideas. Keohane regards international relations as more mutable than do realists, viewing a significant degree of cooperation among actors through international regimes as both possible and desirable. He is relatively sanguine about postwar developments, while taking pains to preclude accusations of "idealism," and he views global society through less elitist and competitive lenses than did his realist precursors.

Will these new concepts and ideas provide the bases for a new paradigm for international relations in the Kuhnian sense? If our analysis of the sources of intellectual change is correct, the answer is probably no. Even as major syntheses of postrealist theory are emerging, such as Keohane's *After Hegemony*, it appears that the agenda of global issues is once more in transition, with military security concerns and East-West relations beginning to assume greater salience since the late 1970s. Concomitantly, an upturn in economic conditions in the West and the prolonged oil glut have reduced anxieties about these matters even though the international economic system continues to face serious threats (for example, debt repayment). Barring major war or some other systemwide catastrophe, we would anticipate a partial return to realist norms, though realism is unlikely to achieve the dominance it once enjoyed. Its resurgence was in part forecast by the impact that Waltz's *Theory of World Politics* and its reassertion of the primacy of structural realism had on the discipline when it appeared in 1979.[78]

Keohane's own work is another harbinger of this trend. While retaining some of the language and insights of scholars who had predicted a decline in the autonomy of nation-states, the growing irrelevance of military security issues, and the inevitable growth of regional and global cooperation on functional or neofunctional lines, he carefully asserts his debt to realism. "My analysis has assumed that governments calculate their interests minutely on every issue facing them. It has not relied at all on assumptions about the "public interest" or the General Will; no idealism whatever is posited."[79]

CONCLUSION

This brief analysis of the sources and nature of evolving theory in international relations is self-consciously gloomy about the prospects for developing a cumulative science in the discipline. Notwithstanding significant advances in data collection and method, it views the discipline as mired in an unceasing set of theoretical debates in which competing empirical assertions grow out of competing normative emphases that have their roots in a broader sociocultural milieu. Dominant norms tend to vary through time, along with shifts in perceptions of the sources of value deprivation and satisfaction; such norms therefore reflect the hierarchy of issues on the global political agenda.

This analysis suggests, therefore, that what we believe to be the dominant theories of an age are more the products of ideology and fashion than of science in the Kuhnian sense. If the natural sciences somehow evolve in linear fashion regardless of their social and cultural context, "knowledge" generation in the social sciences—including international relations—may more closely resemble that in the humanities, which is inevitably infused by the ethos of its era. International relations will therefore continue to be characterized by a welter of competing theories that reflect significant political, subjective, and normative differences until the global system enters a new period of rapid and stressful change.[80] At that point, a dominant theory, resembling a Kuhnian paradigm, may emerge for some period of time, after which the cycle will resume.

NOTES

1. Some of the same issues that we address here echo concerns expressed by Stanley Hoffmann almost 25 years ago. Hoffmann, "International Relations: The Long Road to Theory." *World Politics* 13 (April 1961):346-77.

2. Thomas Kuhn, *The Structure of Scientific Revolutions*, expanded ed. (Chicago: University of Chicago Press, 1970), p. 175.

3. Ibid., p. 165.

4. Ibid., p. 163.

5. James N. Rosenau, *The Scientific Study of Foreign Policy* (New York: Free Press, 1971), p. vii.

6. See Klaus Knorr and James N. Rosenau (eds.), *Contending Approaches to International Politics* (Princeton, NJ: Princeton University Press, 1969).

7. Kuhn, *Structure of Scientific Revolutions*, p. 164.

8. Ibid., p. 164.

9. E. H. Carr, *The Twenty Years' Crisis 1919-1939* (New York: St. Martin's Press, 1962), p. 2.

10. By norms, we refer to considerations that are viewed as morally compelling.

11. Carr, *Twenty Years' Crisis*, p. 4

12. R. J. Rummel, "The Roots of Faith," in James N. Rosenau (ed.), *In Search of Global Patterns* (New York: Free Press, 1976), p. 11.

13. "The State Idea," in M. G. Forsyth, H. M. A. Keens-Soper, and P. Savigear (eds.), *The Theory of International Relations: Selected Texts from Gentili to Treitschke* (New York: Atherton Press, 1970), p. 327.

14. Jacob Bronowski, *The Origins of Knowledge and Imagination* (New Haven, CT: Yale University Press, 1978), pp. 127-29.

15. Ibid., p. 129.

16. For a similar approach, see F. Parkinson, *The Philosophy of International Relations: A Study in the History of Thought* (Beverly Hills, CA: Sage, 1977). The varied normative cleavages in classical Greece are discussed in E. R. Dodd's *The Greeks and the Irrational* (Berkeley: University of California Press, 1964).

17. See Friedrich Meinecke, *Machiavellism: The Doctrine of Raison d'Etat and Its Place in Modern History*, trans. Douglas Scott (New Haven, CT: Yale University Press, 1957). Significant idealists in the European tradition might include Dante, Emeric Cruce, the Duc de Sully, William Penn, the Abbe de Saint Pierre, Rousseau, and Kant.

18. See Jose Ortega Y Gasset, *The Dehumanization of Art and Other Essays on Art, Culture and Literature* (Princeton, NJ: Princeton University Press, 1948), p. 4.

19. See Lionel Trilling, *Beyond Culture* (New York: Harcourt Brace Jovanovich, 1965), p. 81.

20. See James E. Dougherty and Robert L. Pfaltzgraff, Jr., *Contending Theories of International Relations: A Comprehensive Survey*, 2nd ed. (New York: Harper & Row, 1981), pp. 10 and 45, fn. 38.

21. Hans J. Morgenthau, *Politics Among Nations*, 5th ed. (New York: Alfred A. Knopf, 1973), pp. 128-49.

22. Ibid., p. 152.

23. Relatively little has been written regarding the utility of Kuhn's framework to international relations. For contrasting views concerning its utility, see Richard Smith Beal, "A Contra-Kuhnian View of the Discipline's Growth," in *In Search of Global Patterns*, pp. 158-61, Arend Lijphart, "The Structure of the Theoretical Revolution in International Relations," *International Studies Quarterly* 18 (1974):41-74. However, the "paradigm" concept is increasingly accepted, though often in a purely metaphorical sense. Of special interest in this regard is the recent work of Hayward R. Alker, Jr. See Alker and Thomas J. Biersteker, "The Dialectics of World Order: Notes for a Future Archeologist of International Savoir Faire," *International Studies Quarterly* 28 (1984):121-42.

24. Kuhn, *Structure of Scientific Revolutions*, pp. 52-53.

25. See Morgenthau, *Politics Among Nations*, p. 169. Realists were especially enamored of European balance-of-power practice, frequently alleging that Americans had been able to ignore this practice—at their peril—because of the fortunate circumstances of geography. See Robert E. Osgood, *Ideals and Self-Interest in America's Foreign Relations* (Chicago: University of Chicago Press, 1953).

26. Morgenthau, *Politics Among Nations*, p. 3.

27. Ibid., p. 16.

28. Hans J. Morgenthau, "Another Great Debate: The National Interest of the United States," *American Political Science Review* 46 (December 1952):961-88.

29. Realists have correctly pointed out that a people's self-image is not always compatible with the "realities" of power. This insight has provided the basis of theories based on status equilibrium and disequilibrium.

30. Morgenthau, *Politics Among Nations*, p. 11.

31. See Robert A. Packenham, *Liberal America and the Third World: Political Development Ideas in Foreign Aid and Social Science* (Princeton, NJ: Princeton University Press, 1973), p. 245.

32. Bernard Brodie, *War and Politics* (New York: Macmillan, 1973), pp. 368, 365.
33. Richard J. Barnet, *The Roots of War* (New York: Atheneum, 1972), p. 65.
34. David Halberstam, *The Best and the Brightest* (New York: Random House, 1972), p. 69.
35. Arnold Wolfers, *Discord and Collaboration* (Baltimore: Johns Hopkins University Press, 1962), p. 147.
36. Barnet, *Roots of War*, pp. 109-120.
37. Morgenthau, *Politics Among Nations*, p. 7.
38. Kuhn, *Structure of Scientific Theories*, p. 34. Perhaps the best analysis of the work of behavioral and quantitative scholars in this context is by John Vasquez, *The Power of Power Politics: A Critique* (New Brunswick, NJ: Rutgers University Press, 1983).
39. See Robert Jervis, *Perception and Misperception in International Politics* (Princeton, NJ: Princeton University Press, 1976).
40. See Charles F. Hermann, *Crises in Foreign Policy* (Indianapolis: Bobbs-Merrill, 1969).
41. See Graham Allison, *Essence of Decision: Explaining the Cuban Missile Crisis* (Boston: Little, Brown, 1971); Morton H. Halperin, *Bureaucratic Politics and Foreign Policy* (Washington, D.C.: Brookings Institution, 1974).
42. See Robert O. Keohane and Joseph Nye, Jr., *Transnational Relations and World Politics* (Cambridge, MA: Harvard University Press, 1972), and *Power and Interdependence: World Politics in Transition* (Boston: Little, Brown, 1977).
43. See Richard W. Mansbach, Yale H. Ferguson, and Donald E. Lampert, *The Web of World Politics: Nonstate Actors in the Global System* (Englewood Cliffs, NJ: Prentice-Hall, 1975).
44. See Edward L. Morse, *Modernization and the Transformation of International Relations* (New York: Free Press, 1976); Richard W. Mansbach and John A. Vasquez, *In Search of Theory: A New Paradigm for Global Politics* (New York: Columbia University Press, 1981).
45. Kuhn, *Structure of Scientific Revolutions*, p. 182. See also his "Second Thoughts on Paradigms," in F. Suppe (ed.), *The Structure of Scientific Theories* (Urbana: University of Illinois Press, 1971), pp. 462-63, and *The Essential Tension* (Chicago: University of Chicago Press, 1977), pp. xvi-xxiii.
46. See Harold D. Lasswell, *World Politics and Personal Insecurity* (New York: McGraw-Hill, 1935).
47. See Samuel P. Huntington, *The Common Defense* (New York: Columbia University Press, 1961); Warner R. Schilling, Paul Hammond, and Glenn Snyder (eds.), *Strategy, Politics, and Defense Budgets* (New York: Columbia University Press, 1962).
48. See Ernst B. Haas, *The Uniting of Europe: Political, Social and Economic Forces* (Stanford, CA: Stanford University Press, 1958).
49. See Bruce M. Russett, *Trends in World Politics* (New York: Macmillan, 1965); Raymond Vernon, *Sovereignty at Bay: The Multinational Spread of U.S. Enterprises* (New York: Basic Books, 1971).
50. For a discussion of these variables and the manner in which they function, see Mansbach and Vasquez, *In Search of Theory*, pp. 59-63, 87-124.
51. "Actor" in this context should not be equated with "state" or "government." Rather the concept refers to any purposive group that behaves in a colletive and autonomous fashion.
52. "Values" are subjective constructs that express human aspirations for self-improvement. Cf. Harold J. Lasswell and Abraham Kaplan, *Power and Society* (New Haven, CT: Yale University Press, 1950), pp. 55-56 and Ted Robert Gurr, *Why Men Rebel* (Princeton, NJ: Princeton University Press, 1970), pp. 24-26.
53. Morgenthau, *Politics Among Nations*, p. 4.

54. *Ibid.*

55. Kenneth N. Waltz, *Man, the State, and War* (New York: Columbia University Press, 1959), p. 18ff.

56. Among natural scientists, Freudian psychologists may be viewed as relative pessimists owing to the dark forces that they see as inherent in the human psyche and the putative intractability of these forces. Nevertheless, even this relative pessimism has been recently and eloquently challenged by Bruno Bettelheim. See Bettelheim, *Freud and Man's Soul* (New York: Knopf, 1983), esp. p. 103ff. See also Erich Fromm, *Beyond the Chains of Illusion* (New York: Simon & Schuster, 1962), p. 174ff.

57. See Waltz, *Man, the State, and War.* Richard K. Ashley characterizes "neorealist" theory as lending "itself wonderfully well to becoming an apologia for the status quo, an excuse for domination." "The Poverty of Neorealism," *International Organization*, 38 (Spring 1984):257.

58. George Soule, *The Coming American Revolution* (New York: Macmillan, 1935), p. 20. See also Crane Brinton, *The Anatomy of Revolution* (New York: Norton, 1938).

59. By contrast, Edmund Burke in his *Reflections on the Revolution in France* represented the views of a pessimist whose conservatism would not allow him to accept uncontrolled change.

60. See Kenneth N. Waltz, "The Stability of a Bipolar World," *Daedalus* 93 (Summer 1964): 881–909, and his *Theory of International Politics* (Reading, MA: Addison-Wesley, 1979).

61. Robert Heilbroner, *An Inquiry into the Human Prospect* (New York: W.W. Norton, 1975), pp. 136–37.

62. Morgenthau, *Politics Among Nations*, p. 231.

63. George F. Kennan, *American Diplomacy 1900–1950* (Chicago: University of Chicago Press, 1951), p. 82.

64. James Burnham, *The Machiavellians* (Chicago: Henry Regnery, 1943), p. 34.

65. For an effort to find a middle path, see Hedley Bull, *The Anarchical Society: A Study of Order in World Politics* (New York: Columbia University Press, 1977). For his part, Robert O. Keohane seeks to provide a less stringent and abstract definition of self-interest based on "a less egotistical formulation of the concept" in his *After Hegemony: Cooperation and Discord in the World Political Economy* (Princeton, NJ: Princeton University Press, 1984), pp. 110, 110–32.

66. The distinction between these two emphases reflects the problem of private versus collective benefits. See Mancur Olson, Jr., *The Logic of Collective Action* (Cambridge, MA: Harvard University Press, 1965).

67. Kenneth N. Waltz, "International Structure, National Force, and the Balance of World Power," *Journal of International Affairs* 21 (1967): 215–31, and his "Stability of a Bipolar World. "

68. For an excellent critique of Morgenthau's version of balance of power that shows how its empirical and prescriptive elements become entangled, see Inis L. Claude, Jr., *Power and International Relations* (New York: Random House, 1962), pp. 25–37.

69. Walter Lippmann, *The Public Philosophy* (New York: Mentor, 1955), p. 29.

70. Alexis de Tocqueville, *Democracy in America, Vol. 1* (New York: Alfred A. Knopf, 1945), p. 234.

71. Kennan, *American Diplomacy*, p. 81.

72. Morgenthau, *Politics Among Nations*, p. 547

73. See Mansbach and Vasquez, *In Search of Theory* pp. 110–13. The concept of "critical issue" has been analyzed largely in the context of U.S. politics and has to date received little attention in international relations. At present, the process in which a single all-encompassing issue arrives at the apex of the global agenda is only poorly understood.

74. See Dennis Pirages, *A New Context for International Relations: Global Ecopolitics* (North Scituate, MA: Duxbury Press, 1978).

75. See Richard K. Ashley, "The Poverty of Neorealism," *International Organization*, 38 (Spring 1984): 232.

76. See Keohane and Nye, *Transnational Relations*, Ole R. Holsti, Randolph M. Siverson, and Alexander George (eds.), *Change in the International System* (Boulder, CO: Westview/Praeger, 1980); Stephen D. Krasner (ed.), *International Regimes* (Ithaca, NY: Cornell University Press, 1983); John Gerard Ruggie (ed.), *The Antinomies of Interdependence: National Welfare and the Division of Labor* (New York: Columbia University Press, 1983).

77. Keohane, *After Hegemony*, esp. pp. 5-17.

78. Kenneth N. Waltz, *Theory of International Politics* (Reading, MA: Addison-Wesley, 1979). In "The Poverty of Neorealism," Ashley argues that a new synthesis—"neorealism"— has already emerged to replace classical realism, and he declares: "In the United States of the 1980s, neorealism and its structural theory of hegemony frames the measured discourse and ritual of a generation of graduate students in international politics" (p. 227). In addition, Ashley provides something of a *Weltgeist* interpretation for this development by viewing it as paralleling "structuralist triumphs in such fields as linguistics, sociology, anthropology, and philosophy" (p. 234). While some of his criticisms of neorealism are telling (for example, reliance on economic logic and revival of state centricity), his argument is diluted by a self-conscious polemicism and opacity of style. See Robert G. Gilpin's response, "The Richness of the Tradition of Political Realism," *International Organization*, 38 (Spring 1984): esp. p. 289. Nevertheless, Ashley correctly sees a renewed emphasis upon immutability (structural dominance), pessimism, competitiveness, and elitism (hegemony).

79. Keohane, *After Hegemony*, p. 105.

80. Training in the discipline will therefore continue to be characterized by diversity, and this in turn will tend to perpetuate competition among theories.

2
From Systems Physics to World Politics: Invitation to an Enterprise
David Wilkinson and Arthur S. Iberall

BRIDGING THE GAP BETWEEN THE "TWO CULTURES"

Bacteria make rational decisions according to precepts of philosophy. Machines calculate; so do natural systems. Clouds remember. Words are catalysts; catalysis is language. Primitive humans diffuse fluidly. Geopolitics and nucleate boiling are stability analogues. Genes imagine. Gyroscopes, stars, organisms, markets, and balances of power are homeostatic. Self-consciousness evolved. Organisms are factories, as are societies. Apes have culture...

These statements, some of which will seem incongruous and paradoxical, reflect some flavor of our fundamental assertions: Snow's two cultures (1959) are already antiques; traditional barriers between intellectual fields are as ready to collapse as archaic dynasties (faster than the Manchus, less abruptly than the Romanovs); new cross-disciplines will link and are linking researchers who cannot yet communicate and see no reason to do so. The study of politics may consume more of the benefits of this linking than it produces, but is not parasitic: Concepts of gaming and bargaining have already begun to migrate from politics to evolutionary theory. Connections already made between fields suggest further productive possibilities. The strategy that we believe is most likely to maximize and speed broad-spanning interdisciplinary hybrid ideas to the benefit of political science is one of fairly radical physical reductionism. Let us follow that strategy and see where it leads us.

In the physicalist–reductionist view we here expound, there is only one scientific foundation for the operation of all nature, not more; and "human," "society," "mind," and "politics" (and "world politics") are natural phenomena whose scientific study must be built on that single foundation. Past attempts to do so have not succeeded, for reasons we consider ephemeral, special, rather than necessary. The limited scope of the available foundational physical science available for such attempts (the Enlightenment social scientist imagined he had only the physical force of gravity to organize his theories) led in the nineteenth century to the extreme differentiation of various social sciences to deal with complex, apparently non-Newtonian processes. Since that time, however, the social sciences have not been able to discover a universal set of underlying, unifying principles that might justify their separation. Meanwhile physical science has developed enormously, with only modifications of Newtonian thought. We therefore suggest that the time is ripe for a return to the physical sciences for fundamental principles (and criteria for specifying them). We propose to augment these principles with, and with them to augment, the findings of the social sciences during their period of splendid isolation. But we believe that the utility of social science isolationism is past, that interdependence will now prove more profitable to both parties, despite the inevitable costs of the dependency relations implicit in interdependence.

Physicists often prefer to seem self-effacing and unaggressive in public (though not to each other), and may not wish to be held individually responsible for our imperious claims on behalf of their belief system. Our call for the unification of all science upon physics as a base is not instantaneously in tune with the existing scientific paradigm, which encourages independent developments in each field of study, so that nonliving systems are explained differently from biosystems, and both differently from human sociosystems. Nevertheless, we assert the unity of the basic principles of movement and change as among all these various systems found operating in nature, whether nature itself, life, humans, mind, society, polity, world.

Our assertion is general; our current argument is limited to showing the link between physics and macrolevel politics, politics at its largest spatial scale, "world politics." We seek to turn physical concepts into political concepts—or to connect politics and physics—or to reduce politics to physics—or to provide the former with a foundation in the latter. Why should students of politics care whether we succeed? Because political science, like all science, needs a firm paradigmatic foundation; because most who wish to treat it as a science would accept that it now lacks such a foundation; and because we can point to one in physics.

We shall propose physical reductions, and defend physical reductionism. Let it be clearly stated that by "reducing" we mean grounding, deriving, and encompassing, but not replacing. We propose, then, to reduce politics to physics (to ground it upon physics, to derive it from physics, to encompass it within physics), so far as that is possible. Our primary definition of "physics" is both Aristotelian and contemporary: the science of motion and change in all entities, all material-energetic entities, all that exists, everywhere, through all time. We do not propose to replace political science by physics. Every subject matter distinguishable within physics will retain its special science, while acquiring its particular place within the general science, physics. Politics is thus distinguishable. Politics in general is the command, control, management, and regulation of any complex social system, living or not; human politics, the control of such systems composed of human beings.

To "reduce politics to physics" successfully, we must build from a "physics" recognizable as such to physicists to a "politics" recognizable to political scientists, without overtly or covertly introducing terms, concepts, presuppositions, or axioms incompatible with and irreducible to those of physics. This we believe we can accomplish. But we cannot carry out our reduction without thereby broadening the narrow, historically derived common-sense concepts of both "physics" and "politics." Since the direction of our reduction is politics to physics, most of our terms and arguments will look more "physical" than "political."

Our reduction begins with the thumbnail description of a physics applicable to all matter fields—a set of principles, a collection of types of "atomistic" entities and the assemblages of such entities, and an account of one of the standard physical strategies for understanding their actions and interactions. We shall attempt, while asserting no more than a contemporary physicist would allow, to show that from this thumbnail physics, politics (as we have defined it) emerges without word magic through the stipulation of a few, parsimonious, physical addenda—that is, on criteria of reasoning commonly considered necessary and proper by physicists seeking normally to enlarge the discipline of physics.

A THUMBNAIL PHYSICS FOR POLITICS

What exists, exists atomistically. Entities are composed of atomisms, smaller internal physical entities, perhaps to some smallest entities. The universe is a nested hierarchy of natural, physical systems. Each entity at each level of this hierarchy is a field system, which appears both as a continuum (at large scale and long duration), and as an interacting combination of atomisms (at small scale and short duration). The level of analysis problem in international relations [see, for example, Waltz (1959, 1979)] is precisely the reflection in world politics of the atomistic structuring of the universe. At every level of the natural hierarchy (in which humans, states, and civilizations are located), an ensemble of atomistic entities forms a continuum-like field, which under critical conditions becomes unstable and forms larger atomistic entities, which interact to form a larger continuum-like field.

A physical-reductionist strategy for all systems takes a unitary stock of principles of physics and applies them to the field systems under study. Mechanics, statistical mechanics, fluid mechanics, and thermodynamics are the most productive sources of physical principles for application to the world-political field. Every such application of principles simultaneously involves an extension of the principles applied, since every reality is as fully binding on physical law as that law is on such reality. Human society, a real system, must have a social physics—principles of structure, motion, and change—and sociophysics will be both an application and an extension of known physical principles.

The physical science doctrine of conservations among certain essential processes teaches that the behavior of all ensembles of interacting atomisms may be described in terms of a very limited number of quantities that are conserved in, during, and despite the interactions, varying only over a longer time scale and larger space scale than such local interactions, during which processes from afar affect the measures. The advantage in attending to these local conservations is that a scale can be defined at which the atomistic motions drop out of the measurement process and only local field averages need be observed.

The commonly accepted conservational variables in the physics of simple nonliving systems are mass, momentum, and energy. To extend this physics so as to apply to complex living and nonliving systems that have boundaries shielding their interiors from easy exchange with their environments—stars, planets, cells, brains, humans, states—it is necessary to replace the conservational variable of "momentum" with that of "action". Complex systems transform and dissipate energy, acting and producing in self-serving ways that support their existence, form, and function, and delay their dissolution into the environment. In so doing they expend energy over time to survive. Action in a physical sense is measured by the product of a rate of energy expenditure and a time over which energy is spent at that rate; action in a literary sense implies an agent doing deeds to serve its purposes. Our concept of action involves the agent, the physical measure of energy and time, and the self-servingness. And the idea of conservation of action is that all complex systems, within the time scales and space scales at which they survive, repetitively and periodically go through certain performance repertoires at measurable energy-time costs in order to maintain themselves, and are to be known by their repertoires (Iberall and Soodak 1978; Soodak and Iberall 1978; Iberall et al. 1980.)

Not just world systems (Modelski 1972) and economies (Kondratieff 1984) but all complex physical systems display "long" cycles: action cycles, factory days, lifetimes, population turnover times, species turnover times. Complex systems in general are observed spatially by finding interior-exterior boundaries (hence forms, patterns, morphology) and temporally by tracking their actions, energy budgets, activity spectra, factory days, biographies/histories, evolutions—their temporal process spectroscopies [for example, Iberall and McCulloch (1969)].

The theory of complex systems impels us to ask of whatever complex systems we study what its atomisms with boundaries and interiors are. [This question is the general version of the question specifically raised for world politics, with respect to war, by Waltz (1959)] What flows cross what boundaries? [Compare for world politics Rummel (1975-81) and Taylor and Jodice (1983).] Which diffusivities are controlled at what boundaries? (What persons, ideas, and goods are let across, and not let across, which state borders?) By what resistivities? What ultrastable set of phases are switched between (Kaplan 1957; see Ashby 1965)? What fast-moving external events are time delayed into what interiors, leaving what memory traces [see Richardson (1960) on war recursion]? What factories produce what for what other factories, over what factory days (Wallerstein 1974, 1980)? What is the characteristic description of the factory's action spectrum as integrated over the factory day? (Yet to be attacked for world politics. What is the factory day of a polity? A civilization?) How does the factory use the factory day action spectrum to maintain its conservations, to persist, to survive, to retain its internal conditions under external gradient changes? What is its duration expectancy? How does it fail? How do its failure modes yield differential survivorship, and evolution?

Living systems are finitely more complex than complex nonliving systems. One more conservational variable must be watched, mapped, and tracked: population number. Near invariance in bionumber despite complete (generational) turnover of a population is the physically distinctive characteristic of life. (Only at true irreversible thermodynamic equilibrium would true invariance in bionumber be required.) Physicalist biology therefore concentrates on the study of the actions and strategies and sheafs of strategies by which living systems manage to conserve their bionumber despite vicissitudes [see Iberall and McCulloch (1969)].

Until that point in human history where human social systems show the rapid and gross density increment associated with settlement, cities, agriculture, etc., the four conservational variables of mass, energy, action, and bionumber are sufficient to describe the field system of human atomisms for human sociophysics. Human movement patterns, densities, and distributions can be effectively modeled via Brownian "random walk" diffusion (Iberall and Wilkinson 1984). The larger, denser, slower-moving societies and processes of settled civilizations can have their origins physically modeled as criticality transitions of the same general character as condensation, eddy formation, stellar formation, etc. (Iberall and Wilkinson 1985, 1987).

But it appears to us that one further conservational variable is needed, and suffices, to account for the differences between stably settled human societies and other complex system condensative forms: conservation of "value in trade." The immense convective flow that is required to sustain the remarkably increased human bionumber in settled societies and their cities is driven by a counterflow of money among people otherwise "strangers," by an abstract symbol of value, evolved, brain invented, self-organized. Production for sale not use, the commodity concept, the impersonal market, gigantic impersonal trade nets—these represent not primarily an "alienation" but a "conservation."

Human politics, in our view, is not reducible to economics, or to biology; but neither is it irreducibly derived from a unique entity, "political man." Taxonomically, human politics belongs to a family (the control of complex systems that emerge from, remain apart from, and at last diffuse back into their environments—are "born," survive, and "die"), a genus (control of complex living systems that conserve bionumber), and a species (control of complex living systems that conserve value in trade). The range of "comparative politics" should therefore extend to questions such as, How do human and nonhuman systems maintain (and fail to maintain) their mass, energy, and action fluxes? How do human and nonhuman living systems regulate their numbers? What difference must and does it make that human politics in civilized societies also regulates money, exchange, trade, and production?

As an alternative approach to the interpretation of human society, the argument we have just made can be labeled "social system thermodynamics." To compete successfully, social thermodynamics must prove to be more complete, more fundamental, more predictive, more parsimonious, than any competing construct—Marxian or classical economics, Odom's energetics (Odom is an ecologist who has proposed this governing parameter, 1971), Harris's cultural materialism (1979), autonomous demography (a single-variable theory), Freudian social theory, Weberian social theory (1946,1947), pure economics, etc. The claim to completeness and parsimony rests upon the correctness of the particular set of key variables we have chosen—energy, matter, action, bionumber, value in trade—and the correctness of our claim that they are conserved.

Centering social theory around the five conservational variables does not mean that other aspects of human society are thereby amputated. They remain instead to be properly correlated with the fundamental conservations. The uniquenesses of human politics, of command control regulation of human beings in social life, we would not abolish; we suggest only that it can be assimilated to social thermodynamics as obligatory to maintain the conservation of value in trade (and the associated renormalized bionumber) and the productions, flows, exchanges, and storages requisite thereto.

IS POLITICS NECESSARY?

Alternatively, we can ask traditional and fundamental questions of political science, but try to see them in a different way. For instance, Why should the classic phenomena of human politics as we know it (states, government, bureaucracies, ruling classes, elites, power, law) exist at all? Why do they persist? How far might they be changeable? To be of any interest for most political scientists, a physics of politics must have something to say to such questions.

Christian, Muslim, Buddhist, anarchist, socialist, libertarian, egalitarian, and other utopias have signally failed (when they have sought) to eliminate elites, class, rule, oligarchy, power, and other apparently irrepressible political phenomena, as they have failed to eliminate value-conserving economic exchange in favor of some analogue drawn from pre-fifth-conservation experience, for example, the equipartition of energy in simple systems, the sharing of goods in traditional hunter-gatherer systems. Instead, the reformist utopias have been assimilated as ideologies for the phenomena they sought to eliminate, which endure, as documented, for example, by Michels (1915), Mosca (1939), Pareto (1980), and Orwell (1964, 1977). Such results lead us to suggest that the inegalitarian division of labor whereby perhaps 1 or 2 of 100 human atomisms are in the command control structure initiating processes and catalyses, paid for out of the running energetics of the rest of the system, "charging" one-eighth or one-quarter or one-half off the top of total "wealth" (whether measured by control of money, goods, actions, energy, people, or a composite), may be neither deliberate nor conspiratorial nor bioinstinctive, nor even sociobiological, but biophysically–sociophysically driven by physical requirements for command control subsystems of complex systems generally.

This conjecture, based on first principles, is not yet "provable" in ways customarily acceptable to social scientists; but should research political scientists continue to find that the old intractables of politics remain intractable, we believe physical principles allow us to point them to analogues, not just in animal dominance hierarchies, but, for example, in the size and priority of the human brain's resource demand vis-à-vis the rest of the body. (The brain is, in control terms, one giant energy sink that consumes so much of the body's energy in preventing things from being done as to resemble Washington, D.C., more than coincidentally.) Theology provides an alternative source to explain the irreformability of power politics; Niebuhr (1966) quotes with approval the proposition that "the doctrine of original sin is the only empirically verifiable doctrine of the Christian faith" (p.16). Those who accept an evolved, rather than created, human nature may prefer our formulation.

Where should we look to account for the peculiarities of human politics? We point to the fifth conservational variable, value in trade. The development of value in trade conservation necessarily has a great impact on a living species. Human economics is also unique for Marx, who treats the economic variable as the essential connecting variable in social science; non-Marxian believers in a pure theory of economics could doubtless agree. For us, however, what is peculiar about human economics is the development of a world economy and an exchange system of (eventually) global reach, with accompanying division of labor and specialization by comparative advantage, which from the days of an obsidian trade must have linked far-distant strangers, producers who never met their customers, groups who could easily trade farther than they could raid, rob, threaten, rule, or tax. Specialization and arrangement of the division of labor permit—or are required to permit—very large increases in bionumber or per capita wealth: Surely Smith, Ricardo, Malthus, and Marx would not dissent. But they must be governed, controlled, regulated, sustained; and in multistate civilized world systems they have been so governed, but not by a world state, or by a hegemon (the *deus ex machina* of hegemonic stability theory simply does not exist), or by a "world market" (even classic laissez-faire markets require a "nightwatchman state," which is obviously missing at the world market level). But a worldwide symbol of value might well suffice.

At the largest sociodemographic scale, one might consider trade systems and universal conquest empires to be the only viable alternative political forms in which a human bionumber in the billions could be sustained. (See Wallerstein's world economy versus world empire 1974 and 1980.) Why, then, does comparative civilizational history show a multistate world economy almost always, a clear-cut "universal empire" only rarely (Wilkinson 1983)? We would explore this question in terms of fourth-conservation (bionumber) versus fifth-conservation (value-in-trade) patterns; by contrasting survival strategies humans share with other life forms with strategies available only to a species that symbolizes value. One can immediately sense a fluctuating difference of advantage between local and more global integrative processes.

People get goods by trade with each other; they also rob each other (burglarize, extort, swindle, tax, etc.). The relative viability of strategies of trading versus taking by force will be proportional to their relative cost. The existence of intraspecific predation is explicable in fourth-conservation terms. The invention of human collective political organization and state structure improves efficiency of collective intrahuman predation to some degree, but to some degree hardens the target, raising the risks of predatory life styles, classes, groups, states, etc. (How many generations does it take for a predatory community to teach its neighbors to defend themselves and/or counterraid?) The net economic effect of the evolution of human states seems to have been to render relatively less advantageous a human action strategy that treats conspecifics mainly as repositories of matter, energy, and action to be hunted and gathered from. When your neighborly enemies "do unto you" about as much and as often as you "do unto them," rendering your attacks costly or inconclusive, or imposing as many defeats as they suffer [consider the paired histories of states that have been habitual enemies in the last few centuries—see Wilkinson (1980) for a list], you may eventually learn that you (state, nation, individual) cannot afford to express all your hostilities all the time. At best you can afford ultrastable switching between briefly stable conditions of peaceful trade and predatory or destructive war. (Locally increased intrahuman predation is usually diagnosed as a symptom of political decay. What looks to the local observer like migratory flight from war zones or high-crime areas may be more abstractly the local breakdown of the apparatus for supporting value conservation.)

Local trade is an alternative to (economically predatory) local war, and global trade to (semipredatory) global empire, at a given (high) bionumber. If an anonymous world trade net is an advantageous alternative to world empire, it ought to support a wealthier population in the short term and a larger population in the long. In its turn, a universal empire ought to support a wealthier larger population than a world organized primarily by war relations rather than trade relations. Rule, including empire, is not simply reducible to exploitation. Purely exploitative rule will rapidly depopulate a state. Most rule embodies some exchange, even that which treats subjects as managed domesticata to be fleeced, shorn, plucked, etc. Civilized human politics allows exchange to be stabilized, by the state and law or, we hypothesize more cost-effectively, by value symbols, to a degree that permits the achievement and maintenance of an enormously expanded bionumber in a high-order, thermodynamically precarious equilibrium. Accordingly, the true "specter" that haunts human society is that of a failure of high-order political stabilization of the trade economy, a collapse of the viability of remote trade and production for trade, a depopulation of cities, and a restoration of animal band levels, densities, and life styles to human populations.

If we see the political systems of human civilization as, in their net effect for the species, the control regulation mechanisms that maintain the conservational balance of the trade convection, which in turn permits maintenance of otherwise implausible species bionumber (and in the demographic patterns of civil society), a somewhat different interpretation of political problems, actions, strategies, processes, and institutions follows. Many seemingly distant political issues—plan failures in socialist societies, urban crime, aftereffects of nuclear war, faltering educational standards, diplomatic bargaining strategies—may fruitfully be examined with similar conceptual tools, without recourse to "economic man" or dialectical materialism.

If we treat rulers as conveniences (not least to themselves) but rule as a necessity (only) for the maintenance of the conservational balance of the trade convection of civil society, if we treat class structure as an opportune form of a stabilizing process that is not simply opportune but obligatory if sedentary society, dense populations, and intense trade convection are to be maintained, it becomes possible to try for scientific and engineering treatment of issues otherwise ideological and utopian, or hopeless. We need not love our ruling elites (nor they us; not even if we are they), but we cannot do without them (nor they us), and we properly demand certain performances of them (as they us), which it is useful to us for them to perform well (and vice versa), so that we ought to try to compel-persuade-bargain-teach them good performance (and vice versa).

As we have shown, we are like most of our reductionist predecessors, and unlike some theorists who ground politics in a theory of "political man" and economics in a theory of "economic man," in linking the phenomena of human politics (command control regulation subsystems and activities in human social systems) very intimately to economics. But we link politics even more intimately to physics—to all the variables suggested by physics (material goods, energetics, stereotypic human actions, demography—and parallel to these economics as the process of exchange via value in trade) and to models derived from the physics of complex nonhuman systems. We cannot reduce politics to economics. If politics is a "superstructure," it is so only in the sense of the superstructure of a naval vessel, which contains the control centers. The substructure carries the superstructure; the superstructure controls, directs, governs the substructure.

So much as riposte to attempts to reduce politics to economics; let it then be noted that political systems are not best understood as solid-state "structures," but rather as patterned processes in flow fields. "Politics" is not limited to "the state," some specimens of which are fairly solid and structural. A system of states is not a state, or a structure, but a pattern. Even within state boundaries, political "superstructure" in a cultural solvent is a higher renormalized patterning over the mere movement of atomistic people, involving fairly fluid parts of the action patterns of people who are traders, raiders, factory owners, workers, and soldiers, as well as kings, senators, and bureaucrats.

We would argue that we have here demonstrated that our physicalist approach gives an answer to a traditional and fundamental political question; that the answer is not the same as that provided by extant political theories, whether reductionist or nonreductionist; and that it may reasonably be expected to lead to still further questions, hypotheses, answers, and even strategies, all of which should be competitive with their rivals. Archeologists, civilizationists, macrohistorians, macroeconomists, and political scientists will all agree that trade, dense sedentary populations, cities, division of labor, states, and ruling classes are somehow related. If we are correct, all will eventually find it more fruitful to treat them as related in the physicalistic sense we have asserted.

PROBLEM AXES IN THEORIES OF WORLD POLITICS

We think that, among political scientists, students of world politics may have "membranes" relatively more permeable to physical science ideas of politics than some of their colleagues, not simply because of their continuing paradigm crisis, but because of their mixed feelings about the concept of the state. One significant barrier to a political physics is the notion of command control systems as quasi-homunculi, necessarily either conscious, mindful, and deliberate, or nonexistent. The homunculus, expelled from genetics by microscopy, lingers on in the state-centric political science at the polity level of analysis because some rulers and many "ruled" have homuncular remnants in their images of rule, and therefore fail to look for or find control mechanisms in force fields once they have located "rulers" and their "power." Students of world politics (excepting searchers for Illuminoids, gnomes of Zurich, Trilateralists, Elders of Zion, etc.) are more likely to be able to accept that if some political conditions continues, especially over lifetimes, what is required to account for its continuance need not be a mind; it may be a mechanism.

Macropolitical theory has undoubtedly flourished over the last two generations, partially because of its leakage into intellectual-academic circles following the creation of a Marxist-Leninist state that "established" such a theory as official, disseminated it vigorously, provoked dissatisfaction with utopian liberalism and pessimistic political realism, but failed to convince social scientists (beyond the reach of its officialdom) of the scientific legitimacy of its answers even as it convinced them of the propriety of its questions, or at least of some of its social scalings.

In post-Marxist and non-Marxist macropolitics, there have been some isolated if suggestive achievements, a certain amount of local cumulation, but no fieldwide integration, or even fieldwide mutual recognition among researchers. Let us review some major efforts.

Contributions to Macropolitical Theory

Spengler (1926, 1928) constructed a lifespan model of the development of a civilization that included sequences of settlement types (villages, towns, cities, megalopolis, cosmopolis), social groups (folk, people, nation, mass, cosmopolitans/provincials), classes (folk, nobles/priests, bourgeoisie/intelligentsia, urban masses, familistic rural masses), war types (rural, feudal, class, imperialist, private), and regimes (anarchy, feudalism, absolutism, plutocracy, Caesarism).

Sorokin (1937–41) discerned a millennial alternation between Ideational and Sensate culture types in which transitional phases showed more frequent and intense violence, crystallized systems more general stability. Kahn (1979) derived "Basic Long-Term Multifold Trends of Western Culture" over the last millennium to a significant degree from Sorokin.

Wight (1946) identified a "series of powers that have tried to dominate Europe, by war and diplomacy, and have only been prevented by a coalition of the majority of other powers, at the cost of an exhausting general war." (pp. 11-12) England, Spain/Austria, Sweden (in the North) and France (in the West), France again, Germany, and Russia formed the sequence. Later (1978) he added a separate sequence of naval dominant powers, Spain, Holland, Britain, the United States. But it was still among the land powers that he perceived "the series of efforts, by one power after another, to gain mastery of the states-system—efforts that have been defeated only by a coalition of the majority of other powers at the cost of an exhausting general war." (p. 30)

Toynbee (1954, p. 287) identified cycles between "spells of peace" and "bouts of war" in Western, Hellenic, and Sinic civilizations, with wavelengths (cycle times) of about 40 to 50 years, and noted an overlap with the Kondratieff (1984) "long" economic cycle of 40 to 60 years.

Kaplan (1957), using Ashby's cybernetic ideas (1965), identified behavioral rules, stability conditions, and mechanisms maintaining and restoring equilibrium in multipolar and loose bipolar systems with hypotheses for a variety of other system types. Martin (1970) tested the utility of Kaplan's "balance-of-power" model for explaining sixteenth-century Western European international politics, finding it largely satisfactory.

Organski (1958, 1968) developed a theory of world political dynamics resting on a three-stage economic world model (preindustrial, transitional, industrial), in which the differential spread of industrialization between states creates sudden increases in wealth, population, efficiency, and national capability, sequentially producing "challengers" to an established international order headed by a most powerful "dominant" state and consequent wars and shifts of leadership. Organski and Kugler (1980) produced data to buttress the "power transition" theory that the differential growth rates of the two most powerful states in the system, "dominant" and "challenger," and more particularly the overtaking of the dominant by the challenger, destabilize the system and eventuate in a change of leader and/or world war.

Richardson (1960) derived a model for generating the worldwide distribution of complexity of wars since about 1500 in terms of the numbers, power classes, and contiguities of actors.

Hoffmann (1960) called for the comparative study of historical international systems in the manner of Aron's historical sociology (1966), and developed (1965) a typological and legal contrast of stable versus revolutionary systems.

Modelski (1961) carried on Comte's (1896) and Spencer's (1899–1901) developmental sociologies, using Almond and Coleman's structural-functional concepts (1960), to contrast primitive, agrarian, and industrial international systems in terms of population size, class homogeneity, system maintenance, expansion, and war.

Quigley (1961) discerned seven stages in civilizational development, most notably multistate economic expansion, multistate economic stagnation–political conflict, universal empire, and decay; the staged development was driven by innovation, degradation, and reform of economic institutions.

Rosecrance (1963), fusing aspects of Aron's historical sociology and Ashby's cybernetics, distinguished nine international systems or system types from 1740 to 1960 by diplomatic style and constellation: unipolar/bipolar/quasi-bipolar/tripolar/multipolar, compensatory/dissentient/disharmonious/diametrically oppositional, conceived as subject to national disturbance, systemic regulation, and environmental adequacy/scarcity/abundance.

Black (1966) identified phases and types of modernization from the seventeenth century to the twentieth, estimating a period of transitional violence and instability of 150 to 300 years' duration.

Wesson (1967) produced a comparative and ideal-typical study of imperial orders.

Melko (1969) constructed a civilization development model that combined Spenglerian feudal–state–imperial stages with Sorokinian alternation between crystallized and transitional periods and social orders.

Forrester (1971) created a dynamic model of the world system's kinematics since 1900, using demographic rate and level variables (population, birth rate, death rate); economic stocks, rates, and levels (wealth, resources, food, investment); and ecological ratios (crowding, pollution) to explore implications of expansion, limits to growth, models of catastrophic collapse, and system sensitivity to controllable changes. The effort spawned a substantial successor literature, analytical, polemical, critical, and revisionist, beginning with Meadows et al. (1974).

Modelski (1972, 1983) discerned a pattern of long cycles of world leadership in the oceanic global system since 1500, with the leading role played successively by Portugal, the Netherlands, Britain, and the United States, insular or semiinsular seapowers with lead economies and lead polities, and with five demonstrated cycles begun by global wars.

Wallerstein (1974, 1980), drawing from Marxist and dependency literature, has inspired a large and vigorous school of world system analysis [see McGowan and Kegley (1983) or Hopkins et al. (1982)], integrating concepts of socialism–capitalism, core–semiperiphery–periphery, expansion–stagnation, empire and world economy, in a complex account of the expansion of the "capitalist world economy." A Kondratieff cycle is of theoretical importance to the Wallerstein paradigm, as to Kahn (1979).

Choucri and North (1975) related the growth of state population per unit of state area and of state income per person, through expansion and lateral pressure mechanisms, to wars and crises at the international level.

Wight (1977) developed an agenda for the comparative study of systems of states; Wesson (1978) developed a comparative and ideal-typical study of state systems, but in different terms.

Hord (n.d.), continuing an aspect of Toynbee's work, has examined the long-term evolution of groups of polities with a shared constitutional system through periods of free growth (increasing participation) and ordered breakdown (decreasing participation), with particular attention to the breakdown sequence.

A different selection of theorists might have been made. We could have gone back farther; any partners in dialogue can be interesting, and if the dialogue is about politics in general, Plato's and Aristotle's propositions about the transitions among political command control forms (one, few, many) and Confucius's and Mencius's doctrines of principles of command control would be quite proper topics of scientific discussion, and might serve as sources of world systems speculation (when the members of a states system will tend to be collapse prone; what the stability criteria are for a universal state). We could have been more exclusive. Certain cycles are current items on the political-spectroscopic comparative anatomy table, for example, Kondratieff cycles, Modelski's long cycles of world leadership, and various fluctuations in measures of war underway (Wilkinson 1980); others' cycles, for example, Spengler's, seem to occur in bodies politic, some of which are of doubtful status; and Platonic and Aristotelian governmental cycles are hypotheses for which the empirical evidence is either lost or was never collected.

Major Macropolitical Arguments

Nonetheless, a brief conspectus of the kinds and axes of argument in the theory of world politics will testify to its variety, vitality, or desperation.

Among typologies: Is there a fundamental distinction to be drawn between homogeneous and heterogeneous states systems (Aron, after Papaligouras)? Revolutionary and stable systems (Hoffmann)? States systems and imperial orders (Wesson, Wight), perhaps with a feudal variant (Melko)? Agrarian and industrial international systems (Modelski)? World economies and empires (Wallerstein)? Multipolar and bipolar systems (Aron), with bloc structure and weapons systems variants (Kaplan) or unipolar, tripolar, bimultipolar alternatives (Rosecrance)? Which, if any, of these distinctions should be rejected for, subsumed under, subordinated to, or crossed with which others?

Among stagings: Is there succession, cycling, or progression between such system types? Between periods of general war and ecumenical peace (Toynbee); of expansion and conflict (Quigley); of feudalism, capitalism, socialism (Marx-Engels); ideational and sensate cultures (Sorokin); crystallized and transitional societies (Melko); peasant, feudal, national, mass, and despotic societies (Spengler); free growth and scheduled breakdown (Hord)?

Within the last 500 years, in the Western-global states system, do we observe a sequence of dominant powers—Spain/Austria, France-Sweden, France, Germany, Russia (Wight 1946); a parallel sequence of dominant seapowers—Spain, Holland, Britain, the United States (Wight 1978); a sequence of dominant powers—France, England, the United States; and a parallel sequence of challengers—England-the United States/

Germany, Germany/Japan, Russia/China (Organski; Organski and Kugler); or a sequence of world leaders—Portugal, the Netherlands, Britain, the United States (Modelski)?

Macropolitical Hypotheses: Some Choices

We do have some preferences in these discussions, inclining to treat the states system-universal empire contrast as of primary importance (Wilkinson 1983); general war as a periodic restabilizing mechanism; heterogeneity as a function of the engulfment of all other world systems by one of their number (Wilkinson 1984a); agrarian and market economies as distinct from and slower changing than their feudal-marketive-statist command control political orders; economic expansion and stagnation as wave phenomena whose drivers and drivens are as yet uncertain but likely to prove of great significance; and the Wight (1946) sequences as primary within the expanding world system, the Modelski sequence at that system's external boundaries, and the Wight (1978) sequence and the Organski sequence as subordinate in importance to the Wight (1946) sequence (Wilkinson 1985). Modernization appears to rank as the major political destabilizing and later restabilizing phenonenon internal to the world system in the last semimillennium.

We would, in fact, go farther. There are two long cycles, only weakly time driven, but involving institutional learning and aging processes and therefore time dependent. There is one very long cycle alternating between (ideally) "universal empire" and "multistate system," with average lifetimes of each form on the order of hundreds of years (rather than tens or thousands, which are extremes of the lifetime range). For multistate systems, the more common form, there is a shorter cycle, not most centrally of world "leadership" or of "hegemony" in the hegemonic stability sense, but of "dominance" in Martin Wight's usage. This cycle has a period whose average deviation is high, but that is of the order of generations rather than decades or centuries (though these are, again, the range's extremes). For universal empires there may be a third cycle, a crisis cycle (extending the Chinese "dynastic cycle") of several centuries, with more pulsations than one—but not tens of pulsations—per millennium.

We theorize that the holocivilizational social system is politically ultrastable as a two-phase system; microscopically, the multistate phase is cyclically destabilized by the emergence of a dominant state and, lately, restabilized by learned balance-of-power operations; the one-state phase is cyclically destabilized by institutional and bureaucratic aging and semiparasitization processes (Quigley's "institutionalization of the instrument of expansion") and restabilized by large-scale elite turnover through "revolution."

These are nontrivial cycles. If accepted even in part, they imply an agenda for what theoretical political science needs to discover (the drivers of these cycles) and what practical political engineering at the system level needs to control.

THE INTERSECTION OF SYSTEMS PHYSICS AND WORLD POLITICS

We are less concerned at this point, however, with staking out a substantive position in the political and world political dialogues than with suggesting that a systems physics approach has much to offer in terms of criteria and models for the discussion. Without such an approach, we could do no more than suggest a need for greater clarity in definitions, clearer delineation of the space-time boundaries of the phenomena under discussion, and more specification of the kinds of empirical evidence or practical application that should govern choice among macrotheories and macroconcepts. With such an approach, however, we may assert that dynamic systems analysis is the appropriate tool for the study of a dynamic factory, including the human society.

Scalings

To carry out dynamic analysis of any system, we must decide what are the shortest and longest process times and the widest and narrowest spatial scalings of concern. It seems unlikely that political cycles briefer than the daily rounds of a ruler or bureaucrat, or much longer than the two millennia or so of the longest-lived multistate systems thus far, can be expected to have organized political content. Both these cycles clearly do. This is then the political time domain, from about 1 day to 1 million days (around 3,000 years), six orders of magnitude.

Though politics in a meaningful, restricted sense exists even in the male-female pair bond (and in an equally meaningful though extended sense within the human organism), most political study involves units with populations from some thousands to billions, and spatial scalings from city-states and island-states to the earth surface.

The temporal and spatial scales are closely related. World politics properly specializes in the larger spatial scales. We would assert that it should also work at the longest temporal scales, necessarily, not arbitrarily.

Within the space and time domain that represents a whole society, its characteristics can be presented spectrally, mapping frequency against energy in a near-exact analogue of the original "spectroscopy" for atomic or molecular structure. In general, higher-frequency behavior is highly unstable, with rapid switching of states in no easily predictable order. As frequency falls and time domain lengthens, stereotyping, patterning, ritualizing increase. At still longer periods, sequences of flaring instabilities—birth, mastery, integration into larger systems, death—dominate.

Spectroscopy

We would like to be able to identify the structure of major near-cyclic world political processes whose physical causality can be ensured. An extensive art of such process identification has an engineering–physical history of some extent. At the same time (nineteenth to twentieth centuries) that the social sciences were struggling to develop typologies, the physical sciences and engineering began to develop the techniques of dynamic and stability analysis—of elastic systems, of acoustic systems, of electrical systems, of hydrodynamic systems, of electromechanical systems, of atomic nuclear systems. In its current, explosive mathematical form, this approach is found in what is known as qualitative and/or nonlinear dynamical systems analysis. Fundamental to it is spectroscopy.

A spectrum, roughly, is an arrangement of vibratory phenomena, for example, light or radiation, separated (usually) according to wavelength or frequency, used to measure relative intensity or density via frequency. Spectroscopy in a more general sense is a clocking of cycles, rhythms, periodicities. Biospectroscopy is therefore the measuring of the dominant frequencies/cyclic wavelengths at which the dynamic processes of living systems take place—pulse rate, brain wavelength, breath frequency, and temperature swings are biospectroscopic measures.

The major components of such spectroscopic analysis of complex systems are as follow: (1) identification of the processes that are strongly driven by external causality, for example, the daily rotation of the earth, the yearly revolution of the earth around the sun; (2) identification of self-generated strong nonlinear autonomous oscillations, for example, air cells in the atmosphere; (3) identification of a "noise" background of small-amplitude stochastic processes that are too broad band to associate with a sharply located unitary process (particularly "random" in its phasing), for example, the backgroud noise in the electromagnetic spectrum of a radio receiver; (4) identification of intermittent or very distinctly aperiodic stability transitions from one dynamic state of operation to another, for example, transition from laminar to turbulent flow, the buckling or fatigue failure of a structure; (5) identification of a broad field process that seems to have an ergodic character, namely, that the field of processes is so densely filled that the space averages at a fixed time and the time averages at a fixed point in space are hardly distinguishable, for example, that the average that any one person does in his/her life (for example, daily ingests calories) is not far removed from what the entire human population is doing all over the world.

If social processes are repetitive (hence "vibratory"), sociospectroscopy becomes an important form of social measurement. There will be no difficulty in asserting the existence of daily and yearly cycles in human social systems. Police arrests will attest to the social reality of a wholly artificial weekly cycle; U.S. politics and U.S. external relations are observed to alter in time with equally artificial two-, four-, and six-year election cycles, whose appropriateness can be defended or attacked only from some idea of nonarbitrary human social periodicities.

If our principles are correct, sociophysical and biophysical oscillatory "engine" processes will be found to exist in the complex social organism at every scale examined. As in any other application of irreversible thermodynamics, each system and process will be found to have a minimum atomistic scale in space and time over which near equilibrium occurs and a maximum scale in space and time over which the system maintains coherence (it is, after all, also an atomism in another system). The various processes will be found to have largely independent causality, with bivariate cross-correlations between various cycles negligible, even though they are often coupled in very complex ways to produce joint effects. It is important, therefore, to begin to approach human political processes spectroscopically, searching for time scalings, accepting that the first series of measurements may no doubt be wildly mistaken and the processes wrongly identified, hoping only to be somewhat mistaken in imperfect identifications—respecting and continuing the efforts of such as Vico (1984), Spengler (1954), Sorokin (1937-41), Huntington (1915), Quigley (1961), and Dewey and Dakin (1947) et al. without at all being committed to their conclusions or process identification. Singer and Small (1972), Denton (1966), Hord n.d., Melko et al. (1973, 1981, 1984) deserve mention in this connection as contemporaries who have attempted politicospectral analysis of wars, moods, constitutions, and political order.

Spectroscopy is the fundamental, first rudimentary form of dynamic physical analysis of any complex system. (Microscopy is the fundamental form of static or morphological analysis.) The time scalings appropriate to the system under study ought to be estimated a priori to permit meaningful examination or testing of such systems. (Initial estimates of the maximum and minimum relevant spatial scale, and the greatest and least disturbances that are of interest, are also necessary, but obviously so as part of microscopy.) If oscillatory processes and their possible causalities are to be distinguished from quasi-static self-regulatory processes and feedback control "progresses," the systems under study must be examined over a long enough period to determine many of their dynamic characteristics, for example, the longest relaxation or settling time, the fundamental lowest-frequency thermodynamic cycle, etc. Observation over one or more equilibrium thermodynamic cycles (during which the first and second laws of thermodynamics are seen to be complied with) is required if "normal" operations are to be specified and distinguished from perhaps transitory "deviational states."

We suggest that the fundamental lowest-frequency political cycle likely can be identified at the largest (world political) scale, that its phases are similar to those stipulated by Wesson (1967, 1978) [states system versus imperial order], that its time scalings (still to be specified) are on the order of centuries to millennia, with high average deviation from the mean. The next lowest-frequency cycle may be either that cited by Wight (succession of dominant powers) or the appearance and disappearance of independent states in a multistate system, the latter certainly having a much greater variance than the former. Will physics affect the study of politics? A sustained attempt to measure lowest-frequency oscillations would certainly entail a significant change in the main direction of contemporary political science, which, having abandoned progressivist assumptions, now tends to seek islands of stability in a sea of chaos.

Cascades

Furthermore, the set of identified spectra ought to be energetically bound together as a sheaf. What one ought to see in the whole via system spectroscopy, over the life of any system, is a cascade spectrum of processes that indicate how the major energy flows through all the conservations of the system and descends from the lowest-frequency near-stationary and ergodic processes to the highest-frequency such processes. That descent in time is what constitutes the cascade spectrum.

The prototypic example of such processes is the cascade spectrum of the meteorological cycle on earth over most of its 4.5 billion-year history (or the hydrological cycle, or the lithospheric cycle, or the biochemical cycle). All such processes up to and including galactic processes (possibly even cosmological processes) exhibit historicity and evolution. The telling of the tale of any of their histories is comparably difficult, no less, no more, than the telling of the history of life or humans. However, while the former cases have accepted or demanded the aid of the physical scientist, the latter field (of human social science) has not yet done so. So we will have to look very closely at the existing notions of the social sciences, for example, world politics, to see what we can make of them.

Restating Macropolitical Hypotheses in Systems Physics Terms

As a preliminary approach to the reduction of the theoretical dialogue in world politics, we might try the following. It is traditional in social science literature to distinguish between trends and cycles [see, for example, Braudel (1982-84, vol. 3)]. In the literature of world politics, modernization or industrialization tends to be seen [outside Forrester's school (1971)] as a "trend," while Kondratieff cycles, business cycles, war cycles, dominant power cycles, and challenger cycles are variously posited. For our purposes, it seems more useful to distinguish between longer and shorter waves that, when perceived simultaneously and compared, will look to the relativity-bound observer like a "trend" versus a "cycle"; between "open" and "closed" systems in a weak sense, for example, between systems that have not yet expanded to fill their container-niche-ecumene-resource space and those that have done so and have begun to rebound from the walls, the former systems tending perhaps to show what look like trends, the latter what look like cycles; between newly emergent systems that, performing their new factory day ring for the first time, seem to display unilinear successions, and long-established systems whose first apparent successions have begun to ring round; and even between short memory systems, always young, always born yesterday, "American," amnesiac, always perceiving themselves as on a trend and a unique trend at that, and systems with long memories (at least a cycle or two), memory driven, thixotropic, "European," knowing it all and having seen it all before.

In these terms, it seems that the unequal modernization or uneven development that in different ways drives or could be seen as driving Black's phases of national order and chaos, Choucri and North's sequence of lateral pressures, Organski's challengers, Lenin's imperialist wars, and Modelski's sequence of world powers has a "reducible" look to it. It appears to resemble a wavefront phenomenon, a transformation passing through a conceptual space, perhaps at a constant rate, impacting suddenly on and sharply changing the behavior of a few atomisms at a time. There are resemblances in the transformation both to the first-time trend of a newly emergent structure and to a phase change. We are (at least since Forrester) properly concerned with when and whether we should expect a backwave, with sudden collapses and demodernizations of members of the world system (and, possibly, a later cycling process), or rather Black's snug harbor of integration, Marx-Engels's socialism–communism, a phase change if not irreversible at least non-self-reversing. A system physics approach to this problem may point us to the places, times, events, processes, and scales needing to be observed to distinguish one from the other phenomenon.

Another aspect of the world politics debate that may look different in a system physics context is the common element in the distinction between, for example, Wallerstein's world economies and empires, between capitalist long waves and socialist planning failures, between the political disasters specific to a Kaplan balance-of-power system, Wesson's state system, Quigley's stages of expansion and conflict, etc., versus Kaplan's universal system, Wesson's universal empire, Quigley's stages of universal empire and decay, etc. Error processes in the former might in a general sense turn out to be mappable as waves of higher frequency and lower amplitude than in the latter, with fast shifts and continuous crisis characteristic of the former, a longer reaction time, less frequent changes of course, later perception of more imminent disaster, characteristic of the latter.

Yet another change in the world politics debate that systems physics suggests is a relation between past (retrodiction) and future (prediction-control) time scales for systems as such, and therefore for world political systems. Complex systems have a long memory trace. Thus, to make, say, a 3-generation forward prediction, one needs, say, a 40-generation historical, stereotypic, and evolutionary account. To look forward one century, one needs to look back one or two millennia. Studies of world politics that take us back only to World War II are not likely to provide— and rarely aspire to provide—more than a few years' leverage on the future. Studies that go back to 1500 A.D. may reasonably claim about a generation's worth of forward anticipation. But it is possible to push the history of world politics' stereotypic and evolving patterns back 5,000 years, to the Sumerian city-states (Wilkinson 1982, 1983, 1984a,b). The typologies, trends, cycles, and mechanics of a 5,000-year past might have several centuries' worth of forward value. Only demographers, energeticists, and Marxians have as yet taken this proposition seriously; and because the first two have tended to produce univariate models, and the Marxians a decycled staged dialectic, their projections are not convincing beyond a few years or decades at best.

Political cycles in a world of states, and economic cycles in a world of firms, may both be describable as products of a system of many small entities with short memories, limited capacities, fast but incoherent response; political, economic, or politicoeconomic cycles in a single, poorly integrated entity may be abstractly and satisfactorily describable as products of a long memory, coherent reactions, long reaction time, and slow learning (selective turnover of personnel, tools, images of self and world, etc.). Most of these processes would seem to be transient, though not accidental, flow patterns, rather than necessary causal sequences.

Toward Political Engineering

Among other effects, this conception of the failure problems of such political and economic structures (and phases) might lead to fully justifiable technical engineering solutions to apparently political-ideological or ethical-valuational problems. A political engineer hired to straighten out the error cycles of entities like those we have abstractly described might attempt to tinker with the information-processing structures of the decisional mechanisms of the failing states, firms, or planning agencies [see, for example, Iberall and Cardon (1975, 1978)]. With the multiple entities, one might want to prolong their memory trace; with the single entity, to soften its memory drivenness and strengthen its future imaging capabilities and drivings. Slowing the turnover time for the circulation of political-economic elites might be to the point for the first set of entities, speeding it up for the second. In both cases, a speeding up of reaction time might seem indicated, likewise an increase in the proportion of their political resources devoted to data acquisition and processing.

Here the ideas of Deutsch (1963) are perhaps in point. Political science cannot do without the concept of power; still, the implicit metaphor is in some ways distracting, and cybernetic, communicative steering needs also to be thought of. The metabolic energy supply of the most "dynamic" or "powerful" is no greater on average than that of the average follower. Rulers spend only a tiny part of their own action in directing enormous volumes of their subjects' action. Contrast, as an extreme example, the action budgets of Mao Tse-tung's production of a few slogans, and the ten-year Cultural Revolution thereby entrained. Effective rule is a relatively small-energetic process, catalytic, linguistic, power amplified. Language, evoking switchings from mode to mode, is the general basis for command control; human language is the human basis for command control. Confucius insisted upon correct language. Should courses in rulership perhaps emphasize "language" and Confucius, or "power" and—whom? Charles Atlas?

In a more general sense, systems physics may be expected to present new ways of reflecting on engineering political systems. The question of how to manage a political system is, in physical terms, the question of the conservations that must be satisfied for the system to endure for some time versus the freedoms that are available. The richer the system is energetically, the freer its members, the looser the structures that must form to share for survival.

PHYSICAL-REDUCTIONIST POLITICAL MODELING

By politics we now mean, in general, regulation and control of any complex system in the face of both its internal and its external vicissitudinal fluctuations, although as usual our parochial interests direct us particularly toward living systems, and more particularly toward study of systems of humans living in society. Every complex self-maintaining system and every living organism faces the problem of command control maintenance of existence against fluctuations, in which its language and culture become involved; the human "body politic" also has the same problem. A physical-reductionist ethology would suggest political scientists should study how command control and governance emerge throughout the living kingdom. Physics itself, more primitive, says: Look at all complex systems.

Homeostasis

One generally useful lesson is that the things we more or less intuitively think need explaining are not necessarily the things that actually need explaining. Political scientists often behave as if they were driven by Newtonian world images in conceiving their objects of study and seeking the causes of things and events. It is easy to accept the idea that motion and change imply force, that "if something moves (changes its motion), something has pushed." It is more difficult to get acceptance of the corresponding principle from Cannon's (1939) biological-physical ideas: "If nothing moves, something has pushed—and something else has pushed back"; or "If disturbances exist, but the system continues to maintain its form, then the disturbances have been compensated for." Apparent nonchange, in a complex fluid-like system under disturbance, may be more complex than change. A nonevent is not satisfactorily disposed of by a nonexplanation; the failure of the dog to bark in the night required a more intricate explanation than its barking would have (Doyle 1930, p. 397.) The continuation of near-equilibrium conditions in complex, disturbance-prone systems must be dynamically explained. Since the systems are not "dead," unmoving, their continuing motion must have been hidden, and needs to be revealed.

The concept of homeostasis (and, we shall argue, the dynamic concept of homeokinesis) must, in our view, be thoroughly integrated into the working vocabulary of political science. Cannon pointed out that the human body is made up of extraordinarily unstable material, readily disturbed by application of slight external forces, which material perishes with great ease and rapidly decomposes when no longer "living," yet persists over decades in normal use though open to exchange with and disturbance from the "outer world." He more particularly drew attention to the maintenance of body temperature within a narrow range despite wider external temperature fluctuations. The temperature of a carcass does, and of a living body does not, "decay" to the equilibrium temperature that is its surrounding local field average, that is, fluctuates with a decay in synchrony with the ambient temperature. The living body's temperature continues to fluctuate independently of the ambient temperature [see, for example, Iberall (1960)]. Many other body conditions, too, continue despite disturbances that might reasonably be expected to end them, or vary within limits despite variations and fluctuations beyond those limits outside body boundaries such that mere decay to equilibrium would take the body outside the internal limits and approximate it to the field average of self and milieu.

Cannon designated the constant conditions maintained by the body as homeostases, steady states established, returned to, preserved, regulated, and controlled, and proposed that the means employed to preserve them would be suggestive for social organizations subjected to stress and disturbance, which would also be found to have means of "self-righting adjustment" that might be studied and perfected (pp. 19-25). Steady states involving materials were preserved by storage and dumping (for example, of glucose); those involving processes were maintained by speeding up and slowing down the rates of continuously functioning countervailing processes [for example, heat production and heat shedding (ch. 18)]. Cannon posited that any constancy in an open system of unstable material implied the existence of agencies that resist change. Kaplan and Rosecrance followed these leads into politics, but incited few successors. Cannon also proposed that the closest analogue to the animal organism fluid matrix stream was the flow of goods, currency, reserves, rates of production and distribution, and their automatic processes of adaptation. We suggest that the extension of homeostatic concepts from polity to political economy might escape the dead-end to which homeostatic applications to politics seem to have led in the past.

How can homeostasis occur? It suggests the existence of some regulatory mechanisms that perceive the internal variables and the external disturbances (coincidental, cyclic, progressive, steady state, etc.)

and that cause behavior that ends in the maintenance of the values of the internal variables. How can this be accomplished? Within physical laws, by an ensemble of thermodynamic engines including nonlinear active catalytic switches, themselves comprising thermodynamic engine parts, which by inhibition or release from inhibition shift the engines, including the fluxes and potentials of the complex system, moving it through a ring of operational modes, oscillatory processes, thermodynamic engine cycles, each of which performs particular bits of internal work at frequencies (in the human body) from 0.1 second (nerve impulse) to once in a lifetime (Iberall 1960, 1972; Iberall and Cardon 1964; Iberall and McCulloch 1969; Iberall and Soodak 1978; Soodak and Iberall 1978; Iberall et al. 1980.) The system rings through its internal state space with the *telos* of its not being moved beyond the boundaries of its ultrastable equilibrium space. This process of dynamic maintenance of equilibrium variables by thermodynamic engine processes we have called "homeokinesis." ["It takes all the running *you* can do to keep in the same place" (Carroll 1888).]

We would cite as homeostases with highly complex and dynamic regulators (that is, homeokineses) not simply the internal milieu of the biological system and the weather system, but also Smith's invisible hand in the marketplace (1776), Inis Claude's "automatic" version of the balance-of-power system (1962, pp. 43–47), the maintenance of visible bodies apparently at rest by the action of invisible molecules in rapid motion (Lucretius, Maxwell), the maintenance of independence in a state system and of the tenure of an imperial dynasty, the regulation of a household, the management of a firm or church or a political science department, etc.

Tactics of Physical Reductionism in Politics

As our discussion of human sociogeophysics conveys, when presented with a phenomenon to be explained, our first inclination is to try to reduce it to processes explicable in terms of the first three conservations, in terms of statistical mechanics, thermodynamics, and the physics of complex systems with long time-delayed internal atomistic processes. Our next inclination is to inspect it via the fourth conservation of demography—is it related to the fact that living social systems, made up of atomisms that are born and soon die, nonetheless maintain populations of such atomisms over enormous periods of time? Our last try is to complete the program by bringing in the fifth conservation and its equilibrating exchanges at a distance. As a heuristic for political reductionists, we recommend the following principles and procedures.

Entities survive for a limited time and hence are selected, eventually, for, among other things, the efficiency of their political command control systems in manipulating their freedoms against their environmental disturbances and toward survival. (The appearance of neural systems in the evolution of living organisms, for example, made possible a multicellular command control much more complex than that available to more primitive colony-type organisms.)

In explaining any political process, try, therefore, first of all, to reduce it to command control manipulation of freedom in satisfying the first three conservations, in controlling forms and flows of energy, materials and action, in driving trends, cycles and rings, in using time delays for factory processes, as an exercise in statistical political mechanics and mechanistic entity-level survivorship.

Next, try to reduce the unreduced elements to command control over-actuated by the fourth conservation to management of demographics and biological group-level survivorship.

Finally, try to reduce the unreduced remnant to the fifth conservation, to maintenance of massive cities and far-flung massive populations via delayed equilibrated exchanges through a large trade net, to mass survivorship in and self-organizing survival of a network entity linking individual components that are strangers to each other and exchange at a distance, through intermediaries, without contact, contract, reciprocity, or community consciousness—to economic and ecumenical survivorship.

What we have just said in general is again true in particular for our approach to political phenomena and to their relations to economics. Command control processes, even command control over production and exchange processes, speaking in a strict but generic sense of each of these key terms, exist in nonmonetary, nonhuman, and even nonbiological forms. Given our priorities, we will choose the metaphors and models from the most distant disciplines possible, rather than those nearest to political (as is traditional even among scientific political theorists, who tend to go next door to the economics department, and no farther, for their models and metaphors). The rationale is evident: If we can show a human political process to be generically homologous to an evolved or human-created machine-regulatory, factory-regulatory, production-regulatory, or exchange-regulatory process, we have reduced it farther than if the only applicable models are biological, or come from within the human-invented symbol countertrade network.

Priority must be given to the more universal processes, and accordingly to processes least familiar to contemporary political scientists. To make this habitual, it would seem advisable as a general rule to choose one's models and metaphors not from the nearest but from the most distant levels and systems so as to facilitate the most complete reduction. Thus, nonliving systems have similarities to human politics that ought to be treated as more compelling (and hypotheses drawn therefrom as more poignant and crucial) than nonhuman biological systems, and these than human social systems. This diametrically inverts the customary order of priorities in political metaphor making.

Remote Physical Models: Boiling Instability

Before beginning such complex dynamic analyses, it is useful to have at least a simplified mental image of what a complex mobile field system, like human beings and their social and political systems on earth, might be like. We can provide one by considering a very elementary model for the physics of the atmosphere. We will use a system no more complex than the physics of a bubble chamber and/or that of a pot of boiling water. (Both, incidentally, are useful models of some central properties of the atmosphere, one of the closest physical analogues to complex social systems; we anticipate that other fluid mechanical models will also have social applications.) A bubble chamber is filled with a liquid just below the boiling point, and sealed. The pressure within is reduced, lowering the boiling point, leaving the liquid on the verge of transition to gas. An intruding charged particle produces bubbles all along its path. Very little energy is required to trigger a full trajectory "signature" of the intruding particle, because the liquid is already near instability. The bubble chamber is deliberately designed as an exquisite display of small disturbances by arranging large effects for them. Bubble chamber-like phenomena are, in this sense, opposites of homeostatic phenomena, which have arranged that large disturbances shall have small effects. Where we find large, ineffective disturbances, we must look for homeokinetic regulators. What should we look for when we find small, highly consequential disturbances?

A better model is a boiling pot, in which nucleate bubbling at a particular place can be triggered by almost any tiny disturbance, so that the location of the bubble is quite unpredictable even though the frequency of bubbling may be constant. Frequencies and locations of small wars appear to be of similarly differentiated predictability (Richardson 1960; Wilkinson 1980). In the boiling pot, two input fluxes, one of heat and one of water, if maintained within related limits and kept within the bounds set by the pot and the atmospheric pressure, will support the indefinite continuation of boiling—will result in a "sustained instability," in which minor disturbances continually produce major consequences.

We can show that the boiling pot resembles the hydrological and meteorological cycles more closely than one might think. Pay attention to the lid of the pot. We will imagine some disturbance that cools the lid. Water is still boiling; vapor will condense on the lid. The disturbing force (electrical in the real atmosphere) will cause precipitation. At equilibrium the boiling evaporation will equal the precipitation. The gas atmosphere will not be 100 percent saturated, but less (for example, 60 percent of the earth's atmosphere) to support the evaporation. The stability of the system will be exquisitely sensitive to storming disturbances.

The general concept of a boiling unstable field appears to be of wide applicability. The heat input to the pot, represented as an external temperature, supports the continuation of the boiling instability, as the solar temperature and solar flux bring the earth to a boiling-like, or subliming-like, continuing hydrologically and biologically unstable state. The processes possess essentially the same instability, though at the same time scale the earth processes are damped—in slow motion clouds boil visibly, in far slower motion the biosphere "boils" (transforming, for example, through the incoming mutation-producing cosmic radiation principally of galactic origin). Any small disturbance in any boiling unstable field can trigger local forms and processes, for example, be a catalyst or serve as the "language" trigger of disproportionately energetic behavior.

If the boiling fluid is a solvent, it may carry cyclic processes for many other constituents, for example, of earth with boiling to atmosphere hydrologically driving the geochemical cycles of materials such as carbon, phosphorus, and calcium, etc., which have differential reactivities and solubilities, and differentially precipitate out, appear for a while, and dissolve.

The total picture of stable instability with many metastable states, for example, clouds, weather systems, can be viewed as analogous to the conditions governing the appearance and disappearance of life forms, of social forms, of civilizations, of regimes, etc. Where large causes are not observed to trigger large effects, delicately balanced opposed forces (and, if the effects are repetitive, fluxes) should be assumed and searched for.

At proper time-space scalings, a sequence of annual geopolitical maps of the earth surface, each a static one-frame shot, will appear to boil, and the lifetime scale of the boiling process is greater than that of the evanescent precipitates [see, for example, the atlases of McEvedy (1961, 1967, 1972, 1982) or Barraclough (1984)]. The continued boiling instability survives, precipitates, and dissolves states, empires, state systems, and universal empires and therefore requires description independent of those, its products, and, on its own scale, larger than any of theirs. The same ought to be true of the small war-generating system, for whose macroscopic portrait the boiling image is thus superior to the more usual burning image of brushfire and wildfire, containment and control (although the boiling and burning solar surface might provide a doubly apt metaphor).

We do not wish readers to elect the inference that pots of boiling water are sufficient models for political events! They provide an apt physical metaphor, a "flavor." The totality of processes in the physical atmosphere provides a great number of such physical metaphors and "flavors." We think physics has much more to offer than metaphors—but these, too, are worth pursuing, to derive a sense of the fantastically large complex of processes that can emerge from a few forces, for example, electrical forces interacting with matter. And the degree of complexity and intricacy required for a real model of the earth's atmosphere is fully comparable with that required for a real model of the political systems of humans on earth.

Other Remote Physical Models

Four complex nonliving systemic cycles that might be examined to seek surprise analogues and models to the human–political are the weather, the lithosphere, the hydrological cycle, and the geochemical sphere. One does not copy from these systemic exemplars; one learns from them. They provide insight into a great variety of analogous processes that can emerge and the kind of mechanisms that can make them emerge. One does not argue by analogy—although one may name by analogy—one argues by dynamic mechanism.

One point that may provide an entry is that all display a cascade spectrum of processes. A cascade spectrum contains linked processes that emerge at many space–time scales, as energy "cascades" down through them from lower-frequency (longer-time) into higher- and higher-frequency (shorter-time) processes. We are perhaps more inclined to assume that high-frequency political processes drive low-frequency processes; observing systems in which the converse holds may allow us to perceive comparable instances in politics more easily. Contemplating the cascading hydrological cycle, seeing that it may parallel a cascading war cycle, with its infrequent high-energy large-scale events and its high-frequency low-energy wars (Wilkinson 1980), one wonders whether the customary perception of large wars as escalations of small ones may not have the energetics of the problems wrong end up.

The relative abundance, distribution, and movement of elements from place to place in diffusive geochemical processes provide us with models for the description of human densities, distributions, and migrations (Iberall and Wilkinson 1984)—and for the movement of technologies, of ideas, of behaviors. It may well be that the kind of theory that leads to the analysis and prediction of atmospheric pressure, temperature, and disturbance patterns, flows and circulations via the mathematical physics of L. F. Richardson as meteorologist (1922), carried onward by Charney, Fjörtoft, and von Neumann (1950) and now modeled to be used as the basis for current synoptic meteorology, has something to offer to the analysis and prediction of war patterns, flows, and distributions, also based on the mathematics of L. F. Richardson as political scientist (1960), the available basis for synoptic polemology.

Stellar dynamics and fundamental particle "sociology" may also prove suggestive, in that the thermodynamics of these systems all provide comparable clues as to how complexity is effected [see, for example, Iberall and Cardon (1980)]. We need not dwell on such complex systems—nor on others such as cosmos, galaxies, or the so-called vacuum—except to say that each of them has a comparably complex behavioral description, culture, and anthropic utility. Each of the systems exhibits its complexity in using up the dynamic space associated with its few conservations. A modest number of atomic species play out their games of interactions to create a considerable amount of molecular form. From the molecular form arises the matter system—plates, air masses, rivers, cells, vortices, storms, eruptions, organisms, societies—that are so rich in their macroforms. And their histories and evolutions last for billions of years (for example, the living systems). One cannot view human politics and society against any lesser background than the entire set of anthropic, encultured, behaviorally complex, richly formative systems.

It is to be realized that a physical typology that can deal with social phenomena in cosmos, galaxies, stars, weather systems, organ systems, animal and human social systems, organelle systems in the cell, atoms in molecular association, is not going to be a trivial "comparative anatomy." It will cast light on right and wrong principles. The very generality with which these systems have to be attacked provides some notions of the metaprinciples that are relevant. While the locally scaled players may change, the physics tends to remain basically the same. Thus, the principles that are common, as well as the occasional mistake that is made, are fairly quickly identified. Phlogiston was a doctrine that did not last long. A theory of pure economics impresses very few scientists. The incompleteness of biological principles seems quite apparent.

Coda

One might characterize the physicopolitical problem as the game of connecting the laws of physics to the laws of humanity. We are of the belief that this Enlightenment task—which the Enlightenment and post-

Enlightenment would-be sociophysicists (La Mettrie, Saint-Simon, Comte, Marx, Engels, Spencer) were not capable of achieving for want of an adequate underlying physics—is now ready to be attacked. This is the promise. As tentative moves from promise to performance, we offer the following:

> Iberall, et al. (1980), "Homeokinetic Physics of Societies—A New Discipline"
> Iberall (1986) "On the Thermodynamics of Demography"
> Iberall (1985), "Outlining a Social Physics for Modern Societies—Locating Culture, Economics and Politics, (The Enlightenment Reconsidered)
> Wilkinson (1980), *Deadly Quarrels*
> Iberall and Wilkinson (1984, 1985, 1987), "Human Sociogeophysics—Phases I, II, and III"

REFERENCES

Almond, Gabriel A., and James S. Coleman. *The Politics of the Developing Areas.* Princeton, NJ: Princeton University Press, 1960.

Aron, Raymond. *Peace and War.* Trans. by Richard Howard and Annette Baker Fox. Garden City, NY: Doubleday, 1966.

Ashby, W. Ross. *Design for a Brain: The Origin of Adaptive Behavior.* 2nd ed. New York: Methuen, 1965.

———. *An Introduction to Cybernetics.* London: Methuen, 1964.

Barraclough, Geoffrey (ed.). *The Times Atlas of World History.* Rev. ed. Maplewood, NJ: Hammond, 1984.

Black, C.E. *The Dynamics of Modernization.* New York: Harper & Row, 1966.

Braudel, Fernand. *Civilization and Capitalism.* 3 vols. New York: Harper & Row, 1982-84.

Cannon, Walter B. *The Wisdom of the Body.* 2nd ed. New York: W.W. Norton, 1939.

Carroll, Lewis. *Through the Looking-Glass and What Alice Found There.* New York: Macmillan, 1888.

Charney, Jules G. R. Fjörtoft, and John von Neumann. "Numerical Integration of the Barotropic Vorticity Equation." *Tellus* 2 (1950): pp. 237-54.

Choucri, Nazli, and Robert C. North. *Nations in Conflict.* San Francisco: W.H. Freeman, 1975.

Claude, Inis L. *Power and International Relations.* New York: Random House, 1962.

Comte, Auguste. *The Positive Philosophy of Auguste Comte.* London: G. Bell & Sons, 1896.

Denton, Frank H. "Some Regularities in International Conflict 1820-1949." *Background* 9, (1966). pp. 283-96.

Deutsch, Karl W. *The Nerves of Government*. New York: Free Press of Glencoe, 1963.

Dewey, Edward R., and Edwin F. Dakin. *Cycles, The Science of Prediction*. New York: Holt, 1947.

Doyle, Sir Arthur Conan. *The Complete Sherlock Holmes*. Garden City, NY: Garden City Books, 1930.

Forrester, Jay. *World Dynamics*. Cambridge, MA: Wright-Allen, 1971.

Gulick, Edward Vose. *Europe's Classical Balance of Power*. Westport, CT: Greenwood, 1982.

Harris, Marvin. *Cultural Materialism*. New York: Random House, 1979.

Hoffmann, Stanley. "International Systems and International Law." pp. 88–122 in *The State of War*. New York: Frederick A. Praeger, 1965.

———. (ed.). *Contemporary Theory in International Relations*. Englewood Cliffs, NJ: Prentice-Hall, 1960.

Hopkins, Terence K., Immanuel Wallerstein et al., *World-Systems Analysis*. Beverly Hills, CA: Sage, 1982.

Hord, John. "The Tie That Binds: Dynamics of Constitutional Development." Unpublished manuscript, n.d.

Huntington, Ellsworth. *Civilization and Climate*. New Haven, CT: Yale University Press, 1915.

Iberall, Arthur S. "On the Thermodynamics of Demography." *American Journal of Physiology; Regulatory, Integrative, Comparative Physiology* 1986, (in press).

———. "Outlining a Social Physics for Modern Societies—Locating Culture, Economics and Politics (The Enlightenment Reconsidered)." *Proceedings of the National Academy of the Sciences* 82, (1985): 5582-4.

———. *Contributions Toward a Vigorous Systems Science*. Upper Darby, PA: General Technical Services, 1975.

———. *Toward a General Science of Man Systems*. General Technical Services. Report to U.S. Army Research Institute, Washington, D.C., May 1973.

———. *Toward a General Science of Viable Systems*. New York: McGraw-Hill, 1972.

———. "The Human as an Inconstant Heat Source." *Journal of Basic Engineering*. 82, (1960): 96-102, 103-112, 513-27.

Iberall, Arthur S., and S. Cardon. *Contributions to a Thermodynamic Model of Earth Systems: On Rivers*. Final Contractors Report to NASA, contract NASW-3378, February 1981.

———. *Contributions to a Thermodynamic Model of Earth Systems: Linking Lithosphere, Hydrosphere, Geochemical Field, Biochemical Field, Civilization*. First Quarter Contractors Report to NASA, contract NASW-3378, May 1980.

———. "Why the Prince Needs a Scientific Advisor: Executive Summary of a Physical Science Base for Policy Decisions." Report to Office of Policy, Plans, International Affairs, U.S. Dept. of Transportation, 1978.

———. "Systems Models for Transportation Problems." Report to Transportation Systems Center, U.S. Dept. of Transportation, Cambridge, MA: report no. TSC-946-75, 1975.

_____. *Application of Systems Science to Man Systems.* General Technical Services Report to U.S. Army Research Institute, Washington, D.C., December 1973.

_____. "Control in Biological Systems—A Physical Review." *Annals of the New York Academy of Sciences* 117 (1964): 445-515.

_____. "A Study of the Physical Description of the Hydrology of a Large Land Mass Pertinent to Water Supply and Pollution Control," Four Reports to HEW, Washington, D.C., contract SAPH 78640, 1961-62.

Iberall, Arthur S., and W. McCulloch. "The Organizing Principle of Complex Living Systems." *Journal of Basic Engineering* 91 (1969): 290-94.

Iberall, Arthur S., and H. Soodak. "Physical Basis for Complex Systems—Some Propositions Relating Levels of Organization." *Collective Phenomena* 3 (1978): 9-24.

Iberall, Arthur S., H. Soodak, and C. Arensberg. "Homeokinetic Physics of Societies—A New Discipline." in *Perspectives in Biomechanics.* Edited by H. Reul, D. Ghista, and G. Rau. pp. 433-527 in Vol. 1, Part A. New York: Harwood Academic, 1980.

Iberall, Arthur S., and David Wilkinson. "Human Sociogeophysics—Phase II (continued): Criticality in the Diffusion of Ethnicity Produces Civil Society." *GeoJournal* 1986 (in press).

_____. "Human Sociogeophysics—Phase II: The Diffusion of Human Ethnicity by Remixing." *GeoJournal* 9 (1985): 387-91.

_____. "Human Sociogeophysics—Phase I: Explaining the Macroscopic Patterns of Man on Earth." *GeoJournal* 8 (1984):171-79.

Kahn, Herman. *World Economic Development.* New York: Morrow Quill, 1979.

Kaplan, Morton A. *Towards Professionalism in International Relations Theory.* New York: Free Press, 1979.

_____. "The Systems Approach to International Politics." pp. 209-42 in *Macropolitics.* Chicago: Aldine, 1969.

_____. *Systems and Process in International Politics.* New York: John Wiley & Sons, 1957.

Kinder, Hermann, and Werner Hilgemann. *The Anchor Atlas of World History.* 2 vols. Garden City, NY: Doubleday, 1974, 1978.

Kissinger, Henry A. *A World Restored.* New York: Grosset & Dunlap, 1964.

Kondratieff, Nikolai. *The Long Wave Cycle.* New York: Richardson & Snyder, 1984.

Lenin, V.I. *Imperialism, the Highest Stage of Capitalism.* New York: International Publishers, 1939.

Malthus, T.R. *An Essay on the Principle of Population.* New York: W.W. Norton, 1976.

Martin, Anthony D. "The Unstable Balance: A Systems Analysis of the Politics of Sixteenth Century Western Europe." Ph.D. dissertation, University of Chicago, 1970.

McEvedy, Colin. *The Penguin Atlas of Recent History (Europe Since 1815).* Baltimore: Penguin, 1982.

_____. *The Penguin Atlas of Modern History (to 1815).* Baltimore: Penguin, 1972.

_____. *The Penguin Atlas of Ancient History.* Baltimore: Penguin, 1967.

_____. *The Penguin Atlas of Medieval History*. Baltimore: Penguin, 1961.
McEvedy, Colin, and Richard Jones. *Atlas of World Population History*. New York: Penguin, 1978.
McGowan, Pat, and Charles W. Kegley, Jr. *Foreign Policy and the Modern World-System*. Beverly Hills, CA: Sage, 1983.
Meadows, Donella H., Dennis L. Meadows, Jorgen Randers, and William W. Behren III. *The Limits to Growth*. 2nd ed. New York: Universe, 1974.
Melko, Matthew. *52 Peaceful Societies*. Oakville, Ontario: CPRI Press, 1973.
_____. *The Nature of Civilizations*. Boston: Porter Sargent, 1969.
Melko, Matthew, and John Hord. *Peace in the Western World*. Jefferson, NC: McFarland, 1984.
Melko, Matthew, and Richard D. Weigel. *Peace in the Ancient World*. Jefferson, NC: McFarland, 1981.
Michels, Robert. *Political Parties*. New York: Hearst International, 1915.
Modelski, George. "Long Cycles of World Leadership." pp. 115–39 in *Contending Approaches to World System Analysis*. Edited by William R. Thompson. Beverly Hills CA: Sage, 1983.
_____. *Principles of World Politics*. New York: Free Press, 1972.
_____. "Agraria and Industria: Two Models of the International System." pp. 118–43 in *The International System*. Edited by Klaus Knorr and Sidney Verba. Princeton, NJ: Princeton University Press, 1961.
Mosca, Gaetano. *The Ruling Class*. New York: McGraw-Hill, 1939.
Niebuhr, Reinhold. *Man's Nature and His Communities*. London: Bles, 1966.
Odum, Howard T. *Environment, Power and Society*. New York: Wiley, 1971.
Organski, A.F.K. *World Politics*. 2nd ed. New York: Alfred A. Knopf, 1968.
_____. *World Politics*. New York: Alfred A. Knopf, 1958.
Organski, A.F.K., and Jacek Kugler. *The War Ledger*. Chicago: University of Chicago Press, 1980.
Orwell, George. *1984*. New York: New American Library, 1977.
_____. *Animal Farm*. New York: Harcourt Brace, 1964.
Pareto, Vilfredo. *Compendium of General Sociology*. Minneapolis: University of Minnesota Press, 1980.
Quigley, Carroll. *The Evolution of Civilizations*. New York: Macmillan, 1961.
Ricardo, David. *On the Principles of Political Economy, and Taxation*. London: J. Murray, 1821.
Richardson, Lewis Fry. *Statistics of Deadly Quarrels*. Pittsburgh and Chicago: Boxwood and Quadrangle, 1960.
_____. *Weather Prediction by Numerical Process*. Cambridge: Cambridge University Press, 1922.
Rosecrance, Richard N. *Action and Reaction in World Politics*. Boston: Little, Brown, 1963.
Rummel, R.J. *Understanding Conflict and War*. Beverly Hills, CA: Sage, 1975–81.
Saint-Simon, Claude-Henri, comte de. *Selected Writings*. New York: Holmes & Meier, 1975.
Singer, J. David, and Melvin Small. *The Wages of War, 1816–1965*. New York: John Wiley & Sons, 1972.

Small, Melvin, and J. David Singer. *Resort to Arms: International and Civil Wars, 1816-1980.* Beverly Hills, CA: Sage, 1982.

Smith, Adam. *An Inquiry into the Nature and Causes of the Wealth of Nations.* London: W. Strahan and T. Cadell, 1776.

Snow, C.P. *The Two Cultures and the Scientific Revolution.* Cambridge: Cambridge University Press, 1959.

Soodak, H., and Arthur S. Iberall. "Homeokinetics: A Physical Science for Complex Systems." *Science* 201 (1978): 579-82.

Sorokin, Pitirim I. *Social and Cultural Dynamics.* 3 vols. New York: American, 1937-41.

Spencer, Hebert. *The Principles of Sociology.* 3rd ed. New York: Appleton, 1899-1901.

Spengler, Oswald. *The Decline of the West.* Trans. by Charles Francis Atkinson. 2 vols. in 1. London: George Allen and Unwin, 1954.

Taylor, Charles Lewis, and David A. Jodice. *World Handbook of Political and Social Indicators.* 3rd ed. 2 vols. New Haven, CT: Yale University Press, 1983.

Thompson, William R. "The World-Economy, the Long Cycle, and the Question of World-System Time." pp. 35-42 in *Foreign Policy and the Modern World-System,* Edited by Pat McGowan and Charles W. Kegley, Jr. Beverly Hills, CA: Sage, 1983.

Toynbee, Arnold J. *A Study of History.* New edition revised and abridged by the author and Jane Caplan. New York: Weathervane Books, 1972.

———. *Reconsiderations.* Vol. 12 of *A Study of History.* Oxford: Oxford University Press, 1961.

———. *A Study of History.* Abridgement by D. C. Somervell. 2 vols. Oxford: Oxford University Press, 1946, 1957.

———. *A Study of History.* 12 vols. Oxford: Oxford University Press, 1934-61.

Vico, Giambattista. *The New Science of Giambattista Vico.* Ithaca, NY: Cornell University Press, 1984.

Wallerstein, Immanuel. *The Modern World-System II: Mercantilism and the Consolidation of the European World-Economy, 1600-1750.* New York: Academic Press, 1980.

———. *The Modern World-System: Capitalist Agriculture and the Origin of the European World-Economy in the Sixteenth Century.* New York: Academic Press, 1974.

Waltz, Kenneth N. *Theory of International Politics.* Reading, MA: Addison-Wesley, 1979.

———. *Man, the State, and War: A Theoretical Analysis.* New York: Columbia University Press, 1959.

Weber, Max. *The Theory of Social and Economic Organization.* New York: Free Press, 1947.

———. *From Max Weber: Essays in Sociology.* New York: Oxford University Press, 1946.

Wesson, Robert G. *State Systems: International Pluralism, Politics, and Culture.* New York: Free Press, 1978.

———. *The Imperial Order*. Berkeley: University of California Press, 1967.
Wight, Martin. *Power Politics*. Edited by Hedley Bull and Carsten Holbrad. New York: Holmes & Meier, 1978.
———. "De systematibus civitatum." pp. 21–45 of *Systems of States*. Edited by Hedley Bull. Leicester: Leicester University Press, 1977.
———. *Power Politics*. London: Royal Institute of International Affairs, 1946.
Wilkinson, David. "States Systems: Ethos and Pathos." Unpublished manuscript, 1985.
———. "Encounters Between Civilizations: Coexistence, Fusion, Fission, Collision." Unpublished manuscript, 1984a.
———. "Kinematics of World Systems." Unpublished manuscript, 1984b.
———. "Civilizations, States Systems, and Universal Empires." Unpublished manuscript, 1983.
———. "A Definition, Roster, and Classification of Civilizations." Unpublished manuscript, 1982.
———. *Deadly Quarrels*. Berkeley: University of California Press, 1980.
Wilkinson, David, and Arthur S. Iberall. "Macropolitical Scalings." Unpublished manuscript, 1986.

II
Sources and Patterns of Conflict and Violence

3
The Structure of the International System and the Relationship Between the Frequency and Seriousness of War
T. Clifton Morgan and Jack S. Levy

The belief that the seriousness of war is inversely related to its frequency of occurrence has been incorporated into numerous theories of international politics. It has been used to describe the nature of warfare under various sets of theoretical conditions and in particular historical eras, and it is also a basic assumption underlying several important policy-relevant propositions. In an earlier article (Levy and Morgan 1984), we empirically tested this hypothesis at the systemic level of analysis, and found that over the last five centuries there has been a moderate inverse relationship between the frequency of wars that occur in a given period and their seriousness. No effort was made, however, to test alternative theoretical explanations for the observed empirical generalization. The purpose of this study is to determine the extent to which two system-level variables, the polarity of the system and the availability of outlets for expansionist activity, can account for the observed relationship between the frequency and seriousness of war. It has been argued that these variables affect both the frequency and the seriousness of wars by determining whether the great powers fight among themselves in a few cataclysmic wars or fight a large number of extrasystemic wars interspersed by a few minor great power wars. Although there are plausible theoretical arguments predicting that this relationship should also exist at the nation–state level of analysis, that has yet to be confirmed empirically, and this chapter will be restricted to international structural explanations for the observed systemic-level

---

The authors would like to thank Bruce Russett for his comments on an earlier version of this essay and the College of Liberal Arts at the University of Texas at Austin for the financial support of the first author's research.

relationship. After discussing the theoretical arguments and specifying the research hypotheses, we will test the hypotheses over the modern great power system since 1500.

THEORETICAL CONSIDERATIONS

One of the structural variables most widely believed to have an impact on the nature of war is the polarity of the system.[1] The primary impetus for much of the work linking polarity to war came from the familiar debate between Waltz (1964) and Deutsch and Singer (1964) over whether bipolar or multipolar sysems are more "stable."[2] Others have joined this debate, and in the process have generated arguments bearing on the relationship between the frequency and seriousness of war. Rosecrance (1966), for example, has argued that wars may be more frequent in multipolar systems because there are more opportunities for war to break out, but that this is compensated for by the fact that the wars that do occur are less serious. His analysis and that of others have been limited, however, by the absence of an adequate conceptualization of polarity.

Recent studies, particularly quantitative ones, have given more attention to the meaning of polarity (Bueno de Mesquita 1975; Nogee 1975; Jackson 1977; Rapkin et al. 1979; Wayman 1984). Rather than defining polarity as the number of independent centers of political power comprising either single powerful states or tightly aligned groups of states (Haas 1970; p. 99), it is now more common to use polarity to refer to the distribution of military capabilities in the system (Snyder and Diesing 1977, p. 420; Li and Thompson 1978, p. 1292; Waltz 1979, pp. 167-69; Levy 1985b). Although the concept of polarity will be operationally defined below, a brief definition would be useful at this point. For the purposes of this study, we will consider polarity to be a trichotomy: If a single state, unmatched by any other, attains a position of dominance in the system, then the system is unipolar (for example, Napoleonic Europe). If military capabilities are concentrated primarily in the hands of two "superpowers," separated by a considerable gap from all other states, then the system is defined as bipolar (for example, the Cold War period). Finally, if military capabilities are more widely distributed among a larger number of states, with no significant gap separating one or two great powers from others, the system is defined as multipolar (for example, eighteenth-century Europe).[3]

Our general hypothesis is that wars should be most frequent but least serious in a multipolar system, least frequent and most serious in a unipolar system, and of moderate frequency and seriousness in a bipolar system. First consider unipolarity. The concentration of military capabilities in the hands of a single dominant power poses an unambiguous threat to other powers and one that no single state can handle alone. Consequently, a general coalition will form against the leading power. Thus, we would expect there to be a single war, or a series of major wars, that involves all or nearly all of the great powers (Claude 1962, ch. 2; Dehio 1962; Morgenthau 1967).

In a multipolar system, we would expect there to be a large number of relatively minor wars. This results both from the increased number of opportunities for war deriving from the increased number of states and from the fact that the more powerful states have historically had a greater proclivity toward war (Wright 1965; Singer and Small 1972; Levy 1983, chs. 1–2). Since there are several states of roughly equal strength, however, an increase in power for one poses relatively little direct threat to any other single power. States should thus be less apt to intervene in an ongoing war, so that those that do occur are fairly minor. Since wars between a great power and a minor power or wars between two great powers are less likely to escalate than in a bipolar system and since no great power is threatened with elimination by any other single actor, there are few disincentives for engaging in minor wars. Therefore, a multipolar system should be characterized by a relatively large number of minor wars.

The two leading states in a bipolar system have roughly equal capabilities and can generally hold each other in check. Consequently, a coalition of all other states is rarely necessary to defeat an aggressor, and there is no reason to expect a general war involving all of the great powers. The great powers will be relatively free to fight among themselves and with minor actors. Furthermore, each of the two leading great powers may be able to add peripheral territories to its sphere of influence without increasing its capabilities to such an extent that it threatens the other superpower. Thus, we would expect more wars than in a unipolar system, and these wars should generally be fairly mild. There are limits to this, however, and the potential for a major conflagration is higher than in a multipolar system. Since a dramatic increase in either superpower's capabilities would enable it to become dominant, each must be prepared to block the other's attempts at establishing hegemony. In fact, since small changes in the status quo can have symbolic consequences affecting actors' perceptions regarding the relationship between the superpowers, each of the two leading powers must direct a sizable proportion of its resources to defending itself against the other, and each may have to resist (if it is unable to compensate for) even small increases in the other's capability. Thus, the superpowers (and their allies) can come into direct confrontation that can lead to a general war. This prospect serves to moderate the number of minor wars in which the great powers engage. Therefore, we would expect there to be a few more wars in a bipolar system than in a unipolar system. Although most would be fairly minor, the potential for a serious war is high; thus, these wars should be, on the average, more severe than in multipolar systems.

Another variable that should affect the frequency and seriousness of war is the relative availability of outlets for expansionist activity. If great powers can satiate their expansionist desires only at the expense of other great powers, a few serious wars among great powers are likely. On the other hand, if outlets for "cheap" expansion are available, each great power can engage in wars with minor powers or peripheral actors without posing a direct threat to the interests of other great powers. These wars would be relatively mild and fairly numerous. Balance-of-power theorists and many historians have traditionally equated this variable with the "openness" of the "colonial frontier," which is generally defined as being inversely related to the degree to which the European great powers have partitioned the rest of the globe into their respective spheres of influence (Morgenthau 1967, pp. 340-43; Hoffmann 1968; Thompson 1962, ch. 20). It is argued that in systems characterized by an open colonial frontier, wars are frequent but limited, since imperial expansion and minor conflicts on the periphery serve as a "safety valve" for the system. They divert competition for power from the core to the periphery, where it does not involve the vital interests of the great powers and where it can more easily be moderated (Morgenthau 1967, pp. 341-42; Hoffmann 1968). When the territory on the periphery has been completely partitioned among the great powers, however, the situation becomes a zero-sum game. Low-risk and low-cost expansion on the periphery is no longer possible, and further expansion by any single power can occur only at the expense of another great power (Lenin 1939, ch. 6; Chatterjee 1975, pp. 150-51).[4] In terms of the framework suggested by Choucri and North (1975), increases in "lateral pressure" generate an increase in the "intensity of intersections" and consequently in the likelihood of war between the great powers.[5] This increases the costs and risks of expansion, so that attempts at expansion become less frequent. Those expansionist moves that do occur, however, are perceived to affect the vital interests of the great powers, and the likelihood of war between them rises accordingly. Thus, the frequent but limited wars of an open colonial frontier give way to the less frequent but more serious great power wars of a system with closed peripheries. Since the availability of territory for imperial conquest has historically served as the outlet for relatively low-cost great power expansion, we will treat the "openness of the colonial frontier" as equivalent to the "availability of outlets for expansionist activity" for the purpose of our empirical analysis. This does not preclude the possibility that some other mechanism (for example, space colonies or seabed mineral rights) could serve a similar function in the future.

There is another path by which colonial expansion may affect the likelihood of wars between the great powers. Although this expansion into the periphery may introduce new conflicts between some great powers, it may also create issues over which other great powers share similar interests. If these patterns of conflict and cooperation in the periphery are not congruent with those in the core, the resulting cross-cutting pressures among the great powers will generally reduce the likelihood of war between them. It has been argued, for example, that the colonial expansion of the late nineteenth century actually reduced the likelihood of a major European war by generating cross-cutting pressures (Britain versus France in Africa and Britain versus Russia in Asia, for example, which cut across the rivalries in Europe), and these helped delay the rigid polarization of opposing alliance systems (Thompson 1962, p. 473). If the patterns of colonial rivalry are congruent with existing rivalries, however, conflicts between the great powers are reinforced and the likelihood of war increases. In the absence of a detailed picture of the interests of each of the great powers, it is impossible to predict whether colonial rivalries are cross-cutting or reinforcing. In addition, more work would be necessary to determine exactly how the impact of these cross-cutting or reinforcing pressures is affected by the open or closed nature of the colonial frontier. For these reasons, we have not attempted to incorporate these relationships into our model.

It is particularly interesting to speculate how these variables might interact to affect the frequency and seriousness of war. It is likely that the variables are not equally important, and that under some conditions the nature of war may be determined almost entirely by one dominant variable. When the system is unipolar, for example, it should not matter whether the colonial frontier is open or closed since the attention of all would be directed at defeating the hegemon. Thus, if the system is unipolar, we would expect a single, extremely serious war regardless of the openness of the colonial frontier. On the other hand, when the system is bipolar or multipolar, the openness of the colonial frontier will be more important in determining the nature of war.

In a bipolar system with an open frontier, we would expect a moderate number of, on the average, moderately severe wars. The open frontier would allow each of the leading great powers to extend its sphere of influence without directly threatening the other. Each could compensate for the other's gains by pursuing its own colonial policies, making war between the great powers less necessary and presumably less likely. Since only the great powers would have sufficient resources to seek colonies aggressively, there should be relatively few colonial wars.[6] The great powers' colonial policies would occasionally bring them into direct conflict, however, either because they both seek the same territory or because one fears that the other may be gaining too much of an advantage. In this case, a fairly severe war between the leading great powers may occur. Thus, wars in a bipolar system with an open frontier may be moderately frequent and moderately severe, on average.

In a bipolar system with a closed frontier, wars should be fairly infrequent and fairly severe. Conflicts in the periphery would be more likely to assume a zero-sum character, where any potential gain for one great power is perceived as a potential loss for another. This would enormously increase the symbolic dimensions of any colonial rivalry. Perceptions of any dyadic shifts in national strength in the eyes of allies and potential allies would be particularly important. For these reasons, it is very likely that any move by one leading great power would be resisted by the other. The potential seriousness of any resulting conflict, however, should contribute to deterrence and hence reduce their frequency. Because the leading powers in a bipolar system are roughly equal in strength, the danger of hegemony is far less then in a unipolar system, and other great powers are far less likely to intervene. Thus, major wars in bipolar systems should be less serious than those in unipolar systems. In addition, the lower likelihood of intervention by other great powers tends to remove some deterrent effects, so that the frequency of these wars in bipolar systems should be greater than that in multipolar systems.

In a multipolar system with open colonial frontiers, we would expect there to be a large number of relatively mild wars. There would exist several great powers capable of pursuing colonies, and the openness of the colonial frontier would enable them to extend their influence without threatening other powers. We would thus expect a large number of small colonial wars. Any war that did erupt between two great powers over a colonial issue would probably remain localized and therefore relatively mild. If the colonial frontier were closed, on the other hand, we would expect fewer, more serious wars. The great powers would be coming into direct conflict more often, making wars that do occur fairly serious and potentially very serious, which should in turn reduce their frequency.

Alternative Causal Models

It is important to distinguish the two possible patterns of casual linkages involving polarity, the colonial frontier, and the frequency and seriousness of war that are inherent in these arguments. First, the frequency and seriousness of war in a given period may individually and simultaneously be determined by the system-level variables. It may be, for example, that in a multipolar system wars are numerous because there are a greater number of interaction opportunities and relatively mild because the proportion of the military resources available to the warring parties is fairly low. In a bipolar world, however, there are fewer opportunities for war, and thus fewer wars; but those that do occur involve a substantial proportion of the world's military might and are perceived to threaten the very existence of the combatants and thus are relatively serious. This implies that the observed correlation between the frequency and seriousness of war is due to these causal linkages and can be fully explained by the system-level variables, and that any inference regarding a casual link between the frequency and seriousness of war would be spurious. This pattern of linkages is presented in Figure 3.1a, where the solid arrows represent causal links and the dashed line indicates an observed correlation due to these causal links.

Alternatively, the structure of the international system may determine seriousness of war, which in turn determines the frequency of war. That is, the system determines whether a war occurring in a given period is likely to be a colonial war, great power war, or hegemonic war. The

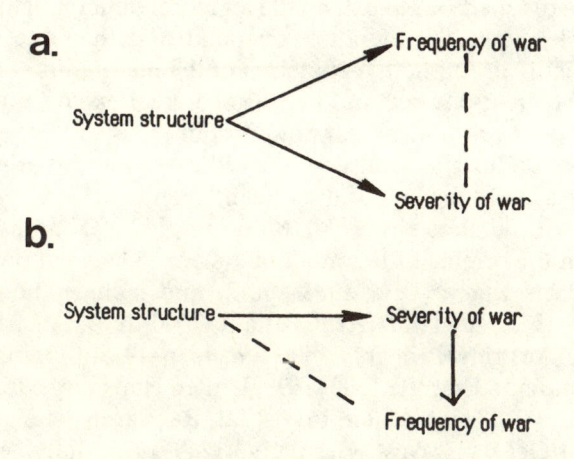

FIGURE 3.1. a: The linkages among the variables if system structure determines the frequency and severity of war. b: The linkages among the variables if system structure determines the severity of war, which in turn determines the frequency of war. Solid arrows indicate causal links; dashed lines indicate correlations.

likely severity of those wars that might occur in turn affects the frequency with which they actually occur through some mechanism that affects the decision-making processes of national leaders. One such mechanism is the cost-benefit calculations of decision makers: The perception that war is likely to be serious results in fewer cases in which the expected costs exceed the expected gains, and hence a diminished frequency of war. It may also be that the expectation of serious war means that it is possible to fight fewer wars with fixed natural resources, also leading to a diminished frequency of war. This pattern of relationships is depicted in Figure 3.1b. In this case, the structure of the system is a direct cause of the severity of war and an indirect cause of the frequency of war (through the intervening variable, severity), but it does not really explain the observed inverse relationship. The task of this study is to determine which of these models, if either, accurately characterizes the relationship between the structure of the international system and the nature of war.

RESEARCH DESIGN

Because of the slow rate at which our system-level variables change and because of the desirability of maximizing the variance in the variables of interest as well as the randomization of extraneous influences, it is advantageous to extend the temporal domain of the study as far as possible. Since the literature on polarity defines the concept—whether explicitly or implicitly—in terms of the distribution of capabilities among the great powers, and because colonial expansion has been primarily the behavior of the great powers,[7] our focus will be restricted to the great powers. Our temporal domain will extend to the origins of the great power system at the end of the fifteenth century (Levy 1983), which is consistent with Wallerstein (1974), Modelski (1978), Thompson (1983), and others on the origins of the modern system.[8] The great powers have been defined elsewhere (Levy 1983, ch. 2) and include the following: France, 1500-1975; England/Great Britain, 1500-1975; Austrian Hapsburgs/Austria/Austria-Hungary, 1500-19, 1556-1918; Spain, 1500-19, 1556-1808; Ottoman Empire, 1500-1699; United Hapsburgs, 1519-56; the Netherlands, 1609-1713; Sweden, 1617-1721; Russia/Soviet Union, 1721-1975; Prussia/Germany/West Germany, 1740-1975; Italy, 1861-1943; United States, 1898-1975; Japan, 1905-45; China, 1945-75.

Definition and Measurement of the Variables

The conceptualization of the frequency of war involves two major questions: (1) What classes of wars should be included? (2) What is the minimum threshold of violence, if any, for inclusion? Since the hypotheses involve small wars and since imperial wars are explicitly included in some of the hypotheses, imperial as well as interstate wars must be included in analysis. However, the hypotheses generally speak in terms of "wars," so that border disputes and other uses of force short of war should not be included. This leaves the more difficult question of the minimum threshold defining a war. We cannot rely exclusively on the Singer/Small 1,000 battle deaths criteria (1972), because it is too high for imperial wars. Since any lower threshold involves problems of data accuracy and availability, we have relied on multiple sources to determine whether a conflict excluded by the Singer/Small criterion went beyond minor skirmishing to open warfare. Existing compilations of war data are not adequate for our purposes, so a new data set of international wars involving the great powers has been generated. A discussion of our data-generating procedures can be found in Levy (1983) and Levy and Morgan (1984).

The best and most widely used indicator of the seriousness of war is its "severity" in terms of battle deaths (Richardson 1960; Singer and Small 1972, p. 130; Levy 1983). Since the "seriousness" of war is to be related to its frequency in a given period, the concern must be not with the severity of a single war but instead with some aggregate measure of the severity of all wars in a given period. While the total number of battle deaths in a period is a good measure of the total severity of war, it must be supplemented with other indicators because it is partially dependent upon the number of wars occurring (which is the variable with which it is to be correlated). The average number of battle deaths per war is perhaps the best measure of the seriousness of the wars occurring in a given period and is also used. This indicator does not discriminate, however, between a period characterized by several large wars and a period with one enormously destructive war and many smaller wars. This distinction can be tapped by the frequency of wars above a certain threshold. The number of wars between great powers ("great power wars") that exceed 50,000 battle deaths is a fairly discriminating measure of severity, including only about 10 percent of all cases in this study. An even more discriminating indicator is the number of "general" or "hegemonic" wars occurring in a period. These are history's most serious wars, involving nearly all the great powers and enormous casualties. For our purposes, a general war is defined as one in which the decisive victory of at least one side is both a reasonable possibility and one that would be likely to result in the leadership or dominance by a single state over the system, or at least in the overthrow of an existing leadership or hegemony (Levy 1985a).[9]

We thus have four indicators of the seriousness of war in a given period: the total number of battle deaths, the average number of battle deaths per war, the number of great power wars exceeding 50,000 fatalities, and the number of general wars. These indicators cover a range of seriousness, which is useful given the inherent ambiguity in the meaning of the concept in the literature. The consistency of results across this range of indicators will increase our confidence in the validity of the findings.

The battle death data are taken from Levy (1983), whose data are based on the Singer and Small data (1972) for the post-1815 period and on the Sorokin data (1937) for the earlier period. Given our focus on the great power system, only the fatalities of the great powers are included in the severity indicator. Because fatality estimates for imperial wars are often unavailable or unreliable, and also because these make a marginal contribution to total fatalities as compared with interstate wars involving the great powers, only fatalities from the latter are used to approximate the severity indicator. From this list of all international wars involving the great powers, the four indicators of the seriousness of war can easily be constructed.

The availability of outlets for expansionist activity is defined as the "openness" of the colonial frontier, which refers to the availability of territories on the periphery of the international system. When there exist vast amounts of territory available for colonization by the great powers, the frontier is open. Conversely, when the great powers can extend their influence only at the direct expense of other system members, the frontier is considered to be closed. Measuring the relative openness of the colonial frontier over nearly five centuries is an exceedingly difficult task. In the absence of a more direct indicator, we have relied on a surrogate measure: the amount of colonial activity. The "safety valve" hypothesis implies that the establishment of new colonies is critical to the avoidance of a major war among core powers, so that the number of colonies established in a given period is one indirect measure of the openness of the colonial frontier in that period. The assumption is that when a large section of territory becomes accessible, and therefore open to colonization, a flurry of colonial activity will follow.[10] The data on this colonial activity indicator are taken from Bergesen and Schoenberg's compilation (1980) of the number of colonies established and terminated each year from 1415 to 1969. Their compilation is based on Henige's list (1970) of colonial governors for that period.

Let us now turn to polarity, which was defined earlier in terms of the distribution of military capabilities in the system. In the absence of interval-level data on the military capabilities of all of the great powers during the last 500 years, it is necessary to use an alternative measurement procedure for polarity. Standard historical sources are used to generate a trichotomous classification of the distribution of power in the system for each year since 1500, reflecting unipolarity, bipolarity, and multipolarity. The resulting classification, together with further discussion of some difficult analytical problems, can be found in Levy (1985b).

For the purposes of this analysis, the data on the frequency and seriousness of war, the openness of the colonial frontier, and polarity have been aggregated by 20-year periods.[11] In our previous article, the majority of the analysis was performed using 25-year periods of aggregation; however, the analyses were replicated with similar results using 20-year periods. The 20-year periods are used in this study in order to increase the number of data points.

Methods of Analysis

Our first task will be to determine the effect the systemic variables taken singly have on the nature of war. First, we must determine whether the predictor variables correlate in the expected direction with each of the war variables. If the hypotheses are correct, (1) the number of colonies established should be positively correlated with the frequency of war and inversely related to the severity of war, and (2) the polarity of the system should be positively correlated with the frequency of war and inversely related to the severity of war. These hypotheses will be tested using bivariate correlation analysis.

The bivariate correlational analysis, however, will not answer the primary question of how the relationship between the frequency and seriousness of war changes according to the value of the predictor variable. To answer this question, we must use causal modeling techniques designed to test for spurious relationships (Blalock 1968). This will be accomplished by determining how the regression estimators relating the frequency of war to the severity of war are altered when the predictor variables are introduced into the equation as controls. We can perform this type of analysis statistically by using analysis of covariance for the nonmetric predictor variable polarity. The effects on the severity/ frequency relationship brought about by the metric indicator of the openness of the colonial frontier can be examined in a similar fashion using multiple-regression techniques. Finally, an analysis of covariance will be performed in which we introduce both system-level variables as controls and determine an adjusted regression coefficient associating the frequency and seriousness of war. If these systemic variables do explain the relationship between the frequency and seriousness of war, then the regression coefficients relating the frequency of wars in 20-year periods to their severity should be substantially reduced in magnitude and significance when we statistically control for the effects of polarity and the openness of the colonial frontiers.[12]

We can also analyze the partial correlation coefficients associating the frequency and severity indicators when the system variables are introduced as controls. Partial correlation coefficients provide the correlations between two variables once the effects of some other variable, or variables, have been partialed out. If, for example, the partial correlation coefficient between the frequency and seriousness of war is substantially reduced when a systemic variable is introduced as a statistical control, we could conclude that the observed frequency/seriousness correlation is spurious. This analysis provides essentially the same information as that provided by the regression techniques and it has the advantage of being more easily interpreted in terms of the question in which we are interested. Recall from the discussion of Figure 3.1 that our general question involves the determination of which, if any, pair of variables is correlated only because both variables are associated with the third. If the system variables determine both the frequency and the severity of war, the correlation between them would actually be due to these relationships and not because of some causal link between them. On the other hand, if the structure of the system determines the severity of war, which in turn determines the frequency of war, the correlation between the system variables and the frequency of war would be substantially reduced. This analysis can thus be used to determine whether the frequency and seriousness of war are "spuriously" correlated or the severity of war is an intervening variable through which the structure of the system indirectly affects the frequency of war.

DATA ANALYSIS

The first set of hypotheses to be tested are those dealing with the predicted correlations between the variables describing the structure of the international system and those reflecting the nature of war. Recall that the polarity and colonial frontier variables are expected to be positively correlated with the frequency of war and inversely correlated with the severity of war. The product/moment correlation coefficients indicating the association between the variables are provided in Table 3.1. The coefficients in the first row of the table reflect the inverse relationship between the frequency and the severity of war that we are attempting to explain. Regardless of the indicator of severity chosen, there is a moderate inverse correlation that is highly significant.[13]

TABLE 3.1
Simple correlations (r) between systemic variables and war*

	Number of Wars	Log (Battle Deaths)	Log (Average Battle Deaths)	Great Power War > 50,000 Battle Deaths	General Wars
Number of wars	—	−0.53	−0.70	−0.34	−0.53
	—	(0.005)	(0.001)	(0.056)	(0.004)
Polarity	0.20	−0.14	−0.15	−0.22	−0.14
	(0.185)	(0.264)	(0.247)	(0.156)	(0.264)
Colonies established	0.57	−0.25	−0.33	−0.30	−0.10
	(0.002)	(0.123)	(0.060)	(0.081)	(0.327)

*The p values are given in parentheses.

The coefficients relating the polarity indicator to the war indicators are all in the predicted direction, but they are relatively weak and none is statistically significant. One possible explanation for the weakness of these coefficients is that one of the assumptions underlying the statistical technique is violated by the nonmetric character of the polarity variable. The results of other tests are fully consistent with these, however. When the tau-b correlation coefficient is used, the results are nearly identical, and a one-way analysis of variance shows that the polarity indicator accounts for only a very small proportion of the variance in the war indicators. The indicator of the openness of the colonial frontier also correlates in the predicted direction with the war indicators.[14] It is significantly associated with the frequency of war and moderately associated with three of the severity indicators.

In order to answer fully the question of why an inverse relationship between the frequency and severity of war exists, it is necessary to determine how the severity and frequency of war are statistically related when we control for the effects of the system variables. We will examine the effects of the polarity and colonial frontier variables through analysis of covariance and multiple-regression techniques, respectively. Given the plausibility of theoretical arguments suggesting that the frequency of war is a function of their expected seriousness, the frequency indicator will be used as the dependent variable in the regression equations. The resulting regression coefficients and their significance levels for these models are presented in Table 3.2.

The first row in the table provides the regression coefficients for the frequency of war when regressed only on the severity indicators. These coefficients will provide a useful standard of comparison by which to judge the effects of the system variables. The standard errors for these

TABLE 3.2
Regression coefficients relating the frequency of war to the severity indicators controlling for the system variables

| | | | Severity Indicator | |
Control Variable		Log (Battle Deaths)	Log (Average Battle Deaths)	General War	Great Power War > 50,000 Battle Deaths
[None]	β	−3.30	−3.75	−5.29	−2.33
	SE	1.15	0.82	1.83	1.41
	p value	(0.009)	(0.000)	(0.009)	(0.112)
Colonies established	β	−2.57	−3.09	−4.78	−1.27
	p value	(0.021)	(0.001)	(0.004)	(0.335)
Polarity	β	−3.20	−3.72	−6.30	−2.22
	p value	(0.016)	(0.001)	(0.008)	(0.155)
Polarity + colonies established	β	−2.51	−3.07	−5.56	−1.39
	p value	(0.003)	(0.002)	(0.001)	(0.319)

simple regression coefficients have also been provided, as have the significance levels. The standard errors will provide a useful "unit" by which to compare changes in the regression coefficients when the system variables are introduced as controls.

Rows two and three show the coefficients associating the severity of war with the frequency of war when the system variables are introduced into the equation singly. While seven of the eight coefficients are lesser in magnitude than those found when no controls are used, none of these is more than 0.8 standard error below the simple regression coefficient. Notice also that when both system variables are simultaneously included as control variables, the results are virtually the same. Since the system variables are correlated in the predicted direction with the nature of war variables, we would expect there to be some reduction in the coefficients even if the system variables do not account for the frequency/severity relationship. Given the weakness of these findings, we cannot conclude that the openness of the colonial frontier or the polarity of the international system is an important determinant of the frequency/severity relationship. Regardless of which indicator of severity is used, the relationship between the frequency and seriousness of war remains substantially constant regardless of the structure of the international system.

The same conclusion can be drawn by examining the partial correlation coefficients between the frequency of war and the severity indicators when the structure of the system is introduced as a control variable. These coefficients are presented in Table 3.3 where the simple correlation coefficients are also provided for the purposes of comparison. Notice that in no case does the introduction of a system variable as a control substantially reduce the correlation between the war variables. In the case of the general war indicator, the correlation actually increases when the number of colonies established serves as a control, suggesting that this aspect of the frequency/seriousness relationship is actually somewhat masked by the structure of the system. The only severity variable for which the introduction of a control brings about even a moderate reduction in the coefficient is the number of great power wars having over 50,000 battle fatalities. This correlation is relatively weak to begin with (and not statistically significant at the 0.05 level), however, and the maximum reduction is only from -0.34 to -0.22. These results provide fairly strong support for the argument that the inverse relationship between the frequency and severity of war is not a statistical artifact produced by the variables' association with the structure of the international system.

We may also use this technique to determine if the other hypothesized set of causal linkages presented in Figure 3.1 is a more

TABLE 3.3
Correlations (r) between frequency of war and severity of war, controlling for the systemic variables

	Log (Battle Deaths)	Log (Average Battle Deaths)	General War	Great Power War > 50,000 Battle Deaths
Frequency	−0.53	−0.70	−0.53	−0.34
Control for colonies established	−0.49	−0.67	−0.58	−0.22
Control for polarity	−0.52	−0.70	−0.52	−0.31
Control for both	−0.49	−0.67	−0.59	−0.22

TABLE 3.4

Correlations (r) between frequency of war and systemic variables, controlling for severity

	Colonies Established	Polarity
Frequency	0.57	0.20
Control for log (battle deaths)	0.53	0.15
Control for log (average battle deaths)	0.51	0.13
Control for general war	0.61	0.15
Control for great power war > 50,000 battle deaths	0.52	0.13

appropriate characterization of the relationship among these variables.[15] The partial correlation coefficients between the frequency of war and the system variables when the severity of war is introduced as a control are presented in Table 3.4. If these coefficients are substantially reduced when the controls are included, we could conclude that the severity of war acts as an intervening variable between the frequency of war and the structure of the system. As can be seen in the table, this is not the case. Once again, the introduction of the control variables brings about little reduction in the correlation coefficients. We are thus led to the conclusion that neither of the possible patterns of causal linkages pictured in Figure 3.1 is correct.

These results suggest that the pattern of causal linkages among these variables corresponds with neither of the hypotheses represented in Figure 3.1. Two logical possibilities remain: Either none of the correlations is spurious or the correlation between the system variables and the severity of war is due to these variables' association with the frequency of war. The results obtained thus far would be consistent with either possibility, but there is some evidence to suggest that the latter hypothesis may be correct. In particular, recall from Table 3.1 that the correlations between the system variables and the frequency of war were stronger than those linking the system variables to the severity indicators. It may be that the structure of the international system affects the frequency of war and is spuriously correlated with the severity of war. We can determine if this is the case by calculating the partial correlation coefficients linking the structure of the system with the severity of war after the frequency of war has been introduced as a control variable. If these coefficients are substantially less than uncontrolled coefficients, we could conclude that the system structure/severity of war association is a product of these variables' relationship with the frequency of war. The results of this analysis are presented in Table 3.5.

TABLE 3.5
Correlations (r) between severity of war and the systemic variables, controlling for the frequency of war

	Log (Battle Deaths)	Log (Average Battle Deaths)	General War	Great Power War > 50,000 Battle Deaths
Polarity	−0.14	−0.15	−0.14	−0.22
Control for frequency	−0.04	−0.02	−0.04	−0.17
Colonies established	−0.25	−0.33	−0.10	−0.30
Control for frequency	0.07	0.13	0.30	−0.14

The results presented in this table suggest that the relationship between the system variables and the severity of war is, in fact, due to the association between these variables and the frequency of war. The associations between polarity and all but one of the severity of war indicators virtually disappear when the frequency of war is introduced as a control variable. The correlations between the severity indicators and the number of colonies established (again with the one exception) actually reverse signs when the control is included. In each case, the coefficient associating the system variable with the number of great power wars of over 50,000 battle fatalities is anomalous. The initial correlation is modestly reduced, but the results are not consistent with those for the other severity indicators. The most obvious explanation for this anomaly is that the severity of war is a multidimensional concept, and that variables other than those included in this study are more closely associated with the severity of war once war begins.

Since these findings conform to none of the theoretical arguments advanced earlier, they require some degree of explanation. These results would be consistent with two patterns of causal linkages. It may be that the system variables affect the frequency of war, which in turn influences the severity of wars. Conversely, it is possible that the system variables and the severity of war (which is determined by factors not included in this study) independently influence the frequency of war. Unfortunately, we are unable to perform a critical test within the bounds of this study that would determine which of these explanations better fits the data.

For theoretical reasons, however, we prefer the latter explanation. We have suggested several reasons why both the structure of the system and the severity of war should affect the frequency of war. It is more difficult to explain how the frequency of war in a given period should causally affect the severity of those wars. It may be true that resource limitations force states to keep their wars limited if they engage in war frequently, but the reverse link would be equally plausible: After engaging in a large war, states have few resources for numerous other wars. The same logic holds for the functionalist argument that the equilibrium of the system can be maintained by either a major adjustment through a major war or a series of minor adjustments effected by more limited wars. Although the frequency of war would affect its seriousness, the effect of the seriousness of war on its frequency should be equally great. In cost/benefit terms, however, it is much more plausible that the expected costs of war will affect decision makers' proclivities for war than the frequency of war somehow affecting its seriousness. Thus, our tentative conclusion is that both systemic structure and the seriousness of war in a given period moderately affect the frequency of war in that period.

CONCLUSION

The purpose of this study has been to attempt to explain the observed inverse relationship between the frequency and seriousness of wars. We have restricted this research to explanatory variables characterizing the polarity of the international system and the availability of outlets for expansionist activity. It has been argued that a few severe wars among the great powers are more likely to occur in periods when the system structure is such that the vital interests of the great powers are threatened. When the polarity of the system is such that one power is perceived to threaten hegemony, or when no outlet for expansionism exists, bringing the great powers into direct conflict, major wars should occur. Conversely, if no great power poses an overwhelming threat to the existence of the others and the extension of one power's influence does not necessarily come at the direct expense of another great power, wars may be frequently but mild as the great powers fight primarily with minor states or nonstate groups. The results of our statistical analyses, however, indicate that these variables do not account for the observed relationship.

It is important to note that our failure to explain the frequency/seriousness relationship is not the product of an absence of relationships among the variables included in this study. To the contrary, there appears to be a consistent pattern of relationships among these variables that serves to disconfirm the hypotheses guiding our study. The failure to account for the observed relationship is thus probably due to the fact that the models we have tested are incompletely specified. We know, for example, that the "seriousness" of war is a multidimensional concept. On the one hand, wars between great powers are more "serious" in terms of their political effects and their potential for escalation than are wars between a great power and a nongreat power. On the other hand, long wars involving many battle deaths are more "serious" than shorter, less destructive wars, regardless of the status of the belligerents. The theoretical arguments guiding this study suggest that the variables we have considered should influence the former type of severity. The frequency/seriousness linkage may be better explained by variables that determine whether wars that do occur will expand and escalate. These include not only systemic variables such as alliance configurations and the nature of military technology, but also such national-level variables as ideological fervor, public opinion, bureaucratic politics, and the idiosyncracies of individual decision makers (Iklé 1971; Smoke 1977). Furthermore, the theoretical arguments linking the severity of war to the frequency of war often cut across levels of analysis; that is, the inverse correlation observed at the systemic level may be at least partially a product of factors operating at the nation-state level of analysis. In short, a complete explanation of the frequency/seriousness relationship will require further analysis incorporating a number of other variables at all levels of analysis.

Clearly, the overwhelming conclusion is that we are a long way from fully understanding the relationship between the frequency and seriousness of war. As we pointed out in our previous study (Levy and Morgan 1984), this question has policy relevance in that it bears on the oft-repeated claim that we must be prepared to fight small wars now to avoid more serious wars later. One aspect of the argument in the preceding paragraph is undoubtedly correct—we do not yet know why the relationship between the frequency and seriousness of war exists, and thus we cannot totally predict when a small war may turn into the big war it is supposed to avoid. Considering this, until the severity/frequency relationship is more clearly understood, we should be quite circumspect about policy prescriptions advocating small wars.

NOTES

1. Since nearly all the literature on polarity implicitly adopts a traditional realist perspective, which incorporates a Eurocentric, great power bias, the concept of "the system" will refer to the modern great power system in which military/security interests are central (Levy 1983).

2. Although stability has been conceptualized in terms of both the maintenance of the status quo and the relative absence of war in the system (Zinnes 1967), most of the theoretical literature on the polarity/stability question defines stability in terms of war proneness, conceived as some combination of the frequency of occurrence of wars and their seriousness (Levy 1985b).

3. This follows Levy's conceptualization of polarity (1985b).

4. Thompson (1962), Craig and George (1983, p.46), and others make this argument explicitly with respect to the pre-World War I period. Thompson states: "It was when the world's resources of such 'cheap compensations' were exhausted, in the decade after 1904, that European tensions reached breaking point. [This period] brought a limit to the expansion of the world's colonial frontiers in general and forced the powers back upon their more dangerous rivalries in Europe where no freedom of maneuver remained" (pp. 473-74).

5. Note that the "safety valve" effect operating at lower levels of lateral pressure or colonial expansion is not incorporated into the dynamic model of conflict created by Choucri and North (1975).

6. Colonial wars (which we shall also refer to as imperial wars) are defined as those involving a great power against a smaller entity on the periphery of the system. They are historically equivalent to Singer and Small's category (1972, pp. 31-32) of extrasystemic wars involving a great power for the 1816-1980 period (Levy 1983, pp. 61-63).

7. Portugal for many centuries is one obvious exception.

8. For purposes of convenient temporal partitioning, we use the year 1500 rather than Levy's 1495 as the starting point for our analysis.

9. The list of general wars is as follows: War of Dutch Independence/Spanish Armada, 1585-1609; Thirty Years' War, 1618-48; Dutch War of Louis XIV, 1672-78; War of the League of Augsburg, 1688-97; War of the Spanish Succession, 1701-13; War of Jenkins' Ear/Austrian Succession, 1739-48, Seven Years' War, 1755-63; French Revolutionary and Napoleonic Wars, 1792-1815; World War I, 1914-18; World War II, 1939-45 (Levy 1985a). In this study, the French Revolutionary and Napoleonic Wars have been treated as two distinct general wars (1792-1800, 1803-15), since they overlap into two temporal periods and since each of the two main phases of the wars individually satisfies the criteria for a general war. In addition, because the Thirty Years' War satisfies our criteria only after 1625, it will be treated as such only in that period.

10. We have also performed the analyses below using an alternative measure of the openness of the colonial frontier: the sum of the number of colonies established and terminated in each period. If the results were stronger for the alternative indicator, it would suggest that the openness of the colonial frontier affects the nature of war by drawing attention away from disputes at the core of the system rather than by creating an outlet for expansionist activity. As one would expect, the indicators are moderately correlated ($r = 0.56$, $p = 0.03$), but this correlation is sufficiently low to suggest that they are measuring different concepts.

11. Any temporal aggregation of this kind raises a question regarding the measurement of polarity. Since the analysis is to be performed on 20-year periods of aggregation, each period must be categorized according to its polarity. In 17 of the 23 periods, this presents no problem because the polarity of the system remained unchanged throughout the 20 years. A change in polarity occurred during the other six periods, however, making the classification of these periods more difficult. There are several possible ways in which this problem can be handled.

One means would be to categorize a period according to the value of polarity it took on during the majority of its years. This would classify the periods on the basis of the polarity that presumably would have had the longest influence. Another strategy would be to classify the entire period as the polarity at which it began. This could be reasonable since the effects on the nature of war brought about by a change in polarity could be felt only after a lag. Furthermore, if changes in polarity are often coincident with a major war, that war should be attributable to the polarity under which it began. Thus, the warfare occurring in a given period could be most closely associated with the polarity when the period began. This argument is less valid if the change in polarity occurs within the first year or two of a period, however. A third prospect represents a synthesis of the previous two. We can categorize a period as being the polarity at which it began, unless the change occurs within five years of its onset. In four of the six cases in question, all three methods provide the same coding. In categorizing the other two periods, we have relied on the third method. In both cases, the other methods provided different answers, so this scheme served as something of a "tiebreaker."

12. Conversely, if the adjusted regression coefficients are higher when the system variables are included as controls, we could conclude that our predictor variables actually serve to mask the strength of the frequency/seriousness relationship. If the coefficients show little change, it would indicate that the system variables have no bearing on the relationship.

13. These results are consistent across indicators, whether 20- or 25-year periods are used, and when the partitioning of the data is shifted by beginning the analysis in years other than 1500 (Levy and Morgan 1984).

14. Performing this, and the remaining, analysis using our alternative measure of the openness of the colonial frontier provides results that are fully consistent with those presented here. The results are somewhat weaker, however, suggesting that the openness of the frontier affects the nature of war by providing an outlet for expansion.

15. The analysis based on the regression equations actually provides a more appropriate test of the hypotheses than does the partial correlation analysis (Blalock 1968, p. 176). In addition, none of the statistical assumptions of the analysis of covariance test are violated by the nonmetric indicator of polarity as are those underlying the partial correlation analysis. Throughout the remainder of this study, we will focus our attention on the partial correlation coefficients, however, because these are easier to present and interpret in light of our hypotheses. We have performed the regression analyses for each of the remaining tests with identical substantive results; therefore, our confidence in our findings remains high.

REFERENCES

Bergesen, A., and R. Schoenberg. 1980. "Long Waves of Colonial Expansion and Contraction, 1415-1969." In A. Bergesen (ed.), *Studies of the Modern World System*. New York: Academic Press, pp. 231-77.

Blalock, H. M. 1968. "Theory Building and Causal Inferences." In H. M. Blalock and A. B. Blalock (eds.), *Methodology in Social Research*. New York: McGraw-Hill, pp. 155-98.

Bueno de Mesquita, B. 1975. "Measuring Systemic Polarity." *Journal of Conflict Resolution* 19 (June):187-216.

Chatterjee, P. 1975. *Arms, Alliances and Stability*. Bombay: Macmillian.

Choucri, N., and R. C. North. 1975. *Nations in Conflict: National Growth and International Violence*. San Francisco: W. H. Freeman.

Claude, I. L., Jr. 1962. *Power and International Relations*. New York: Random House.

Craig, G. A., and A. L. George. 1983. *Force and Statecraft*. New York: Oxford University Press.

Deutsch, K., and J. D. Singer. 1964. "Multipolar Power Systems and International Stability." *World Politics* 16 (April):390-406.

Dehio, L. 1962. *The Precarious Balance*. New York: Vintage.

Haas, M. 1970. "International Subsystems: Stability and Polarity." *American Political Science Review* 64 (March):98-123.

Henige, D. 1970. *Colonial Governors*. Madison: University of Wisconsin Press.

Hoffmann, S. 1968. "Balance of Power." In *International Encyclopedia of the Social Sciences, Vol. 1*. New York: Macmillan, pp. 506-10.

Iklé, F. C. 1971. *Every War Must End*. New York: Columbia University Press.

Jackson, W. D. 1977. "Polarity in International Systems: A Conceptual Note." *International Interactions* 4:87-96.

Lenin, V. I. 1939. *Imperialism*. New York: International.

Levy, J. S. 1985a. "Theories of General War." *World Politics* 37 (April): pp. 344-74.

―――. 1985b. "The Polarity of the System and International Stability." In A. N. Sabrosky (ed.), *Polarity and War: The Changing Structure of International Conflict*. Boulder, CO: Westview.

―――. 1983. *War in the Modern Great Power System: 1495-1975*. Lexington: University Press of Kentucky.

Levy, J. S., and T. C. Morgan. 1984. "The Frequency and Seriousness of War: An Inverse Relationship?" *Journal of Conflict Resolution* 28 (December):731–49.

Li, R. P. Y., and W. R. Thompson. 1978. "The Stochastic Process of Alliance Formation Behavior." *American Political Science Review* 72 (December):1288–1303.

Modelski, G. 1978. "The Long Cycle of Global Politics and the Nation State." *Comparative Studies in Society and History* 20 (April):214–35.

Morgenthau, H. 1967. *Politics Among Nations.* New York: Alfred A. Knopf.

Nogee, J. L. 1975. "Polarity: An Ambiguous Concept." *Orbis* 18 (Winter): 1193–1224.

Rapkin, D. P., W. R. Thompson, and J. A. Christopherson. 1979. "Bipolarity and Bipolarization in the Cold War Era." *Journal of Conflict Resolution* 23 (June):261–95.

Richardson, L. F. 1960. *Statistics of Deadly Quarrels.* Chicago: Quadrangle.

Rosecrance, R. N. 1966. "Bipolarity, Multipolarity, and the Future." *Journal of Conflict Resolution* 10 (September):314–27.

Singer, J. D., and M. Small. 1972. *The Wages of War, 1816–1965.* New York: John Wiley and Sons.

Smoke, R. 1977. *War: Controlling Escalation.* Cambridge, MA: Harvard University Press.

Snyder, G. P., and P. Diesing. 1977. *Conflict Among Nations.* Princeton, NJ: Princeton University Press.

Sorokin, P. A. 1937. *Social and Cultural Dynamics, Vol. 3: Fluctuation of Social Relationships, War and Revolution.* New York: American.

Thompson, D. 1962. *Europe Since Napoleon,* 2nd ed. rev. New York: Alfred A. Knopf.

Thompson, W. R. 1983. "Uneven Economic Growth, Systemic Challenges, and Global Wars." *International Studies Quarterly* 27 (September): 341–55.

Wallerstein, I. 1974. *The Modern World System I: Capitalist Agriculture and the Origins of the World-Economy in the Sixteenth Century.* New York: Academic Press.

Waltz, K. N. 1979. *Theory of International Relations.* Reading, MA: Addison-Wesley.

———. 1964. "The Stability of a Bipolar World." *Daedalus* 93 (Summer): 882–86.

Wayman, F. W. 1984. "Bipolarity and War: The Role of Capability Concentration and Alliance Patterns Among Major Powers, 1816–1965." *Journal of Peace Research* 21 (April):61–78.

Wright, Q. 1965. *A Study of War.* Chicago: University of Chicago Press.

Zinnes, D. 1967. "An Analytical Study of the Balance of Power Theories." *Journal of Peace Research* 4: 270–88.

4
The Vietnam War and Generational Differences in Foreign Policy Attitudes
Robert A. Wells

INTRODUCTION

One decade has passed since the collapse of the South Vietnamese government, thereby terminating U.S. participation in a long and costly war. However, the legacy of Vietnam in terms of its long-term impact and consequences for U.S. foreign policy remains unclear. The widespread opposition and discontent produced by U.S. involvement in Indochina led Henry Kissinger to observe in 1975 that Americans, particularly the young, "have been traumatized by Vietnam as we were by Munich" (quoted in LaFeber 1985, p. 280). In the words of Norman Podhoretz, "Whatever other 'lessons' Vietnam might have been thought to yield, the one that seemed to take deepest root in American culture was that military force had become, or at any rate was on the way to becoming, obsolete as an instrument of American political purposes in the Third World" (1985, p. 452). Thus, it has been argued, the United States' failure in Vietnam had been sufficiently demoralizing for a sizable number of U.S. citizens to question the utility of military power as an instrument of U.S. foreign policy.

An alternative view suggested by Chomsky and Herman (1979) maintains that "the basic institutions of U.S. society survived the Indochina crisis undamaged and unchanged" (pp. 17-18). Consequently,

---

The author wishes gratefully to acknowledge and thank Terry W. Sloope, Paul Allen Beck, and Ole R. Holsti for their useful comments and suggestions.

Chomsky and Herman believe that since the sources of foreign policy "in domestic U.S. society have undergone no significant change... There is every reason to suppose that the traditional U.S. government policies of international subversion and—when circumstances warrant—overt aggression will continue" (p. 21). Not surprisingly, given the very diverse interpretations of the consequences of the Vietnam War for U.S. foreign policy, the topic has received a substantial amount of attention from scholars.

The predominant view among analysts of U.S. foreign policy is that Vietnam led to the breakdown of the post-World War II consensus that had been forged out of the experience of the United States in World War II. Prior to U.S. involvement in Vietnam, mass public and elite attitudes were structured within an internationalist-isolationist framework. Since internationalists far outnumbered isolationists, an "age of consensus" existed concerning the proper goals of U.S. foreign policy and the means by which those goals were to be achieved. However, a number of scholars (Bardes and Oldendick 1978, 1980; Holsti 1979; Holsti and Rosenau 1980a,b, 1984; Maggiotto and Wittkopf 1981; Wittkopf 1981; Wittkopf and Maggiotto 1983) have provided evidence to suggest that the old internationalist-isolationist dichotomy is no longer an adequate framework for understanding or explaining the attitudes of the U.S. public in the post-Vietnam era. In short, Vietnam served as the catalyst for the breakdown of the old foreign policy consensus and the formation of a new attitudinal structure to replace it. This new attitudinal structure is multidimensional, resulting in competing and conflicting belief systems as to the extent and nature of U.S. global interests and responsibilities. Thus, rather deep cleavages characterize the U.S. public regarding various foreign policy issues.

A corollary of the breakdown of consensus perspective is the generational thesis. This interpretation explains the present lack of consensus as, in part, a consequence of the differential impact that the Vietnam experience had on different age cohorts. Specifically, speculation has centered on the proposition that the Vietnam War served as a dramatic socialization event for those individuals who reached the age of maturity during the period of U.S. involvement in Southeast Asia. Just as an earlier generation's world views had been shaped by the experience of World War II, it has been hypothesized that a Vietnam generation has emerged with a rather distinctive foreign policy outlook. The purpose of this study is to examine the impact of generation on the foreign policy attitudes of the U.S. public and to note if generational differences occur according to theoretical expectations.

THE CONCEPT OF GENERATION

The term "generation" has a variety of meanings. One definition is simply biological, that is, the time period necessary for sons to become fathers (and daughters to become mothers). Within this context, age would not have any political significance in the sense that generational succession would not involve political or social change, but a continuation of the past. A second perspective, associated with Eisenstadt (1956), offers a definition of generation based on changes of attitudes that occur as a consequence of the maturation process. Attitude differences between age groups are a function of what position or stage one occupies in the life cycle. The life cycle theory also leads to the conclusion that generational succession will not necessarily entail fundamental social change because the young will eventually change their attitudes as they mature and assume familial, career, and social obligations or responsibilities.

A third view of generation, most clearly explicated by Mannheim (1952), directly assigns generation the role of a potential agent of social change. For Mannheim, the concept of generation has a political-sociological basis. "The fact of belonging to the same class, and that of belonging to the same generation or age group, have this in common, that both endow the individual with a common location in the social and historical process, and thereby limit them to a specific range of experiences, predisposing them for a certain characteristic mode of thought and experience, and a characteristic type of historically relevant action" (p. 291). Mannheim's basic thesis, then, is that each generation experiences a unique set of social-historical events that shape that generation's attitudes as well as differentiate it from preceding and succeeding generations.

However, the existence of generation is not sufficient to endow it as an important factor in the process of social change. "Whether a new generational style emerges every year, every thirty, every hundred years, or whether it emerges at all, depends entirely on the trigger action of the social and cultural process" (Mannheim 1952, p. 310). Therefore, the significance of generation emerges only in reaction to the historical and social forces operating during a given era. In brief, it is the historical and social setting that determines whether generation becomes a factor in the historical process.

A central question regarding the impact of Vietnam is whether or not it was an historical event of sufficient magnitude to serve as a socializing event for those who reached the age of maturity during U.S. involvement in Southeast Asia. The question being raised here is not whether Vietnam had an impact on U.S. foreign policy and the general public, but the extent to which it had a differential impact between age groups. A theory of generational change suggests not only that the events of a particular era shape the thinking of those who experience it, and as a result certain lessons of history are derived from the experience, but also that the impact will be greatest on those in their early adulthood years. Since the conditions that prevailed while one was growing up carry greater weight than later life experiences, a generation with distinct views emerges when the youth of a particular historical period are socialized by a unique or radically different set of common experiences.

The concept of generation has been utilized by a number of scholars to explain variation in the foreign policy beliefs of U.S. citizens. Klingberg (1979), for example, has identified a cyclical pattern in U.S. foreign policy. According to him, for the last 200 years U.S. foreign policy has alternated between "extrovert" and "introvert" moods. Klingberg argues that these moods are related, at least in part, to the ascendancy of new political generations (p. 39). Similarly, Roskin (1974) maintains that during the last 100 years U.S. foreign policy has consisted of alternating paradigms: An interventionist orientation by elites is followed by a trend toward isolationism. These shifts occur during generational intervals and are due to the specific cohort experiences of each generation. Roskin also speculates that the impact of Vietnam will serve as the catalyst for the return to an isolationist trend in the United States.

In addition to these historical and interpretative analyses, studies more focused on the post-World War II period have provided evidence to support the existence of age or generational differences. Jeffries (1974) found that the acceptability of nuclear war varies between generations. Those persons reaching adulthood during the 1960s most strongly reject nuclear warfare, while the greatest acceptance of nuclear war is among those who reached maturity before or during World War II. One study of college students offered evidence that U.S. involvement in Vietnam might have created a more pacifist generation of Americans (Handberg 1972-73). Comparing 1962 and 1972 samples of college students, Handberg found that students of the early 1970s were dramatically more inclined to accept a pacific philosophy than were college students of the early 1960s.

In examining research utilizing public opinion polls, several scholars have also reported findings demonstrating age differences, although the findings are somewhat contradictory. For example, Converse and Schuman (1970, p. 24), Mueller (1973, pp. 136-40), and Lunch and Sperlich (1979, pp. 32-34) have found that, when compared with the older cohort, the younger respondent was consistently more supportive of the Vietnam War. These authors observed that the popular image of the young being in the forefront of the opposition to the war was not supported by the data. In contrast, Ferree (1980) found that when education is controlled, "surveys from the 1970's suggest that something did indeed happen to college students of the 60's that left real, if not overwhelming traces a decade later" (p. 38). According to Ferree, the college-educated generation of the 1960s is relatively less supportive of defense spending than other college-educated generations. Similarly, Kriesberg and Klein (1980) trace public opinion on the issue of defense spending from 1973 to 1978. Employing generation as one explanatory variable, they report support for the generational thesis in 1973 and 1975, finding the Vietnam cohort less supportive of military spending than older cohorts. But they note that by 1978 the Vietnam generation was no longer distinctive.

Other recent studies report age to be a discriminating variable in explaining foreign policy attitudes (Bardes and Oldendick 1978, 1980; Maggiotto and Wittkopf 1981; Wittkopf 1981; Wittkopf and Maggiotto 1983). However, Bardes and Oldendick (1978) and Wittkopf (1981) disagree on the relationship between age and militarism. The former conclude that old people tend to be the most militaristic age group and young people the least. Conversely, Wittkopf found that opposition to military involvement was strongest among those aged 50 and over.

Admittedly, research of the generational thesis based on public opinion polls reveals ambiguous findings. However, whether or not generational differences exist within the mass public, it is plausible to hypothesize that generational cleavages would be more pronounced among the elites in U.S. society since the elite would be more interested and knowledgeable regarding the conduct and issues surrounding U.S. foreign policy. Holsti and Rosenau (1980a, 1984) have investigated the nature of foreign policy beliefs in the post-Vietnam period among an elite sample of citizens. In regard to generational differences among the elite, Holsti and Rosenau report modest support for the generational thesis. However, their findings suggest that the greater cleavages exist between occupation groups rather than between generations.

This brief review suggests that present research has not yet provided a clear answer to the generational issue and related questions. Did Vietnam create a generation with distinct foreign policy views? Or was the impact more in the nature of period effects and thus likely to diminish with the passage of time, as suggested by Kriesberg and Klein (1980)? If the Vietnam War did create a generation with distinct views, is it pacifist or militarist? Isolationist or internationalist?

DATA AND METHOD

The investigation of generational change immediately raised two questions for the researcher. First, at what age does an individual begin to acquire political attitudes and beliefs? Second, which historical events and time periods most likely distinguish unique periods of socialization for young people? There appears to be no clear consensus regarding either question (Adler 1983, pp. 6–7). The decision is somewhat arbitrary, often reflecting the constraints of the data and the assumptions made by the researcher. Therefore, the cutoff dates used in this essay require a note of explanation as to both the theoretical assumptions and the constraints of the data.

For the purpose of this study, I have identified four generational groups. This classification scheme reflects the belief that the recent history of U.S. foreign policy has been characterized by four rather distinct periods that were sufficiently different to result in possible generational cleavages. These periods were (1) the period prior to World War II, (2) World War II to the early 1960s, (3) the mid-1960s to the early 1970s, and (4) the mid-1970s to the present.

The selection of World War II as a benchmark is self-evident. The period of U.S. involvement in World War II not only represented a fundamental shift in U.S. foreign policy, but also a dramatic personal experience for millions of U.S. men and women. In contrast to the isolationism of the interwar years, U.S. leaders in the post-World War II period were advocates and architects of an internationalist posture for the United States. This internationalism was manifested in a political-military policy of containment vis-à-vis the Soviet Union and, through the institutions created at Bretton Woods, an open international economic system dominated by U.S. economic strength. As the Cold War hardened, a public consensus emerged around the core of these policies that was not fundamentally challenged until the Vietnam War. Thus, I view it as justifiable to consider the entire period from World War II to Vietnam as a distinct and continuous period of socialization.

The second benchmark is the period of U.S. involvement in Vietnam, roughly the mid-1960s to the early 1970s. This period was characterized by domestic unrest and opposition to the war, doubt and reevaluation concerning the wisdom or capacity of the United States to pursue its traditional foreign policies. Consequently, it was during this period of U.S. involvement in Southeast Asia that the basic axioms of U.S foreign policy came under challenge, thereby providing a rather unique set of common experiences for those young Americans who came of age during this turbulent time.

Finally, I have identified a post-Vietnam generation. It seems likely that the period from the middle 1970s to the early 1980s is sufficiently distinctive to warrant classification as a generational grouping. In contrast to the Vietnam period, this was an era of nonmilitary involvement, the end of détente, and increasing tension between the United States and the Soviet Union. This generation is more likely to draw its historical lessons from the Soviet intervention in Afghanistan and the seizure of the U.S. embassy in Iran rather than vague recollections of Vietnam.

This study will utilize three surveys of the U.S. mass public conducted for the Chicago Council on Foreign Relations (CCFR) in 1974, 1978, and 1982.[1] The surveys are national probability samples, with the 1974 survey containing 1,513 respondents, the 1978 survey 1,546, and the 1982 sample 1,547.

The cutting points selected in the CCFR data sets reflected, as far as possible, the analysis outlined above. The only difficulty arose in regard to a cutting point between the pre-World War II and the World War II generations. Assuming that the socialization process begins in the late teens and continues well into one's twenties, the ideal date to divide these two age cohorts would have been approximately 1916–18. Since the 1974 CCFR survey did not contain that option, 1910 was selected as perhaps the best alternative. The remaining cutting points were 1940 and 1954. Thus, the generational groups are as follows:

Pre-World War II, includes those born prior to 1910
World War II, includes those born between 1910 and 1939
Vietnam, includes those born between 1940 and 1953
Post-Vietnam, includes those born in 1954 and after.

This classification scheme leads to certain expectations regarding generational differences on foreign policy issues. For example, we might expect the pre-World War II generation to be the most isolationist generation. This age group achieved political maturity during the interwar years when U.S. foreign policy was relatively isolationist compared to the internationalism of the postwar period. Also, the 1930s witnessed the Great Depression where certainly domestic economic problems were the most salient issues of this age cohort's early adulthood.

It would also be plausible to assume that the World War II generation would be strongly anticommunist. This generation came of age during the era of greatest tension between the United States and the Soviet Union, whereas during the formative years of the pre-World War II generation the fascism of Germany, Italy, and Imperial Japan was viewed as the main threat to peace in the international system. The Vietnam and the post-Vietnam generations are also likely to perceive communism as less threatening than the World War II generation, viewing it as a divided movement rather than a unified monolithic movement directed from Moscow. Furthermore, one can speculate that the World War II generation would be more supportive of defense spending and the use of military force than the other age cohorts.

An additional hypothesis would be that the Vietnam generation is atypical in its lack of support for defense spending and its opposition to the use of military force. That is, one legacy of the Vietnam conflict for this generation would be suspicion of the use of military power as an instrument of U.S. foreign policy since this age group was socialized during a period when the application of military power resulted in military defeat. For the post-Vietnam generation, deteriorating U.S.-Soviet relations and increasing concern over Soviet military strength are two major aspects of their early adulthood.

Of course, other differences could be (and have been) advanced. Roskin (1974), Allison (1970-71), and Holsti and Rosenau (1980b, 1984) are useful sources for additional generational axioms. However, those listed above should provide a sufficient basis for examining the generational thesis.

To test these hypotheses, the surveys were first analyzed by crosstabulating generation with the responses to a number of foreign policy questions. Many of the questions were identical in each survey, thereby providing an opportunity to examine the continuity of opinion across time. Cross-tabulations were also performed controlling for attention-interest to foreign affairs issues. Indexes were constructed for each of the surveys to create a subsample of respondents who were the most interested and attentive to foreign affairs. Education was also used as a control by assigning respondents into either a college or a noncollege group. The college group consisted of those respondents who had attended college (although not necessarily obtaining a degree). The noncollege group consisted of those respondents who had no formal education beyond high school or a technical-trade school.

Finally, five additive-type scales were created from survey items specifically designed in both surveys to tap a particular dimension of foreign policy attitudes (see Appendix for explanation of scale construction and reliability scores). Analysis of variance was then employed to analyze generational differences among the various foreign policy dimensions. A 0.05 significance level was adopted when referring in the text to a relationship as being statistically significant.

THE FINDINGS

Table 4.1 displays the results for generational differences on a number of foreign policy questions. Question 1 asks whether the United States should take an active role in world affairs. This item appears to be almost a pure indicator of internationalism, although it does not differentiate what type of internationalism. Nevertheless, differences do emerge between generations concerning whether the United States should take an active role in world affairs. Within the general public, the post-Vietnam generation was relatively isolationist in 1974 and this isolationism persisted in 1978 and 1982. The pre-World War II generation also emerged as relatively isolationist in 1982 compared with 1974. However, this isolationism was not shared by the attentive members within these age groups (with the exception of the attentive members of the post-Vietnam generation in 1978). While U.S. citizens of all generations are generally supportive of an active role for the United States in world affairs, there appears to have been some erosion of internationalist sentiment from the mid-1970s to the early 1980s. In 1982, it should be noted, the Vietnam generation was the most supportive age group for an active U.S. role in world affairs. More interesting, perhaps, is the relative isolationism of the post-Vietnam generation. But, clearly, isolationism was not a lesson learned by the Vietnam generation as a consequence of the Indochina war; instead, it is actually the most internationalist age group.

Questions 2 to 7 all deal in one way or another with a military aspect of foreign policy. Question 2 elicits a response from the respondent regarding his/her general attitude toward military aid. Only among the general public in 1974 did statistically significant differences emerge, with the post-Vietnam generation the least supportive of military aid and the World War II generation the most supportive of it. By 1978 generational cleavages had diminished. The period from 1974 to 1978 also witnessed a moderate rise in support for military aid, which cut across age groups. Subsequently, support for military aid remained fairly stable during the period between 1978 and 1982. Questions 3 and 4 address a possible benefit and drawback to military aid. Question 3 asks respondents whether military aid is a good substitute for U.S. troops. Interestingly, while generational differences did not characterize this issue in 1974, by 1978 generational differences had arisen. Specifically, the post-Vietnam cohort was least inclined to view military aid as a good substitute for troops. However, it was the Vietnam age group that was least likely to agree that military aid was a good substitute for troops in 1982. Furthermore, in contrast to the other age groups, the Vietnam gen-

TABLE 4.1
Percentage by generation

Question Text	Year of Survey	Post-Vietnam	Vietnam	World War II	Pre-World War II	(N)	Significance	Gamma
1. Do you think it will be best for the future of the country if we take an active part in world affairs, or if we stay out of world affairs? (percent = "active part")	1974GP	50.7	74.5	76.3	74.6	(1,351)	0.00	−0.11
	1974AP	a	77.7	85.3	79.7	(327)	0.00	−0.20
	1978GP	61.1	70.2	71.3	60.6	(1,362)	0.01	−0.02
	1978AP	56.7	87.5	82.8	85.7	(392)	0.01	−0.15
	1982GP	55.1	69.5	65.7	52.0	(1,345)	0.00	−0.02
	1982AP	76.8	80.6	73.6	72.4	(367)	0.57	0.11
2. On the whole, do you favor or oppose our giving military aid to other nations? (percent = "favor")	1974GP	15.6	25.9	29.2	22.4	(1,301)	0.03	−0.03
	1974AP	a	26.7	30.9	23.3	(312)	0.15	−0.03
	1978GP	33.9	31.3	37.4	33.3	(1,345)	0.24	−0.06
	1978AP	43.3	40.2	45.9	39.2	(390)	0.73	−0.02
	1982GP	27.4	31.9	34.3	32.7	(1,371)	0.26	−0.08
	1982AP	33.9	37.6	41.7	46.4	(364)	0.61	−0.12
3. Do you think that giving military aid to other countries generally is a good substitute for the use of U.S. troops and manpower? (percent = "Yes")	1974GP	49.3	55.1	60.1	55.2	(1,167)	0.21	−0.05
	1974AP	a	58.9	60.8	50.0	(294)	0.50	0.07
	1978GP	51.7	54.9	67.6	69.0	(1,278)	0.00	−0.23
	1978AP	64.3	59.3	70.5	66.7	(391)	0.25	−0.13
	1982GP	58.8	55.6	66.7	73.4	(1,248)	0.00	−0.17
	1982AP	60.7	53.6	74.1	79.3	(344)	0.00	−0.29

4. Do you think that giving military aid to other countries generally gets us too involved in other countries' affairs? (percent = "Yes")	1974GP	80.2	86.0	84.9	90.5	(1,341)	0.08	−0.11
	1974AP	a	85.3	84.3	92.1	(321)	0.41	−0.14
	1978GP	86.1	88.0	83.2	90.0	(1,401)	0.06	0.05
	1978AP	86.7	81.5	78.3	82.4	(410)	0.67	0.07
	1982GP	85.7	86.7	83.7	86.2	(1,375)	0.61	0.05
	1982AP	87.3	79.6	78.5	82.8	(364)	0.53	0.09
5. Do you feel the role of the military should be more important than it is now, less important, or about as important as it is now? (percent = "more important")	1974GP	26.7	15.6	20.4	29.4	(1,274)	0.00	−0.00
	1974AP	a	9.9	20.9	22.6	(309)	0.04	−0.03
	1978GP	30.2	25.2	32.0	35.6	(1,409)	0.02	−0.02
	1978AP	36.7	26.6	34.4	36.7	(406)	0.66	−0.03
	1982GP	27.6	24.5	26.0	31.9	(1,417)	0.22	0.01
	1982AP	23.3	25.7	30.6	38.7	(384)	0.15	−0.02
6. Here is a list of present federal government programs. For each, I'd like you to tell me whether you feel it should be expanded, cut back, or kept about the same ... defense spending? (percent = "Expand")	1974GP	16.9	10.5	14.9	22.7	(1,406)	0.00	0.01
	1974AP	a	15.2	23.2	27.4	(338)	0.57	−0.06
	1978GP	30.9	33.2	41.8	40.6	(1,421)	0.00	−0.08
	1978AP	65.5	41.0	50.9	58.3	(410)	0.02	−0.01
	1982GP	28.4	22.5	23.8	24.7	(1,435)	0.34	0.03
	1982AP	32.2	28.6	28.7	19.4	(380)	0.40	0.10
7. At the present time, which nation do you feel is stronger in terms of military power, the United States or the Soviet Union—or do you think they are about equal militarily? (percent = "U.S.S.R. stronger")	1982GP	41.0	28.8	28.8	27.4	(1,394)	0.00	−0.03
	1982AP	32.8	18.2	29.7	31.3	(375)	0.36	0.01

GP, general public; AP, attentive public. [a] Deleted owing to small *N*.

(continued)

TABLE 4.1
(Continued)

Question Text	Year of Survey	Post-Vietnam	Vietnam	World War II	Pre-World War II	(N)	Significance	Gamma
8. On the whole, do you favor or oppose our giving economic aid to other nations for purposes of economic development and technical assistance? (percent = "favor")	1974GP	55.1	63.1	58.7	51.1	(1,347)	0.02	0.10
	1974AP	a	64.6	61.7	58.9	(328)	0.90	0.06
	1978GP	63.1	54.3	56.4	44.9	(1,346)	0.01	0.09
	1978AP	65.4	67.3	67.0	66.7	(393)	0.99	-0.00
	1982GP	55.5	60.4	58.0	43.9	(1,352)	0.03	0.05
	1982AP	64.9	67.0	64.3	65.4	(360)	0.96	-0.02
9. Do you feel U.S. economic aid to other countries generally gets us too involved in other countries affairs? (percent = "Yes")	1974GP	77.3	81.8	79.6	84.7	(1,354)	0.30	-0.04
	1974AP	a	77.3	79.5	80.0	(329)	0.96	-0.04
	1978GP	77.0	81.8	83.4	78.6	(1,401)	0.19	-0.05
	1978AP	72.4	78.4	82.9	77.1	(401)	0.45	-0.08
	1982GP	83.3	77.9	81.5	80.0	(1,393)	0.31	0.00
	1982AP	75.0	67.0	78.2	80.0	(369)	0.17	-0.15
10. Here is a list of possible foreign policy goals that the U.S. might have. For each one, would you please say whether you think that should be a very important foreign policy goal of the U.S., a somewhat important foreign policy goal, or not an important goal at all . . . containing communism? (percent = "very important")	1974GP	48.7	54.3	61.4	59.4	(1,400)	0.14	-0.10
	1974AP	a	54.2	60.4	60.0	(331)	0.38	-0.11
	1978GP	54.7	59.8	71.2	67.3	(1,443)	0.00	-0.17
	1978AP	45.2	57.7	72.1	74.0	(418)	0.02	-0.27
	1982GP	59.5	56.0	65.2	68.6	(1,436)	0.01	-0.12
	1982AP	60.0	49.6	71.7	81.3	(385)	0.00	-0.28

11. Here is a list of international events that the U.S. has been involved in recent history. For each, please tell me whether you think it was a proud moment in U.S. history, a dark moment, or neither a proud moment nor a dark moment... Vietnam? (percent = "dark moment")	1974GP 1974AP	72.2 a	76.0 74.0	73.8 75.8	81.5 78.7	(1,418) (335)	0.32 0.84	−0.05 −0.11
12. The Vietnam War was more than a mistake; it was fundamentally wrong and immoral. (percent = "agree strongly")	1978GP 1978AP 1982GP 1982AP	45.7 34.5 52.6 51.7	48.5 51.4 45.7 43.4	50.2 48.9 47.5 53.4	56.3 55.8 55.6 67.7	(1,406) (417) (1,408) (380)	0.04 0.84 0.00 0.17	−0.03 −0.07 0.02 −0.07
13. Which of these statements comes closest to describing your own view of what the U.S. should do if friendly countries are attacked? (percent = "send military and economic aid, and if necessary U.S. troops and manpower)	1974GP 1974AP	24.3 a	31.0 31.6	25.3 29.1	19.9 25.0	(1,367) (335)	0.01 0.33	0.11 0.02

GP, general public; AP, attentive public. [a]Deleted owing to small N.

eration's attitude remained stable between 1974 and 1982. We shall return to the differences noted here later.

Question 4 raises the issue of military aid leading to excessive involvement in the affairs of other countries. There is widespread agreement among all generations in 1974, 1978, and 1982 that indeed military aid does lead to excessive involvement. Consequently, no significant differences are present on the issue.

Question 5 asks the respondent's view on the role that the military should play in determining U.S. foreign policy. In 1974 and 1978, the Vietnam cohort was significantly less supportive of a more important role for the military. However, by 1982 these generational differences had largely disappeared. Support for the military generally increased from 1974 to 1978, but then dropped slightly from 1978 to 1982. A similar pattern arises in regard to the public's attitude toward defense spending (Question 6). As with support for a more important role for the military, the Vietnam generation was least supportive of defense expenditures in 1974. In 1978, generational differences were significant for both the general and the attentive public. The post-Vietnam generation was the least supportive of defense spending among the general public, while the attentive members of this same age group were also the most supportive of expanding defense expenditures. But again, by 1982 the differences between age groups had diminished. There was also a general trend toward increased support for defense or military spending among both the general and attentive publics from 1974 to 1978 and then a decline in support for defense spending from 1978 to 1982.

Differential support for defense spending may reflect somewhat divergent perceptions of Soviet and U.S. military power. Question 7 inquires as to whether the respondent believes the United States or the Soviet Union was militarily stronger in 1982. The post-Vietnam generation had the most ominous view of Soviet military strength among both the attentive and the general public. But also among the attentive public, it was the Vietnam generation that saw the Soviet Union as least threatening militarily.

Turning to support for economic aid (Question 8), modest generational differences emerge among the general public, with the Vietnam generation the most supportive in 1974 and 1982 and the pre-World War II age group least supportive in each year. Opinion regarding economic aid remained essentially stable in the period between 1974 and 1982. However, like military aid, U.S. citizens of all generations view economic aid as having the drawback of getting the United States too involved in the affairs of other countries (Question 9). No statistically significant differences emerge on this question.

Next, Question 10 asks respondents about the foreign policy goal of containing communism. Generational differences were not significant in 1974 for either the general or the attentive public. However, in 1978 and 1982, generational differences were significant for both the general and the attentive public. In 1978 the containment of communism was least important for the post-Vietnam generation. The Vietnam generation was least likely to feel that the containment of communism was a very important goal in 1982. At the same time, the pre-World War II generation was most likely to rate the containment of communism as a very important goal in 1982. Furthermore, a comparison of the attentive publics of 1974 and 1982 reveals an increase in importance for the containment of communism in all but one of the generational groups. Only the Vietnam generation assigned decreased importance to this goal in 1982 as compared with 1974.

Since this study is concerned with detecting generational differences on foreign policy issues resulting from U.S. involvement in Indochina, it is useful to examine a number of items that deal specifically with attitudes regarding the Vietnam War. The 1974 respondents were asked whether the Vietnam War represented a dark or proud moment in U.S. history (Question 11). U.S. citizens of all generations were in agreement that Vietnam represented a dark period in U.S. foreign policy. Consequently, no significant generational cleavages were present on this issue. However, this is somewhat misleading as the question fails to distinguish between a number of possible motivations for labeling the Vietnam conflict as a dark period. This is illustrated by Question 12 asked in 1978 and 1982. Respondents were asked if Vietnam was not only fundamentally wrong, but also immoral. In 1978 it was the post-Vietnam generation (among both the attentive and the general public) that was least likely to agree with this statement. For the general public, the differences were statistically significant. Generational differences were also significant in 1982. But surprisingly, in 1982 it was the Vietnam generation that was the age group least willing to view the Vietnam War as wrong and immoral. Obviously, this finding is contrary to commonly held beliefs about the nature of the impact of the Vietnam War on those who were socialized during that era. Namely, it is the Vietnam generation that is least likely to view the Vietnam War as a mistake. Also, an examination of the attentive publics in 1978 and 1982 reveals a noticeable shift in perception regarding the Vietnam War. For all but the Vietnam generation, the perception that the Vietnam War was a mistake has increased with time. Among the attentive members of the Vietnam generation, the perception that the Vietnam War was wrong has diminished with time.

Question 13 perhaps provides a partial answer to the generational cleavage concerning the Vietnam War as well as the benefits to be derived from military aid as a substitute for troops (see Question 3). The CCFR asked respondents in 1974 to select one of four possible options that best described their view of what the United States should do if a country friendly to it were attacked. The options were (1) send military and economic aid and U.S. troops if necessary, (2) send military and economic aid but no troops, (3) send economic aid but no military aid or troops, or (4) send no economic or military aid and no troops. Therefore, the response listed as (1) is the most hawkish of the four possibilities. The Vietnam generation emerged as the age group most willing to support the initial introduction of U.S. troops in the event a state friendly to the United States were attacked. Although the differences between generations are modest, the belief that military aid is not a very good substitute for troops may explain the greater propensity of the Vietnam generation to sanction the use of U.S. troops.

In order to examine the structure of foreign policy attitudes in more depth, five scales were created to capture particular dimensions of foreign policy attitudes. Analysis of variance was then used to discern possible generational differences. For the purpose of interpretation, the scores reported for each generation represent the mean score of the particular age cohort. Since the number of items used to construct the scales vary from survey to survey, it is not the absolute scores that can be compared across time, but the relative position of the score for an age group that should be compared.

Scale 1 (Table 4.2) provides a measure of the extent to which the respondent views the expansion of communism abroad as a threat to the United States. In 1974 and 1978 generational differences were significant for all groups except the noncollege. In 1974 it was the pre-World War II age group that viewed communism as the most threatening. Similarly, in 1978 the pre-World War II generation was the age group most threatened by the expansion of communism in two of the three groups where the differences were significant. Among the general public in 1982, it was the Vietnam generation that viewed communism as the most threatening, but the differences were not significant. Interestingly, among the attentive public in 1982, generational differences were significant and it was the Vietnam generation that was least threatened by communism. It is also interesting to note some intragenerational shifts between 1974 and 1982. In 1974, within each age cohort, the mean score for the attentive public was lower than that for the general public. By 1982, however, this pattern was reversed for each age group except the Vietnam generation, where the

TABLE 4.2.
Scale 1: Communist threat. Mean score by generation

Group	Post-Vietnam	Vietnam	World War II	Pre-World War II	(N)	Significance of F
Year 1974	Scale Range = No threat (−6) to Threat (+6)				Grand Mean = 1.82	
General Public	1.33	1.26	2.03	2.53	(1,494)	0.001
Attentive Public	0.29	0.61	1.97	2.20	(411)	0.016
College Educated	−0.11	0.50	0.90	2.17	(544)	0.044
Noncollege	2.02	2.09	2.50	2.64	(950)	0.397
Year 1978	Scale Range = No threat (−10) to Threat (+10)				Grand Mean = 3.42	
General Public	2.90	2.99	3.88	3.37	(1,526)	0.007
Attentive Public	3.29	2.97	4.59	4.77	(424)	0.023
College Educated	2.61	2.43	3.68	4.11	(527)	0.041
Noncollege	3.07	3.38	3.97	3.09	(999)	0.083
Year 1982	Scale Range = No Threat (−12) to Threat (+12)				Grand Mean = 4.34	
General Public	3.75	4.53	4.48	4.29	(1,509)	0.149
Attentive Public	4.33	3.64	5.56	4.91	(39)	0.021
College Educated	3.58	4.13	4.06	5.33	(592)	0.456
Noncollege	3.97	4.94	4.71	4.02	(905)	0.179

Results based on one-way analysis of variance.

TABLE 4.3.
Scale 2: Military involvement. Mean score by generation

Group	Post-Vietnam	Vietnam	World War II	Pre-World War II	(N)	Significance of F
Year 1974	*Scale Range = Favor (12) to Oppose (24)*				*Grand Mean = 20.81*	
General Public	20.68	20.59	20.71	21.53	(1,465)	0.001
Attentive Public	21.15	20.39	20.09	21.09	(403)	0.051
College Educated	21.19	20.48	20.66	21.25	(536)	0.207
Noncollege	20.44	20.71	20.72	21.62	(929)	0.001
Year 1978	*Scale Range = Favor (10) to Oppose (20)*				*Grand Mean = 16.51*	
General Public	16.51	16.43	16.44	17.02	(1,526)	0.105
Attentive Public	15.58	15.87	15.82	15.81	(424)	0.968
College Educated	16.41	16.23	16.68	16.14	(527)	0.317
Noncollege	16.54	16.57	16.33	17.26	(999)	0.014
Year 1982	*Scale Range = Favor (10) to Oppose (20)*				*Grand Mean = 17.08*	
General Public	16.82	16.78	17.33	17.45	(1,509)	0.001
Attentive Public	15.62	16.30	16.43	16.56	(390)	0.132
College Educated	16.49	16.62	17.18	16.95	(592)	0.024
Noncollege	17.07	16.99	17.41	17.57	(905)	0.102

Results based on one-way analysis of variance.

attentive public continued to perceive communism as less threatening than the general public. Consequently, whereas the Vietnam generation was the least threatened by the expansion of communism among the general public in 1974, it had become the age group most threatened by the expansion of communism in 1982.

Scale 2 (Table 4.3) measures the willingness to employ U.S. troops abroad. Among the general public in 1974, 1978, and 1982, the Vietnam age group was the generation most willing to sanction the use of troops. For 1974 and 1982, the differences were statistically significant. The pre-World War II generation was the age group least willing to approve of military involvement among the general public for both years as well. No significant differences emerged among the attentive public or the college-educated group in 1974 or 1978. However, among the noncollege group in 1974 and 1978, age differences were significant, with the post-Vietnam generation most willing to support the use of troops in 1974 and the World War II cohort most likely to favor the use of troops in 1978. By 1982 significant differences had arisen between the college educated, with the post-Vietnam generation most willing to support military involvement and the World War II generation least likely to favor it. This latter finding is somewhat surprising, given the theoretical expectations discussed earlier.

In regard to détente with the Soviet Union [Scale 3 (Table 4.4)], little in the way of generational cleavage emerges. Only among the general public in 1974 did statistically significant differences arise. The post-Vietnam generation was the most supportive and the pre-World War II generation least supportive of détente. Nonetheless, détente appears to be an issue on which the U.S. public is not divided along generational lines.

A similar lack of generational division characterizes the public's attitudes toward economic aid [Scale 4 (Table 4.5)]. No statistically significant differences were present concerning economic aid for 1974, 1978, or 1982. In regard to military aid [Scale 5 (Table 4.6)], only in 1978 and 1982 did any generational differences become significant. These differences were among the general public and the noncollege group in 1978 and the college-educated and the attentive public in 1982. For both years, the pre-World War II generation was most inclined to ascribe benefits to military aid. In contrast, this view was least shared by the Vietnam generation in 1978 and the post-Vietnam generation among the college educated in 1982. However, it was the Vietnam age group among the attentive public in 1982 that was least supportive of military aid.

TABLE 4.4.
Scale 3: Détente. Mean score by generation

Group	Post-Vietnam	Vietnam	World War II	Pre-World War II	(N)	Significance of F
Year 1974	*Scale Range = Favor (9) to Oppose (18)*				*Grand Mean = 10.61*	
General Public	10.08	10.34	10.80	10.91	(982)	0.004
Attentive Public	10.27	10.43	10.87	10.65	(281)	0.524
College Educated	9.62	10.03	10.17	10.33	(404)	0.450
Noncollege	10.32	10.79	11.08	11.14	(578)	0.242
Year 1978	*Scale Range = Favor (6) to Oppose (12)*				*Grand Mean = 8.14*	
General Public	8.02	8.10	8.14	8.41	(1,050)	0.203
Attentive Public	8.11	8.13	8.13	8.36	(352)	0.836
College Educated	7.77	7.86	7.86	7.96	(414)	0.944
Noncollege	8.21	8.32	8.30	8.57	(636)	0.420
Year 1982	*Scale Range = Favor (7) to Oppose (14)*				*Grand Mean = 9.45*	
General Public	9.51	9.45	9.43	9.31	(1,052)	0.841
Attentive Public	8.74	9.36	9.46	9.22	(320)	0.066
College Educated	9.26	9.40	9.18	9.20	(454)	0.628
Noncollege	9.73	9.50	9.57	9.37	(591)	0.565

Results based on one-way analysis of variance.

TABLE 4.5.
Scale 4: Economic Aid. Mean score by generation

Group	Post-Vietnam	Vietnam	World War II	Pre-World War II	(N)	Significance of F
Year 1974	*Scale Range = Aid Is Not Beneficial (−13) to Aid Is Beneficial (+13)*					*Grand Mean = 0.34*
General Public	0.18	0.74	0.39	−0.49	(1,443)	0.053
Attentive Public	0.36	0.84	0.44	−0.17	(396)	0.689
College Educated	1.46	0.95	1.44	0.37	(522)	0.614
Noncollege	−0.41	0.50	−0.03	−0.77	(921)	0.147
Year 1978	*Scale Range = Aid Is Not Beneficial (−9) to Aid Is Beneficial (+9)*					*Grand Mean = 0.38*
General Public	0.67	0.46	0.32	0.03	(1,526)	0.499
Attentive Public	1.23	1.37	0.62	1.06	(424)	0.510
College Educated	1.12	1.00	0.72	0.97	(527)	0.861
Noncollege	0.40	0.09	0.13	−0.23	(999)	0.696
Year 1982	*Scale Range = Aid Is Not Beneficial (−7) to Aid Is Beneficial (+7)*					*Grand Mean = 0.73*
General Public	0.74	0.88	0.68	0.41	(1,509)	0.661
Attentive Public	1.45	1.70	1.08	1.22	(390)	0.640
College Educated	0.85	1.38	1.05	2.10	(592)	0.376
Noncollege	0.68	0.36	0.56	0.03	(905)	0.546

Results based on one-way analysis of variance.

TABLE 4.6.
Scale 5: Military aid. Mean score by generation

Group	Post-Vietnam	Vietnam	World War II	Pre-World War II	(N)	Significance of F
Year 1974	Scale Range = Aid Is Not Beneficial (−15) to Aid Is Beneficial (+15)					Grand Mean = 2.63
General Public	−2.71	−2.94	−2.16	−3.11	(1,429)	0.079
Attentive Public	−2.79	−3.48	−2.50	−4.21	(385)	0.217
College Educated	−2.44	−3.62	−2.41	−3.43	(516)	0.218
Noncollege	−2.83	−2.21	−2.07	−3.01	(913)	0.255
Year 1978	Scale Range = Aid Is Not Beneficial (−12) to Aid Is Beneficial (+12)					Grand Mean = −1.07
General Public	−1.43	−1.77	−0.62	−0.54	(1,526)	0.001
Attentive Public	−1.06	−0.37	0.11	0.48	(424)	0.580
College Educated	−1.41	−1.33	−0.25	−0.71	(527)	0.167
Noncollege	−1.44	−2.07	−0.80	−0.49	(999)	0.003
Year 1982	Scale Range = Aid Is Not Beneficial (−7) to Aid Is Beneficial (+7)					Grand Mean = 0.36
General Public	0.08	0.12	0.55	0.89	(1,509)	0.053
Attentive Public	0.23	−0.14	1.31	1.47	(390)	0.012
College Educated	−0.12	0.01	0.71	1.67	(592)	0.040
Noncollege	0.26	0.28	0.53	0.71	(905)	0.663

Results based on one-way analysis of variance.

CONCLUSION

The results of this study support the existence of generational differences on a number of foreign policy issues. However, where generational cleavage was present, it generally was moderate in nature. Additionally, the generational differences detected frequently did not conform to theoretical expectations. These two observations merit further comment.

First, Holsti and Rosenau (1980a, p. 20) have noted the substantial policy implications underlying the generational thesis. If the present lack of foreign policy consensus is in large measure generational, then the process of generational succession implies the possibility of not only major foreign policy shifts resulting from older elites being replaced by younger elites with different foreign policy beliefs, but also the emergence of a new foreign policy consensus. The findings reported here do not provide much support for the argument that generational succession will entail fundamental policy change. This does not necessarily imply that the impact of generation will be negligible. On certain issues, generational differences may be sufficiently important to have an impact. Overall, however, there is little evidence to suggest that generational succession will result in substantial policy change or signal the end of dissensus.

Second, it was noted that generational differences on foreign policy issues at times were not consistent with theoretical expectations. In most respects, the attitudes of the pre-World War II generation were consistent with expectations. This age group was relatively isolationist, but also generally supportive of defense spending and an important role for the military. However, the pre-World War II generation was not supportive of direct military involvement abroad. The attitudes of the World War II generation were also largely consistent with expectations. This generation was relatively internationalist and generally supportive of military and economic aid. However, on a few issues, the attitudes of this age cohort did not conform to expectations. For example, the World War II generation was less supportive of military involvement than either the Vietnam or post-Vietnam generations, and among the college educated in 1982 was the age group least supportive of military involvement.

Another finding of some interest is the relative isolationism of the post-Vietnam generation. On a number of single items (U.S. world role, economic aid, and military aid, for example), this generation exhibited attitudes closer to those of the pre-World War II generation than the Vietnam or World War II age groups. Perhaps this is a response to the lack of foreign policy consensus that has characterized the post-Vietnam period. It may also represent a reaction to the economic difficulties of the

1970s when recession, inflation, and unemployment focused attention away from international affairs to domestic concerns. However, the events of the late 1970s and the early 1980s left their mark on the post-Vietnam generation in other ways. For example, this generation's perception of Soviet military power and its support for U.S. defense expenditures are likely a consequence of the more hostile superpower relationship of the late 1970s and early 1980s.

However, it was the Vietnam generation whose views were least consistent with expectations. For example, compared with the other age cohorts, the Vietnam generation was the most willing to approve of the use of military force. Perhaps the most frequent assertion concerning the impact of Vietnam on the young adults who were socialized during that era was that the Vietnam experience would lead to a more pacifist generation of U.S. citizens, less willing to support the involvement of the U.S. military abroad. However, the results of this study suggest that the Vietnam cohort was consistently the age group most willing to sanction the use of U.S. troops. The Vietnam age group was also the generation least likely to view U.S. involvement in Indochina as wrong and immoral in 1982. Additionally, in 1982 the Vietnam generation was the age group most likely to interpret the expansion of communism as a threat to the United States (although this perception was not shared by the attentive members of the Vietnam generation). There is also no evidence to suggest that the Vietnam generation has become relatively isolationist. The Vietnam generation, in comparison with other age groups, was relatively supportive of an active role for the United States in world affairs, providing economic assistance, and, as mentioned above, military involvement. Therefore, to the extent that the attitudes of the Vietnam generation were distinctive, it casts some doubt on the popular image of the foreign policy lessons that this generation derived from the experience of U.S. involvement in Southeast Asia.

The results reported above raise a number of questions concerning the legacy of the Vietnam War for U.S. foreign policy. Specifically, what is the reason for the moderate relationship between age and foreign policy attitudes? Second, what accounts for the relative hawkish foreign policy orientation of the Vietnam generation? Several possible explanations can be advanced. For example, the absence of stronger generational cleavage may be a result of the impact of Vietnam having been overestimated. That is, while Vietnam is perhaps viewed as a foreign policy mistake, it did not fundamentally alter perceptions concerning foreign policy in the same manner that World War II served as a watershed event. As a consequence, Vietnam failed to serve as a dramatic socialization event for those who reached early adulthood during that era. A second possible explanation for modest generational differences is that while the Vietnam

War had a major impact on the U.S. public, it essentially cut across age groups rather than between them. In short, all age groups were affected by the Vietnam War, thereby muting generational differences. It is also possible that stronger generational cleavage is masked by intragenerational polarization within age groups. That is, the foreign policy lessons that Vietnam provided for a particular age cohort were conflicting foreign policy lessons. Consequently, the Vietnam War resulted in both intragenerational and intergenerational cleavage.

The above discussion and the rather surprising foreign policy attitudes of the Vietnam generation are suggestive of a complex interpretation of the generational impact of the Vietnam War on the U.S. public. This complexity implies elements of both continuity and change for U.S. foreign policy in the future. It was noted earlier that the process of generational succession is unlikely to lead to the formation of a new foreign policy consensus. Thus, the present dissensus that characterizes U.S. foreign policy is likely to persist. However, it is also likely that the distinctiveness of the Vietnam and post-Vietnam generations will result in some foreign policy change. In the case of the Vietnam generation, the nature of the impact may be somewhat unexpected.

APPENDIX

The following provides a brief description of each scale and Cronbach's alpha, which was used to assess the reliability of the scales.

Communist Threat: includes items asking whether it would be a threat to the United States if certain regions or countries became communist. 1974, six times, alpha = 0.91; 1978, five items, alpha = 0.87; 1982, six items, alpha = 0.79.

Military Involvement: consists of items posing hypothetical situations that might justify the use of U.S. troops. 1974, 12 items, alpha = 0.88; 1978, 10 items, alpha = 0.75; 1982, 10 items, alpha = 0.78.

Détente: consists of items covering various aspects of U.S.-Soviet relations (for example, trade, arms control, etc.). 1974, nine items, alpha = 0.86; 1978, six items, alpha = 0.42; 1982, seven items, alpha = 0.53.

Military Aid: includes items depicting possible benefits and drawbacks to military aid. 1974, 15 items, alpha = 0.72; 1978, 12 items, alpha = 0.75; 1982, 7 items, alpha = 0.72.

Economic Aid: includes items depicting possible benefits and drawbacks to economic aid. 1974; 13 items, alpha = 0.73; 1978, 9 items, alpha = 0.74; 1982, 7 items, alpha = 0.77.

NOTE

1. The data utilized in this study were made available by the Inter-University Consortium for Political and Social Research and the Chicago Council on Foreign Relations. Neither the collector of the original data nor the Consortium bears any responsibility for the analyses or interpretations presented here.

REFERENCES

Adler, Kenneth P. 1983. "The Successor Generation: Why, Who, and How." In *The Successor Generation: International Perspectives of Postwar Europeans*, edited by Stephen F. Szabo, pp. 4-16. London: Butterworths.

Allison, Graham T. 1970-71. "Cool It: The Foreign Policy of Young Americans." *Foreign Policy* 1:144-60.

Almond, Gabriel A. 1960. *The American People and Foreign Policy*. New York: Praeger (originally published in 1950).

Bardes, Barbara, and Robert Oldendick. 1980. "The Dimensions of Mass Opinion on Foreign Policy." Paper delivered at the Annual Meeting of the Southwestern Political Science Association.

———. 1978. "Beyond Internationalism: A Case for Multiple Dimensions in the Structure of Foreign Policy Attitudes." *Social Science Quarterly* 59:496-508.

Chomsky, Noam, and Edward S. Herman. 1979. *After the Cataclysm: Postwar Indochina and the Reconstruction of Imperial Ideology*. Boston: South End Press.

Converse, Philip E., and Howard Schuman. 1970. "Silent Majorities and the Vietnam War." *Scientific American* 222:17-25.

Cutler, Neal E. 1970. "Generational Succession as a Source of Foreign Policy Attitudes." *Journal of Peace Research* 1:33-47.

Eisenstadt, S. N. 1956. *From Generation to Generation: Age Groups and Social Structure*. Glencoe, IL: Free Press.

Ferree, G. Donald, Jr. 1980. "Gaping at the Generation Gap." *Public Opinion* (February-March) 3:38-39.

Handberg, Roger B. 1972-73. "The Vietnam Analogy: Student Attitudes on War." *Public Opinion Quarterly* 36:612-15.

Holsti, Ole R. 1979. "The Three Headed Eagle: The United States and System Change." *International Studies Quarterly* 23:339-59.

Holsti, Ole R., and James N. Rosenau. 1984. *American Leadership in World Affairs: Vietnam and the Breakdown of Consensus*. Boston: Allen and Unwin.

——— 1980a. "Does Where You Stand Depend on When You Were Born? The Impact of Generation on Post-Vietnam Foreign Policy Beliefs." *Public Opinion* Quarterly 95:1-22.

_____. 1980b. "Cold War Axioms in the Post-Vietnam Era." In *Change in the International System*, edited by Ole R. Holsti, Randolph M. Siverson, and Alexander L. George, pp. 263-301. Boulder, CO: Westview Press.

Jeffries, Vincent. 1974. "Political Generations and the Acceptance or Rejection of Nuclear War." *Journal of Social Issues* 30:119-36.

Klingberg, Frank L. 1979. "Cyclical Trends in American Foreign Policy Moods and Their Policy Implications." In *Challenges to America: United States Foreign Policy in the 1980's*, edited by Charles W. Kegley, Jr., and Patrick J. McGowan, pp. 37-55. Beverly Hills, CA: Sage.

Kriegel, Annie. 1978. "Generational Differences: The History of an Idea." *Daedalus* 107:23-38.

Kriesberg, Louis, and Ross Klein. 1980. "Changes in Public Support for U.S. Military Spending." *Journal of Conflict Resolution* 24:79-111.

LaFeber, Walter. 1985. *America, Russia, and the Cold War 1945-1984*. 5th ed. New York: Alfred A. Knopf.

Lunch, William L., and Peter Sperlich. 1979. "American Public Opinion and the War in Vietnam." *Western Political Quarterly* 32:21-44.

Maggiotto, Michael A., and Eugene R. Wittkopf. 1981. "American Public Attitudes Toward Foreign Policy." *International Studies Quarterly* 25:601-31.

Mannheim, Karl. 1952. "The Sociological Problem of Generations." In *Essays on the Sociology of Knowledge*, edited by Paul Kecskemeti, pp. 276-322. London: Routledge and Kegan Paul.

Mueller, John E. 1973. *War, Presidents, and Public Opinion*. New York: John Wiley and Sons.

Podhoretz, Norman. 1985. "The Reagan Road to Detente." *Foreign Affairs: America and the World 1984* 63:447-64.

Roskin, Michael. 1974. "From Pearl Harbor to Vietnam: Shifting Paradigms and Foreign Policy." *Political Science Quarterly* 89:563-88.

Wittkopf, Eugene R. 1981. "The Structure of Foreign Policy Attitudes: An Alternative View." *Social Science Quarterly* 62:108-23.

Wittkopf, Eugene R., and Michael A. Maggiotto. 1983. "The Two Faces of Internationalism: Public Attitudes Toward American Foreign Policy in the 1970's—and Beyond?" *Social Science Quarterly* 64:288-304.

5
The War-Weariness Hypothesis: An Empirical Test
Jack S. Levy and T. Clifton Morgan

It is now commonplace to argue that the United States' proclivity toward military intervention in the Third World in the period immediately following the Vietnam War was lessened by a "war weariness" induced by its Vietnam experience (Holsti and Rosenau 1984). Britain and France also appear to have been affected by war weariness immediately after World War I, and undoubtedly other examples could be cited in support of the argument that a state's tendency toward war or perhaps even the use of force short of war may be tempered by a recent war experience. In addition, there are good theoretical reasons for expecting that a nation's war involvement might, for a time at least, inhibit its subsequent war behavior. This is expressed by Richardson (1960a) in his version of the well-known "war-weariness hypothesis": "A long and severe bout of fighting confers immunity on most of those who have experienced it" (p. 232). But in spite of the Vietnam syndrome and comparable examples for other states, and in spite of the inherent plausibility of the war-weariness hypothesis, numerous empirical studies have concluded that there exist no regularized patterns of war weariness in the international system (Singer and Small 1972, 1974; Levy 1982a; Garnham 1983). This tension between the apparently obvious implications of particular cases and the conclusions of systematic empirical studies has led to continued attempts to discover regularized patterns of war contagion.

The authors acknowledge the helpful comments of Bill Thompson and Bruce Bueno de Mesquita. The research of the second author has been supported by the College of Liberal Arts at the University of Texas at Austin. Reprinted with minor alterations from the *American Journal of Political Science*, Vol. 30, No. 1, February 1986, by permission of the University of Texas Press.

Although recent findings of the absence of systemic-level contagion are consistent with a long line of empirical research on contagion and periodicity going back to Richardson (1960b, pp. 128-31) and Sorokin (1937, pp. 352-60), they do not necessarily rule out the existence of a regularized pattern of war weariness on the national level. Since most theoretical discussions of the war-weariness hypothesis per se treat it as a national-level phenomenon, the aim of this study is to test the war-weariness hypothesis and other hypotheses of addictive contagion by examining the national war behavior of the great powers.[1]

THEORETICAL CONSIDERATIONS

There are several theoretical reasons why a nation's war involvement might reduce the likelihood of its participation in another war in the period immediately following. As the war-weariness hypothesis suggests, war may induce a general revulsion against war and an immunity against subsequent military action until the memory of war fades, when a new generation may approach war with a new enthusiasm. As Richardson (1960a) notes, "This acquired immunity is not permanent but fades out after a decade or two.... There arises a new generation, not rendered immune by experience" (p. 232). This argument was advanced previously by Toynbee (1954):

> It is manifest that the survivors of a generation that has been of military age during a bout of war will be shy, for the rest of their lives, of bringing a repetition of this tragic experience either upon themselves or upon their children, and that therefore the psychological resistance to any move towards the breaking of a peace that the living memory of a previous war has made so precious is likely to be prohibitively strong until a new generation that knows War only by hearsay has had time to grow up and to come into power (p. 322).

Toynbee carries his generational hypothesis to its logical end, however, and suggests that for the next generation war may actually beget war: "A bout of war, once precipitated, is likely to persist until the peace-bred generation that has lightheartedly run into war has been replaced, in its turn, by a war-worn generation whom these inexperienced war-mongers have sent to the shambles" (p. 322). In Toynbee's scheme, then, addictive contagion may be either negative or positive depending on a society's generational cycle.[2] As a result, his version of the war-weariness hypothesis is weakened considerably.

There are a number of theoretical problems with the war-weariness hypothesis. Both the Toynbee and Richardson versions assume that war weariness is induced by any war, or at least any long or destructive war, regardless of whether the state was victorious and regardless of the territorial, economic, or political gains. A victorious war might actually increase the likelihood of a later war by increasing a state's power and hence its ability to fight again; by inflaming the nationalistic passions and jingoistic attitudes of society as a whole; by bringing to power an elite whose political power is based largely on its successful conduct of war and that may have an incentive to continue the bellicose policies that brought it to office; or by creating or reinforcing a cultural norm that regards war as a legitimate instrument of national policy. Even an unsuccessful war might increase the likelihood of a subsequent war, by generating throughout society demands for revenge, as the post-World War I German case indicates (Grathwol 1980). Particularly costly wars might intensify revanchist sentiment and the desire to revenge earlier losses, rather than increase war weariness. It should also be recognized that the reaction to war may not be the same for all segments of society. A costly and unsuccessful war might induce weariness in some but demands for revenge in others. The critical questions concern what segments of society share the hypothesized war weariness, whether these attitudes are also shared by the decision-making elite, and how much influence each of these groups has in the policymaking process. The war-weariness hypothesis is theoretically incomplete in that it fails to provide the linkages between war weariness conceived as a social phenomenon and subsequent decisions regarding war and peace by political decision makers.

It should be emphasized that if war weariness is defined as a war-induced revulsion against subsequent war among certain segments of society, then the "war-weariness hypothesis" is only one of several causal mechanisms leading to negative addictive contagion. The depletion of a nation's resources by war, leaving it incapable of the rational initiation of another war, might have the same result. A decisive and victorious war might resolve all outstanding issues and leave a state so satisfied with its new position that a subsequent war is unnecessary, and it might also deter the initiation of wars by others. Alternatively, an unsuccessful war might induce a change in the political elite and bring to power those committed to a more peaceful policy.[3] Thus, war weariness is only one of several paths by which war might inhibit subsequent war, so that an empirical finding of a reduced propensity toward war in the period following an earlier war would not necessarily confirm the war-weariness hypothesis.

War weariness and other sources of a reduced propensity toward war are conceived here as intervening variables in hypotheses that predict that after one war a state is less likely to become involved in a subsequent war. This status of war weariness as an intervening variable between the occurrence of one war and the outbreak of a second leads to yet another problem. Even if it were true that somehow war weariness or other considerations induce inhibitions in decision makers that leave them disinclined to initiate a war, it does not necessarily follow that they would be less likely to become involved in a war. Such a psychological inhibition against war may actually make war more likely by creating an appearance of weakness and undermining deterrence. Other states might be tempted to take this opportunity to resolve long-standing disputes or advance other interests by increasing their coercive pressure. While such pressure might be effective in extracting the desired concessions from the weary state, it might also backfire and lead to a conflict spiral and war by miscalculation. Similarly, a state whose military and economic resources are depleted by one war may be unprepared to initiate another war during its period of recovery, but this does not mean that its probability of war involvement is diminished. Its very weakness may increase the likelihood of war by providing an incentive for others to attack.

Thus, under certain conditions the consequences of war weariness may be precisely the opposite of the predicted reduction in the likelihood of war. In conjunction with our earlier survey of propositions suggesting why war might beget war, this suggests that theoretical arguments for positive addictive contagion are as plausible as those for war weariness or other forms of negative addiction. These processes need not act independently, of course, and the simultaneous or sequential operation of both positive and negative addictive processes only increases the complexity of the question of contagion. Furthermore, positive and negative contagion processes may each be the product of distinct social/psychological, political, or economic responses to a previous war. There is neither adequate theory nor adequate data to permit a thorough empirical analysis of the interaction of all of these distinct processes. Whether the net effect of all of these contagion processes is positive or negative, to beget war or to inhibit war, is an important question in itself, however. The establishment of an empirical law, even if we lacked a complete theoretical explanation, would increase our descriptive knowledge of international behavior and enhance our predictive power. In addition, the discovery of a consistent pattern of contagion may have some bearing on several hypotheses regarding specific contagion processes and thus aid in our testing of those hypotheses.

Empirical Studies of War Contagion

There have been several empirical studies of war contagion, but these have yet to resolve the debate. Most studies have found that the occurrence of one war has no impact on the likelihood of subsequent war in the international system (Richardson 1960b, pp. 128-31; Singer and Small 1972, pp. 205-7, 1974, pp. 279-82; Levy 1982a). There is more evidence that the expansion of war follows an infectious process (Davis et al. 1978), and that alliances (Siverson and King 1979) and borders (Richardson 1960b, pp. 273-87; Most and Starr 1980, p. 932) play key roles in this process. However, neither the absence of contagion on the systemic level nor these findings of infectious contagion are directly relevant to the question of addictive contagion in general or war weariness in particular.

Of greater interest are the few national-level studies of contagion, but these findings are somewhat mixed. Singer and Small (1974, pp. 283-84) find that neither initiators nor defenders in war in the nineteenth or twentieth century are very likely to initiate another war within a decade, though winners are far more likely to initiate another war than losers. This leads them to conclude that victorious war begets war. But they also conclude that this "simple proposition is in fact a rather complex one, and that the alternative ways of interpreting and testing it (via many alternative indicators) lead to rather different conclusions. The evidence, then, is far from complete" (Singer and Small 1974, p. 284). In a later article Singer and Cusack (1981) make only limited headway in resolving the question of the contagious effects of victory and defeat in war. Using the length of the interwar peace as the measure of contagion, they find some propensity of victorious states toward early reentry into war, but find no inhibition against war for defeated states (pp. 413-15). In fact, they find that the mean interval to the next war is even shorter for defeated states than for victorious states; while this difference is not statistically significant, it does point toward a revenge rather than the war-weariness hypothesis. In a similar study, Garnham (1983) finds that victorious major powers are no more likely than losers to initiate a subsequent war. Singer and Cusack (1981, pp. 415-17) also examine the impact of the outcome and cost of war on the question of addictive contagion. They find that high fatalities have a very slight prolonging effect and that a high magnitude (nation-months) has a very slight shortening effect, though neither is statistically significant. For defeated states, however, wars costly in fatalities result in a longer interval until the next war, which is consistent with the war-weariness hypothesis. Garnham (1983, p. 11) confirms that there is no relationship between the cost of war and the time until the next war, but argues that evidence in support of the war-weariness hypothesis is somewhat stronger (though not significant) for democratic states. He concludes, however, that "neither earlier empirical work nor [his] analyses confirm the war weariness hypothesis" (p. 11). Finally, in a study that examines the contagious impact of a nation's threats to use military force as well as actual use of force, Bremer (1982) concludes that "the resort to force, or the threatened use of force, by nations does not appear to be addictive" (pp. 51-52).

The mixed results of empirical studies of war contagion highlight the complexity of contagion hypotheses and suggest that further work is necessary to resolve the question of the net effects of contagion. Given our focus on war weariness and other mechanisms by which a state's war involvement affects its subsequent war behavior, the national level of analysis is the appropriate one. Systemic-level findings incorporate infectious as well as addictive processes and thus have no direct implications for war weariness or other forms of national contagion. Although there appear to be no net contagion effects at the systemic level, it is entirely possible that war is positively addictive for some states and negatively addictive for others. The following analysis will have direct bearing on this possibility.

One unique aspect of this study will be its focus on the contagious effect of war between the great powers, or great power wars. The great powers are the most important states in the system in terms of the systemic consequences of their actions (Keohane 1969; Waltz 1979; Levy 1983); their general behavior may be distinct from that of other states; great power wars are particularly likely to induce weariness because of their seriousness; and the addictive contagious effects of great power wars on their participants have not been investigated previously. Singer and Cusack (1981) and Garnham (1983) each look at wars involving great powers but not at the distinctive class of wars between the powers. One reason for the failure of most contagion studies to examine the contagion of great power war is that adequate data are not widely available. The Singer and Small correlates of war data begin in 1816 and incorporate fewer than ten cases of great power war, too few to examine contagion effects with confidence, even for a national-level study. One of the strengths of Levy's study (1982a) is that by covering five centuries of international history it permits a more thorough analysis of the contagion of great power war, but its relevance to the contagion of national war behavior is limited by its systemic-level focus.

This study aims to build on earlier work by focusing specifically on the phenomenon of addictive contagion in great power war behavior. It will attempt to answer the question of whether the net contagious effects of a state's war involvement are to increase or decrease the likelihood of its involvement in a subsequent war. These net effects reflect the interaction of numerous distinct contagious processes, but these processes are too complex and their data requirements too stringent to permit an empirical analysis of the distinct causal mechanisms involved.

RESEARCH DESIGN

Our study is organized around several specific hypotheses, each of which represents a different operational perspective on the general proposition that war inhibits subsequent war. The first hypothesis is that a state's participation in one war reduces the likelihood that it will become involved in a subsequent war in the period immediately following the first. The second hypothesis is that the greater the seriousness of the first war, the greater the inhibition against subsequent war. The third hypothesis, reflecting the possibility that it is not an individual war but instead a series of wars over a relatively short period that induces an inhibition against subsequent war, is that the higher the frequency of war in one period, the lower the frequency of war in the following period.[4]

Given the focus on the contagion of great power wars over several centuries, the analysis will begin in 1500, the approximate origin of both the modern great power system (Levy 1983, ch. 2) and the modern global system (Modelski 1978). This extended temporal domain will incorporate a large number of great power wars and will therefore permit an aggregate data analysis of their contagion effects. The diversity of conditions subsumed by this five-century span will also allow the generalization of empirically based findings on contagion beyond the particular historical circumstances of the nineteenth and twentieth centuries. Given the nature of our temporal partitioning, the analysis will cover 475 years, to 1975. The identity of the great powers over this period is taken from Levy (1983, ch. 2).[5]

This study investigates the contagious effects of great power war, the occurrence of which essentially serves as the independent variable. The question now is what classes of wars should be taken as evidence of these contagion effects. The war-weariness hypothesis suggests that long and costly great power wars should inhibit not only other great power wars, but also less serious wars. The standard 1,000 battle-death criterion suggested by Singer and Small (1972) and widely adopted sets too high a threshold. It would exclude from the data too many lesser conflicts that should be inhibited by the weariness induced by earlier great power war, and that therefore must be included in the analysis as data bearing on contagion hypotheses. For the same reason, the analysis must not be restricted to interstate wars. As suggested by references to the post-

Vietnam inhibitions against U.S. intervention in the Third World, military activity on the "periphery" of the system, removed from the central European core, should also be included. For the pre-1945 period, this means that the occurrence or nonoccurrence of imperial and colonial wars must also be considered as evidence relevant to addictive contagion hypotheses. Separate analyses will be conducted for the effects of contagion on all wars and on great power wars.

The data on great power wars for the 1500–1975 period are taken from Levy (1983). For the dependent variable, however, which includes imperial wars and smaller European wars, existing compilations of war data are not adequate. The revised Small and Singer (1982) data go back only to 1815; the Wright (1965) and Sorokin (1937) data are not based on systematic criteria and contain numerous inconsistencies; and Levy (1983) excludes imperial wars and smaller European wars. Thus, a new data set of international wars involving the great powers must be generated. Interstate and imperial wars involving the great powers during the post-1815 periods are taken from the revised Small and Singer (1982) lists of interstate and extrasystemic wars, with some modifications. Richardson (1960a), Langer (1972), and Dupuy and Dupuy (1977) are consulted for the inclusion of imperial wars and other wars involving fewer than 1,000 battle deaths but significant hostilities nevertheless. For the pre-1815 period, a combination of the Wright (1965), Sorokin (1937), and Woods and Baltzly (1915) data sets are used. While these are individually unreliable, together they provide mutual validity checks. Any war listed in two of these is included in our compilation. Cases involving single-source wars are resolved by reference to Dupuy and Dupuy (1977) and Langer (1972). These two references are also important sources for the identification of imperial wars, which are only sporadically included in our main sources. Further ambiguities are resolved with reference to standard historical sources such as *The New Cambridge Modern History* (1957), Mowat (1928), and Hill (1914).[6]

The war-weariness hypothesis and other hypotheses of negative addiction suggest that contagion is a function not only of the incidence of war but also of the seriousness of war, with longer and more costly wars expected to have a stronger contagion effect. The length or duration of war for each great power is defined in terms of elapsed time from beginning to end and is measured in years. The severity of war for each great power is measured in battle deaths and is the best indicator of the human cost of war. A third dimension of the seriousness of war is its extent or number of participating great powers. Finally, a state's total number of battle deaths may be less significant than its yearly average during a war; this severity/duration ratio will be referred to as the concentration of war. The data on these dimensions of great power war are taken from Levy (1983). Since hypotheses of negative addiction put far more emphasis on inhibitions against the outbreak of subsequent war than on the seriousness of the wars that might occur, the dependent variable will be measured only by the incidence of war and the elapsed time from the termination of one war to the onset of another.

As emphasized, each of the hypotheses will be tested at the national level. This will involve two sets of analyses. First, the national war behavior of all great powers will be aggregated and analyzed. The focus of this aggregate-level analysis is on the great power role without regard for the identities of particular powers. Each great power war will generate N cases, where N is the number of powers participating in the war, and the duration, severity, and concentration of the war will be distinct for each participant. Next, the analyses will be conducted separately for each great power in order to determine whether the aggregate pattern holds individually for each of the great powers in the system. If the aggregate patterns hold for each of the individual great powers, our confidence in their validity will be enhanced.[7]

DATA ANALYSIS

The central prediction of the war-weariness hypothesis and other hypotheses of negative addictive contagion is that war induces an inhibition against war and thus reduces the likelihood of subsequent war. It follows that the time interval between wars would be greater than if war weariness were absent. This hypothesis can be tested directly by comparing the observed distribution of elapsed times between wars with the theoretical distribution that would be expected in the absence of war weariness or other forms of contagion. In the absence of contagion or other extraneous influences, wars would occur randomly over time. We know from probability theory that random events follow a Poisson distribution, and that the time intervals between random events follow an exponential distribution.[8]

The Distribution of Interwar Intervals

In the presence of war weariness, the distribution of time intervals between wars would deviate from the exponential distribution in one of three ways. First, the distribution could have the same exponential shape but be shifted to the right, reflecting a short-term "dead time" induced by contagion before the normal pattern is resumed. Alternatively, the shape of the distribution could change in such a way that a significant proportion of the area under the curve shifts to the right, reflecting a shift in the likelihood of war from the short-term to the long-term period after a great power war. Finally, the distribution may be altered in both ways.

The actual distribution of elapsed times between a great power war and the subsequent war is presented in Figure 5.1, and that for the time to the next great power war in Figure 5.2. These data represent the combined results for all great powers, aggregated over ten-year periods.[9] The observed data certainly appear to conform to the exponential distribution predicted by our null hypothesis of no contagion. This can be confirmed by a χ^2 goodness-of-fit test, based on a comparison of the observed and expected distributions. The theoretical distribution of intervals between random events can be calculated from the probability density function of the exponential distribution, $f(t) = \lambda e^{-\lambda t}$, where $1/\lambda$ is the mean time between events. The observed and predicted distributions of elapsed times, for subsequent wars and for great power wars, are presented in Table 5.1, along with the χ^2 statistics and their associated p values. Neither of the χ^2s is statistically significant at 0.10, so the null hypothesis cannot be rejected. There is no evidence of the effects of any

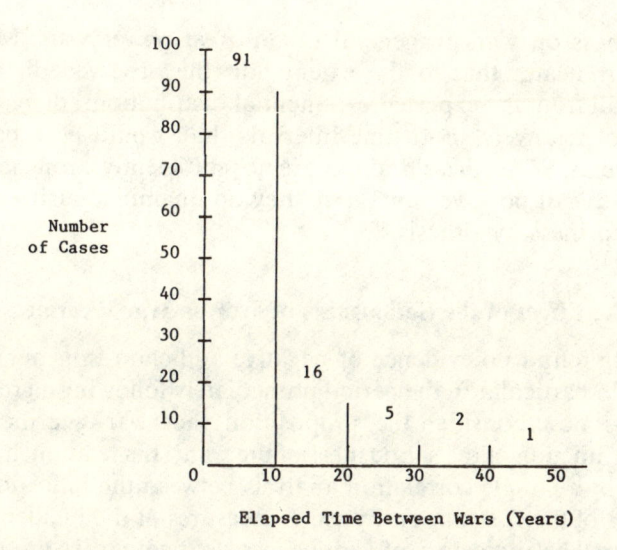

FIGURE 5.1. Distribution of interwar intervals after great power wars.

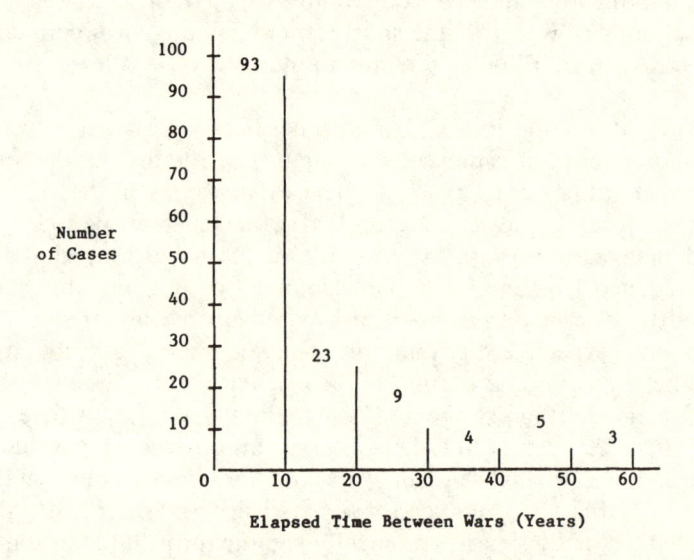

FIGURE 5.2. Distribution of elapsed time between great power wars.

war weariness on wars in general or on great power wars. Moreover, Table 5.1 indicates that to the extent that the observed distributions deviate at all from the expected exponential distributions, there are more instances of relatively short time intervals than would be expected for random events. While these findings are not sufficiently strong to support the hypothesis of positive contagion, they do unambiguously contradict the war-weariness hypothesis.[10]

The Effect of the Seriousness of War on War Weariness

Having found no evidence of negative addiction in general or war weariness in particular in the period immediately following a great power war, let us now consider the proposition that war weariness is an increasing function of the seriousness of the war. This relationship can be examined by a simple correlation analysis between the indicators of the seriousness of the first war and various measures of the incidence of the second war. The indicators of seriousness defined earlier are duration, extent (number of participating great powers), severity [log (battle deaths)], and concentration [log (battle deaths per year)]. The dependent variable will be the number of wars (and great power wars) occurring in the five-year period following the end of a great power war and the

TABLE 5.1.
Observed and expected frequencies of elapsed time between wars

All Wars*			Great Power Wars**		
Elapsed Time (years)	Observed	Expected	Elapsed Time (years)	Observed	Expected
1–10	91	86	1–10	93	84
11–20	16	22	11–20	23	33
⩾21	8	7	21–30	9	12
			⩾31	12	8

*$\chi^2 = 2.069$, $df = 2$, $p > 0.3$
**$\chi^2 = 5.99$, $df = 3$, $p > 0.1$

elapsed time until the next war (and great power war). The resulting product/moment correlation coefficients are presented in Table 5.2.

There appears to be no meaningful relationship between the seriousness of great power war and the outbreak of subsequent war. None of the correlation coefficients exceeds 0.24, indicating that none of the war indicators accounts for more than 6 percent of the variance in the subsequent outbreak of war, and only two exceed 0.20. While many of the coefficients are in the same direction as predicted by the war-weariness or other negative addiction hypotheses, only three are statistically significant, and these appear to follow no meaningful pattern. It is

TABLE 5.2.
Correlations (r) between war indicators and measures of subsequent war, aggregated for all great powers

	War Indicators[a]			
Indicators of Subsequent War	Dur	Ext	Sev	Con
Number of wars within 5 years	−0.08	−0.20[b]	−0.02	−0.03
Number of great power wars within 5 years	0.01	−0.24[b]	−0.02	−0.07
Elapsed time to next war	−0.11	0.12	−0.02	0.13
Elapsed time to next great power war	−0.07	0.10	0.09	0.21[b]

[a]The indicators of the first war are, respectively, duration, extent (number of participating powers), severity (battle deaths), and concentration (battle deaths per year). The logarithmic transformations of the severity and concentration indicators are used.
[b]Statistically significant at the 0.05 level.

interesting that the severity of war, which in theory should have the greatest immunizing effects, appears to have the least, with its coefficients being smallest on average and none being significant. It is seen that the results are roughly the same regardless of whether all wars or great power wars are used as the dependent variable. It can be concluded that the coefficients are far too weak to support the hypothesis that the more serious the great war, the greater the inhibition against subsequent war.

These results are confirmed if we examine the coefficients for individual great powers.[11] Of the 112 coefficients for France, England, Spain, Austria, Turkey, Russia, and Prussia/Germany, only 9 are statistically significant at 0.05 and 4 of these point to positive addiction rather than to war weariness. Most of the coefficients are relatively small, and only about one-half are in the predicted direction. The results are mixed both for individual states and for specific indicators. The coefficients for the elapsed time indicators often point in the opposite direction from those for the incidence of war during or after a previous war, and the indicators for all wars are often opposite from the indicators for great power war. The contagion effects of the duration of war are positive for some states (Austrian Hapsburgs), negative for others (Prussia), and mixed for the rest. Most of the patterns have no obvious theoretical explanations. Differences across indicators for a given power are as large as differences between powers. The coefficients are so small that their directions are highly unstable. For these reasons we must conclude that the contagion effects of great power war are basically independent of the seriousness of the war.[12]

To this point we have found that there is no evidence that war has any contagious effects on its participants, except that the likelihood of a second great power war may be increased slightly, directly contrary to hypotheses of war weariness and other forms of negative reinforcement. In addition, longer, more extensive, more severe, and more highly concentrated wars are no more contagious for their participants than less serious wars, and general wars are no different in their addictive contagious effects from other great power wars. The question that remains is whether the incidence of war might be affected not by the existence or seriousness of a single preceding war, but instead by a series of earlier wars.

The Contagious Effects of a Series of Wars

The question here is whether the frequency of a great power's wars in one period has any impact on the frequency of its wars in the following period. War weariness and other forms of negative addictive contagion would predict a negative relationship. A ten-year period of aggregation is examined in order to capture short-term contagion effects but exclude intermediate-term cyclical phenomena, and a product/moment correlation coefficient is used as the measure of association. The results, including an aggregate measure for all great powers as well as the coefficients for individual powers, are presented in Table 5.3. Great powers in the system for less than a century or so are excluded from the table and from the individual (but not aggregate) analyses.

If the national war behavior of all states is aggregated, we find a small negative relationship between the frequency of a great power's wars during one period and its frequency of wars during the following period, and a very small positive relationship involving the frequency of great power wars in the following period. These relationships are very weak, however, with the frequency of great power war explaining at most 1 percent of the variance in the frequency of subsequent war.[13] It is interesting that great power wars tend to inhibit, however slightly, the occurrence of subsequent war but tend to increase slightly the incidence of great power war.

This conclusion is supported by an analysis of the individual great powers. There is a negative relationship between the frequency of great power war in one period and the frequency of war in the following period for all but one of the powers, but these relationships are all very weak except for the case of England. The war-weariness hypothesis would predict more strongly negative contagion effects on subsequent great power wars, but Table 5.3 shows that this is not the case. There are more positive than negative coefficients, but these are far too small to be substantively meaningful. Nor do there appear to be any obvious patterns for individual states. England's significant negative relationship involving all wars vanishes for great power wars. There appears to be some negative reinforcement for both types of wars in the case of Spain, but neither of the coefficients is statistically significant and in neither case can this explain more than 8 percent of the variance in the frequency of subsequent war.

On the basis of this analysis, we must conclude that a great power's involvement in several wars with other great powers in one period has no effect on its likely frequency of war involvement in the following period.[14] Taken together, these analyses suggest that the historical evidence contradicts hypotheses of negative addictive contagion, but is not strong enough to support hypotheses of positive addiction.

The Stability of the Findings over Time

One potential problem with the analyses performed to this point is that the finding of no war contagion may not be constant over the entire

TABLE 5.3.
Correlations (r) between frequencies of great power war and subsequent war*

	10-Year Periods	
	All War	Great Power War
Aggregate (n = 266)	−0.10	0.06
France (N = 47)	0.03	0.07
England (N = 47)	−0.37[a]	0.00
Spain (N = 26)	−0.25	−0.27
Austrian Hapsburgs (N = 37)	−0.15	−0.10
Ottoman Empire (N = 20)	−0.07	−0.03
Russia (N = 24)	−0.16	0.05
Prussia/Germany (N = 23)	−0.11	0.11

[a]Statistically significant at the 0.05 level.

five-century span of the modern great power system. For example, if we make the plausible assumption that the impact of societal variables has increased over the last five centuries (Osgood 1967; Howard 1976), then we should expect that the existence of war weariness and its impact on war behavior have been increasing over time. If this (or some other mechanism) has altered the impact of contagion processes, it is possible that our finding of no contagion is masking a true relationship of negative contagion in the more recent historical era and positive (or no) contagion in the earlier years of the great power system.[15] Our concern regarding this potential problem of time-associated spuriousness is deepened by the fact that the frequency of war is considerably lower in the more recent period (Levy 1982b). In order to control for any such spuriousness associated with time, we will repeat several of our analyses separately for the periods before and after 1815.[16]

First, consider the question of whether a series of great power wars has any impact on the frequency of war or great power war in the following period. If we aggregate the war behavior for all great powers in each ten-year period, we get a total of 178 national ten-year periods before 1820 and 88 national ten-year periods for the 1820–1970 period.[17] The correlation between the frequency of great power war in one ten-year period and the frequency of all wars in the following ten-year period is $r = 0.07$ for the 1500–1820 era and −0.12 for the 1820–1970 era (versus −0.10 for the 1500–1970 era). Similarly, the correlations involving subsequent great power war are $r = 0.06$ for the earlier era and −0.15 for the more recent era. Each of these coefficients is relatively small and none is statistically significant at the 0.05 level. While the coefficient for each type of war is slightly more negative for the period since 1820, the differences are too small to be meaningful, particularly given the relatively few independent cases for the recent period. It can be concluded, therefore, that the absence of contagion effects from a series of great power wars remains basically unchanged during the five-century span of the modern system.

Another comparison of the periods before and after 1815 can be made with respect to the hypothesis that the more serious a war, the greater its negative addictive effects. The same indicators are used as previously, and the aggregate results for all great powers are presented in Table 5.4. For most of the pairs of indicators, the differences between the correlations for the periods before and after 1815 are relatively small. If we focus on the number of wars or great power wars occurring within five years of a great power war, or the elapsed time to the next war, we see that 11 of the 16 pairs of coefficients differ by 0.10 or less, suggesting the absence of significant changes over time. It is particularly interesting that the correlations involving the elapsed time indicators suggest a tendency for a slight negative addiction in the pre-1815 period to be replaced by a slight positive addiction in the last century and a half. This is the opposite of the increasing war weariness or negative reinforcement that would be predicted by the war-weariness hypothesis on the basis of the increasing democratization of political systems and the presumed increase in the impact of societal variables on state behavior. Note also that the indicator for which these tendencies are most pronounced is not the severity or concentration of war for a particular state, as the war-weariness hypothesis would predict, but instead the total number of great powers involved in the war.

If we repeat out analysis of the distribution of elapsed times between wars for each of these periods using χ^2 goodness-of-fit test between the observed data and the theoretical exponential distribution predicted by the null hypothesis, we find no significant differences in contagion over time. For the elapsed time between great power war and subsequent war, aggregating the elapsed times by five-year periods, we find that the χ values are about 2.5 and both P values are about 0.4 to 0.5 for the periods before and after the Congress of Vienna.[18]

Taken together, these different statistical tests suggest that there is no systematic evidence pointing to significant changes in the patterns of addictive contagion over time. There is no reason to believe that our general conclusion of the absence of addictive contagion masks a pattern of positive contagion in one period and negative contagion in another, and thus no reason to question the validity of our findings for the entire 1500-1975 period.

TABLE 5.4.
Correlations (r) between war indicators and measures of subsequent war, for periods before and after 1815[a]

Indicators of Subsequent War		Dur	Ext	Sev	Con
			War Indicators[b]		
Number of wars within 5 years	Pre-1815	−0.12	−0.21[c]	−0.00	0.03
	Post-1815	−0.07	−0.11	−0.04	−0.04
Number of great power wars within 5 years	Pre-1815	−0.09	−0.23[c]	−0.00	0.04
	Post-1815	−0.02	0.01	0.08	0.11
Elapsed time to next war	Pre-1815	−0.07	0.22[c]	−0.03	0.03
	Post-1815	−0.21	−0.15	−0.06	0.08
Elapsed time to next great power war	Pre-1815	0.06	0.30[c]	0.17[c]	0.17[c]
	Post-1815	−0.31	−0.46[c]	−0.12	−0.00

[a]There are about 130 cases prior to 1815 and about 40 cases afterward.
[b]The indicators of the first war are, respectively, duration, extent (number of participating powers), severity (battle deaths), and concentration (battle deaths per year). The logarithmic transformations of the severity and concentration indicators are used.
[c]Statistically significant at the 0.05 level.

CONCLUSION

The war-weariness hypothesis holds that a state's involvement in war, and particularly long and destructive war, reduces the likelihood of its involvement in subsequent wars for a certain period of time. This empirical study of war contagion differs from earlier ones in several key respects. It focuses exclusively on the addictive contagion effects of wars between the great powers; it analyzes whether the hypothesized negative addictive contagion inhibits imperial wars as well as interstate wars involving the great powers; it examines the hypothesis over the full five-century span of the modern system; and it examines the hypothesis for each of the great powers individually as well as for the aggregate national-level behavior of all of the great powers combined. We have examined the impact on contagion of various dimensions of the seriousness of war in addition to its incidence or frequency. Finally, we have examined possible changes in patterns of contagion over the five-century span of the modern system.

The results have been relatively consistent, regardless of precisely how the hypothesis is operationalized. After being involved in a war with another power, a great power tends to be no more likely to become involved in another war or great power war. If anything, there is a short-term increase in the likelihood of war, but this tendency is not sufficiently strong to provide conclusive support for a positive reinforcement hypothesis. If the time intervals between wars are examined, the data conform fairly well with the exponential distribution associated with the null hypothesis of random events with no contagion. Moreover, any deviations from the expected theoretical distribution are in the direction of positive addiction. The probability of war is independent of the period of time since the last war. In addition, the hypothesis that more serious wars generate a greater inhibition against subsequent war (or great power war) is not supported by the evidence, and general wars involving nearly all the great powers are no different in their contagion effects than the average great power war. Finally, there is no support for the hypothesis that a series of great power wars induces an inhibition against subsequent war. These conclusions of the absence of negative contagion in general and war weariness in particular hold for the individual great powers as well as for the aggregate of all national great power war behavior. There appear to be no distinctive and consistent patterns involving individual great powers, but because of relatively small N values it is difficult to generalize. There is no consistent evidence of any significant changes in these patterns of contagion over the five-century span of the system.

These findings of the absence of war weariness are consistent with a wide range of empirical studies on contagion in the outbreak of war. They confirm other national-level studies that find no convincing evidence of addictive contagion (Singer and Small 1974, pp. 283-84; Singer and Cusack 1981; Bremer 1982, pp. 51-52; Garnham 1983), and extend these earlier findings by demonstrating their validity for great power wars and for the entire span of the modern system. By examining the addiction hypothesis for individual great powers as well as for the aggregation of all national great power behavior, this study also has some relevance for earlier systemic-level studies of contagion, which generally find no contagion in the outbreak of war (Richardson 1960; Singer and Small 1974, pp. 278-82; Singer and Cusack 1981; Levy 1982a). One possible explanation for the absence of systemic-level contagion is that war may be positively contagious for some states and negatively contagious for others, but this study has found no clear and consistent evidence in support of such a proposition.[19] Instead, the more likely explanations are either that there are no contagion effects of any kind, that multiple but opposing contagion effects cancel each other out, or that under some conditions war is positively contagious while under other conditions it is negatively contagious. The testing of these alternative explanations would be a potentially useful avenue for subsequent research.

NOTES

1. This follows the analytical distinction between "addiction" and "infection" (Davis et al. 1978, p. 777) or "reinforcement" and "spatial diffusion" (Most and Starr 1980, p. 933). Addiction or reinforcement refers to the contagious effects of a war on the probability of a subsequent war involving one of the belligerents in the first war, whereas infection or spatial diffusion affects the subsequent war behavior of other actors. Each form of contagion can be either positive or negative.

2. Toynbee concedes, however, that the hypothesized generational cycle of war and peace cannot fully account for the "complete War-and-Peace Cycle" consisting of general wars, breathing space, supplemental wars, and general peace. This complete cycle spans 100 years, or four generations, and Toynbee (1954, pp. 251-54) suggests that these complete cycles can be better explained in terms of the balance of power and the underlying dynamics of the international system. Similarly, long-cycle theory and related theories of world system dynamics suggest that the probability of war is largely a function of the changing structure of the international system or a state's changing power position within that system (Modelski 1978; Doran 1983; Thompson 1983b).

3. Or, a victorious war might bolster the political position of an existing regime and increase its proclivity to resort to bellicose policies in the future as a means of increasing domestic political support. Many of these tendencies can be further reinforced by a variety of other variables, including the cognitive beliefs and psychological processes of decision makers. For example, Jervis (1976 ch. VI) emphasizes the importance of the last major war in shaping the lessons decision makers learn from history.

4. It should be emphasized that while these hypotheses are stated in the form of negative addictive contagion, this analysis is equally open to the possibility of positive addiction.

5. The great powers include France, 1500-1975; England/Great Britain, 1500-1975; Austrian Hapsburgs/Austria/Austria-Hungary, 1500-19, 1556-1918; Spain, 1500-19, 1556-1808; Ottoman Empire, 1500-1699; United Hapsburgs, 1519-56; the Netherlands, 1609-1713; Sweden, 1617-1721; Russia/Soviet Union, 1721-1975; Prussia/Germany/West Germany, 1740-1975; Italy, 1861-1943; United States, 1898-1975; Japan, 1905-45; China, 1949-75.

6. See Levy and Morgan (1984) for further discussions of this data set.

7. Patterns of contagion for individual great powers also have bearing on hypotheses regarding the determinants of contagion. Similar patterns could be explained by the nature of the system or great power role. Significantly different patterns of contagion for individual powers would suggest, however, that national-level variables or the unique environments of individual powers are important sources of addictive contagion.

8. This is the basis of queuing theory (Wadsworth and Bryan 1960) and waiting time analysis (Mood et al. 1974).

9. Since our focus is on war weariness, we analyze only those wars occurring after the first war has terminated. This excludes 54 cases of war and 26 cases of great power war that occur while the first great power war is underway. For this reason, the number of great power war cases in Table 5.1 exceeds the number of all war cases.

This analysis was also performed using one- and five-year periods of aggregation with virtually identical results. The ten-year periods are presented to simplify the visual presentation and to "smooth" the downward curves.

10. These analyses were also performed using five-year periods of aggregation and for the pre- and post-1815 period separately. In every case the results were consistent with those presented here. Of the ten additional tests, in only one did χ^2 approach statistical significance. For the entire period, using a five-year period of aggregation, the distribution of the elapsed time until the next great power war was significant at $p < 0.10$. The only category in which the observed frequency was greater than the expected frequency was the first five-year period. But this, once again, is the direct opposite of what the war-weariness hypothesis would predict.

Analyses of this type performed separately for Britain and France produced identical patterns. The number of cases for each of the other great powers is too small to provide meaningful results, however.

11. The analyses of individual powers is restricted to seven states, for only they provide a sufficient number of cases to permit us to generalize about the contagion in their war behavior. Each state included was in the system for at least 200 years and was involved in at least nine great power wars, whereas each state excluded was in the system for at most 105 years and (except for the United Hapsburgs, 1519-56) was involved in no more than seven wars.

12. It is conceivable that the relationship between the seriousness of war and the degree of contagion is not linear, but instead involves a threshold effect—once the seriousness of war reaches a certain level, war weariness and therefore a period of relative peace are induced. This hypothesis can be tested by examining the effects of general or hegemonic wars. These conflicts involve nearly all of the great powers and largely determine the structure and transformation of the international system. Because of their high severity and length, they should be most likely to induce war weariness and other forms of negative addiction. For a definition of general war and list of the ten general wars since 1500, see Levy (1985).

Whether general wars have distinctive contagion effects is determined as follows. Difference-of-means tests are used to compare general wars with the great power wars examined earlier (with general wars removed from the latter), using the following indicators of subsequent war: yearly number of wars and great power wars occurring within ten years and elapsed time to the next war and great power war. If the results are aggregated over all states, we find the differences are all in the predicted direction but are very small, with only one of the four being statistically significant at 0.05 and the other P values being relatively high. The results for the individual great powers are similar and support the conclusion that general wars have no distinctive contagion effects, though these findings must be treated with caution because of the small number of cases.

13. The absence of a relationship involving the frequencies of great power wars in successive periods is confirmed by a Durbin-Watson test for autocorrelation. If the frequency of great power war is regressed against time, an analysis of the residuals generates a Durbin-Watson coefficient of $D = 2.03$, which falls within the range of no serial correlation (Yamane 1973, p. 1096; Ostrom 1978, pp. 32-34). The coefficient for all wars has a fairly low P value of 0.054, but this is due in part to the large number of cases involved (an aggregate total of 266 ten-year periods).

14. The results of this analysis are no different if a 20-year period of aggregation is used.

15. This problem is well known by those familiar with the studies produced by the Correlates of War Project. In a number of cases, variables that are uncorrelated over the entire period are moderately correlated (but in opposite directions) in the nineteenth and twentieth centuries [see, for example, Singer and Small (1968) and Singer et al. (1972)].

16. The date 1815 is used because it is the beginning point for most quantitative studies of contagion (since the Singer-Small data begin in 1816), because it represents the most obvious turning point in most indicators of great power war (Levy 1983, ch. 6), and because it is often taken as the beginning of the period of modern democratic states (so that changes in societally induced war readiness should be most readily detected at this point). For purposes of convenience in the temporal aggregation of the data, the year 1820 rather than 1815 is used, but this has no effect on the identity of the wars included in the study.

17. Note that the 88 ten-year periods since 1820 are somewhat misleading, and do not represent 88 truly independent cases. Owing in part to infectious contagion, nearly 40 percent of all great power involvements in great power wars since 1820 consist of the experiences in the two world wars. The fact that they do not occur in adjacent periods produces a negative bias in the resulting correlations.

18. An analysis of the elapsed times between great power wars for the pre-1815 period gives a $\chi^2 = 9$, $P > 0.1$, compared with $P > 0.5$ for the later period. The main deviation from the theoretical exponential distribution, however, is the greater number of very short elapsed times, directly contrary to the war-weariness hypothesis.

19. This finding should be regarded as tentative until it is confirmed by subsequent research.

REFERENCES

Blainey, Geoffrey. 1973. *The Causes of War*. New York: Free Press.

Bremer, Stuart A. 1982. "The Contagiousness of Coercion: The Spread of Seriousness International Disputes, 1900-1976." *International Interactions* 9:29-55.

Davis, William W., George T. Duncan, and Randolph M. Siverson. 1978. "The Dynamics of Warfare: 1816-1965." *American Journal of Political Science* 22 (November):772-92.

Doran, Charles F. 1983. "Power Cycle Theory and the Contemporary State System." In W. R. Thompson (ed.), *Contending Approaches to World System Analysis*, Beverly Hills, CA: Sage, ch. 7.

Dupuy, R. Ernest, and Trevor N. Dupuy. 1977. *The Encyclopedia of Military History*, rev. ed. New York: Harper and Row.

Erikson, Robert S. 1976. "Is There Such a Thing as a Safe Seat?" *Polity* 8 (Summer): 623-32.

Garnham, David. 1983. "Explaining Major Power Bellicosity and Pacifism." Paper presented at the 24th annual convention of the International Studies Association, Mexico City, April 5-9.

Gilpin, Robert. 1981. *War and Change in World Politics*. Cambridge: Cambridge University Press.

Grathwol, Robert P. 1980. *Stresemann and the DNVP: Reconciliation or Revenge in German Foreign Policy, 1924-1928*. Lawrence: Regents Press of Kansas.

Hill, David Jayne. 1914. *A History of Diplomacy in the International Development of Europe*, 3 vols. London: Longman's Green.

Holsti, Ole R., and James N. Rosenau, 1984. *American Leadership in World Affairs*. Boston: Allen and Unwin.

Howard, Michael. 1976. *War in European History*. Oxford: Oxford University Press.

Jervis, Robert. 1976. *Perception and Misperception in International Politics*. Princeton, NJ: Princeton University Press.

Keohane, Robert O. 1969. "Lilliputian's Dilemmas: Small States in International Politics." *International Organization* 23 (Spring):291-310.

Langer, William L. 1972. *An Encyclopedia of World History*, 5th ed., rev. Boston: Houghton Mifflin.

Levy, Jack S. 1985. "Theories of General War." *World Politics* 37 (April): 344-74.

———. 1983. *War in the Modern Great Power System, 1495-1975*. Lexington: University Press of Kentucky.

———. 1982a. "The Contagion of Great Power War Behavior, 1495-1975." *American Journal of Political Science* 26 (August):562-84.

———. 1982b. "Historical Trends in Great Power War, 1495-1975." *International Studies Quarterly* 26 (June):278-300.

Levy, Jack S., and T. Clifton Morgan. 1984. "The Frequency and Seriousness of War: An Inverse Relationship?" *Journal of Conflict Resolution* 28 (December):731-49.

Modelski, George. 1978. "The Long Cycle of Global Politics and the Nation-State." *Comparative Studies in Society and History* 20 (April):214-235.

Mood, Alexander M., Franklin A. Graybill, and Duane C. Boes. 1974. *Introduction to the Theory of Statistics*. New York: McGraw-Hill.

Most, Benjamin A., and Harvey Starr, 1980. "Diffusion, Reinforcement, Geopolitics, and the Spread of War." *American Political Science Review* 74 (December):932-46.

Mowat, R. B. 1928. *A History of European Diplomacy*. London: Edward Arnold. *The New Cambridge Modern History*, 14 vols. Cambridge: Cambridge University Press, 1957-70.

Osgood, Robert. 1967. "The Expansion of Force." In Robert Osgood and Robert W. Tucker (eds.), *Force, Order, and Justice*. Baltimore: Johns Hopkins University Press, 41-120.

Ostrom, Charles W., Jr. 1978. *Time Series Analysis.* Beverly Hills, CA: Sage.
Richardson, Lewis F. 1960a. *Arms and Insecurity.* Chicago: Quadrangle.
_____. 1960b. *Statistics of Deadly Quarrels.* Chicago: Quadrangle.
Singer, J. David, and Thomas Cusack. 1981. "Periodicity, Inexorability, and Steermanship in International War." In Richard Merritt and Bruce M. Russett (eds.), *From National Development to Global Community.* London: Allen and Unwin, pp. 404-22.
Singer, J. David, Stuart Bremer, and John Stuckey. 1972. "Capability Distribution, Uncertainty, and Major Power War, 1820-1965." In Bruce M. Russett (ed.), *Peace, War, and Numbers.* Beverly Hills, CA: Sage, pp. 19-48.
Singer, J. David, and Melvin Small. 1974. "Foreign Policy Indicators: Predictors of War in History and in the State of the World Message." *Policy Sciences* 5 (September):271-96.
_____. 1972. *The Wages of War, 1816-1965.* New York: John Wiley and Sons.
_____. 1968. "Alliance Aggregation and the Onset of War, 1815-1945." In J. David Singer (ed.), *Quantitative International Politics.* New York: Free Press, pp. 247-86.
Siverson, Randolph M., and Joel King. 1979. "Alliances and the Expansion of War, 1815-1965." In J. David Singer and Michael Wallace (eds.), *To Augur Well.* Beverly Hills, CA: Sage., pp. 37-49.
Small, Melvin, and J. David Singer. 1982. *Resort to Arms: International and Civil Wars, 1816-1980.* Beverly Hills, CA: Sage.
Sorokin, Pitrim A. 1937. *Social and Cultural Dynamics: Fluctation of Social Relationships, War, and Revolution, Vol. 3.* New York: American.
Thompson, W. R. 1984. "Cycles of General Hegemonic, and Global War." Presented at the Conference on Dynamic Models of International Conflict, Boulder, CO, October 31-November 3.
_____. 1983a. "The World-Economy, the Long Cycle, and the Question of World System Time." In Pat J. McGowan and Charles W. Kegley, Jr. (eds.), *Foreign Policy and the Modern World System.* Beverly Hills, CA: Sage., pp. 35-62.
_____ (ed.) 1983b. *Contending Approaches to World System Analysis.* Beverly Hills, CA: Sage.
Toynbee, Arnold J. 1954. *A Study of History, Vol. 9.* New York: Oxford University Press.
Wadsworth, George P., and Joseph G. Bryan. 1960. *Introduction to Probability and Random Variables.* New York: McGraw-Hill.
Wallerstein, Immanuel. 1984. "The Three Instances of Hegemony in the History of the Capitalist World Economy." In Immanuel Wallerstein (ed.), *The Politics of the World-Economy.* Cambridge: Cambridge University Press, ch. 3.
Waltz, Kenneth. 1979. *Theory of International Politics.* Reading, MA: Addison-Wesley.
Woods, Frederick Adams, and Alexander Baltzly. 1915. *Is War Diminishing?* Boston: Houghton Mifflin.
Wright, Quincy. 1965. *A Study of War*, 2nd ed. Chicago: University of Chicago Press.
Yamane, Taro. 1973. *Statistics.* New York: Harper & Row.

6
Persisting Patterns of Repression and Rebellion: Foundations for a General Theory of Political Coercion
Ted Robert Gurr

Repression and rebellion are persisting features of political life in most of the contemporary world. There is little justification now for theories prevalent 30 years ago that interpreted rebellion and revolution as aberrations in a worldwide process of economic and political development. Nor is there any longer much optimism about the prospects for stable democracy in the Third World based on the consent of the governed, nor faith in the capacity of democratic political arrangements to minimize violent conflict in any nations, old or new. In most of the contemporary world, repression is the price paid for political order, even in regimes that preserve democratic forms. And violent forms of resistance—mass uprisings, revolutionary guerrilla warfare, terrorism—are part of a global repertoire of political actions available to groups that oppose the prevailing distributions of wealth and power.

This essay sketches a theoretical framework for comparative research on the uses of coercion by groups in and out of power. It incorporates in a single conceptual scheme rebels' use of violent political action and the reliance of regimes on agencies and policies of repression. One postulate developed in this framework is that there is a general tendency toward equilibrium in the intensity of coercion used by regimes and their opponents; the equilibrium will be at a high level in societies that are sharply differentiated along segmental and class lines. It also is proposed that partisans who successfully seize power ordinarily must

---

I am indebted to Michael Nicholson, Michael Stohl, and Margaret P. Karns for their thoughtful comments.

establish "structures of repression" as the instrument of retaining power in the face of renewed challenges by partisans out of power.[1]

Testing these and other propositions derived in this framework has substantial implications for the kinds of information that should be recorded in cross-national compendia such as Charles Lewis Taylor's accounting of political "events" (Taylor and Jodice 1983, vol. 2) and Raymond Gastil's ratings of political rights (1984). What is required is the collection of systematic data on the identity of the partisan groups that initiate coercive political action, and the groups that are the targets of state coercion and deprivations of rights. More generally, convincing answers to some of the key substantive and theoretical questions in contemporary conflict analysis require research on actual and potential partisan groups at both the micro- and macrolevels of analysis.

PARTISAN VIOLENCE AND STATE COERCION IN EMPIRICAL CONFLICT THEORY

Critics of empirical theory and research on civil conflict have repeatedly pointed out that the use of violence by rebels is closely linked to the state's use of coercion. Galtung in 1969 objected to the exclusive identification of "violence" with the physical acts of protesters and insurgents, and promoted the concept of "structural violence" to refer to the kinds of deprivation and repression inflicted by institutions, including the state. Violence by rebels, in this conception, is resistance to structural violence. In another theoretical commentary, Nardin in 1971 criticized theories that treated the violent acts of partisans as a political problem and the use of violence by authorities as conflict management. Instead, he proposed that inquiry should focus on "how violent interactions among partisan groups, including the state, originate, escalate, and become managed" (p. 64).

A related set of empirical problems plagues empirical studies of the presumed effects of regime "coercion" on collective violence, including those by Gurr (1968), Feierabend and Nesvold (1970), Markus and Nesvold (1972), and Hibbs (1973, ch. 6). One problem noted in Snyder's 1976 review is that "partisan violence" as measured in aggregate studies includes violence used by the authorities against opposition groups and mutual violence instigated by authorities' use of violence against such groups. Theory and empirical analysis should treat government coercion along two dimensions: its timing (whether preemptive or responsive) and the extent of violence used by government forces (Snyder 1976).

One of the few general theories of state coercion has been proposed by Charles Tilly (1978) as part of his larger theory of conflict processes.

When challenged by groups seeking to improve their positions, regimes may respond with repression, toleration, or facilitation. The character of the political regime partly determines the response: Facilitation is somewhat greater in democracies than in repressive regimes; toleration is much greater in weak regimes than in totalitarian states. The characteristics of the challengers are equally important: The weaker or less acceptable the challengers and the larger their scale of action, the more likely they are to be repressed (Tilly 1978, ch. 4). A limitation of the analysis is the assumption that state coercion is reactive; no consideration is given to proactive violence.

Duvall and Stohl (1983) have focused more narrowly on the circumstances in which states resort to terrorism, which stipulates one general circumstance in which elites initiate the use of violence. They propose a cost-benefit analysis that takes into account the expected relative costs and effectiveness of state terrorism. There are two "syndromes" of political conditions in which elites are likely to regard terrorism as cost-effective: in militaristic states (where the means are available) and in those with an ideological mission (which provides justification for unrestrained repression of ideological opponents). Harff (1985) offers a general explanation of why regimes engage in the most extreme form of state coercion, genocide, against whole groups of ethnic or political opponents. The essential internal conditions, she proposes, are political upheavals in polarized societies that bring to, or confirm in, power elites with radical and exclusionary ideologies. Such elites choose to destroy rather than merely repress as a demonstration of their power and convictions.

This author has proposed a general multivariate theory of conditions that increase the likelihood that rulers will use violence as a means of political control, a theory incorporating both situational and structural variables that affect cost-benefit calculations (Gurr 1986). Situational variables are characteristics of regimes and challengers that affect elites' decision-making calculus: The greater the immediate political threat attributed to actual or potential challengers, and the weaker the regime, the more likely elites are to rely on coercion rather than accommodation. Structural conditions are those that define elites' relations with opponents and constrain their options: Elites are most likely to choose violent means of control in heterogeneous and highly stratified societies and during periods of involvement in international conflict. The crucial dispositional factors are elites' norms about the acceptability of coercive strategies. Elites who have seized and held power through violence are likely to be habituated to its use; secret police and similar agencies established during such conflicts provide means and reinforcement for persisting reliance on state violence and terror.

Such theories still fall short of Nardin's goal of a general theory of political violence. Theories of "why states coerce" complement theories of "why people rebel," but there remains a need for a higher-order, integrating theoretical framework that encompasses the uses of coercion and violence by all parties contending for power, whether they hold it or seek it, and the interactions among them.

One step in the direction of an interactive theory is Jackson et al.'s action-reaction model of "conflict and coercion in dependent states" (1978). It is formally demonstrated that equilibria can be reached between regimes and opposition at either high or low levels of coercion. No analytic distinctions are made among the different dimensions of coercion and violence, however, and the analysis is specific to dependent Third World states. An empirical study by Lichbach and Gurr (1981) takes a similar approach: Time-lagged cross-national data are used to model the action-reaction relations between the extent of political opposition and violent government responses, without specification of conditions that initiate such sequences.

More recently, Lichbach (1985) criticizes the limitations of action-reaction models, arguing instead for a strategic model in which opposition groups select among a repertoire of violent and nonviolent tactics using an "optimizing decision calculus" that takes into account government response strategies, in particular the mix of repression and accommodations used in response to opposition tactics. He draws the paradoxical inference that increased governmental repression of an oppositional tactic that is relatively effective increases the overall level of opposition. In a parallel analysis of regimes' decision calculus, he assumes that elites want to minimize both political violence and potential revolutionary overthrows. Formal analysis suggests that these are inconsistent goals: Up to some point, both accommodation and repression will reduce violence, but with the unintended consequence of increasing the potential for revolution (Lichbach 1984a). Whether or not these specific deductions are valid, the common assumption is that all parties to conflict make ongoing strategic analyses of the costs and benefits of coercive versus other tactics. The theoretical argument that follows builds on this assumption.

TOWARD A GENERAL CONCEPTION OF THE USE OF COERCION IN THE PURSUIT AND PRESERVATION OF POWER

Most of the theoretical approaches reviewed above make the assumption, implicitly or explicitly, that coercion used by those in power is intrinsically different from violence used by those who oppose or seek concessions from them. The fundamental premise of the present analysis is that the violence of opposition and the violence or repression used by states are two different facets of the same general phenomenon, which is the use of coercion in the pursuit and preservation of political power. They are, in effect, different tactics in the general repertoire of coercive actions that is available to all participants in the political process. A general theory of political coercion should, among other things, (1) define the parameters of the repertoire, (2) propose distinctions among different kinds of coercive tactics, and (3) say something about the circumstances that influence the choices of tactics by groups in and out of power. The remainder of this section sketches the beginnings of such a theory.

One initial qualification: The use of the phrase "choices of tactics" in the preceding paragraph does not imply a narrow commitment to a microeconomic or rational choice framework such as those used by Jackson et al. (1979) and Lichbach (1985). The rational choice framework used here is an expanded one that accommodates the effects of non- or quasi-rational factors in the calculus of coercion. In particular, the motivational roles of anger and reaction to threat must be incorporated [see Gurr (1970) and Gurr and Duvall (1976)], and also the effect of normative commitments based on peoples' historical experiences and ideological convictions. The role of such normative commitments in the explanation of state violence is discussed in several of the theories of state violence cited above (Duvall and Stohl 1983; Harff 1985; Gurr 1986).

As a point of departure, it is worth asking why so many scholars assume that the use of violence by those in power should require a different theoretical explanation than does violence used by those who oppose them. The critical theorist's approach to explanation is that many scholars value the state and political stability (at least in its Western manifestations) more than those who actively oppose it. Therefore, there is a latent normative disposition to regard the two kinds of violence as qualitatively different from one another [see Nardin (1980)].

There is also a major substantive consideration: Political control of opposition in most modern states is achieved more through dissuasion than the open use of violence. That is, much of the coercion used by states is exercised subtly, in the form of warnings, surveillance, and deprivations of liberty, whereas those who would oppose the state coercively usually find it necessary to use mass action and acts of violence. This may be reinterpreted in the strategic choice terms suggested above: The repertoires of coercive action available to the state are significantly different from those available to oppositions. In particular, most states have more institutional capacity to use coercion; the main exceptions among opposition groups are revolutionary organizations with "parallel structures" and widespread support.

For a general theory of coercion, we need both a general definition of coercion and distinctions among its forms or types. Coercion is the use or threat of harmful action to alter the target's behavior. Harmful actions are "negative sanctions," or in other words any overt action that does physical or psychological hurt to the target. Here we are concerned with coercion in the political arena: Political coercion aims at altering the target's politically relevant behavior. What constitutes punishment, or threat, or "politically relevant behavior" is to some degree culturally and situationally determined. Therefore, the context of a particular act, and perceptions of it, may have to be judged by an analyst before concluding that it is or is not "political coercion." Nonetheless, at the core of the concept are relatively unambiguous acts, such as a regional liberation front's assault on a police barracks or the imprisonment of 43 opposition politicians, whose meaning is as clear to the partisans as to the observer.

Political coercion, so defined, refers to a property of some acts, and policies, of both regimes and their opponents. It is useful to distinguish a number of dimensions or types of political coercion. First, coercive actions may be systematically or sporadically applied. If they are applied in a patterned and persistent way by a regime, they can be characterized as a policy of repression. Patterned and persistent acts of coercion by opposition groups are more often characterized as "campaigns"— of antigovernment demonstrations, bombings, guerrilla warfare, etc. Sporadic coercive acts usually have less political significance, unless they are accompanied by warnings that make it clear they are terroristic, that is, designed to induce sharp fear in a target audience, thereby altering their political behavior (Duvall and Stohl 1983, p.182; Schmid 1983, p. 111).

A second essential distinction is between coercive acts that are violent, in the sense of doing immediate physical harm to the targets, and those that are nonviolent. Violent coercion may be carefully targeted and highly selective, as in the assassination of a parliamentarian or execution of the leaders of a failed coup; or it may be directed against targets of chance or convenience, as in some kinds of terrorism. Violent coercive acts can be further distinguished between those that are reactive (national guardsmen shooting rioters, demonstrators attacking abusive police officers) and those that are proactive. Proactive violence occurs without any obvious or immediately preceding coercive act by the target. Such acts are both difficult and important to explain: difficult because the immediate causes or reasons are usually obscure, important because they often signal the beginning of a round of deadly violence.

Nonviolent coercion can take many forms, ranging from disruption of routines (for example, by demonstrators who block access to offices or police who impose martial law) to deprivation of valued conditions (ousting officials from office, confiscating rebel supporters' property; imprisoning political opponents). A distinctive form of nonviolent coercion is the use of threats of punishment, threats that have credibility to the extent that those making them have previously shown their willingness and ability to carry them out. Thus, in a police state the simple act of surveillance by security police is a threat to those under observation. Political demonstrations also have the quality of threats in most contemporary polities: They symbolize loss of support by elected officials and noncompliance with policies and hint at more disruptive actions to come.

The most important of these distinctions and their interrelations are shown schematically in Table 6.1. They also can be related to Stohl and Lopez's distinctions (1983) among oppression, repression, and terrorism: Oppression is characterized by denial of privileges to whole classes or groups of people; repression involves the use or threat of coercion; and terrorism "is the purposeful act or threat of violence to create fear and/or compliant behavior" (p. 7). These are portrayed as a series of narrowing concentric circles, the first subsuming the second, etc. In the present analysis, coercion is a generalized set of means; repression is the consequence of their systematic application by the state; terrorism is dramatic, violent coercion used by any partisan group, in or out of power, to alter by shock and fear the state of mind of a target audience.

One other general observation: The repertoire of coercive tactics available to regimes ordinarily is much broader than that of their partisan opponents. This is so because regimes usually command much greater resources to impose sanctions, and because their threats of coercion carry more conviction (evoke more fear) than threats by weaker and more transient opponents. Rebels are more likely to have to rely on repeated and violent acts of coercion to achieve political effects that regimes obtain through consistent application of nonviolent coercion and threats, reinforced by occasional acts of deadly violence. Underlying these qualitative differences in emphases, though, is a common method (reliance on negative sanctions) and a common set of purposes (to alter the political behavior of the targets). Regimes use coercion to help establish and maintain their political power; rebels use coercion in attempts to improve their relative power.

To summarize, political coercion is the use or threat of punishment (negative sanctions) to alter the political behavior of a target group. It is one of the main instrumentalities of power; others are the use of positive sanctions and the invocation of legitimacy. Physical violence in its various forms is only one part of the repertoire of political coercion. (Note that not all acts of violence in the course of political conflict are

TABLE 6.1
Dimensions of political coercion

Type of Partisan Group	Relations Among Types of Political Coercion			Conventional Label
	Violent Sanctions	Nonviolent Coercion		
		Threats	Sanctions	
Regimes	Patterned and persistent violence against subjects and opponents	+ Surveillance (threat of sanctions)	+ Deprivations of liberty, status, property	= Repression
Regimes and oppositions	Unpredictable, sporadic violence against symbolic targets	+ Warnings		= Terrorism
Oppositions	Patterned and persistent violence against regimes	Demonstrations (threatened withdrawal of political support)	and/or Disruption of public routines, general strikes, expropriations (etc.)	= Rebellion
				= Protest

"coercive." That depends on the intentions of the actors, some of whom may use violence spontaneously, and the perceptions of the targets, who may see sporadic violence as accidental or incidental. If an act of violence has neither coercive intent nor effect, then it is not "coercive.") What appear to be qualitative differences in the kinds of coercion used by regimes, rebels, and protestors reflect strategic and normative choices from repertoires of coercive actions. The relative power of groups, and their demonstrated capacity to act, affect both the choice of specific modes of coercion and how the use of coercion is perceived by the target audiences.

STRUCTURES OF CONFLICT AND REPRESSION

It is obvious that political coercion is more widely employed in some societies than others. The essential postulate offered here is that there is a general tendency toward equilibrium in the severity of coercion used by all groups contending for power within politically organized societies. Where regimes rely heavily on coercion, so do their opponents; where regimes obtain compliance mainly by invoking legitimacy and using concessions, their opponents use relatively little coercion. This does not necessarily imply that the extent of opposition rises in proportion to the extent of coercion used by regimes, although this relation should hold up to some fairly high threshold [for theory and evidence on this point, see Snyder (1978) and Lichbach (1985)]. Rather, the essential argument is that, to the extent that rebels do challenge highly coercive regimes, they will tend to rely on highly coercive tactics themselves, and vice versa. Counterexamples can be cited: for example, the episodic occurrence of revolutionary terrorism against the relatively noncoercive regimes of contemporary Italy, France, and West Germany; and the use of peaceful demonstrations to challenge Pinochet's repressive regime in Chile. The postulate asserts only that there is a general tendency toward equilibrium, not a precise uniformity. It does imply, though, that if oppositional terrorism becomes widespread in any nonrepressive regime, that regime is likely to respond in increasingly repressive ways.

The postulate rests on a causal logic that is considerably more complex than the postulate itself. One element in the argument is the assumption of an underlying action-reaction sequence: If one partisan group escalates the intensity of coercion, other partisan groups will tend to respond in kind. The response is not likely to be literally the same kind of coercion, but whatever higher levels of coercion in the group's repertoire seem most justified and cost-effective. Thus, ongoing conflicts, as in Northern Ireland, move through a series of equilibria: One party introduces a new, more intense or threatening tactic, which induces the opponent to introduce an offsetting tactic that reestablishes equilibrium at a higher level. This equilibrium persists for a time before it is again disrupted.[2]

Here again, a general tendency is being asserted that may appear to be contradicted by specific examples. For example, if a regime uses such overwhelming force against its opponents that their existence as a collectivity is destroyed, the possibility of coercive response is eliminated—for that group. But new partisan groups, including dissident factions within the regime, are likely thereafter to place greater reliance on coercion. The underlying mechanism is one of social learning: Tactics seen to work for one group affect the cost-benefit calculations of other groups. The cumulation of a number of episodes in which partisan groups gain advantages through coercion can be expected to contribute to the evolution of "political cultures of coercion" in which there are both normative justifications for relying on coercion and good rational choice grounds for thinking that coercive strategies are cost-effective.

This argument suggests why some political societies experience rising general levels of coercion. The complementary question is whether there are processes that lead in the opposite direction. The successive subordination and incorporation of previously autonomous groups by an expanding state constitute a historical sequence that has led to this outcome in various parts of the world (for example, in Western European kingdoms such as Britain and France, in dynastic China, and in imperial Russia). Once most past and potential rebels have been incorporated or eliminated, resistance declines and so does reinforcement of norms that once justified reliance on coercion. It also is reasonable to assume that in some, but not necessarily all, circumstances, it becomes more costly in an absolute sense to rely on coercion than other means to ensure compliance. If resistance to a regime declines over time, and if more cost-effective means of securing compliance are developed, declining reliance on coercion is likely to follow.

This is the argument seen from the perspective of those in power. From the perspective of potential rebels (including partisan factions within the state), there is a mirror image set of assessments: As the partisans in power come to rely less on coercion and more on positive inducements, it becomes more cost-effective for partisans out of power to shift from openly coercive tactics to reliance on threats, influence, and negotiation.

These are the arguments for the postulate that there is approximate correspondence in the levels of coercion used by partisan groups. But they do not provide an explanation for the substantial variation among societies in existing equilibrium levels of coercion. The general answers to that question have to do with (1) the extent of socioeconomic cleavages in societies and (2) the extent to which partisans in power have institutionalized structures of coercive control.

Socioeconomic Cleavages

Theories of revolution and state violence tend to agree on the postulate that sharp internal cleavages along lines of class and ethnic or religious cleavage contribute to violent conflict. There are various arguments in the literature on revolution and rebellion about why this should be the case, but the essence is that the greater and more invidious are economic and political differentials across groups—socioeconomic classes or segmental groups—the greater the potential for challenges by the less advantaged.[3]

It can be debated whether rebellions are more likely to arise across lines of class division or between segmental ethnolinguistic and religious groups. Stratification by class characterizes all modern political societies, but only some of them are ethnically or religiously heterogeneous. There is probably general agreement, though, that rebellions are likely to be more numerous and intense in societies that have sharp class stratification and ethnolinguistic cleavages, and are likely to be greatest of all where dominant groups are distinguished from others by both class and ethnicity.

The reasons why regimes in heterogeneous and stratified societies are particularly likely to rule coercively have been summarized elsewhere (Gurr 1986). The simple reason is that they more often face violent challenges. By the equilibrium postulate above, this increases regimes' reliance on coercive tactics. Two factors reinforce this tendency. At the normative level, there is probably a lack of empathic identification between partisans in heterogeneous and highly stratified societies: Social distance, whether based on ethnic difference or class barriers, makes it psychologically easier to dehumanize opponents [see Kelman (1973)]. There is also a reinforcing strategic consideration: Partisans in power are likely to perceive—usually correctly—that challengers of different class and ethnic origins pose a high degree of threat, which warrants using all the coercive measures at the regime's disposal.

In the special case in which an ethnic or religious minority holds power in a highly stratified society, as in contemporary South Africa, coercion is used routinely as an instrument of control. Such elites are likely to be repeatedly challenged by partisans representing different segmental groups, making zero-sum demands to displace the ruling minority or to secede from its control. The common result is a coercive "equilibrium" at a high level, in which the regime develops highly institutionalized capacity to use coercion systematically against actual and potential rebels.

Structures of Repression

One of the likely outgrowths of prolonged periods of partisan conflict is the establishment of specialized agencies of state coercion and terror. These agencies and the policies of coercive control that they implement are referred to here as "structures of repression." To the extent that such organizations and policies exist, the levels and intensity of coercion by regimes tend to remain high, although there may a shift in the mix of coercive tactics away from physical violence toward surveillance and nonviolent sanctions. Once such structures are in operation, elites are likely to calculate that the relative costs of relying on coercion are lower and the risks of using noncoercive means greater. These strategic considerations tend to be reinforced by habituation; in other words, the development of elite norms that coercive control is not only necessary but desirable. Moreover, a bureaucratic "law of the instrument" may prevail: The professional ethos of agencies of control centers on the use of coercion to restrain challenges to state authority. Their directors may therefore recommend violent "solutions" to suspected opposition, or use their position to initiate them, as a means of justifying the agencies' continued existence [see Gurr (1986)].

Structures of repression are likely to be established in either of two circumstances: (1) The first generation of leaders who have seized power by violence are particularly likely to be habituated to the political uses of coercion, and to have the means to establish agencies of political control ready to hand in the form of military and special police units manned by former revolutionary fighters and zealots. This combination of circumstances has been associated with policies of "governance by terror" in postrevolutionary Russia, China, Ethiopia, Iran, and elsewhere. (2) Elites who face repeated partisan challenges, for example, the minority elites in stratified societies characterized above, develop specialized agencies of coercive control in a more evolutionary fashion, agencies upon which they rely increasingly to maintain themselves in power.

Secret police have been the archetypical agencies of state repression over the last century. Typically they are established outside the command structure of the military or of the civilian police, and are answerable directly and exclusively to the top political leadership. Twentieth-century examples are the Extraordinary Commission to Combat Counter-Revolution (the Cheka), established by the Bolsheviks in 1917 and soon renamed OGPU, later (in 1934) the NKVD [see Gouldner (1977-78) and Solzhenitsyn (1974-78)]; the Nazi Shutzstaffeln (SS) [see Koehl (1983)];

the Shah of Iran's SAVAK; and the Afrikaaner regime's Bureau of State Security (1969-78), now replaced by the Department of National Security (winter 1981).

To summarize, some political systems are characterized by what may be called a "syndrome of coercion," in which the equilibrium level of coercion remains persistently at a high level. Three kinds of conditions cooccur with this syndrome: high internal stratification across class lines, sharp segmental cleavages among diverse ethnolinguistic groups, and the development of state-directed agencies of coercive control. The syndrome is likely to develop as the result of a process in which repeated conflicts across lines of stratification and/or cleavage generate a series of partisan conflicts for control of political society. The partisan groups that win these struggles come to power with a legacy of violence: They are disposed to use coercion against opponents and have, or soon establish, the organizational means to do so. Partisans who would oppose the winners are then likely to calculate that violent resistance is their only potentially effective alternative to defeat. The victory of partisans in power may be seen by opponents to be only temporary and capable of being reversed through intensified struggle. It is only after partisans in power have demonstrated their staying capacity in the face of repeated challenges that cost-benefit analysis suggests the futility of continued opposition.

IMPLICATIONS FOR EMPIRICAL RESEARCH

The theoretical argument outlined here has implications for empirical work on the strategic calculations of partisan leaders, for the study of interactions between oppositions and regimes in conflict situations, and for the analysis of variability in the general levels of coercion at the societal level.

At the microlevel, the theory rests on assumptions about partisans' repertoires of coercive tactics and the conditions that influence leaders' strategic choices among those tactics. The relevant conditions, for partisans in and out of power, include their own capacities for action, the strategies of opposing groups, and group norms (derived mainly from past experiences in conflict) that affect assessments about the relative (non)acceptability of different tactics. Testing these arguments directly would require detailed information about the judgments and perceptions of the leaders of partisan groups. Such information is more readily obtainable for groups in low-intensity than high-intensity conflicts, and if it is to be developed at all is likely to come from in depth case studies.

One approach is retrospective research using evidence from protest activists in Western societies; it also is possible to use interview techniques for ongoing study of participants in such movements, as Muller and Opp (1984) have done with German antinuclear activists. Another approach is to reconstruct the decision-making calculus of the leaders of well-documented revolutionary and terrorist movements, as Strinkowski (1986) has attempted for the Irgun and the Irish Republican Army.

At the group level of analysis, the focus is on the changing status, evolving strategies, and patterned interactions among partisan groups over time. I proposed above that groups intensify or moderate their coercive tactics in response to the tactics used against them by other partisans. Partisans who succeed in seizing power are a special case: They tend to develop and rely upon structures of repression to control potential opposition. The short-term effect postulated above is intensification of opposition by other partisans who hope to reverse the situation. Eventually all potential partisans may be either eliminated or incorporated in the new coercive order, followed by a decline in the intensity of coercion. Tilly (1978), Zald and McCarthy (1979), Gamson (1975), and other sociologists have developed ample techniques and some data for studying the mobilization and strategies of "challenging groups," that is, of partisans out of power. They could be readily adapted to the analysis of sequential coercive interactions, as proposed by Snyder (1978), for example. However, I know of no comparable body of empirical work on the evolution and uses of state's coercive apparatuses: It is as though partisans, once they have a grip on power, pass out of conflict analysts' line of vision.

The dynamics of partisan combat underlie the general postulate of equilibrium in the intensity of coercion, which is testable at the level of political society. The most feasible approach is to make use of existing cross-national data collections, in particular the third edition of the *World Handbook* (Taylor and Jodice 1983). The intensity of coercion by partisans out of power can be ordered along a continuum from demonstrations (low-intensity threat of coercion) to riots, armed attacks, and all-out revolutionary warfare. The intensity of coercion by regimes ranges from impositions of political restrictions (low-intensity coercion) to political executions of individuals, to mass killings of political opponents. One empirical implication of the equilibrium hypothesis is that any shift in the modal intensity of coercion along one of these continua is likely to be matched by a corresponding shift along the other. Once a new equilibrium is reached, it will tend to persist until one partisan introduces a new tactic. Another implication, with qualifications, is that there should be a positive correlation between the extent of coercive acts by regimes and the extent of partisan opposition—a relation that has, in fact, been observed in most cross-national empirical studies [see the summary by Zimmermann (1980; pp. 191-99)].

Some deductions from the general model can be tested both in simultaneous and lagged cross-national analyses and in longitudinal analyses. Longitudinal analysis is especially appropriate for studying the effects of violent seizures of power on general levels of coercion. The predicted pattern is an increase in the intensity of coercion by the new regime and its opposition, followed by a gradual decline in the equilibrium intensity of coercion and a corresponding institutionalization of structures of repression.

Another set of propositions specifies that equilibrium levels of coercion should be highest in political societies with high stratification and segmentation. An interaction effect was suggested: High levels of inequality across social strata and segments lead to frequent partisan challenges to state power, high levels of coercion by regimes, and the institutionalization of structures of repression. Some of these relations have been tested in empirical macrostudies. Data gathered on separatist and discriminated groups (Gurr and Gurr 1978) have been shown in a series of studies to be strongly correlated with magnitudes of conflict in the 1960s (Gurr and Duvall 1973; Hibbs 1973, ch. 5; Gurr and Lichbach 1979). Other studies have shown positive aggregate relations between material inequalities and levels of political violence. Muller (1985), using new data, has provided the most recent supportive evidence, obtaining bivariate correlations of 0.57 for the mid-1960s and 0.40 for the mid-1970s. His analysis also shows significant relations between regime repressiveness and political violence (that is, violence used by opposition groups) and governmental acts of coercion and political violence during one or both of these periods.

The fundamental limitation of these aggregate studies is that they do not examine directly the group origins and targets of coercion. The theoretical arguments that prompt the use of measures of segmental groups and material inequalities assume that levels of conflict and coercion are high because minorities and the economically disadvantaged are differentially involved. What is not tested directly is whether they initiate cycles of conflict more often than other groups, or whether they are more often the targets of regime repression. This is a reflection of the fact that most cross-national collections of data on the conflict behavior of partisans and the sanctions used by regimes do not identify the specific groups involved. The data on protest and sanctions in the third edition of the *World Handbook* take a step in this direction by identifying the general type of actor responsible for each protest event and the type of target of political sanctions, but the coded data do not take the second and definitive step of identifying the groups by name (Taylor and Jodice 1983, vol. 2).

The theoretical assumptions that underpinned most quantitative comparative research on conflict during the 1960s and 1970s are largely responsible for the limitations of global data collections. One such assumption was that research should aim at explaining an aggregate property of conflict at the national level: deaths from collective violence (Russett 1964), the total number of events of different types (Hibbs 1973), or the total magnitude of conflict (Gurr 1968; Gurr and Duvall 1973). Alternative explananda such as the issues of conflict, the extent to which different groups or classes are involved, and outcomes of conflict for particular groups are now regarded as equally or more important foci of research. A second limiting assumption was that the independent variables explaining for conflict behavior were mainly properties of domestic social and economic systems rather than political variables. Newer theoretical approaches emphasize such internal political factors as state structures, polarization and politicization along lines of intergroup and interclass cleavage, the coercive policies used by elites to create and maintain order, and the capacity of challengers to mobilize opposition [for example, Tilly (1978); Jackson et al. (1979); Duvall and Stohl (1983)].

The crucial implication, then, is that newer theoretical approaches to the study of internal conflict and coercion require a group focus for the collection and analysis of cross-national as well as intranational data. The feasibility of such an approach is not in doubt: Lichbach (1984b) has developed and applied a procedure for identifying and coding information on all actual and potential oppositional groups in a political system. We cannot hope to answer convincingly many of the key substantive and theoretical questions in contemporary conflict analysis without some such information on the identity of the groups involved in conflict and the issues or circumstances that lead particular partisan groups to the use of violence. This is emphatically true of most of the propositions presented in this essay about the origins and uses of coercion by partisans in and out of power.

CONCLUDING COMMENT

This essay has sketched a theoretical framework for comparative research on the uses of coercion by partisans in and out of power. It incorporates in a single conceptual scheme rebels' uses of violent political action and the reliance of regimes on structures and policies of repression. They are the Janus-headed faces of the same general phenomenon, which is the use of coercion in the pursuit and preservation of political power. Coercive tactics are assumed to be chosen by partisans from a repertoire of alternative political actions guided by rational considerations. Their choices are conditioned by social structures, the strategies of opponents, and also normative considerations. The argument has implications for sequences of interactions between partisans, for the general equilibrium of coercion in society, and for the outcomes of seizures of power. It also helps clarify the circumstances under which regimes establish institutions and policies that enable them to exercise coercive control without relying mainly on overt acts of violence.

It is evident that many of the hypotheses generated in this framework can be tested only by focusing on the traits of and interactions among specific partisan groups. Crucial questions in cross-national research on political coercion center on which groups use coercion against which target groups and the lines of cleavage that define and divide those groups. A focus on the group sources and targets of coercion should contribute to the improvement of empirical models used in forecasting the onset and dynamics of large-scale internal conflict. They may also lead to better understanding of the circumstances in which particular groups are singled out as the targets of massive violence by regimes.

The analysis also has pessimistic implications for world trends in rebellion and repression. It is widely recognized that successful revolutions inspire attempted revolutionary seizures of power elsewhere. It seems less widely recognized that strategies of repression that strengthen the position of threatened elites also are likely to be emulated by other regimes. Given the large and growing number of independent states that provide examples of successful revolution and repression, and the proliferation of global networks of rapid political communication, the tendencies of partisan groups in new and poor countries to use coercion are reinforced. When these transnational dynamics are linked to the internal dynamics of escalating coercion, we have strong reasons for anticipating a general increase in aggregate levels of internal coercion, especially in the Third and Fourth Worlds. Contributing to this trend are the major powers' policies of supporting insurgencies in one another's client states. It is further reinforced by recurring episodes of regional and global economic crisis, whose general effect is to intensify internal conflicts [see Gurr (1985)]. Running counter to these pressures are public and private international efforts to mediate deadly internal conflicts and to dissuade repressive regimes from gross violations of human rights. The long-established regimes of the First and Second Worlds also may be insulated to a degree from these tendencies because of their skills at "reformist" and institutional approaches to controlling political conflict. But on theoretical grounds the global outlook is not encouraging.

NOTES

1. The word "partisans" is used throughout this essay as a generic term for groups in coercive contention for power, including those presently in control of the state apparatus as well as their challengers [for a similar usage, see Tilly (1978, passim)]. It should be read as a collective noun for "regimes" and "rebels" in situations of protracted conflict.

2. The idea of multiple, successive equilibria is suggested by Michael Nicholson (personal communication). Escalation is not an inevitable consequence of the introduction of new tactics because some of them may push the equilibrium toward lower levels of intensity.

3. For empirical studies on the role of segmental groups in conflict, see Hibbs (1973, ch. 5), Green (1975), and Barrows (1976). Two recent theoretical and empirical studies of the relation between material inequalities and conflict are by Midlarsky (1982) and Muller (1985).

REFERENCES

Barrows, W. L. 1976. "Ethnic Diversity and Political Instability in Black Africa." *Comparative Political Studies* 9 (July): 139-70.

Duvall, Raymond, and Stohl, Michael. 1983. "Governance by Terror." In Michael Stohl (ed.), *The Politics of Terrorism*, 2d ed., pp. 179-219. New York: Marcel Dekker.

Feierabend, Ivo I., Nesvold, Betty A., with Feierabend, Rosalind L. 1970. "Political Coerciveness and Turmoil: A Cross-National Inquiry." *Law and Society Review* 5: 93-118.

Galtung, Johan. 1969. "Violence, Peace, and Peace Research." *Journal of Peace Research* 6: 167-91.

Gamson, William A. 1975. *The Strategy of Social Protest*. Homewood, IL: Dorsey.

Gastil, Raymond D. 1984. *Freedom in the World: Political Rights and Civil Liberties, 1983-1984*. Westport, CT: Greenwood Press.

Gouldner, Alvin W. 1977-78. "Stalinism: A Study of Internal Colonialism." *Telos* 34 (Winter): 5-48.

Green, C. S. 1975. "Modernization, Cultural Heterogeneity, and Civil Strife." *Human Organization* 34: 69-78.

Gurr, Ted Robert. 1986. "The Political Origins of State Terror: A Theoretical Analysis." In George Lopez and Michael Stohl (eds.), *Government Violence and An Agenda for Research*, Westport, CT: Greenwood Press.

———.1985. "On the Political Consequences of Scarcity and Economic Decline." *International Studies Quarterly* 29 (March): 51-75

———.1970. *Why Men Rebel*. Princeton, NJ: Princeton University Press.

———.1968. "A Causal Model of Civil Strife: A Comparative Analysis Using New Indices." *American Political Science Review* 62 (December): 1104-24.

Gurr, Ted Robert, and Duvall, Raymond. 1976. "Introduction to a Formal Theory of Conflict Within Social Systems." In Louis A. Coser and Otto N. Larsen (eds.), *The Uses of Controversy in Sociology*. New York: The Free Press, pp. 139-54.

Gurr, Ted Robert, and Gurr, Erika. 1978. "Indicators of Group Discrimination and Potential Separatism in 1960 and 1975." Photocopied ms., Department of Political Science, Northwestern University. Subsequently published in abbreviated form in Charles Lewis Taylor and David A. Jodice (eds.), 1983 *World Handbook of Political and Social Indicators, Vol. 1.*, 3d, pp. ed., 50–57, 66–75. New Haven, CT: Yale University Press.

Gurr, Ted Robert and Lichbach, Mark Irving. 1979. "A Forecasting Model for Political Conflict Within Nations." In J. David Singer and Michael D. Wallace (eds.), *To Auger Well: Early Warning Indicators in World Politics.* Beverly Hills, CA: Sage, pp. 153–93.

Harff, Barbara. 1985. "Anticipating Genocides: A Theory with Applications." Paper read to the annual meeting of the International Studies Association, Washington, D.C.

Hibbs, Douglas A., Jr. 1973. *Mass Political Violence: A Cross-National Causal Analysis.* New York: Wiley Interscience.

Jackson, Steven, Russett, Bruce M., Snidal, Duncan, and Sylvan, David. 1978. "Conflict and Coercion in Dependent States." *Journal of Conflict Resolution* 22 (December):627–57.

Kelman, Herbert. 1973. "Violence Without Moral Restraint." *Journal of Social Issues* 29:26–61.

Koehl, Robert Lewis. 1983. *The Black Corps: The Structure of Power Struggles of the Nazi SS.* Madison: University of Wisconsin Press.

Lichbach, Mark I. 1985. "Deterrence or Escalation? A Microeconomic Model of Opposition Responses to Government Coercion." Paper read to the annual meeting of the International Studies Association, Washington, D.C.

———. 1984a. "An Economic Theory of Governability: Choosing Policy and Optimizing Performance." *Public Choice* 44: 307–37.

———. 1984b. "Final Project Report: Forecasting Models of Political Instability." Unpublished ms., Department of Political Science, University of Illinois at Chicago.

Lichbach, Mark I., and Gurr, Ted Robert. 1981. "The Conflict Process: A Self-Generating Model." *Journal of Conflict Resolution* 21 (March):3–29.

Markus, Gregory B., and Nesvold, Betty A. 1972. "Governmental Coerciveness and Political Instability: An Exploratory Study of Cross-National Patterns." *Comparative Political Studies* 5 (July):231–44.

Midlarsky, Manus I. 1982. "Scarcity and Inequality: Prologue to the Onset of Mass Revolution." *Journal of Conflict Resolution* 26 (March):3–38.

Muller, Edward N. 1985. "'Income Inequality, Regime Repressiveness, and Political Violence." *American Sociological Review* 50(1): 47-61.

Muller, Edward N., and Opp, Karl-Dieter. 1984. "Rational Choice and Rebellious Collective Action: Public Good, Psychological Gratification, and Socialist Class Consciousness." Paper read to the annual meeting of the American Political Science Association, Washington, D.C.

Nardin, Terry. 1980. "Theory and Practice in Conflict Research." In Ted Robert Gurr (ed.), *Handbook of Political Conflict: Theory and Research.* New York: Free Press, pp. 460–89.

_____. 1971. *Violence and the State: A Critique of Empirical Political Theory.* Sage Professional Papers in Comparative Politics, No. 01-020. Beverly Hills, CA: Sage.

Russett, Bruce M. 1964. "Inequality and Instability: The Relation of Land Tenure to Politics." *World Politics* 16 (April): 442-54.

Schmid, Alex P. 1983. *Political Terrorism: A Research Guide to Concepts, Theories, Data Bases and Literature.* Amsterdam: North-Holland and New Brunswick, NJ: Transaction Books.

Synder, David. 1978. "Collective Violence: A Research Agenda and Some Strategic Considerations." *Journal of Conflict Resolution* 22 (September): 499-534.

_____. 1976. "Theoretical and Methodological Problems in the Analysis of Government Coercion and Collective Violence." *Journal of Political and Military Sociology* 4: 277-94.

Solzhenitsyn, Aleksandr I. 1974-78. *Gulag Archipelago*, 3 vols. New York: Harper & Row.

Stohl, Michael, and Lopez, George A. (eds.). 1983. "Introduction." In *The State as Terrorist: The Dynamics of Governmental Violence and Repression.* Westport, CT: Greenwood Press, pp. 3-10.

Strinkowski, Nicholas. 1986. "The Organizational Behavior of Revolutionary Groups." Ph.D. dissertation, Department of Political Science, Northwestern University.

Taylor, Charles Lewis, and Jodice, David A. 1983. *World Handbook of Political and Social Indicators*, 3d ed., *Vol. 2: Political Protest and Governmental Change.* New Haven, CT: Yale University Press.

Tilly, Charles. 1978. *From Mobilization to Revolution.* Reading, MA: Addison-Wesley.

Winter, Gordon. 1981. *Inside Boss: South Africa's Secret Police.* Harmondsworth, U.K.: Penguin Books.

Zald, Mayer N., and McCarthy, John D. 1979. *The Dynamics of Social Movements.* Cambridge, MA: Winthrop.

Zimmermann, Ekkart. 1980. "Macro-Comparative Research on Political Protest." In Ted Robert Gurr (ed.), *Handbook of Political Conflict: Theory and Research.* New York: Free Press, pp. 167-237.

III
Breaking the Cycle

7
Nonviolent Alternatives in International Studies: Five Questions
Glenn D. Paige

The most critical source of tension between continuity and change at the end of the twentieth century lies neither in conflict over relative degrees of freedom-unfreedom nor economic equality-inequality. It lies in nonviolent challenges to dysfunctional conventional commitments to violence. These challenges are appearing in widespread global practice (for example, Gandhiism in the Third World, Solidarity in the Second World, and the Greens in the First World) and increasingly in theory (for example, the Mohandas Gandhi-Gene Sharp theory of nonviolent political power[1] and Gene Keyes's theory of nonviolent common defense).[2]

The rise of such challenges, given human experience since the French Revolution, is predictable. Neither liberty nor equality is possible without fraternity. Attempts to impose one or more of the three by violence has produced inauthenticity and instability. Thus, to the American Revolution (Live free or die!) and to the Russian Revolution (Peace, bread, and land!) must be added an increasingly purposive process of nonviolent global transformation into the twenty-first century (Life for all!).

The historical emergence of ideas, leaders, organizations, social movements, and parties dedicated to the attainment of nonviolent ends by nonviolent means results from a combination of subjective and objective factors, both of which must be accorded the status of social reality. All of the great religious and secular teachers in human experience have taught that the most desirable condition of life is peace and that this is not beyond rightly understood human effort.

The subjective goal of peacefulness, encompassing all humanity, is not in error, but the pursuit of it by violent means has proved increasingly dysfunctional, giving rise to worldwide alarm. In security, we have reached the limits of the logic of lethality. We can murder millions but cannot guarantee the sanctity of a single life.[3] The more we waste for unproductive and destructive lethal purposes, the more we are confronted by unmet needs of a rapidly growing global population.[4] In the area of human dignity,[5] righteous readiness to kill creates cultures that glorify one's own atrocities, while villifying those of others, and produces people socialized in violence through political ideologies, religion, education, sports, entertainment, and family life. Under appropriate conditions many persons thus socialized explode in fits of slaughter.[6] Disrespecting human life, it is not surprising that we threaten to destroy the life-bearing capacity of the biosphere—of water, air, and soil, and sea.[7] Stratified within our violence-accepting national and corporate actors, we seek to impose solutions to the problems of the many in the interests of the few.

To liberate ourselves from insecurity, deprivation, indignity, ecocide, and divisive domination, we must make a decisive shift from violence-based to nonviolent modes of local, national, international, and global politics and relations, for none of humankind's pressing problems of survival can be solved through continued commitment to violence. A purposive shift to nonviolence at every level of human organization is the single most important factor that can contribute to mutually supportive, multiple global problem solving.

Creators and users of knowledge in international studies can make contributions to achieving a decisive shift from violence-based to non-violence-based human relations as we approach the twenty-first century. Such a shift will require a new four-part logic of nonviolent analysis and action: understanding and removing the causes of violence; understanding and strengthening the causes of nonviolence; understanding and assisting processes of transition from violence to nonviolence; and understanding and realizing conditions for a stably nonviolent world community that will satisfy human needs for freedom and equality. To make this shift will require raising and seeking answers to some extraordinarily significant questions.

IS A NONKILLING SOCIETY POSSIBLE?

By nonkilling society is meant a society characterized by no killing and no threats to kill, neither human nor technological preparations for killing, and no conditions of psychological or material deprivation that are attributable to actual or threatened lethality. It is a society characterized by the absence of conditions that predispose to kill plus the presence of conditions that predispose not to kill. The conditions of nonlethality must prevail from the family through the local community and nation or its successor to encompass all humankind.

Customary responses among U.S. political scientists are that such a society is unthinkable for three main reasons: First, violence is ineradicably rooted in human nature. Human beings are like animals—treacherous and capable of unspeakable atrocities. Second, violence will always result from inescapable conflict over scarce material resources. Scarcity leads to conflict; conflict leads to killing. Third, one must always be prepared to kill in sexual defense against rape of female relatives and friends (customary male argument) or in defense against threats to the life of one's children (customary female argument). Intellectually these beliefs are reflected in theories that justify the state as monopolist of coercive force, seizure of natural resources, use of lethal threats as a deterrent, justified reciprocal violence (eye for an eye), and armed rebellion against tyranny or armed counterrevolution.

The predominant political science view from the United States is identical to that of the late Hollywood film director Sam Peckinpah who left a proud legacy of violent movies including *Bonnie and Clyde* (1967) and *The Wild Bunch* (1969). Explained Peckinpah, "Man is violent by nature and we have to live with it and control it if we are to survive."[8]

This view is not universally shared. "We know that man is not violent by nature," explained an Arab political scientist in a professional group discussion of nonviolent politics at the University of Jordan in 1981, "but we have to fight in self-defence." During the 1979 International Political Science Association (IPSA) meeting in Moscow, some Soviet social scientists found the idea of nonviolent politics readily thinkable provided satisfactory solutions could be found to the problems of how to cope with violent tragedies and of how to establish an appropriate economic base. Furthermore, O. N. Bykov, a high-ranking Soviet policy science intellectual in the arms control and disarmament field, commented in a public meeting attended by more than 50 IPSA political scientists from various countries, "Some people say that nonviolent politics, Gandhiism, is some kind of fantasy. But we do not agree. It might become reality tomorrow."

Still another viewpoint, neither automatic rejection nor acceptance of the feasibility of a nonviolent society, was expressed by a member of the Swedish Future Studies Society at a meeting in Stockholm in January 1984: "I've never really thought about it. I'll have to give it some thought."

My own view is that a nonkilling society is thinkable and eventually achievable through a combination of nonviolent values and empirical science expressed in research, education, action, and institutional development, drawing upon all sources of knowledge. Not all animals are killers; not all humans kill. If humans by nature were programmed to kill, the world population would be progressively declining instead of increasing—and the human family would be impossible. To be realistic, against humankind's most murderous members must be compared the most nonviolent humans who have ever lived. Against the economic concept of competitive lethality (a recent U.S. book is entitled *The Way of the Warrior: How to Make a Killing in Any Market*)[9] must be considered sharing of limited resources and expanding them through productivity and creation of need-satisfying functional alternatives. As for sexual defense, or defense of one's offspring, why is it necessary to leap immediately to justification of and eternal readiness for life taking? Are there not nonlethal, incapacitating technologies and procedures that might achieve the defensive objectives—and furthermore make possible scientific study of the offenders so that multiple victim-saving preventive measures could become part of customary public policy?

Confidence that a nonkilling society is possible can be gained from a wide variety of scientific and practical accomplishments that will not be argued fully here. The purpose is to raise the question of the feasibility of a nonkilling society as a key issue for the future development of international studies, not definitively to argue the case. But let it be noted that encouragement comes from scientific findings in such fields as animal studies,[10] brain studies,[11] and psychiatry. As one group of 21 Stanford University School of Medicine psychiatrists concluded in 1970 after study of the causes of violence in U.S. society. "Already we may know enough about man to close his era of violence if we determine to pursue alternatives." But they cautioned, "Nothing short of intense determined effort can rid this or any society of violence, an effort similar to the dedicated, cooperative effort of citizens, government, and industry that brought the United States from the tiny Explorer satellite in 1958 to the Apollo moon missions in a scant decade."[12] From their perspective the main obstacle is not insufficient knowledge but the political will to make use of what is already known.

Even if we do not know enough now, I believe we can know enough very quickly to make a nonkilling society possible. But to do so we will have to ask and seek answers to difficult questions that are unlikely to be pursued seriously under the assumption that a nonkilling society is impossible. Our commitment to violence prevents the fundamental shift of thought that is essential for acquiring and using the knowledge that is essential for the attainment of true conditions of peacefulness.

HOW ARE WE TO COPE WITH A MAD DICTATOR (OR WITH A RATIONAL INSTITUTIONALIZED KILLER) USING COMPLETELY NONVIOLENT MEANS?

This will be recognized as the familiar challenge, "Pacifism is admirable, but how are you going to stop Hitler and Jewish genocide by nonviolent means?" Indeed, how are we to do so? Let us take the question seriously and not assume that satisfactory answers are impossible—historically, in the present, or in the future. If we do not take this question seriously, it means that we are condemned eternally to prepare to be more brutal, cruel, and treacherous than any Hitler. If only murder can stop murder, we must all be prepared to be supermurderers or the supporters of such—forever. Furthermore, the combination of Hitler, the Nazi movement, the German state, war, and genocide is not the only murderous atrocity for which humankind must find nonviolent preventive alternatives. One's list tends to depend upon ideological and cultural position. One's atrocity is another's finest hour, as is the case with the world's first use of atomic weapons on the populations of Hiroshima and Nagasaki on August 6 and 9, 1945. Certainly we should add also the atrocities of Stalinism, the genocidal regime of Pol Pot in Cambodia, and the military destruction of the elected Allende government in Chile. A completely universal, "objective" list of life-taking events for which nonviolent alternatives must be found needs to be compiled, and typologies made, as a contribution to comprehensive scientific investigation of this question.

The idea that widespread acquiescence forms the basis of political power provides at least a point of departure. If we do not want Hitler and Nazi-like outcomes, we should not give our support to (elect) aggressive personalities who portray enemies in inhuman dichotomous terms; we should not concentrate our hostilities upon scapegoats; we should not train our progeny to be obedient to military commanders; we should not build up military and intelligence machines indoctrinated loyally to carry out lethal orders from higher bureaucratic authorities; we should not employ our intellects to create and use lethal technologies; we should not give moral and material support to the lethal actions of the violent nation-state; and we should not expect weak victims to save themselves unaided by nonviolent defensive action by the advantaged and the strong throughout the world.

Satisfactory answers to the "mad dictator" issue will require precise basic and applied scientific solutions to problems that occur in three zones of what can be envisaged as a funnel of violent causality: the killing zone, where slaughter is ongoing or imminent; the lethal socialization

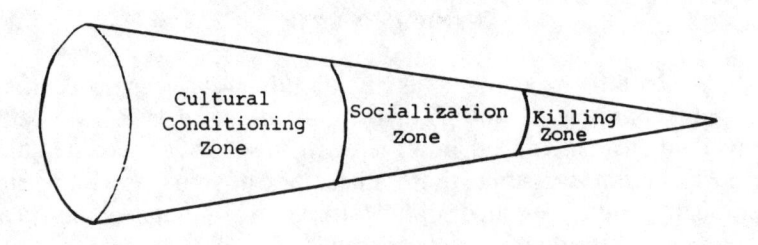

FIGURE 7.1. Funnel of lethal causality.

zone, where potential protagonists are prepared for lethal behavior; and, less immediately, the cultural conditioning zone, in which the cognitions, emotions, and expectations are created and transmitted that make the violent outcomes expectable and acceptable. The funnel and its zones, defined in terms of temporal proximity and number of direct participants in violence, are depicted in Figure 7.1.

The tasks of nonviolent alternative analyses and action are to find preventive, reversive, and postviolence restorative modes of action in each zone that will broaden the field of human capabilities to avoid narrow entrapment in lethality. In effect, the objective is to transform the funnel of lethal causality into a fan of expanding nonviolent alternatives, as suggested in Figure 7.2.

---Nonviolent alternatives

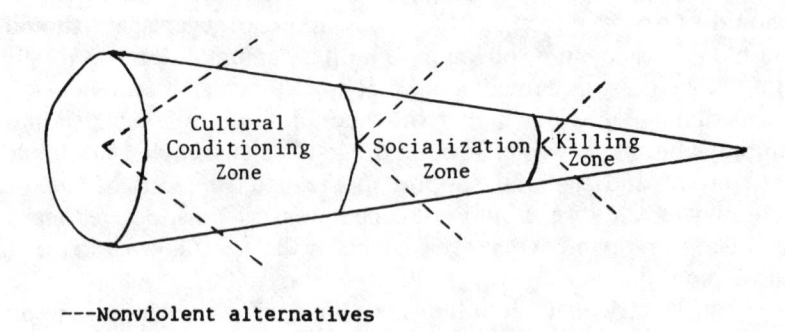

FIGURE 7.2. Expanding fan of nonviolent alternatives.

To achieve transformation, discoveries and inventions must take place in all three zones. Efforts must be made to multiply their nonviolent effects within and across zones. The most difficult area, of course, is the killing zone, where time is short, emotions are high, information is scarce, and control is often limited. Nevertheless, the occurrence of ceasefires among combatants for religious and other reasons, the success of nonviolent negotiations with life-threatening persons, and the refusal to kill of certain combatants suggest that further development of theories for nonviolent killing zone interventions is not impossible.

IS A NONVIOLENT REVOLUTION (AND EVEN A NONVIOLENT CLASS STRUGGLE) POSSIBLE?

For most political scientists the concept of "revolution" is associated with bloodshed, while at the same time the necessity for radical transformation of society under certain conditions is accepted. This means that life-taking transformational action is expected.

But can fundamental political change be accomplished without bloodshed, say, from conditions of low to high freedom and from low to high equality, even involving sharp shifts in class or other power wielder advantages? Certainly most contemporary political scientists are inclined to answer negatively. However, the idea that nonviolent revolution is not unthinkable receives support from no less important theorists in the history of Western political thought than Aristotle and Machiavelli.

Discussing causes of changes in constitutions (chiefly by violent revolutions), Aristotle explains: "Changes of constitution can also take place without violence. Lobbying and intrigue, lack of vigilance, and changes so gradual as to be imperceptible—these are three ways in which this can come about."[13] Continuing Aristotle's inquiry, Machiavelli asks: "Why it is that, in the many changes that carry a state from freedom to tyranny, and from servitude to liberty, some are effected by bloodshed, and others without any." He answers that "when such a change is effected *by the general consent of the citizens* [emphasis added] who have made the state great then there is no reason why the people should wish to harm anyone but the chiefs of state.... Such revolutions are very rarely dangerous."[14] Note that in these classical discussions of the possibility for nonviolent revolution, Aristotle appears more "Machiavellian" than Machiavelli.

In the late twentieth century, Soviet, Chinese, and U.S. theorists are also arguing that nonviolent revolutions are possible. Two Soviet writers, Plimak and Karyakin, assert that a peaceful socialist revolution, involving a sharp shift in class power, can occur under conditions where there is widespread loss of support for existing institutions. They define a peaceful socialist revolution as one characterized by transference of class power, no civil war, no foreign military intervention, and "virtually no bloodshed."[15] They quote General Secretary Brezhnev as saying at the Twenty-Fifth Soviet Communist Party Congress in 1976: "The tragedy in Chile by no means nullifies the conclusions of communists that different paths of revolution are possible, including a peaceful one, if conditions for it are favorable. But it strongly reminds us that a revolution must always be capable of defending itself."[16]

In a similar mode, the Chinese writer Zhang Yiping argues that the possibility of a successful nonviolent movement for national liberation, under certain conditions, ought to be taken seriously. Taking as examples the Gandhian movement in India and the relatively peaceful emergence of new states in Africa, Zhang contends that to deny the possibility of nonviolent national liberation, to insist always on the necessity for armed revolution, is "wrong in theory and harmful in practice."[17]

To these theories of class and national revolution by relatively peaceful means, the North American political sociologist Gene Sharp has been adding a theory of nonviolent revolution that is especially applicable to revolutionary overthrow of dictatorial regimes. Sharp's thesis is that since all political power rests upon massive obedience, any government can be brought down by widespread withdrawal of support.[18]

While nonviolent revolutionary theory has been developed by Marxian and non-Marxian theorists alike, there has been virtually no development of nonviolent counterrevolutionary theory. How, for example, are advantaged, dominant minority groups, classes, or institutions to advance their interests and to seek fulfillment of their needs against aggrieved opponents without threat or use of killing force? There is as yet no theory of nonviolent capitalist counterrevolution to complement those being developed for nonviolent socialist revolution.

A first response is that such a theory is unthinkable: "Everyone knows that the ruling classes never relinquish power, wealth, and status peacefully but always defend themselves and require defeat by force." But must this go on forever? Is it not possible that there could take place a nonviolent class revolution in which rulers and ruled radically change in relative positions of power and wealth through a process by which each follows nonviolent principles of action? In short, is a nonviolent class struggle (or other ruler-ruled struggle) possible?

There is evidence from which to infer a realistic basis for such a theory, although the necessary theoretical elaboration remains to be accomplished. This evidence is simply that among the oppressed and the oppressors there is a propensity to respond positively to appeals for nonviolent political action. For example, it is customary for proponents of violent class revolution to criticize Gandhian and other advocates of nonviolent action on the grounds that it deceives and weakens the militant revolutionary struggle of the oppressed masses. This implies that the oppressed are receptive to appeals for nonviolent resistance. The violence-accepting revolutionaries do not complain that the advocacy of nonviolent revolution weakens the oppressors.

On the other hand, it is striking how sharply the leaders, theorists, and publicists of ruling classes attack and seek to discredit advocacy of pacifist and nonviolent ideals and policy alternatives. This is true of the contemporary leaders of both the United States and the Soviet Union. Both argue that nonviolent approaches fail to appreciate the dangerous lethality of their enemy and undermine the will and determination to fight (kill) among those whose support is most needed. Note that these leaders do not complain that appeals to nonviolence weaken their opponents, but rather that such appeals weaken their own bases of violent power. These two arguments imply that there is responsiveness to nonviolent appeals among both rulers–oppressors and the ruled–oppressed.

Further development of this insight into theories of action applicable within specific political–economic–social–cultural settings can make an extremely important contribution to solving problems of global transformation to the well-being of all in our time.

WHAT IS THE ECONOMIC BASIS OF A NONKILLING SOCIETY, A NONVIOLENT POLITICAL SCIENCE, AND A NONVIOLENT INTERNATIONAL STUDIES?

This is a fundamental question that must be answered along with a similar question directed toward clarifying the psychological and motivational bases of nonviolent action. Beginning with contemporary economies and the global economic system, one thing is clear: Neither capitalist nor socialist economies as now constituted can maintain themselves internally or in their external relations without direct or proxy reliance upon the threat and use of killing force. It is as correct to say that all economies rest upon the substructure of readiness to kill as it is to portray lethality as a product of economy.

Therefore, the question of what kind of economy (local to global) will neither require nor produce lethality to maintain and change itself presents international studies with a question of fundamental importance. To answer it, contributions from basic, experimental, and applied research must be sought from all ideological, scientific, and economic world perspectives. Surely one characteristic will be an economy that takes account of the well-being of all (*sarvodaya* in the Gandhian sense). It will also combine flexibility in response to needs with creativity in producing need-responding resources. Present waste in and profits from production for lethality should be eliminated. The material advantages of life saving must replace those of life taking.

Whereas historical nonviolent movements have been self-financed by member sacrifice and voluntary supporter contributions, the global system of violence is financed primarily by lethally enforced state extractions supplemented by contributions from satellite foundations and corporations.

Some small shifts in the direction of nonviolence are beginning to appear, such as in various state-supported institutes for peace, disarmament, and international security being established in the Soviet Union, Australia, Canada, and the United States.[19] But these are far from the massive commitments of resources that accompany acts of political will to create a superweapon, to place a person on the moon, or to create a national system of transportation.

Future developments of nonviolent knowledge are likely to arise—as in the past—primarily from practical action. Examples include the Gandhian movement for national and social liberation; the movement for racial justice led by Martin Luther King, Jr.; the creation of a nonviolent political movement–party by the Greens of Germany; the organization of a nonviolent labor union by Cesar Chavez; various movements to abolish the death penalty and to recognize rights of conscientious objection to military service; and efforts to stop killing, torture, and oppression by nonviolent action.

To complement, interpret, and extend these practical advances, largely self-financed researchers and writers are beginning to work on nonviolence under varied conditions of toleration. Gradually it is hoped that philanthropists will aid these pioneering humanistic and scientific efforts. Eventually for greatest effectiveness substantial commitments of innovative research and development resources must be dedicated to making truly significant basic and applied breakthroughs in the theory and practice of nonviolence on a global scale. There is an urgent need for resources from truly peace-seeking sources to advance new nonviolent knowledge and action. Are any supporters of international studies responsive to this need?

HOW CAN THE CREATION AND USE OF NONVIOLENT KNOWLEDGE IN INTERNATIONAL STUDIES BEST BE FACILITATED?

In the period since World War II, major innovations in international studies have been firstly methodological and secondly substantive. The first innovation was to encourage the application to intersocietal inquiry of the philosophy and empirical research methods of the natural and social sciences. The second salient change has been to interpret the global system of international and intersocietal relations in terms of transnational economic relationships. For example, in a list of 88 Ph.D. dissertations currently in progress in the field of international relations published by the American Political Science Association in late 1984, some 33 seemed clearly undertaken from a political economy perspective, the largest single category.[20] It is noteworthy that the word "peace" did not appear in any title, nor "disarmament," nor "human rights" (except as a deletion), nor "economic justice," nor "nonviolence" (although one was importantly titled "Alternatives to Violence").

The search for nonviolent alternatives in international studies will require more than scientific methodology and an economic perspective. It will require an unprecedented convergence of normative, scientific, interdisciplinary, and organizational elements.

The achievement of knowledge for nonviolent global transformation will have to abandon the fantasy of single person omniscience–omnicompetence. The limited nonviolent successes of Jesus of Nazareth, Gautama Buddha, Mohandas K. Gandhi, and Martin Luther King, Jr., among others, long ago should have made this clear. On the other hand, the efficacy of large-scale collective action not dependent upon saintly qualities of single individuals is abundantly illustrated in the violent culture-rooted achievements of the Manhattan Project, the U.S. National Aeronautics and Space Administration, national bureaucracies, and transnational corporations. Of course, individual geniuses are urgently needed, but their visions and accomplishments must be advanced through purposive combination of multiskilled basic research, applied research and development, training, institutional innovation, and feedback from the field of nonviolent action. Human violence, like cancer, is a product of multiple causation and reinforcement; no monistic approach to prevention, diagnosis, and treatment is likely to succeed in its elimination. Also, like physicians afflicted by cancer and other diseases, scholars produced by cultures of violence may yet have time to contribute to nonviolent global transformation. If time permits, violence-afflicted researchers of nonviolence can make liberating contributions as well as cancer-afflicted researchers of cancer. Neither study nor practice of nonviolence depends upon sainthood. They are within the range of normal human capabilities. Furthermore, they can be greatly strengthened through institutional modes for combining and amplifying competencies.

Three principles show promise for successful innovation in the organization of nonviolent research and action. The first is convocation around an unambiguous nonkilling ethical core. This was an important reason for the success of two international seminars on Buddhism and Leadership for Peace held in Honolulu (1983) and Tokyo (1984) that brought together Buddhists, peace researchers, and peace leaders from China, Japan, the Republic of Korea, the United States, and the Soviet Union, as well as from Indonesia (Bali), India, Sri Lanka, Thailand, and Mongolia.[21]

A second principle is active encouragement of diverse ethical, professional, national, and, of course, gender participation. Convergence around a nonviolent ethical core does not mean ideological screening of participants beyond willingness to engage in peaceful exchange of ideas and experience. In the Buddhism and Leadership for Peace Seminars, for example, in addition to national diversity, contributions were made by colleagues from different Buddhist sects, plus those of Muslim, Catholic, Protestant, Hindu, atheist, Marxian, non-Marxian, and other beliefs. Participants also differed in acceptance of the universality of a nonkilling ethic. Despite this diversity, respect for the core ethical commitment was maintained and sustained in unanimous hope that the exchange of experience could be continued in the future with increased strengthening of nonviolent knowledge and action.

A third principle is interdisciplinary convergence around the question, What can your discipline tell us about the causes of violence, nonviolence, transition, and conditions of a stable nonkilling society? Note that the integrating question is not how one discipline can become more like the others or dominate the common inquiry. This question provided the focus for a workshop on Nonviolence as a Way to Peace held at the University of Hawaii on November 10, 1984, including colleagues from information science, brain science, anthropology, economics, political science, art, and nonviolent community service (the Quakers). They were joined by 60 other participants of diverse backgrounds from the university and supporting community.

A fourth principle is to apply in group relations, however diverse in participation, growing knowledge of the tenets of successful nonviolent action. At the very least, this means responsiveness to the human needs of all who participate plus commitment to nonviolent service of the most pressing needs of humankind. A possibility for successful organization of a research–teaching–action group in the field of nonviolence is suggested by brain research. One theory is that violence occurs when electrical pathways are interrupted between the cerebellum (motion-controlling subsystem) and the limbic system (emotion-controlling subsystem). Applied research has shown that violence-prone persons can restore themselves to peaceful conditions by self-controlled electrical stimulation of the pleasure pathways between the cerebellum and limbic system.[22] This suggests that an institute for the study of nonviolence might be organized deliberately to facilitate mutually supportive interchanges between its religious–humanistic (ethical), rational–empirical (scientific), and applied (action) components. Whatever terms are given them, these can be recognized as the pervasively useful three dimensions of modern social science (affect, instrumentality, and power) and of the ancient Hindu (and other) religious prescriptions to seek peaceful community with humankind and nature through devotion, knowledge, and action.

The intent of this essay has been to engage the international studies community in seeking answers to five questions that promise contributions to nonviolent global transformation into the twenty-first century: Is a nonkilling society possible? How are we to cope with a mad dictator (or with a national institutionalized killer) using completely nonviolent means? Is a nonviolent revolution (and even a nonviolent class struggle) possible? What is the economic basis of a nonkilling society, a nonviolent politics, a nonviolent political science, and a nonviolent international studies? How can the creation and use of nonviolent knowledge in international studies best be facilitated?

NOTES

1. Gene Sharp, *The Politics of Non-Violent Action* (Boston: Porter Sargent, 1973), especially ch. 1, "The Nature and Control of Political Power," pp. 7–62. See also Krishnalal Shridharani, *War Without Violence* (Bombay: Bharatiya Vidya Bhavan, 1962); and Gene Sharp, *Gandhi as a Political Strategist* (Boston: Porter Sargent, 1979).

2. Gene Keyes, "Strategic Non-Violent Defence: The Construct of an Option," *Journal of Strategic Studies* 4 (June 1981): 125–151.

3. Olof Palme et al., *Common Security: A Blueprint for Survival* (New York: Simon & Schuster, 1982), Report of the Independent Commission on Disarmament and Security Issues.

4. Willy Brandt et al., *North-South: A Program for Survival* (Cambridge: MIT Press, 1980), Report of the Independent Commission on International Development Issues.

5. Amnesty International Staff, *Amnesty International Report 1984* (London: Amnesty International, 1984).

6. Michael Herr, *Dispatches* (New York: Alfred A. Knopf, 1968).

7. Royal Swedish Academy of Sciences, "Environmental Research and Management Priorities for the 1980's," *Ambio: A Journal of the Human Environment* 12 (1983). This special issue lists ten priorities in each category.

8. *Honolulu Advertiser*, January 3, 1985, p. B-2. Quoting Garner Simmons, *Peckinpah: A Portrait in Montage* (Austin: University of Texas Press, 1984).

9. Julian M. Snyder, *The Way of the Warrior: How to Make a Killing in Any Market* (n.p.: Richardson & Snyder Books, 1982).

10. Loh Seng Tsai, "Peace and Cooperation Among Natural Enemies: Educating a Rat-Killing Cat to Cooperate with a Hooded Rat." *Acta Psychologia Taiwanica* 3 (March 1963): 1-5.

11. Richard M. Restak, *The Brain: The Last Frontier* (Garden City, NY: Doubleday, 1979), especially ch. 8, "Cain's Curse," pp. 118-33.

12. David N. Daniels et al., *Violence and the Struggle for Existence* (Boston: Little, Brown, 1970), p. 441.

13. Aristotle, *The Politics, Book V*, trans. T. A. Sinclair (Harmondsworth: Penguin Books, 1978), ch. 3, p. 195.

14. Niccolo Machiavelli, *The Prince and The Discourses*, introd. Max Lerner (New York: Modern Library, 1950), ch. 7, pp. 436-37.

15. E. G. Plimak and Yu. F. Karyakin, "Lenin o mirnoi i nemirnoi formakh revolyutsionnogo perekhoda v sotsializmu" ("Lenin on Peaceful and Nonpeaceful Forms of Revolutionary Transition to Socialism"). Paper presented at the XIth World Congress of the International Political Science Association, Moscow, August 12-18, 1979, pp. 1-2. Translated by the author.

16. Ibid., p. 27.

17. Zhang Yiping, "Dui feibao zhuyi ying jiben kending," ("We Should Positively Affirm Nonviolence"). *Shijie lishi (World History)* 16 (June 7, 1981): 79. Translated by the author.

18. Sharp, *Politics of Non-Violent Action*, especially part I, pp. 34-47; part III, pp. 705-68, 799-810.

19. Scientific Research Council on Peace and Disarmament (Soviet Union), Canadian Institute for International Peace and Security, Peace Research Centre (The Australian National University), and the U.S. Institute of Peace (P.L. 98-525, October 19, 1984).

20. The next largest categories were foreign policy (15) and military and arms control (11), with various additional studies devoted to theory, history, conflict, political behavior, and political socialization. *PS* 17 (Fall 1984): 940-42.

21. The first seminar (October 22-28, 1983) was cosponsored by the Dae Won Sa Buddhist Temple of Hawaii and the Department of Political Science, University of Hawaii at Manoa. The report [Glenn D. Paige (ed.), *Buddhism and Leadership for Peace* (Honolulu: Dae Won Sa Temple of Hawaii, 1984)] may be obtained without charge by writing to the Temple at 2559 Waiomao Road, Honolulu, Hawaii 96816, U.S.A. The second seminar (December 1-7, 1984) was sponsored by the Peace Research Institute of Soka University, Tokyo, Japan, and was coordinated by Associate Professor Tadashige Takamura.

22. Restak, *The Brain*, pp. 122-33.

8
Folie à Deux:
A Psychological Perspective on Soviet-American Relations
Morton Deutsch

There are various definitions of *folie à deux*. As I am redefining and using the term, it refers to the craziness or pathology that exists in the interaction between two people, or groups, or nations that otherwise might not necessarily act irrationally. The actions of the parties toward one another push each of them to engage in offensive-defensive maneuvers that worsen instead of improve their respective situations. Each attempt by either side to make itself feel more secure produces actions from the other that makes it less secure. The irrational actions of either side foster irrational responses from the other. The malignant process that results is increasingly costly and dangerous to the parties involved and to others who may be affected by their irrational actions.

I believe that the relations between the United States and the Soviet Union resemble a *folie à deux* and that it is vital to recognize that their pathological social process is relentlessly pushing us all closer to a nuclear holocaust, in which, as some have noted, "the survivors might well envy the dead." Both the United States and the Soviet Union have spent and plan to continue to spend additional hundreds of billions of dollars on nuclear weapons systems in the illusion that it will be possible to obtain some advantage over the other and thus deter the other from starting a nuclear war. Each, of course, wants to have the advantage in the belief that this will make the country's position more secure. However, the enormous sums already spent on nuclear weapons have worsened the

---

This essay is a modified version of ideas more fully developed in "Preventing World War III: A Psychological Perspective," a chapter in my book *Distributive Justice: A Social Psychological Perspective* (New Haven, CT: Yale University Press, 1985).

situations of both sides: It has increased the chances of a nuclear holocaust and it has seriously wounded the economies of both nations.

Sane and intelligent people, once they are enmeshed in a pathological social process, engage in actions that seem to them completely rational and necessary but that a detached, objective observer would readily identify as contributing to the perpetuation and intensification of a vicious cycle of interactions. We have all seen this happen in married couples and in parent-adolescent relations where the individual people are otherwise decent and rational. They trap themselves into a vicious social process that leads to outcomes—hostility, estrangement, violence—that no one really wants. So can this happen with nations: Otherwise sane, intelligent leaders of the superpowers have allowed their nations to become involved in a malignant process that is driving them to engage in actions and reactions that are steadily increasing the chances of a nuclear war—an outcome no one wants. In such a process, both sides are right in coming to believe that the other is hostile and malevolent: The interactions and attitudes that develop in those involved in such a process provide ample justification for such beliefs.

THE CHARACTERISTICS OF MALIGNANT SOCIAL PROCESS

Here, I want to describe some insights that social science research is developing about malignant social processes, to indicate how the superpowers seem enmeshed in one, and to suggest some ideas for getting out of it. A number of key elements contributing to the development and perpetuation of such processes are depicted below.

Involvement in an Anarchic Social Situation

There are social situations that do not allow the possibility of "rational" behavior so long as the conditions for social order or mutual trust do not exist. Social scientists have conducted many experiments with such situations. A typical one involves two people who play a game called "The Prisoners' Dilemma." Each player has to choose between pressing a green or red button. If both press their respective green buttons, each will win $1; if both press their red buttons, each will lose $1; if one presses red and the other presses green, the one who presses red will win $2 while the one who presses green will lose $2. Each player is "tempted" to press the red button: By doing so, he/she earns more ($2 rather than $1, if the other presses green) or loses less ($1 rather than $2, if the other presses red). Most pairs of players in such situations end up pressing their red buttons and both lose money. Yet they could both win money, if they could have mutual confidence that neither fear nor greed will lead the other to press the red button.

Research by social scientists indicates that when confronted with such social dilemmas, individuals can avoid being trapped in a mutually reinforcing, self-defeating cycle only by attempting to change the situation so that a basis of social order or mutual trust can be developed. Thus, in a Prisoners' Dilemma experiment, if a third party is introduced who has the power to enforce agreements that both players make to choose green, then their confidence in the social arrangement of an enforceable contract will enable them to resolve their dilemma. Also, in such a situation, if the players are given information that leads them to believe that they have similar basic values and attitudes, they will usually develop sufficient mutual trust to cooperate in choosing green.

The current security dilemmas facing the superpowers result from the kind of situation captured in the Prisoners' Dilemma game. A characteristic feature of such "nonrational" situations is that an attempt by any individual or nation to increase its own security (without regard to the security of the others) is self-defeating. For example, consider the United States' decision to develop and test the hydrogen bomb so as to maintain a military superiority over the Soviet Union rather than to seek an agreement to ban its testing and thus prevent a spiraling arms race. This decision led the Soviet Union to attempt to catch up. Soon, both superpowers were stockpiling hydrogen bombs. U.S. leaders believed that if the Soviets had been the first to develop the hydrogen bomb, they would have tested it and sought to reap the advantages from doing so. Undoubtedly, they were right. Both sides are aware of the temptations that the other has to increase its security "by getting ahead." The fear of "falling behind" as well as the temptation to "get ahead" lead to a pattern of interactions that increase insecurity on both sides.

Comprehension of the basic reality that nuclear war would be mutually devastating suggests that mutual security rather than national security should be our objective. The basic military axiom for both the East and West should be that military actions should only be taken that increase the military security of both sides; military actions that give a military superiority to one side or the other should be avoided. The military forces of both sides should be viewed as having the common primary aim of preventing either side (even one's own) from starting a deliberate or accidental war. How? By regular meetings of military leaders from East and West; by establishing a continuing, joint technical group of experts to work together to formulate disarmament and inspection plans; by positioning mixed military units on each other's territory, etc. Crucially, we both must recognize that if military inferiority is dangerous, so is military "superiority"; it is dangerous for either to feel tempted or frightened into military action. Neither the United States nor the Soviet Union should want its weapons or the other's to be vulnerable to a first strike. Similarly, neither side should want the other to have its command, control, and communication systems become so ineffective that the decision to use nuclear weapons would be in the hands of individual, uncontrolled units.

Competitive Orientation

Using many experimental formats and diverse ways of inducing competition, social psychologists have shown that if the participants in a conflict see it as a win–lose, competitive situation, the resulting malignant social process will tend to perpetuate and indeed escalate the conflict. In one series of studies, we employed a two-person bargaining situation in which each person owned a trucking firm and earned $1 each time his/her truck delivered merchandise to a specified destination. The cost of the truck's trip was a function of its duration; if it took much time, the truck could lose money. Each firm had two routes to its destination: a long, two-lane alternate route that took much time and a short, main route. The midsection of the main route was only one lane wide. The two trucks went in opposite directions, so if both went on the main route they would meet on the one-lane section. The bargaining problem was "who would back down" and let the other go through first. We stimulated competition by promising a bonus to the bargainer who earned the most money, and by other methods also.

This research demonstrated that the characteristics of a competitive conflict process are as follows:

1. Communication between the conflicting parties is unreliable and impoverished. Poor communication enhances the possibility of error and misinformation, reinforcing preexisting stereotypes and expectations toward the other. Most important, there is impaired ability to respond to the other's shifts away from a win–lose orientation.

2. The view is stimulated that the solution of the conflict can be imposed by one side or the other only by means of superior force, deception, or cleverness. The attempt by each of the conflicting parties to create or maintain a power superiority tends to change the focus from the immediate issue in dispute to the more abstract issue of "power" for its own sake.

3. A suspicious, hostile attitude develops that increases the sensitivity to differences and threats while minimizing the awareness of similarities. Such an attitude permits behavior toward the other that

would be considered outrageous if directed toward someone like oneself.

In spite of public statements of the leaders of the two superpowers that define the conflict as a confrontation of two irreconcilable ideologies, and it is apparent that basic ideological differences do exist, their conflict need not be viewed as an inherently win–lose, cutthroat struggle. Neither Soviet nor U.S. ideology is consistent or operational enough to guide action in the day-to-day decisions that shape history. Furthermore, both ideologies are vague. Their vagueness provides ample room for both the United States and the Soviet Union (or China) to find a basis of amicable relations.

The resurgence of the Cold War has intensified our perception of ideological differences; but in light of internal conflicts within both "East" and "West" (the Sino–Soviet break and the trade disputes among the Western nations), we have an opportunity to revise our images of the so-called "struggle between communism and freedom." The intensity of the current ideological struggle reflects primarily an outdated power struggle between two continental superpowers that have defined their prestige and security in terms of world leadership. The emergence of such a power struggle between the United States and the Soviet Union was predicted by Alexis de Tocqueville in 1835 and by others long before the latter nation adopted a communist ideology.

Historically, the quest for world power has been closely bound to strivings for national security, economic dominance, and international prestige or influence. It has commonly taken the form of an attempt to establish military supremacy over one's major competitors, but the drive for military dominance in the nuclear age is dangerously anachronistic. So, too, crude economic imperialism no longer provides as much opportunity for economic gain as does scientific research and development. However, the quest for international power and influence can be reasonable for all societies. Later, fair rules for such competition are discussed.

Inner Conflict Within the Parties

Although competitive conflict is necessary for long-lasting malignant conflict, it is not sufficient. The considerable experience of psychotherapists working with troubled couples indicates that malignant conflicts persist because of the internal needs of the conflicting parties. In a vicious circle, the malignant conflict may itself intensify the internal needs that support it. For example, a husband and wife, each of whom has a deep sense of personal failure, may each provoke the other to be abusive: The other's abusiveness provides a rationalization for one's failure, but being victimized also intensifies one's sense of failure.

There is little doubt that the superpower conflict has served important internal functions for the ruling establishments in the United States and the Soviet Union. The Soviet establishment has justified the continuation of its autocratic form of government, the Russian domination of the other nationalities in the Soviet Union, its control of the nations of Eastern Europe, and its subordination of Communist parties in other countries in terms of its struggle against "capitalist imperialism." Under the guise of anticommunism, the U.S. establishment has justified its intervention in other countries to promote the interests of U.S. business; it has supported the continuation and growth of the military-industrial complex; it has rationalized governmental secrecy so that many important governmental decisions are made without informed public discussion; and it has inhibited the development of significant and sustained political opposition to the policies of the national security establishment.

It is hoped that there is growing recognition within each superpower that the escalating dangers and costs of the arms race are dwarfing the gains from having an external devil. Obviously, many of the internal problems of both superpowers would be lessened if they were not engaged in such extravagantly nonproductive expenditures as are involved in their arms race.

Misjudgment and Misperceptions

Most people and groups have an egoistic bias toward perceiving their behavior toward the other as being more well intentioned and legitimate than the other's behavior toward them. For example, research has shown that U.S. students view U.S. espionage activities in the Soviet Union as more well motivated than similar activities by Soviet agents in the United States. If each side in a conflict perceives its own motives and behavior as more benevolent and justified than those of the other side, the conflict is apt to spiral upward in intensity. Such bias leads to a parallel bias in what is considered to be an equitable agreement for resolving conflict. This makes agreement more difficult and thus extends conflict. Some of the difficulties the United States and the Soviet Union have in reaching agreements on arms control reflect their egoistic biases.

There are, of course, other types of processes leading to misjudgments. The intensification of conflict may induce tension beyond a moderate optimal level. This can impair cognitive processes in several ways. It may reduce the range of perceived alternatives; induce one to focus on the immediate rather than the long-term consequences of one's actions; polarize thought so that percepts take on a simplistic cast of being black or white, for or against, good or evil; increase defensiveness; and enhance the pressures for social conformity. Excessive tension or cognitive rigidity reduces the intellectual resources available for discovering new ways of coping with a problem or resolving a conflict. Intensification of conflict is the likely result as simplistic thinking and the polarization of thought push the participants to view their alternatives as being limited to victory or defeat.

There are three basic ways to reduce the misjudgments and misperceptions that typically occur during the course of conflict: (1) Make explicit the assumptions and evidence underlying them and examine how likely they were to have been influenced by any of the common sources of error. (2) Bring in friendly, objective outsiders, to see whether their perceptions of the situation are in agreement or disagreement with one's own. The outsiders should have the independence to ensure that they are free to form their own views and the stature to be able to communicate them so that they will be heard. When this is unfeasible, the use of internal "devil's advocates" has been recommended as a way of challenging the assumptions and evidence underlying one's judgments. Here, too, it is important that the devil's advocates be sufficiently independent and prestigious to present hard challenges that cannot be ignored. (3) There are agreements that can be made with one's adversary to reduce the chances of malignant misjudgment of one another during conflict, such as promoting continuing informal contact and providing for regular feedback of the other's interpretations of one's communications.

Unwitting Commitments

During the course of a malignant social process, the actions that the parties take may strengthen the beliefs that have given rise to the actions, committing the parties to their beliefs unwittingly. This well-investigated psychological process is termed "dissonance reduction." For example, in explaining his opposition to a U.S. proposal made shortly before Pearl Harbor that Japan withdraw its troops from China, Prime Minister Tojo said, "We sent a large force of one million men [to China] and it has cost us well over 100,000 dead and wounded, [the grief of] their bereaved families, hardships for four years, and a national expenditure of several tens of billions of yen. We must by all means get satisfactory results from this."[1] Similarly, the belief by leaders of the U.S. government that the Soviet Union would do us in militarily if it could leads to actions, such as intensifying our military build-up, that will in turn produce increased psychological commitment to the belief: After deciding to build the MX missile, doubts about the beliefs that support the decision will be reduced.

Self-Fulfilling Prophecies

Social scientists have identified "self-fulfilling prophecies" as one of the most important mechanisms involved in pathological social processes. In a self-fulfilling prophecy, distortions are perpetuated because they evoke behavior that makes the originally false conception come true. You hear the false rumor that a friend is saying nasty things about you, you snub him; he then bad-mouths you, confirming your expectation. Similarly, if the policymakers of East and West believe that war is likely and either attempts to increase its military security vis-à-vis the other, the other's response will justify the initial move. The dynamics of an arms race have the inherent quality of a *folie à deux*, wherein the self-fulfilling prophecies mutually reinforce one another. As a result, both superpowers are right to think that the other is provocative, dangerous, and malevolent. Each side, however, is blind to how its own policies and behavior have contributed to the development of the other's hostile attitudes. If each superpower would recognize its own part in maintaining the malignant relations, it could lead to a reduction of mutual blaming and an increase in mutual problem solving.

Gamesmanship

What is so seductive about nuclear weapons and the scenarios of nuclear war that the strategists and decision makers in both of the superpowers seem drawn to them like moths to a flame? There are so many dimensions of power—economic, political, cultural, scientific, sports, educational, etc.—in which the power struggle could be played out. What is the special fascination to playing the international power game with nuclear weapons?

There are two key psychological features that make the power game with nuclear toys a supergame. The game is very tidy and abstract, and it has a tremendous emotional kick for those with strong power drives: The stakes are high (the fate of the earth is at risk), decisions have to be made quickly (there is no time for indecisiveness), and nuclear weapons are superconcentrated power.

To play the game, each side has to make assumptions about how its own weapons (as well as how its command, control, and communication systems) will operate in various hypothetical future nuclear war scenarios as well as how the other side's will operate. There is, of course, very little basis in actual experience for making accurate, reliable, or valid assumptions about these matters, since none of these weapons or systems has been tested or employed in circumstances even remotely resembling the situation of any imaginable nuclear war. However, for the nuclear game to be played and for scenarios to be developed, assumptions about these matters have to be made. Once these assumptions have been made and have, by consensus, been accepted within one side's strategic group, they become psychologically "real" and are treated as "hard facts," no matter how dubious their grounding in actual realities. These "psychological realities" and dubious "hard facts" are then used as a basis for further decisions in the strategic game of preparing for the eventuality of nuclear war. These decisions may entail potential expenditures of hundreds of billions of dollars for new nuclear weapons—as, for instance, on the MX missile and the B-1 bomber—which will require the strategic gamesplayers on the other side to respond (also based on their psychological realities and dubious hard facts) in a way that will prevent them from "losing" the nuclear war game. Citizens and elected officials must vigorously challenge the dubious hard facts underlying the psychological realities of the strategic gamesplayers on both sides.

What can be done to reverse the malignant social process I have described, and how can we begin to reduce the dangers resulting from the military gamesmanship and security dilemmas of the superpowers? Let me address the latter question first.

A bold and courageous leadership in the United States would take a risk for peace. It would announce its determination to end the insane arms race. It would offer to agree on a package of "no first use of nuclear weapons," a nonagression pact between the North Atlantic Treaty Organization (NATO) and the Warsaw Pact, a substantial reduction and equalization of the opposing conventional forces in Europe, and a verifiable freeze on further research, development, testing, and production of nuclear weapons.

At the same time, the United States would initiate a GRIT process, GRIT standing for "graduated reciprocation in tension reduction," a psychological strategy for reducing international tension articulated by Professor Charles Osgood of the University of Illinois, a former president of the American Psychological Association. The United States would announce a unilateral reduction of, for example, 10 percent of its existing nuclear weapons and would invite the Soviet Union and other nations to verify that they were being destroyed. It would request the Soviet Union to reciprocate. The United States has such an excess of nuclear weapons that it could afford to make several rounds of unilateral cuts in case the

Soviets did not initially reciprocate, without losing its capacity to destroy Soviet society, even if they were to attack first. Such repeated unilateral initiatives, if sincere in their intent and execution, would place the Soviet Union under the strongest pressure to reciprocate.

President Kennedy in his "Strategy for Peace" address on June 10, 1963, initiated something like a GRIT process by announcing a unilateral halt to all atmospheric nuclear tests, in the context of asking U.S. citizens to reexamine their attitudes toward the Cold War. This politically courageous action led the Soviet Union to reciprocate and the superpowers agreed to end their atmospheric nuclear tests permanently. If U.S. leaders could now show similar wisdom and courage, we might replace the arms race with a peace race.

UNDOING THE MALIGNANT SOCIAL PROCESS

Arms control and disarmament agreements are only a first step. Since the ability to make nuclear weapons will continue to exist—forever—we must remove the malignancy from the relations between the superpowers and eliminate any possibility that such a condition could develop among other great powers. A major way to do so would be the development of fair rules for international competition.

Fair Rules

As Professor Amitai Etzioni, a distinguished political sociologist, has indicated, a set of rules would include such principles as the following: No nonaligned country would be allowed to have military ties with other countries, particularly not with any of the major powers; no foreign troops, foreign bases, or foreign arms of any sort would be permitted to remain in or enter the nonaligned country; creation of a U.N. observer force consisting largely of personnel from nonaligned countries and equipped with the necessary scientific equipment and facilities (including satellites) to check the borders, ports, airfields, roads, railroads, etc., would be deployed at the request of any of the major powers or by the Secretary-General of the United Nations; violations of the arms embargo—once certified by an appropriate U.N. tribunal—would set in motion a cease-and-desist order aimed at the sender of arms or troops and a disarm order aimed at the receiver. Lack of compliance with such orders would result in appropriate sanctions, for example, a trade and communications embargo, a blockade, the use of armed forces.[2] If some such rules could, in fact, be established, what effects might be expected? Clearly, the revolutionary ferment would not disappear. Communist governments might take power in some countries, but they would have to obtain and remain in power without foreign military aid and they would not be able to provide military assistance to communists in other countries. Such a government might be a tragedy to its people, but the United States would fulfill its moral responsibility if it were to develop and enforce rules that could prevent outside military aid from foreclosing the possibility that the people will overthrow a government that is obnoxious to them.

An agreement on fair rules for competition will require the governments that sell arms to other countries to give up this lucrative form of trade. Currently, it amounts to about $25 to $35 billion a year of which NATO countries originate somewhere over 50 percent, the Warsaw Pact countries about 40 percent. The Western and Soviet blocs should agree to end the arms-peddling business: It is an even more destructive form of trade than drug peddling.

DEVELOPING A COOPERATIVE FRAMEWORK

A cooperative framework must be developed to resist the debilitating effects of the inevitable disputes associated with any system of rules. How can this be done? The psychological key to the development of cooperation can be stated very simply. It is the provision of repeated and varied opportunities for mutually beneficial interactions. One of the most well-established principles in psychology is the tendency for people to seek out and to repeat activities that they find rewarding.

The U.S. reluctance to trade with the Soviet Union and its unsuccessful attempts to get its allies to limit their trade with that country are indicators of an underlying view that hampers the attempt to strengthen cooperative bonds and fosters a malignant relation: the notion that anything that helps the Soviets hurts the United States and vice versa. Clearly, it helps the Soviets if their children have available Sabin polio vaccine, but does this harm the U.S.? Assuredly, it harms the Soviets if they are forced into a costly arms race, but does this help the U.S.? If the United States were to refuse to sell grain to the Soviet Union, it would be harmful to them, but would the U.S. gain in any meaningful way?

For many, appeasement and cooperation are equated. They feel that the only credible stance toward an adversary is a self-righteous, belligerent counterhostility. However, there is a more productive stance: one that combines firmness and cooperativeness. One can communicate both a firm, tough resolve not to allow oneself to be abused, intimidated, or rendered defenseless and a willingness to cooperate to mutual benefit.

"Firmness" in contrast to "belligerence" aborts the development of vicious spirals. It is, of course, difficult to resist the temptation to respond with belligerence to provocations; it requires a good deal of self-confidence not to have to demonstrate that one is "man enough" to be tough, that one is not "chicken." It is just this kind of firm, nonbelligerent, self-confident, cooperative attitude that our experimental research indicates is most effective in inducing cooperation even when the other is initially hostile and provocative.

Can the United States adopt such an attitude? U.S. defensiveness is high. Throughout most of its history, the country has been in the uniquely fortunate position of having pretty much its own way in foreign affairs. Initially, this was due to its powerful isolated position in the Americas, and since World War II it has been the leading world power. The United States faces a loss of status. It can no longer be isolated from the physical danger of a major war, nor can it remain the uniquely powerful nation. The Soviet Union, the nations of Western Europe, as well as other nations will not continue to grant the United States the uncontested primacy it had for several decades after World War II. The United States has to adjust its aspirations to the changing realities or suffer a constant frustration.

From what psychology has learned about malignant social processes, we have reason to believe that a nuclear holocaust is not inevitable. Such a process can be reversed if we recognize clearly its underlying irrationality and are willing to make the sincere, sustained effort necessary to substitute more constructive ways of managing international conflicts.

NOTES

1. Quoted in Robert Jervis, *Perception and Misperception in International Politics* (Princeton: Princeton University Press, 1976) p. 398.
2. Amitai Etzioni, *The Hard Way to Peace* (New York: Collier Books, 1962).

9
Arms Control, Disarmament, and Global Peace and Security
Michael D. Intriligator and Dagobert L. Brito

Arms control and disarmament are two concepts that are often combined and used interchangeably, as in the title of the U.S. Arms control and Disarmament Agency. They are, however, fundamentally different and, in certain respects, conflicting concepts, arms control referring to initiatives that reduce the probability of war (and, secondarily, its severity and the cost of armaments) and disarmament referring to weapons reductions. A further problem relating to the concept of arms control is the narrowing of its meaning to refer to only U.S.-U.S.S.R. bilateral negotiations, when it can refer to unilateral and multilateral as well as bilateral initiatives. This chapter analyzes the nature of the distinctions between these two concepts, compares them in terms of their potential for global peace and security, discusses the current U.S.-U.S.S.R. strategic situation, and develops some additions to the arms control agenda. These additions to the arms control agenda include initiatives to prevent war by accident, miscalculation, or irrational action and initiatives to prevent the erosion of deterrence.

ARMS CONTROL AND DISARMAMENT: CONTRASTING APPROACHES

It sometimes happens that the means to a goal become confused with the goals themselves and are pursued without regard for their ultimate consequences. Battles are sometimes fought without regard to the purpose of the war, and wars are sometimes pursued without regard to the overall political goals. This is the case with arms control and disarmament. Both represent means to global peace and security.

Sometimes they work in a parallel fashion, but at times they can be in conflict.

Arms control and disarmament each represent different approaches to the problems of global peace and security, particularly in regards to the issues of nuclear weapons and nuclear war. The two are sometimes combined, as in the name of the U.S. Arms Control and Disarmament Agency, or even used interchangeably, but they are fundamentally different and, in certain respects, conflicting concepts.

Disarmament refers to reductions in the levels of weapons, whether nuclear or conventional, by unilateral, bilateral, or multilateral initiatives. Its goal is to eventually reach the disarmed state through weapons reductions by one or more of these initiatives.

Arms control, in contrast, refers to changes in the numbers, types, configurations, etc., of weapons that can affect their use or effectiveness. As with disarmament, these changes can be unilateral, bilateral, or multilateral in nature. However, the goal of arms control is primarily to reduce the chance of war, especially nuclear war, and second to limit the damage in case war does occur and to reduce the cost of armaments (Schelling 1960, 1966; Schelling and Halperin 1962).

Sometimes disarmament initiatives coincide with arms control initiatives, such as when arms control agreements call for certain ceilings or reductions in weapons levels. Examples of this are the Washington Naval Agreement, the demobilization following World War II, the explicit and implicit U.S.-Soviet understandings stemming from the 1962 Cuban missile crisis, and Strategic Arms Limitation Talks (SALT) I and II. There have been other cases, however, in which certain initiatives that can be treated as arms control measures did not involve arms reductions or limitations, and even some that called for increases in weapons levels. For example, the hardening of land-based missiles by both the United States and the Soviet Union in the 1960s represented important unilateral arms control initiatives involving changes in the configurations of weapons that reduced the chance of war by strengthening the deterrent capability of both sides. They did not, however, change the levels of weapons. The deployments of missile-carrying submarines by the two superpowers involved increases in weapons on both sides, but also represented important examples of unilateral arms control initiatives, since they, too, lowered the probability of war by strengthening deterrence in providing a secure second-strike retaliatory capability.

One might well ask how arms increases could possibly represent arms control. The reason is that arms control is defined not to be arms reduction (which is the definition of disarmament), but rather to be initiatives that reduce the chance of war. The definition involves the goal of global peace and security rather than the means to the goal. It sometimes happens that the means to the goal, for example, weapons reduction, are confused with the goal itself, for example, global peace and security. Furthermore, there could be a conflict between a goal and the means to the goal. In this case, disarmament, a means to the goal of global peace and security, could be confused with or even be in conflict with the goal itself. If arms increases reduce the probability of war by strengthening deterrence, then such arms increases must be considered arms control initiatives in satisfying the principal definition of "arms control." What is "controlled" in arms control is not the level of arms, but rather their likelihood of use.

A further conceptual problem relating to "arms control" is the fact that many interpret the term as virtually synonymous with U.S.-U.S.S.R. bilateral negotiations leading to a treaty with quantitative limitations on weapons and with verification provisions, as in the SALT/Strategic Arms Reduction Talks (START) process. Given this extremely narrow definition, which again confuses the means to the goal (bilateral agreements on weapons) and the goal itself (reducing the chance of war), it is not at all surprising that many have become skeptical about or even hostile to arms control. While bilateral initiatives can be part of arms control, interpreted in an operational way, as in the above definition, arms control certainly does not exclude unilateral or multilateral initiatives. Examples of unilateral arms control initiatives have already been given. Examples of multilateral arms control initiatives include the Washington Naval Agreement and the development of a nuclear nonproliferation regime. Furthermore, bilateral agreements need not be embodied in treaties as in the already-cited case of the U.S.-Soviet understandings stemming from the 1962 Cuban missile crisis. If arms control is interpreted narrowly as identical to the SALT/START process, it retains little value. Rather it should be interpreted much more broadly, as it has been traditionally, to include all initiatives—whether decreases or increases in weapons; whether bilateral, unilateral, or multilateral; whether quantitative or qualitative; whether negotiated or not; whether involving verification or not; whether explicit or implicit—that can reduce the chances of nuclear war. Given this broader interpretation, one that focuses on the goal rather than the means to the goal, arms control is both significant and valuable.[1]

As to disarmament, small reductions in levels of weapons can have considerable value, particularly if the eliminated weapons are useful only in a first strike or are undependable, and such reductions would represent both disarmament and arms control. Large-scale weapons reductions, however, can create serious potential problems. While such large-scale reductions in the level of weapons might reduce the cost of arms, which is an aspect of arms control, they could increase the chance of war in reducing deterrent capability and thereby conflict with the primary goal of arms control. In a situation of significantly reduced levels of weapons, whichever side could gain even a few weapons could seriously threaten the other. This disadvantage is particularly acute in the case of the two superpowers, since each country has the ability to rapidly produce both nuclear weapons and a variety of delivery systems and thus could quickly assemble a weapons system that it could use to threaten or even to attack the other. Furthermore, if the superpowers each had very few weapons, neither side would be able to deter the other, creating an incentive for each to build weapons systems in order to extract concessions from the other side.

Movements by the superpowers to significantly reduce levels of weapons might be amicable and peaceful if undertaken in a period of goodwill, for example, as part of some type of comprehensive political agreement. Once such a situation is attained, however, political goodwill may not continue. For example, a dispute over even a relatively minor issue could escalate into a major crisis if each side perceived the other to possibly be rearming and also recognized that neither side could deter the other. A very small number of nuclear weapons and delivery vehicles could be decisive in such a situation, and, knowing this, each side would have an incentive to retain such weapons or the means to build them rapidly. Thus, in a crisis situation, there could be an arming race combined with the absence of deterrence—a situation with a grave danger of a nuclear war. Given this prospect, a situation of very few weapons on either side resulting from large-scale disarmament may, in fact, be a highly dangerous one. Thus, a situation in which both countries have very few weapons may not be consistent with the paramount goal of arms control, namely, reducing the chance of war. This situation highlights the potential inconsistency between disarmament and arms control.

The danger is that if weapons levels are too low, then one of the countries involved in a crisis may be tempted to escalate its level of weapons, since relatively few additional weapons could be decisive. Since this could be true for both countries, in a situation of few weapons on both sides, a crisis could lead to an arms race that in turn could trigger a war. An example of this phenomenon was the mobilization race that preceded World War I. War plans for each of the countries involved called for mobilization of their vast reserves. It was felt that the country that mobilized first would be able to win. As a result, the political crisis triggered a mobilization in the countries involved. Once started, no country could afford to stop or slow down its efforts, and contingency war plans became operational before the crisis could be politically defused.

In sum, having very few weapons on either side would result in crisis instability, in that it could in a crisis situation lead to the outbreak of war. Thus, it is inconsistent with the goal of reducing the chances of war. Indeed, in such a situation the best arms control initiative may very well be substantial increases in the levels of weapons so as to attain a situation of mutual deterrence. Such an initiative meets the primary purpose of arms control, namely, lowering the probability of (nuclear) war. Thus, to the extent that the United States and the Soviet Union rely upon mutual deterrence as the primary mechanism for reducing the chances of war, arms control and disarmament represent rather different approaches to the problems of national security and global peace and security. Some selected weapons reductions may be useful as an arms control measure—such as the reduction or elimination of weapons that could be vulnerable to a first strike—and in such instances arms control and disarmament complement each other. In other cases, however, they may move in opposite directions, such as when mutual deterrence calls for increases in the stocks of certain types of weapons.[2]

THE OVERALL GOAL: STABILITY AGAINST THE OUTBREAK OF WAR

The most important objective for arms control, disarmament, or any other such process affecting weapons and how they are used is simple: to ensure against the outbreak of war, particularly nuclear war with its disastrous consequences. Everything else is secondary.

An illustration of the primacy of minimizing the chance of nuclear war is that of cruise missiles. Such missiles, whether ground, air, or sea launched, have frequently been criticized as being nonverifiable. Small and easily hidden, they could be placed in virtually any factory building, airplane, ship, or submarine. Furthermore, it may not be readily determined, even if they are located, whether they carry conventional or nuclear warheads. This lack of verifiability has been used as an argument against their deployment, but the overall goal of arms control is, after all, to reduce the chance of war, not enhance verifiability. Verifiability is only one aspect of one particular kind of arms control initiative. Further, verifiability in and of itself has no value. It is a means to a goal, not a goal itself. If cruise missiles are not verifiable, they may, in fact, contribute to the overall goal, in that since they are difficult or impossible to find, they could actually increase stability by strengthening mutal deterrence. If they could survive a first strike, then they would be available for use in a retaliatory second strike. In this respect, cruise missiles are similar to ballistic missile-carrying submarines. The deployment of mobile or concealed cruise missiles would be particularly valuable in view of the increasing vulnerability of land-based missiles to a first strike. Because of increases in the accuracy of warheads, land-based missiles in fixed silos, including the planned MX deployments, are vulnerable to a first strike. Thus, they would not contribute in the future to the stability of mutual deterrence. Indeed, intercontinental ballistic missiles (ICBMs) could even become a major contributor to instability if they were perceived as primarily first-strike weapons, being both vulnerable and highly accurate. An alternative that could preserve the nuclear triad and also contribute to stability could be the replacement of silo-based ICBMs with mobile or concealed land-based cruise missiles. Such deployments, while admittedly not verifiable, would enhance nuclear stability by ensuring the presence of a retaliatory second-strike capability. It is important not to lose sight of the primary goal, of reducing the chance of war particularly when it is in conflict with other goals or means to the goal, such as verifiability.

THE CURRENT U.S.-SOVIET STRATEGIC SITUATION: THE CONTRIBUTION OF PAST ARMS RACES AND ARMS CONTROL TO STABILITY VIA MUTUAL DETERRENCE

The current strategic situation with respect to the superpowers, as based on the history of the last 40 years of both arms races and arms control, is one of stability via mutual deterrence. As a result of both arms procurements and arms control initiatives, the superpowers have constructed a system that has great stability against the outbreak of war. While the arms race has involved quantitative or qualitative changes in weapons systems, it, together with arms control initiatives, has led to stockpiles of strategic weapons in such configurations that have ensured against the outbreak of war by creating, reinforcing, and ensuring a stabilizing situation of mutual retaliation and deterrence. In such a situation, an attack by either superpower on the other would be equivalent to an attack on itself and thus suicidal.

Since about 1970, the U.S.-Soviet arms race has shifted from a quantitative competition to build more warheads and missiles to the current one of a qualitative competetion involving the development and deployment of newer weapons systems. This arms race, which has involved a virtually continuous interplay of action and reaction, is based in part on misperceptions and heuristic decision-making rules (Intriligator and Brito 1985b). It has also involved enormous costs, owing in part to technological developments, research and development, and the expense of deploying new systems.

Important U.S.-Soviet arms control activities have also occurred over this period, involving both quantitative and qualitative initiatives. In fact, there is an important interplay between the arms race and arms control activities, each stimulating the other. For example, the arms race deployment of counterforce-capable weapons led to such arms control responses as the hardening of missile silos and the deployment of missile-carrying submarines, both of which contributed to deterrence by ensuring retaliatory second-strike capabilities. Fear of the potential instability stemming from the deployment of "MIRVed" (i.e. missiles containing multiple independently targeted reentry vehicle) missiles led to the Anti-ballistic Missile (ABM) Treaty. Actual and potential arms race activities of states other than the superpowers led to multilateral arms control initiatives, including the formation of a nonproliferation regime through such organizations as the International Atomic Energy Agency (IAEA), the Nuclear Nonproliferation Treaty (NPT), and the London Suppliers Group, and the various agreements limiting nuclear testing.

As a consequence of both the arms race and arms control activities, the current situation is one of great stability against the outbreak of war between the United States and the Soviet Union. Each side rightly believes that the chance of a "bolt out of the blue" attack by the other is virtually nil. This situation has been achieved through mutual deterrence, each superpower having enough weapons to inflict unacceptable damage on a retaliatory second strike. Mutual deterrence is fundamental to the stability of the strategic relationship between the superpowers. However, while this may mean that the probability of an attack by one superpower upon the other is very small, it is not zero. Furthermore, it does not eliminate the possibility of nuclear war starting in other ways, for example, through accident or the actions of third parties. Mutual deterrence, however, is currently fundamental to nuclear stability. It has been very successful thus far in averting nuclear war despite the presence of two superpowers with opposing ideologies, each with enormous military capabilities. It is reasonable to assume that it will continue to be successful in the foreseeable future. Conversely, no viable alternative to mutual deterrence has been yet identified.

Ironically, the stability of mutual deterrence requires the presence of large stockpiles of nuclear weapons on both sides. These large stockpiles and the large variety of weapons that stem from the quantitative and qualitative arms race are, in fact, valuable as a hedge against potentially destabilizing technological breakthroughs by either side. Smaller stockpiles or fewer types of weapons systems could run the risk of being inadequate if effective countermeasures were developed against one type of weapon, for example, in antisubmarine warfare (ASW). The presence of a triad of weapons implies that if one weapon becomes unavailable owing to effective countermeasures, the other two can still deter the other side. More generally, there is value to large and varied weapons stocks on both sides to ensure that each can deter the other despite the ongoing development of countermeasures.

The current situation is thus one of an arms race but stability against the outbreak of war. The large stockpiles of nuclear weapons are simultaneously both a cause of the problem of a potential nuclear war and a contribution to its solution. The presence of nuclear weapons and long-range delivery systems has fundamentally and irreversibly changed the global system, and it is impossible to return to the prenuclear world. These weapons and delivery systems give rise to the possibility of nuclear war, but they also deter against premeditated attack, thereby helping to avoid nuclear war. It is not the presence or even the level of stockpiles of nuclear weapons that creates instability. Rather it is the danger of accident or escalation, the actions of smaller nuclear powers, and the possible erosion of deterrence that create actual or potential instability and that should provide the basis for an expanded arms control agenda.

AN EXPANDED ARMS CONTROL AGENDA

The current arms control agenda includes in the U.S.-U.S.S.R. bilateral approaches discussions as to limitations on strategic or intermediate-range weapons systems, troop reductions, etc. Such discussions are valuable, even if they do not lead to formal treaties.[3] Even if they do lead to agreements, implicit or explicit, or formal treaties, however, the inherent limitations of this particular approach to arms control must be recognized. Small reductions or limitations of weapons at close to current levels have little effect, although they could improve the climate. Large-scale reductions or limitations on weapons levels significantly below current levels are probably infeasible politically and are potentially dangerous in undermining the stability that has been achieved via mutual deterrence. Some further problems with the current arms control agenda are the development or deployment of weapons as bargaining chips and the shift, partly due to quantitative limitations, from a quantitative to a qualitative arms race, both of which could contribute to instability (Brito and Intriligator 1981).

While there are inherent limitations and problems with the current arms control agenda, this does not mean that arms control as a process should be abandoned. Rather it means that the agenda should be expanded. An expanded agenda, based on the overall goal of stability against the outbreak of war, should specifically focus on areas of potential instability, and it should lead to initiatives that would stabilize the situation as it now exists or may be developing. In fact, the major problem is not one of reducing or limiting arms, as in the current U.S.-U.S.S.R. bilateral agenda, but rather of stabilizing against their use.

The expanded arms control agenda recognizes the stability of the current situation against the initiation of war, due to mutual deterrence, and it seeks to prevent the outbreak of war due to causes other than a premeditated attack, such as accidents. It also seeks to prevent any erosion of the system of mutual deterrence.

The immediate action items on the expanded arms control agenda are initiatives that would reduce the chances of accidental war. One such type of possible accident is the failure of a communications or control system, such as a computer failure, resulting in the accidental launch of one or a few missiles. A much more dangerous accident is that resulting from the possibility that either superpower might adopt a launch-on-warning posture. Such a posture could trigger a massive retaliatory response on the basis of a false or accidental warning (for example, a failure of communications, computer error, radar error, etc.). In fact, there have been repeated false warnings, including a major accident of potentially cataclysmic import when, in 1980, a training tape of a massive Soviet attack was mistakenly read by U.S. computers as an actual attack. Arms control measures that could be taken to avoid accidents, particularly those involving a launch-on-warning system, include improved command, control, communications, and intelligence; upgraded communications with the potential adversary; advance notification of flight tests and major military maneuvers; increased superpower interaction and discussions; and steps that would eliminate the perceived need for a launch-on-warning posture, such as the elimination of vulnerable weapons systems. Most of these initiatives could be achieved unilaterally, but they could also be supplemented by bilateral or multilateral action, such as agreements on warning and communications systems that would reduce the perceived need for a launch-on-warning posture.

A further set of items on the expanded arms control agenda comprises short-term initiatives. While the present system is one of stability via mutual deterrence, over time this could erode, with a resulting increase in instability. Short-term initiatives would include actions to prevent such an erosion of mutual deterrence, especially that caused by a possible decapitation strike, a breakthrough in ASW, the deployment of an antisatellite system (ASAT), or a comprehensive system of space-based defense. Unilateral actions of this type include improvements in command, control, communications, and intelligence and rebuilding the nuclear triad with weapons systems that could survive a first strike. The latter would include replacing the land-based systems in known fixed sites with mobile and concealed weapons, such as ground-launched cruise missiles. Bilateral agreements would be valuable components of any short-term arms control agenda, including agreements on ASAT and ASW. Both superpowers rely heavily upon submarine-launched missiles as a deterrent and upon space-based assets for warning, communications, navigation, and so forth. Thus, bilateral agreements on ASAT and ASW are important to preserve deterrent capability. At the same time, unilateral measures to hedge against possible breakthroughs in antisubmarine and antisatellite warfare, including research on defenses against such warfare, further weapons diversification, and the deployment of newer systems for communication and navigation, should be part of a new arms control agenda. It would also be useful to modify the ABM Treaty by mutual agreement to allow the superpowers to deploy a limited strategic defense system that would not be effective against a retaliatory strike but would be effective against a small accidental launch or a nuclear attack by a third party (Intriligator 1985).[4]

These items, which are part of an expanded arms control agenda, all focus on areas of current or potential future instability. All lead to specific arms control initiatives as actions that could ameliorate these problems and thereby significantly reduce the chance of war, particularly nuclear war, thus promoting global peace and security.

NOTES

1. Another conceptual problem involving a narrow definition is that of the "arms race." If it is a race, it must have a winner and a loser. However, if in the U.S.–U.S.S.R. strategic interaction there is no war, then both sides "win"; whereas if there is a war, then both sides "lose." Furthermore, the term "arms race" suggests a single measure of performance, for example, how long it takes to complete the course, while, in fact the superpower arms race has many dimensions, with qualitative as well as quantitative features. While one side may be "ahead" in certain dimensions, it may be "behind" in others. Perhaps a more apt sports analogy might be a track meet or a tournament rather than a race.

2. For theoretical developments of mutual deterrence and the relations of arms race to deterrence and security, see Intriligator (1967), Brito (1972), Intriligator and Brito (1984, 1985a,c), and Brito and Intriligator (1985). For a survey of arms races, see Intriligator and Brito (1976), and for a survey of conflict theory, see Intriligator (1982).

3. It is worth recalling that the final "T" in SALT and START is "talks," not "treaties." Discussions and communication are valuable in their own right, even in the absence of treaties.

4. While a complete defensive shield would be extremely dangerous in undermining mutual deterrence, there would be great value in a limited strategic defensive system to defend against accidents, decapitation strikes, and strikes by smaller nuclear powers.

REFERENCES

Brito, D. L. (1972) "A Dynamic Model of an Armaments Race." *International Economic Review* 13:359-75.
Brito, D. L., and M. D. Intriligator. (1985) "Conflict, War, and Redistribution." *American Political Science Review* 79 (December): 943-57.
———(1981) "Strategic Arms Limitation Treaties and Innovations in Weapons Technology." *Public Choice* 37:41-59.
Brito, D. L., M. D. Intriligator, and A. E. Wick (eds.) (1983) *Strategies for Managing Nuclear Proliferation—Economic and Political Issues.* Lexington, MA: Lexington Books.
Intriligator, M. D. (1985) "What 'Star Wars' Is Intended to Prevent," Letter to the Editor. *New York Times,* March 14, 1985.
———. (1982) "Research on Conflict Theory: Analytic Approaches and Areas of Application." *Journal of Conflict Resolution* 26:307-27.
———. (1975) "Strategic Considerations in the Richardson Model of Arms Races." *Journal of Political Economy* 83:339-53.
———. (1967) "Strategy in a Missile War: Targets and Rates of Fire." Security Studies Paper No. 10, Los Angeles: Security Studies Project, University of California, Los Angeles.
Intriligator, M. D., and D. L. Brito. (1985a) "Non-Armageddon Solutions to the Arms Race." *Arms Control* 6:41-57.
———. (1985b) "Heuristic Decision Rules, the Dynamics of the Arms Race, and War Initiation." In M. D. Ward and U. Luterbacher (eds.), *Dynamic Models of International Conflict.* Boulder: Lynne Rienner.
———. (1985c) "The Stability of Mutual Deterrence." In J. Kugler and F. Zagare (eds.), *The Stability of Deterrence,* Denver Monograph Series. Denver: University of Denver Graduate School of International Studies.
———. (1984) "Can Arms Races Lead to the Outbreak of War?" *Journal of Conflict Resolution* 28:63-84.
———. (1976) "Formal Models of Arms Races." *Journal of Peace Science* 2:77-88.
Jones, R., J. Pilat, C. Merlini, and W. Potter. (eds.) (1985) *Nuclear Suppliers and Nonproliferation.* Lexington, MA: Lexington Books.
Schelling, T. C. (1966). *Arms and Influence.* New Haven, CT: Yale University Press.
———. (1960) *The Strategy of Conflict.* Cambridge, MA: Harvard University Press.
Schelling, T. C., and M. H. Halperin. (1961) *Strategy and Arms Control.* New York: Twentieth Century Fund.

IV
Conceptualizing Nonviolence Patterns: Population, Resources, and Economic Performance

10
Social Time and International Policy: Conceptualizing Global Population and Resource Issues
John Gerard Ruggie

It would be difficult to imagine two more contradictory assessments of the emerging global predicament than those advanced in *The Global 2000 Report to the President* (Barney 1980), prepared by the Council on Environmental Quality and the Department of State during the Carter administration, and *The Resourceful Earth* (Simon and Kahn 1984), a response to it organized under the auspices of the Heritage Foundation, a Washington-based conservative think tank. The major conclusion of *The Global 2000*, widely cited, was this:

> If present trends continue, the world in 2000 will be more crowded, more polluted, less stable ecologically, and more vulnerable to disruption than the world we live in now. Serious stresses involving population, resources, and the environment are clearly visible ahead. Despite growing material output, the world's people will be poorer in many ways than they are today. (Barney 1980, vol. 1, p. 1)

To which the Heritage Foundation study retorted:

> If present trends continue, the world in 2000 will be less crowded (though more populated), less polluted, more stable ecologically, and less vulnerable to resource-supply disruption than the world we live in

---

This essay draws on a longer study prepared for the World Resources Institute, Washington, D.C. I am indebted to William T. R. Fox, Ernst B. Haas, Robert O. Keohane, Friedrich V. Kratochwil, and Eugene B. Skolnikoff for comments and suggestions, and to Jay Speakman for research assistance.

now. Stresses involving population, resources, and environment will be less in the future than now. The world's people will be richer in most ways than they are today. The outlook for food and other necessities of life will be better.... Life for most people on earth will be less precarious economically than it is now. (Simon and Kahn 1984, pp. 1-2)

The mere existence of this debate bears witness to the fact that global population and resource issues have become increasingly significant and controversial elements in U.S. foreign policy. But the dialogue of antitheses reflected by the debate also suggests that a good deal of conceptual and empirical work remains to be done before the various issues at stake can be systematically acted upon.

What accounts for these radically different expectations about what is, presumably, the same "real world"? The reasons are many and varied, and include the use of different assumptions in model construction, different baselines for trend data, different methods of extrapolation, as well as errors of commission and omission on the part of both studies. A very different kind of reason is that, to some degree, the two studies are not assessing the same "real world" at all. For example, in the passage cited above, the Heritage Foundation study concludes that the world in 2000 will be less vulnerable to resource-supply disruptions than at present, the specific reference apparently being to the fuel and nonfuel minerals sectors. Indeed, the weight of opinion among analysts tends to support their conclusion. But *The Global 2000* did not argue otherwise. The resource-related vulnerability of which it spoke was not natural or artificial shortages in minerals markets, but the effects of the progressive degradation and impoverishment of the biophysical systems that support life on the planet, as exemplified by ecocatastrophes currently occurring in large parts of Africa.

This apparent misunderstanding of what is meant by resource-related vulnerability is not, alas, an isolated case. The literature, ranging from academic treatises to congressional testimony, is replete with similar instances: Yes, "x" is a problem, no, "x" is not a problem—where "x" refers to the same pressing global issue, but often not to the same aspect of that issue. Now, if it is true, as I believe it to be, that issues regarding the global resource base will become increasingly critical foreign policy concerns, then an effort is warranted to identify means of conceptualizing such issues in a manner that avoids or at least minimizes misunderstandings of this sort. The present essay represents a first step in that direction.

Concepts such as "population" or "resources" are far too aggregated to convey much policy-relevant meaning. They subsume too many issues to which policymakers have to pay attention. At the same time, however, an infinite proliferation of discrete meanings cannot prevail either, since that would make any kind of synoptic view, and therefore policy, impossible. The key to a useful conceptualization, therefore, is some systematic basis for differentiating diverse meanings and then clustering them together again in ways that make sense in policy terms. For reasons that will become clear as we go along, and, it is hoped, persuasive by the time the demonstration concludes, the dimension of time is a particularly appropriate basis for conceptualizing global issues.

The first section of this chapter demonstrates how the dimension of time serves as a basis for conceptualizing global population and resource issues, differentiating them on both substantive and epistemological grounds. The second illustrates the specific global population and resource policy problems that come into focus depending upon the time frame within which they are viewed. The third section, suggests how the criteria for appropriate policy responses also vary as time frames shift. I conclude with a brief summary, together with some general remarks on the growing practical importance of this epistemological dimension of policymaking.

TIME FRAMES AND ISSUE TYPES

A premise that is widely shared among analysts, irrespective of their methodological and ideological proclivities, is that, however they are defined, coping with population and resource issues requires that the time horizons of policy be expanded (Dahlberg 1983). This is so for the obvious reason that the effects of decisions taken or foregone today may not materialize until well into the future, and it may take equally long to reverse such effects should it prove necessary. But beyond this shared premise, it is not simply the sheer length of time that changes as we expand time horizons; entirely new and different factors also come into view as we do so. Donald Kennedy (1984) considers this to be the major lesson derived from scenarios depicting so-called nuclear winter:

> No longer is it acceptable to think of the *sequelae* of nuclear war in terms of minutes, days or even months.... What we have learned from the things biologists and atmospheric physicists are telling us today is that the proper time scale is *years*, and that the processes to which we must look are unfamiliar both in kind and scale. (p. xxxi)

An illustration will help to elaborate this point. Imagine a simple agricultural community, relying on a staple crop and responding to variations in climate. In response to year-to-year fluctuations in temperature and precipitation, this community is likely to keep reserves on hand to compensate for temporary shortfalls. In the face of a succession of climate-induced bad harvests, however, inventory formation by itself will prove inadequate, and a new crop mix as well as a scattering of fields to different sites and elevations may be undertaken. Last, the onset of a progressively inhospitable climate is likely to elicit still more fundamental measures, ultimately including mass migration to favorable climes (Bryson and Murray 1977; Rotberg and Raab 1981).

In this illustration, the duration of time that the community takes into consideration in making its decisions clearly increases from one step to the next. But duration is not the only change that takes place, nor is it the most important. After all, annual fluctuations can go on literally forever without triggering any response over and above emergency stockpiling. Three additional changes also take place: (1) a change in the relevant time frame within which fluctuations in temperature and precipitation are assessed; (2) a change in the nature of the issue that is perceived to require a response, as the time frame shifts; and (3) a change in the type of response that becomes appropriate, as the time frame shifts.

Let us take a closer look at time frames. They, of course, reflect phenomena in the world of nature. But they are also social constructions (Sorokin 1964; Geertz 1973; Le Goff 1980). Time frames serve to structure intersubjective expectations concerning the temporal location of events and processes in society (Durkheim 1912, pp. 14–15). As a result, they constitute "one of the major parameters of the social world" (Zerubavel 1982, p. 2).

In our illustration, the raw datum, fluctuations in temperature and precipitation, remains the same throughout. But the temporal location of this datum changes, and hence also the expectations it engenders, depending on the time frame within which it is considered. Our imaginary community assessed these fluctuations initially in a year-to-year context, then as indicating the possibility of a climatic cycle, and finally as portending fundamental climate change. Thus, the community successively employed three characteristic time frames. We may refer to them as incremental, conjunctural, and secular time frames. Variations of these time frames produced variations in social meaning and social action.

The critical difference among the three time frames lies not in duration, but in the temporal forms that are embedded in them—or to use the awkward term of Emory and Trist (1973), in their "temporal gestalten" (p. 11). To each temporal form there corresponds a particular conception of the elements that go to make up the socially relevant universe. An incremental time frame slices time into a succession of discrete and infinitely divisible units. The corresponding view of the socially relevant universe visualizes its elements as separate and distinct actors, palpable properties, and discontinuous events. A conjunctural time frame depicts the basic units of time as cycles or similar configurations of temporal movement. Here, the corresponding view of the socially relevant universe focuses attention on the processes underlying actors, properties, and events. Secular time is removed still further from everyday experience. It is the temporal form considered basic by, for example, the historians of *la longue durée*. As Jacques Le Goff (1980), one of the leading practitioners of the art, makes clear, *la longue durée* should be regarded not simply as lasting a long time, but "as having the structure of a system" that emerges at one point and dissipates at another (Braudel 1980 p. xi). Similarly, climatologists delineate little and big ice ages, and ecologists make reference to biotic regimes. In each case, the frame of reference is a structural arrangement that governs the functioning of some system within certain boundary conditions. Secular time is measured by change in those structures: Once they are transformed beyond the boundary conditions, a new historical era, climatological age, or ecological regime is said to come into existence.

We can now turn to the task at hand, and apply these notions to our consideration of global population and resource issues. To begin, Figure 10.1 presents a matrix in which population and resources are the column headings, and the threefold differentiation of time frames distinguishes the rows. The first step is to enter into this matrix some specific meanings of the general categories, population and resources, depending on the time frame within which they are assessed.

Which aspects of population and resources are likely to come into focus when viewed through the lenses of an incremental time frame, as we have defined it? In terms of population, the central issue of concern to policymakers no doubt will be changes in the relative size and attributes of their own population as well as in those of strategic and economic competitor and partner nations. By attributes we refer to such factors as age, gender, health and welfare, ethnic composition, spatial distribution, and so on. In short, we have here what the geopolitics literature calls the manpower aspects of population (Sprout and Sprout 1962). What is the analogous characterization of resources? Here, the central issue most likely will be the distribution of and access to strategically and economically important raw materials, including fuel, nonfuel minerals, food, water, and the like. These factors depict what the 1952 Paley Commission called the materials strength of nations (President's Materials Policy Commission 1952).

Now take the second time frame, that of conjunctural movements.

FIGURE 10.1 Time Frames and Issue Sectors

| | Sectors | |
Time Frame	Population	Resources
Incremental		
Conjunctural		
Secular		

The postwar "baby boom" in the United States is an example of a conjunctural movement in population. In retrospect, we understand fully that it affected far more than the relative size and attributes of U.S. population: It also affected the demand for and supply of housing, schools, transportation systems, employment, durable and consumer goods, as well as the cultural landscape, the crime rate, and political processes. In the global context, an analogous phenomenon is the momentum built into current rates of growth in the world population. The most critical issue here is the relationship between such demographic momentum, as it may be described, and the rate at which economic opportunities, social amenities, and physical infrastructure can be supplied (World Bank 1984). On the resource side, the critical issue of a conjunctural nature is the sustainability of resource bases, such as cultivatable land and soils more generally, the marine environment, mineral deposits, gene pools, and the like, given current and anticipated levels of demand (Repetto, 1986).

When we shift to the third time frame, that of secular time, still different dimensions of population and resources are drawn to our attention. On the population side, over the course of human history, some social systems have proved to be too small to maintain themselves as autonomous or even effectively functioning entities, others too large; some have been too densely populated, others too sparsely. We may refer to this issue as the social carrying capacity of different organizational forms. It is a measure of the size of population clusters to be organized, relative to known and acceptable means of social organization (Hawley 1950; Bennett 1976). On the resource side, we may speak of the natural carrying capacity of physical and biological life support systems. This refers to the ability of the biosphere to perform the environmental services on which human (and other) life depends, including the maintenance of heat and energy balances, screening out solar radiation, recycling nutrients, and similar processes (Ehrlich et al. 1977).

By way of summary, then, we can redraw our matrix with these six population and resource issue types entered into the individual cells. The matrix is presented as Figure 10.2. It contains a simple typology, wherein population and resources are differentiated on the basis of time frames. The next step is to identify some current real world analogues of these generic issue types.

ISSUE TYPES AND POLICY PROBLEMS

In the previous section, I argued that when time frames are shifted, generically different aspects of the same issue, such as global population and resources, are identified. The differences are not only substantive, but also epistemological. Here I propose simply to illustrate the different issue types, by describing briefly some actual international policy problems that fall within each. For each case, examples will be provided from the security and the economic fields. But to keep the discussion manageable, it will be limited to those aspects of population and resource issues that could effect major changes in the overall international security order and international economic order, respectively.

FIGURE 10.2. Time Frames and Issue Dimensions

Sectors

Time Frame	Population	Resources
Incremental	Relative Size and Attributes	Distribution and Access
Conjunctural	Demographic Momentum	Sustainable Bases
Secular	Social Carrying Capacity	Natural Carrying Capacity

Relative Size and Attributes of Populations

Notwithstanding the old adage to the contrary, that "God is always on the side of the biggest battalions," there has never been a simple one-to-one correspondence between national population size and international hierarchy. Whatever correspondence there may have existed in the past between the two has become weaker over time, owing to developments in the technology of warfare (Sprout and Sprout 1962). Moreover, there is little evidence that population size in and of itself constitutes a significant source of international conflict behavior (Choucri 1974).

Among the attributes of populations that have proved most potent in triggering violent conflicts in the past are various segmental cleavages within societies. These include, above all, ethnic, religious, and tribal cleavages (Choucri 1974; Enloe 1980), as well as those in the distribution of wealth (Durham 1979; Kleinman 1980). Conflicts triggered by such cleavages may spill over into the international arena. Many regional conflicts that intersect with the global conflict axis today are of this sort, and no change in this situation appears imminent.

Other attributes of national populations that may come to have global security implications include the aging of populations in the industrialized countries. The United States and its European allies will face the prospect of serious shortages of male recruits for their armed forces as early as the late 1980s. The Soviet Union and Eastern Europe face a similar situation, with the problem for the Soviets being in part ameliorated but also complicated by the continued rapid population growth of its Asian minorities (Wilcox 1981; Kutscher 1983). In addition to changes in patterns of recruitment, this development may lead to greater reliance on high-technology war-fighting capabilities and more frequent uses of surrogates.

On the economic side, there appears to be little direct relation between population size per se and location in the international division of labor (World Bank 1984, Appendix, Table 1). Here again, the attributes of populations are a more significant demographic factor. However, insofar as the structure of world industrial production reflects relative labor costs, the combination of relative size and age profiles of labor forces in the industrialized and developing countries will reinforce the growing importance of high-technology and service activities in the industrialized world and the growing role of developing countries as producers and exporters of manufactured products (Organization for Economic Cooperation and Development 1979). The same set of factors will keep migratory pressure on porous national borders, such as that between Mexico and the United States. These developments pose opportunities and constraints for national economic policies in both sets of countries.

Resource Distribution and Access

Gaining control over or securing access to adequate supplies of essential raw materials has long been assumed a necessary condition of becoming and remaining a great power. Moreover, the struggle for raw materials has long been linked to foreign expansionist drives, including warfare and imperialism. There is lively debate about these theses even today (Eckes 1979).

Five industrialized countries—the Soviet Union, the United States, Canada, Australia, and South Africa—possess most of the world's supplies of the 25 minerals that account for over 90 percent of the total value of all minerals consumed (Arad and Arad 1979, p. 64). Hence, it would take an extraordinary confluence of events to alter fundamentally the global balance of strategic power via the raw materials route. This is not to say, however, that conflicts over raw materials are inconceivable.

East-West "resource war" scenarios hinge on the extent to which the West is vulnerable because of its high degree of reliance on raw materials imports, though the United States in most instances relies on imports by volition rather than sheer necessity; whether the Soviet Union is becoming import dependent and is thus compelled to compete for sources abroad; and whether the Soviet Union is pursuing an aggressive resource denial strategy vis-à-vis the West—while also making parts of the West dependent on it, as in the case of the natural gas pipeline (Miller 1980; U.S. Congress 1980, 1981a,b). The regions of greatest concern in this connection are the Persian Gulf, which is both highly unstable politically and the source of a large though declining share of the West's oil; Southern Africa, from the Congo to the Cape, from which the West imports virtually every important nonfuel mineral (in many cases more than half of total consumption), and which also dominates the oil routes around the Cape; and the Indian Ocean, on which the other two border and which contains strategic and commercial sealanes of great importance to the West.

North-South "resource war" scenarios dominated policy debates in the 1970s, following the Organization of Petroleum-Exporting Countries (OPEC) embargo. The central question here is whether the South can manipulate its control over raw materials in such a way as to compel the North to acquiesce to Southern political demands or to react against the South with the threat of force or force itself. The North remains most vulnerable in the area of petroleum, though less to OPEC power than to regional instability. Beyond that, a great deal depends on how the future of South Africa unfolds, but here, too, general instability rather than deliberate supply manipulation is the greater threat (Arad and Arad 1979; Sambunaris 1981; Gilpin 1982).

Intraregional conflicts may affect the supply of raw materials worldwide even if resources are not directly at issue, or intraregional resource conflicts could become internationalized. With two exceptions, the most likely areas in which either might occur have already been enumerated. One of the exceptions is conflict attending resource-induced migration, such as that now taking place in the Himalayan foothills/northern Bangladesh/northeastern India and in the Horn of Africa. The second exception is fresh water as a source of conflict. It is likely to become increasingly salient, involving river diversions (148 of the world's 200 major river basins are shared by two countries), underground aquifers, weather modification, and water augmentation systems (Thompson 1978).

On the economic side, no other raw material is likely to match the impact on the international economic order effected by petroleum after 1973. This is so for three reasons. First, the ratio of minerals consumption to gross domestic product (GDP) has been decreasing steadily throughout the industrialized world, so that the importance of nonfuel minerals to overall economic activity there is declining (Tilton and Landsberg 1983). Second, in the case of the United States, for example, the annual import bill for nonfuel minerals is lower than that for oil on the order of roughly ten to one, so that it is inconceivable for the direct macroeconomic effects of any price increases to be even remotely comparable with the effects that oil price increases had during the last decade. Third, the necessary conditions for successful cartelization of nonfuel minerals markets appear to be met in few if any cases; so that even if cartels were to be formed, they are not likely to be able to sustain themselves for any appreciable length of time (Russett 1984; Tilton and Landsberg 1984).

Temporary interruptions of supplies, however, may well increase as time goes on. One reason is the political instability of supplier countries and regions. Another is the possibility of unforeseen surges in demand as new entrants come into world markets, which in the prevailing climate of low levels of new investment (because of depressed market conditions) and low levels of stockpiles (because of high interest rates) will lead to temporary but ultimately self-correcting shortfalls (Tilton and Landsberg 1984).

For the developing world, the critical resource other than petroleum, of course, is food. Aggregate food availability on a global basis is no longer a constraint on access to food anywhere. Access to food worldwide increasingly has become a matter of effective market demand—which is to say it is a function of social power and government policy, domestic and international (Johnson 1984).

The issues discussed above exemplify the kinds of policy problems that come into view when global population and resource-related factors are viewed through the lens of an incremental time frame. The relevant players and events can be identified with reasonable facility, and in principle the parameters within which they will operate are knowable. When we shift to a conjunctural time frame, very different kinds of policy problems appear.

Demographic Momentum

From about 1750 until 1900, world population grew at about 0.5 percent per annum; from 1900 to 1950, the rate of population increase rose to 1 percent per annum; it reached 2 percent in the 1960s. In the industrialized countries, fertility fell to replacement levels or even below by the 1970s. In the developing countries, however, fertility continued to increase and the death rate to decrease. As a result, the rate of population increase in the developing countries reached 2.4 percent per annum in the 1960s. Owing largely to the impact of China, it has declined to roughly 2 percent since then, but remains between 2 and 4 percent for most low and middle-income countries. Total world population now stands at about 4.8 billion. According to World Bank calculations (1984), the momentum built into the current rate of increase will produce a world population of some 6.3 billion by the year 2000. Because the mothers-to-be themselves are already born, this projection is made with a fair degree of certainty. On standard assumptions, total world population is projected to rise to 9.8 billion by 2050, and to stabilize at around 11 billion in 2150. Even with rapid fertility decline, "the populations of most developing countries are likely to increase by 50 percent or more by 2000; a few, including Kenya and Nigeria, will almost double" (p. 74). In sum, for the next several decades, the world will experience a demographic momentum at a rate and under conditions for which there is no precedent in history.

The most obvious security-related scenario is that of rapid population growth leading to external aggression. In academic parlance, this notion is embodied in the "lateral pressure" model of international conflict (Choucri and North 1975); it used to be known as the struggle for *Lebensraum*. In either guise, its past predictive value has been uncertain at best. It has proved virtually impossible to define the key causal terms, be they scarcity, density, size, or growth rates, in such a manner that the predictions based on them are confirmed with any degree of consistency. It is almost always possible to adduce counterexamples where equal magnitudes have failed to yield expected outcomes (Kleinman 1980). Accordingly, Quincy Wright (1945), in his monumental study of the causes of war, concluded that the effect of population pressure was indeterminate. It is clear, however, that population pressure has, on occasion, served as a pretext or justification for external aggression, as by the geopolitical propagandists in the service of Hitler and Mussolini (Sprout and Sprout 1962, p. 407).

There is a second and closely related indirect link between population pressure and conflict potential. In today's developing countries, populations are likely to encounter institutional barriers long before they encounter absolute physical scarcity—or, perhaps more accurately, segments of populations may encounter physical scarcity because of the existence of such institutional barriers as landholding patterns as well as government policies that favor one population segment at the expense of others. Population pressure then may spill over into international conflict behavior, as it did in the so-called soccer war between El Salvador and Honduras (Durham 1979). Yet it does so not because of population increases per se, but because institutional arrangements deny access to resources to those segments of populations that are often growing most rapidly (Durham 1979; Kleinman 1980). The external spillover may be inadvertent, or it may be deliberate, by the state diverting attention to the international arena or forcing the emigration of the "undesirable" population sectors.

It is also possible to imagine more widespread militarization resulting from large labor surpluses in developing countries, especially among young men. From 1980 to 2000, the working age population of developing countries will increase by 1.15 billion, compared with a corresponding increase of 730 million during the previous 20 years. The record of the recent past is not encouraging with respect to the absorptive capacity of developing countries' economies on such a scale. Increasingly, with the failure of other sectors of the economy to keep pace, governments have become a major employer; for example, in Kenya during the period 1972-80, the public sector accounted for two-thirds of the growth in wage employment (McNamara 1984). For a variety of reasons—the hope of securing domestic stability, the mobilization of mass labor for infrastructural projects, the greater relative availability of security assistance from abroad as compared to economic assistance—the military side of many Third World governments may increase in importance as an employer of manpower. Whether the effects will be benign or malignant, of course, will depend on the overall political situation of individual countries.

Last, rapid urbanization in developing countries has also been cited by observers as a cause for concern. Third World cities have been growing at almost twice the rate of overall populations. UN statistics project an urban agglomeration of some 31 million in Mexico City by the year 2000, 26 million in São Paulo, nearly 23 million in Shanghai, 19 million in Rio, some 17 million in Bombay and Jakarta, and so on, all of which represent unprecedented rates of urban growth. African cities, starting from a smaller base, will not reach those levels of absolute size, but are growing at an even more rapid pace (United Nations 1980). The security-related problem that is feared is social turmoil resulting from an insufficient capacity on the part of cities to service such large increments of population in so short a time. Social turmoil in turn may provide targets of opportunity either for domestic forces to internationalize the problem or for foreign forces to meddle in domestic affairs. The limited evidence available to date is ambiguous (Bienen 1984; Harrod 1986), but it is based on studies of situations that may have been more favorable than those that are now beginning to emerge.

Most of the direct economic effects of this demographic momentum will be felt by the individual countries concerned. Precisely what the effects will be is subject to analytical and empirical dispute, as well as to ideological posturing [cf. Barney (1980) versus Simon (1981)]. Nevertheless, no one argues seriously that countries already characterized by a low per capita income, a heavy dependence on agriculture, insufficient stock of social overhead capital and physical amenities, and a weak institutional infrastructure will be better off with rapid population growth rates than with lower rates. The fact is that many of the developing countries experiencing high rates of population growth fall into this category.

There are likely to be several kinds of international economic effects. First, demographic trends in developing countries will keep their real wages low relative to those in industrialized countries. This sets the stage for increased pressure on the industrialized countries through the mechanisms of international trade and migration, particularly from the middle-income developing countries. Second, barring dramatic international and domestic policy reversals, the recent African initiatives undertaken by international agencies, donor governments, and nongovernmental organizations are likely to be but the first in a series of increasingly permanent "emergency" relief efforts, not only in African but also in other low-income countries.

A third international economic effect that is often postulated is an increase in the global prices of raw materials due to population increases. This is a more dubious proposition. In the case of nonfuel minerals, real production costs have been declining steadily, while current and prospective reserves continue to increase (Tilton and Landsberg 1983). Factors other than population pressure are likely to be responsible for price instability in world oil markets (Russell 1984), though population pressure will continue to raise the private and social costs of such noncommercial sources of energy as fuelwood and dung. Finally, food prices limit access to food for some segments of populations, substantial segments in some countries, but international food prices are not themselves population driven, nor is the share of the world's income devoted to agriculture increasing (Food and Agricultural Organization 1979).

Sustainability of Resource Bases

The question of sustainability here concerns the future of the natural resource capital required to maintain and improve human welfare in an enduring manner. For the purposes of the present discussion, we can divide these resource bases into (1) fossil fuel deposits, (2) nonfuel minerals deposits, and (3) biological resources.

In the area of fossil fuels, a transition away from oil will have to commence within the next 25 years or so, though the margin of error may be considerable as the recent past has shown. Other sources of fossil fuels remain plentiful, as do prospective synthetic fuels based on fossil fuel sources, though their viability will depend on price and environmental effects. The same is true of nuclear power, the major alternative source. Energy conservation continues to offer major supply possibilities (Russell 1984). The key policy problem, then, is one of devising adequate transition strategies.

In the case of nonfuel minerals, most analyses of the quantities likely to be added to current reserves during the next 50 years, even assuming no change in prices, agree that supplies should be adequate. This projection seems to hold for a variety of plausible population scenarios and other changes on the demand side (Ridker 1979). However, difficulties can be expected to arise from such factors as environmental controls, land use restrictions, and the cost of water. These could affect locational decisions of extraction and production, and thus the short-term security of supplies and stability of prices.

In contrast to the previous two, the situation is very different when it comes to what we might call biological resource bases: soils, aquatic systems, forests, biomass fuels, genetic materials, and the like. The problem here is twofold: First, long-term global trend data are either nonexistent or of little use. They are of little use because critical interdependencies—for example, the interrelationships among deforestation, soil cover, fresh water supplies, and the atmosphere, or the impact on this entire set of acid precipitation—either are quite novel or have not been monitored in the past. Second, projections are also problematical, because in many instances they depend almost entirely on assumptions made about the institutional arrangements that will govern these resource bases in the future. Thus, Simon and Kahn (1984) reach the absurdly casuistic conclusion that the "alarms" of the 1960s and 1970s warning of the impending death of the Great Lakes "have turned out totally in error" as shown by the fact that "fishing and swimming conditions there are now excellent" (p. 11). They conveniently neglect to mention that the entire regulatory regime of the Great Lakes was transformed in the interval, largely in response to those "alarms."

At the global level, vast pools of genetic resources, for example, which are situated disproportionately in tropical forests, have yet to be discovered, and many of the fraction that have been discovered are far from having either a market price or a publicly assigned value. Hence, there is no incentive to husband them. Tropical forests themselves are currently treated as though they were a one-time windfall rather than a renewable resource (Guppy 1984). Forestry elsewhere and fisheries everywhere are barely beyond the hunting and gathering stage. The same is true of biomass fuel sources in the developing countries. Tremendous discrepancies exist worldwide between the private gains and social costs of overburdening agricultural soils and aquatic systems. Now, if one assumes that current institutional arrangements will remain as they are, then one is compelled to project unsustainable rates of exploitation with major and possibly global deleterious effects: deforestation, species loss, soil erosion, siltation, salination, and so on—in short, serious biotic impoverishment, together with tremendous economic loss and conflict potential. On the other hand, if one assumes that prices will come to reflect replacement values, that property rights will be adjusted to internalize externalities, and that states will compensate for remaining market failures, then one reaches the conclusion of a virtually limitless and presumably harmonious future. On the historical record, neither set of assumptions merits confidence.

In sum, the fossil fuels sector poses transition problems. The kinds of problems that may emerge in the nonfuel minerals areas are not likely to be shaped uniquely if at all by the sustainability issue in any foreseeable future, but rather by more situational factors affecting distribution and access. Biotic impoverishment would raise quite different kinds of problems. On the security side, seriously degraded resource bases could lead to domestic turmoil and regional conflicts. On the economic side, the possible negative effects run the gamut from opportunity costs (lost genetic resources), to greater vulnerability resulting from more fragile resource bases (soil erosion), to economic dislocation produced by outright depletion of resource bases (forestry, fisheries).

Demographic momentum and the sustainability of resource bases are the types of issues that are raised when one views global population and resources through a conjunctural time frame. As in the previous section, my purpose here has not been to treat these subjects exhaustively, but to provide sufficient illustrative materials so that the more general points can be better appreciated. Both the generic issue types and also the specific policy problems that fall within them differ within this time frame from those that emerge within an incremental time frame. They differ not only substantively but also epistemologically.

Social Carrying Capacity

The issue of what we might call the social carrying capacity of organizational forms arises today at the international level in several forms. One concerns cities, another countries, and a third the state system itself.

With respect to cities, the obvious question is whether the large urban centers projected for the Third World are viable as organizational entities, at a human cost that is acceptable. Urban growth gives rise to economies of scale and agglomeration. But it has not been determined whether there exists any particular urban size at which diseconomies come to outweigh them (Linn 1983; World Bank 1984). Even less is known about the relationship between the urban size and political/ administrative "economies" and "diseconomies." Moreover, for economists there can be no such thing as "overurbanization" in any case, because self-correcting mechanisms would prevent it (Kelley and Williamson 1984). But what is self-correction for the economist may be social turmoil and conflict for the political scientist—not to mention what it is for the individuals involved. As a result, we are left to wonder what a Mexico City of some 31 million inhabitants would look like, to take the most extreme case, in view of how it functions today. But how it functions at its current size may offer little if any guide, one way or the other.

So it is with individual countries. Until recently, the concern was with small and ministates being unviable in an age of ever-larger social formations. But in the light of projected population sizes for some countries, the concern has arisen that they may become too large to be viable as political and administrative entities. It should be noted that the same kinds of conceptual conundrums hold here as in the case of cities. Moreover, the statistics neither inspire confidence nor offer much guidance. For example, on standard fertility assumptions, the population of Kenya, which is 18 million today, is expected to grow to 120 million by 2050; on the assumption of rapid fertility decline, the total is projected to be 50 million fewer (World Bank 1984). Presumably this is a difference with a difference, even in the context of the already "soft" African state (Callaghy 1985), but it is impossible to say if it is a decisive one.

The inadequacy of the state system in the face of global problems has long been an article of faith among visionaries and some practitioners of international affairs, though arguments in defense of the state system have become both more frequent and elegant (Bull 1977; Waltz 1979). The current "crisis of multilateralism" (De Cuellar 1984), however, raises the question of how durable some of the compensatory mechanisms are, such as international regimes (Krasner 1983), that have been designed to attenuate the institutional shortcomings of the international political system. These surely are problems in social ecology, broadly defined (Hawley 1950), but they are not the product of population growth per se. Hence, this is not the place to explore them further.

Natural Carrying Capacity

Nothing better introduces this last set of issues than the hypothesized phenomenon that has come to be known as "nuclear winter" (Turco et al. 1983; Sagan 1983–84; Ehrlich et al. 1984). This is so because nuclear winter crystallizes in extreme form the disruptions of planetary life support systems that can result from certain human intrusions into the biosphere, most of which are the cumulative byproducts of normal, everyday activities.

The notion of nuclear winter refers to the projected effects on the biosphere of the particulate matter that would be a byproduct of nuclear exchange, in addition to the direct effects of blast, fires, and radiation. In brief, as a result of nuclear dust, soot, and smoke, the amount of sunlight reaching the earth would be reduced. A prolonged darkness is projected, followed by a drop in temperatures. The settling of the particulate matter, perhaps after a period of some months, would be accompanied by increased exposure to ultraviolet light, since the nuclear blasts would have resulted in ozone depletion. All the while, ionizing radiation from nuclear fallout would spread. This combination of atmospheric, climatic, and radiological consequences would have directly destructive effects on human, animal, and plant life, but in addition would also impair the normal functioning of natural ecosystems in the longer run. As a result, there would be interruptions in the services provided by these ecosystems, including photosynthesis, maintaining the gaseous composition of the atmosphere, regulating climates, producing fresh water, disposing of wastes, recycling of nutrients, generating and preserving soils, and so on.

Far short of nuclear war or other cataclysmic changes, these life-supporting resources can be degraded by industrial processes and products, agricultural practices, the burning of fossil fuels, deforestation, and a host of other human activities. Much of the attention of policymakers has been devoted to immediate or acute problems, such as the health effects of air and water pollution and toxic waste disposal. Far less attention has been paid to the degradation of natural life support systems. These problems in the first instance are predominantly local or national in scope. But some, such as acid rain, also have transborder and regional effects. Moreover, even local problems may have cumulative effects that may ultimately be global in scope; the buildup of carbon dioxide in the atmosphere is one case in point. Some problems, such as ozone depletion, are global in effect to begin with.

The buildup of carbon dioxide is fairly typical of the kinds of issues that fall into this category: It is the product of the cumulative effects of dispersed processes, no single instance of which may seem—or indeed may be—important in and of itself. It is evolving slowly, and therefore does not force itself onto the policy agenda. In addition, there are enormous uncertainties concerning its dynamic and above all its full range of potential consequences. The evidence suggests that carbon dioxide buildup may have a direct impact on climate and weather via its so-called greenhouse effect, and that it will alter the balance of nature because of its impact on photosynthesis (Eckholm 1984; Schneider and Thompson 1986). The performance of environmental services will be affected worldwide. The extent to which the performance of these services will actually be impaired, as it is on a limited scale with acid rain and much more seriously with ozone depletion, is not known at this time.

The possible international political and economic consequences of disrupting environmental services vary not only in intensity but also in type. For example, to date, the effects of acid rain have been a diplomatic irritant, and they have externalized production costs, thereby subsidizing the production of goods in one place while taxing it in another and reducing overall economic efficiency. Not much is known yet about the specific consequences of carbon dioxide buildup, except that some areas will gain while others will lose. If these shifts are of a sufficient magnitude, then not only the balance of nature but also the balance of power among states could be affected, as agricultural capacity, for instance, is globally redistributed. The effects of ozone depletion are potentially the most serious. Of a sufficient magnitude, they could place in jeopardy the security of nations by directly attacking the health, welfare, and lives of their people.

In sum, this last time frame, secular time, draws our attention to certain aspects of the organization of communities—social, on the one hand, and natural, on the other. With respect to population, it raises the issue of the social carrying capacity of organizational forms; with respect to resources, it raises the issue of the natural carrying capacity of planetary life support systems. These are the most elusive issues by far.

APPROPRIATE POLICY RESPONSES

The U.S. national defense establishment, including its civil defense branch, traditionally viewed the consequences of nuclear war in terms of how much devastation would be caused by any given primary blast and its collateral damage, such as local radioactive fallout. The delayed effects of fallout transported over long distances were subsequently discovered, but their magnitude and scale continue to cause surprises. Only recently has official concern been drawn to such problems as the electromagnetic pulse effects of nuclear blasts on command and control capabilities. The issues raised by nuclear winter are expanding the horizon still further, in terms of both duration and the kinds and scale of phenomena that are taken into consideration. We might say, then, that in assessing the effects of nuclear war, the thinking of military planners has been moving slowly from an incremental time frame, to a conjunctural time frame, and most recently to a secular time frame.

As such a shift takes place, new policy problems are discovered; hence, new policy responses have to be devised. But I have suggested that, as time frames shift, new problems differ from the old not only substantively but also epistemologically. A world composed of discrete time increments and distinct actors having palpable properties is inherently more knowable than one composed of aggregate processes that work themselves out only over the course of the unfolding of some dynamic. Complex systems and their laws of transformation are the most difficult of the three to comprehend with any degree of certainty. In this section, I briefly suggest some of the characteristic implications of these epistemological differences for the formulation of global population and resource policies.

In the world that we see through an incremental time frame, the relevant players and events can be readily identified, their attributes assessed, and judgments made about their significance. Precise calculation and prediction of specific outcomes may never be possible, but the basic parameters of situations can be known and their likely trajectory projected. In principle, information is plentiful. The key analytical problem for policymaking in this domain, therefore, is the standard one of choice under the constraint of how much time and energy can be devoted to any particular decision. Hence, care must be taken that the usual cognitive and institutional mechanisms that reduce information to manageable proportions do not at the same time distort it.

For example, David Baldwin (1985) shows in his thorough and provocative study that there exists a general tendency to underestimate the efficacy of economic instruments of statecraft and, by implication, to overrate the utility of the role of force. Even a casual reading of congressional hearings on possible resource wars, which were referred to in the previous section, underscores Baldwin's argument. In addition, the same congressional sources indicate that the East-West dimension of strategic minerals is weighted far more heavily than any other, though the justifications may be questionable; that such likely triggers of resource-related conflict as struggles over fresh water supplies are overshadowed by a preoccupation with strategic minerals; and that the attributes of populations as an indigenous source of conflict are poorly understood.

Formulating policy in response to the phenomena that appear within a conjunctural time frame is subject to more fundamental constraints. To begin with, there are some unknowns here. Moreover, factors that are assumed to remain constant within an incremental time frame become variable here. And it is inherently more difficult to produce an intended effect on processes than it is on actors and events. Nevertheless, as we saw in the previous section, the key factor that will determine the outcomes of the various conjunctural movements we examined is the adequacy of institutional mechanisms. Hence, it should serve as the thematic focal point for policymaking.

Let us take U.S. policy as an illustration again. On the population side, concern has been limited largely to family planning, and even this commitment has been called into question by the present administration. There has been little official strategic or economic thinking devoted to the broader demographic issues that we examined above, or to the social, economic, and political arrangements on which their impact will hinge. As for securing sustainable resource bases, the United States has relied largely on the institution of the market. This seems to have worked reasonably well in the nonfuel minerals sector. It might work in the realm of commercial fuels if governments, including the U.S. government, allowed the market to operate effectively. But by definition, market forces are not going to take care of the problem of noncommercial fuels. Moreover, future progress in the world food system depends on institutional and policy changes primarily within but also among countries. Last, in the realm of biological resources, direct intervention is required to compensate for the absence of any pricing mechanism for many of these resources, and for the disjunction between the private and social costs of others, so as to begin to institute the conditions under which market forces could play an effective role in the future.

The population and resource issues that emerge within a secular time frame reflect very much an agenda that is still in the making. A good deal of effort will continue to be devoted to articulating the dimensions of this agenda. At the intergovernmental level, the process was begun at the Stockholm environment conference in 1972, and different strands were introduced at the subsequent U.N. conferences on population (1974, 1984) and human settlements (1976). On the other hand, beyond this stage of agenda setting, there is a core problem that increasingly has come into focus. It concerns the effects of human scale on the productive and regenerative capacities of ecosystems. These effects, if deleterious, in principal could be countered either by modifying the factor of human scale, which would include modifying forms of social organization, or by attempting directly to manage ecosystems. Obviously, neither can be accomplished extensively, because humankind lacks both the knowledge and the policy instrumentalities to do so.

The range of policy options therefore narrows down to various interim measures designed to limit seriously disruptive human intrusions into the biosphere. Even this is a herculean task at the present. The key analytical problem for decision making is the trade-off between potentially high risks and inadequate knowledge about them. The problem is compounded by the fact that complete information in many instances may never be at hand, and even adequate information in some instances may be produced either too late or perhaps only as a byproduct of the very outcomes that one is seeking to avoid. Analytically, what is called for, therefore, is a "bias shift" in decision making, away from a conventional problem-solving mode, wherein doing nothing would be favored on burden-of-proof grounds, toward a risk-averting mode, wherein prudent contingency measures would be undertaken to avoid risks we would rather not face or to compensate for them if they arose—much as we do in the realm of national security.

Appropriate policy instrumentalities follow from this proposed "bias shift." To say that they are appropriate, however, is not to imply that they can be easily put into place. First of all, the collective knowledge base on which more informed decisions can be based must be expanded. This entails research, monitoring, modeling, information exchange, and the like. The major difficulty here, aside from expense, is the adversarial context within which knowledge will be produced and used—akin to the never-ending debates between the tobacco industry and the public health establishment in the United States, but without the possibility of closure being imposed by a central arbiter. Second, in most instances, the costs of responding will be direct and visible, whereas the benefits are likely to be diffuse and longer term. As a result, mechanisms will have to be evolved to cope with the inevitable "free rider" problem and to establish schemes of burden sharing. Both are extraordinarily difficult to achieve in the decentralized international polity. The national policies of individual states, and even more so the collective policies of the international community as a whole, remain in a very early stage of development in this domain.

In sum, it is possible to conceive in broad terms certain characteristic features of appropriate policies in the population and resources fields, deriving from the epistemological dimensions of the three time frames through which we viewed population and resource problems. Our theoretical discussion of social time, then, does have practical policy consequences.

CONCLUSION

The ecology of international conflict and of international economic relations is changing today, as it always has. The major difference between past and present in this regard is that the ever-evolving interplay between socioeconomic forces and biophysical factors has reached planetary proportions. To the extent that policymakers express any explicit concern with the issues arising from this transformation, they would prefer to handle them as thoroughly conventional issues. The more visionary advocates outside of government, for their part, prefer to believe that conventional aspects of these issues no longer exist, or are not as important, as the novelty that they seek to have us embrace. If the former is akin to apprehending the future through a rearview mirror, in McLuhan's inimitable phrase, the latter is an instance of looking right over the horizon altogether and not keeping one's eyes on the road directly ahead. The gap between the two is enormous; and it must be narrowed if policy responses are to deal effectively with emerging global realities.

It has been a premise of this essay that the manner in which we conceptualize policy problems has direct practical consequences. I have suggested that the dimension of time serves as a particularly useful basis for conceptualizing global population and resource issues. Now, any set of categories ultimately is arbitrary. But the conceptualization developed here allows us, through one and the same analytic operation, to display the diversity of the socially relevant meanings of global population and resource issues, and to group these diverse meanings in such a way that they immediately convey some policy strategies.

Focusing on the dimension of time has two other advantages over possible alternatives. First, time frames as depicted earlier in this essay are not idiosyncratic to the observer. They are, to borrow Durkheim's apt language (1912), "représentations collectives" that express "réalités collectives" (p. 13). That is to say, they are primordial aspects of social structure. Second, in the light of the current global ecological transition, there are few deeply embedded aspects of social structure that it is more important to bring closer to the surface of conscious concern. Of all the inchoate mental imageries that shape society's approach to international order (Ruggie 1972, 1978), few can do greater real world damage to our collective future than the effects of assessing ecological developments around us within the wrong time frame.

Having said all that, I must conclude by acknowledging that this essay has made but a modest beginning. My discussion has considerably simplified the complex relations that go on within and among time frames. I have focused on only three characteristic time frames; of course there are others. Even more seriously, my discussion may give the impression that the three are distinct and separate. They are distinct, but they are not separate. As Emory and Trist (1973) have put it: "Any person or group is at any instant in many 'presents', each corresponding to what is a phase of the temporal gestalten in which he or it is embedded" (p. 11). Obviously there is only one present, but different time frames place it in different temporal locations and thus alter its signification. Last, I have ignored the systematic interrelationships that may exist among the different time frames, whereby acting on phenomena that are highlighted within one affects phenomena in the others, or whereby trade-offs and perhaps even contradictions may exist between what is desirable in one time frame as opposed to what is desirable in others. These are important issues that will have to be dealt with—all in good time.

REFERENCES

Arad, R. W., and U. B. Arad. (1979) "Scarce Natural Resources and Potential Conflict." In Arad et al. (eds.), *Sharing Global Resources*, pp. 25-104. New York: McGraw Hill, for the Council on Foreign Relations.

Baldwin, D. A. (1985) *Economic Statecraft*. Princeton, NJ: Princeton University Press.

Barney, G. O. (ed.) (1980) *The Global 2000 Report to the President of the U.S.*, 2 vols. New York: Pergamon Press.

Bennett, J. W. (1976) *The Ecological Transition*. New York: Pergamon Press.

Bienen, H. (1984) "Urbanization and Third World Stability." *World Development* 12:661-91.

Braudel, F. (1980) *On History*, trans. by Sarah Matthews. Chicago: University of Chicago Press.

Bryson, R. A., and T. J. Murray. (1977) *Climates of Hunger: Mankind and the World's Changing Weather*. Madison: University of Wisconsin Press.

Bull, H. (1977) *The Anarchical Society: A Study of Order in World Politics*. London: Macmillan.
Callaghy, T. M. (1985) "The Patrimonial Administrative State in Africa." Prepared for "Symposium on African State in Transition," Georgetown University, February 22-23.
Castle, E. N., and K. A. Price. (eds.) (1983) *U.S. Interests and Global Natural Resources: Energy, Minerals, Food*. Washington, D.C.: Resources for the Future.
Choucri, N. (1974) *Population Dynamics and International Violence*. Lexington, MA: Lexington-Heath.
Choucri, N., and R. C. North. (1975) *Nations in Conflict*. San Francisco: W. H. Freeman.
Dahlberg, K. (1983) "Contextual Analysis: Taking Space, Time, and Place Seriously." *International Studies Quarterly* 27:257-66.
DeCuellar, J. P. (1984) "What Future for Multilateralism?" Speech to the Geneva Diplomatic Club and the Centre d'Etudes Pratiques de la Negociation Internationale, Geneva, July 3.
Durham, W. H. (1979) *Scarcity and Survival in Central America: Ecological Origins of the Soccer War*. Stanford, CA: Stanford University Press.
Durkheim, E. (1912) *Les Formes Elémentaires de la Vie Religieuse*. Paris: Felix Alcan.
Eckes, A. E., Jr. (1979) *The United States and the Global Struggle for Minerals*. Austin: University of Texas Press.
Eckholm, E. (1984) "New Predictions See Rise in CO_2 Transforming Earth." *New York Times* (August 7):C1-2.
Ehrlich, P. R., A. Ehrlich, and J. Holdren. (1977) *Ecoscience: Population, Resources, Environment*. San Francisco: W. H. Freeman.
Ehrlich, P. R., et al. (1984) *The Cold and the Dark: The World After Nuclear War*. New York: W. W. Norton.
Emory, F. E., and E. L. Trist. (1973) *Towards a Social Ecology: Contextual Appreciation of the Future in the Present*. London: Plenum.
Enloe, C. H. (1980) *Ethnic Soldiers: State Security in Divided Societies*. Athens: University of Georgia Press.
Food and Agriculture Organization. (1979) *Agriculture: Toward 2000*. Rome: Food and Agriculture Organization.
Geertz, C. (1973) "Person, Time, and Conduct in Bali." In C. Gertz (ed.), *The Interpretation of Cultures*, pp. 360-411. New York: Basic Books.
Gilpin, S. (1982) "Minerals and Foreign Policy." *Africa Report* 27: 16-22.
Guppy, N. (1984) "Tropical Deforestation: A Global View." *Foreign Affairs* 62:928-65.
Harrod, J. (1986) *The Unprotected Worker: The Social Relations of Subordination*. New York: Columbia University Press (in press).
Hawley, A. H. (1950) *Human Ecology: A Theory of Community Structure*. New York: Ronald Press.
Johnson, D. G. (1984) "World Food and Agriculture." In J. L. Simon and H. Kahn (eds.), *The Resourceful Earth: A Response to "Global 2000,"* pp. 67-112. New York: Basil Blackwell.

Kelley, A. C., and J. G. Williamson. (1984) *What Drives Third World City Growth? A Dynamic General Equilibrium Approach*. Princeton, NJ: Princeton University Press.

Kennedy, D. (1984) "Introduction." In P. R. Ehrlich et al. (eds.), *The Cold and the Dark: The World after Nuclear War*, pp. xxv–xxxv. New York: W. W. Norton.

Kleinman, D. S. (1980) *Human Adaptation and Population Growth*. Montclair, N J: Allanheld, Osmun.

Krasner, S. D. (ed.) (1983) *International Regimes*. Ithaca, NY: Cornell University Press.

Kutscher, G. (1983) "The Impact of Population Dynamics on Military Manpower Problems: An International Comparison." *Armed Forces and Society*. 9:265–75.

Le Goff, J. (1980) *Time, Work, and Culture in the Middle Ages*, trans. by Arthur Goldhammer. Chicago: University of Chicago Press.

Linn, J. (1983) *Cities in the Developing World*. New York: Oxford University Press.

McNamara, R. S. (1984) "Time Bomb or Myth: The Population Problem." *Foreign Affairs* 62:1107–31.

Miller, J. A. (ed.) (1980) *The Resource War in 3D—Dependency, Diplomacy, Defense*. Pittsburgh: World Affairs Council of Pittsburgh.

Organization for Economic Cooperation and Development. (1979) *Facing the Future*. Paris: Organization for Economic Cooperation and Development.

President's Materials Policy Commission. (1952) *Resources for Freedom. Report of the President's Materials Policy Commission*. Washington, D.C.: U.S. Government Printing Office.

Repetto, Robert. (1985) *The Global Possible: Resources, Development, and the New Century*. New Haven, CT: Yale University Press (in press).

Ridker, R. G. (1979) "Resource and Environmental Consequences of Population and Economic Growth." In P. H. Hauser (ed.), *World Population and Development*, pp. 99–123. Syracuse: Syracuse University Press.

Rotberg, R. I., and T. K. Raab. (eds.) (1981) *Climate and History: Studies in Interdisciplinary History*. Princeton, NJ: Princeton University Press.

Ruggie, J. G. (1978) "Changing Frameworks of International Collective Behavior: On the Complementarity of Contradictory Tendencies." In N. Choucri and T. Robinson (eds.), *Forecasting in International Relations*, pp. 384–406. San Francisco: W. H. Freeman.

———. (1972) "The Structure of International Organization: Contingency, Complexity, and Post-Modern Form." In *Peace Research Society (International) Papers, The London Conference, 1971, Vol.18*, pp. 73–91.

Russell, M. (1984) "Energy Is an International Good." In E. N. Castle and K. A. Price (eds.), *U.S. Interests and Global Natural Resources: Energy, Minerals, Food*, pp. 10–47. Washington, D.C.: Resources for the Future.

Russett, B. (1984) "Dimensions of Resource Dependence: Some Elements of Rigor in Concept and Policy Analysis." *International Organization* 38:481–99.

Sagan, C. (1983–84) "Nuclear War and Climatic Catastrophe: Some Policy Implications." *Foreign Affairs* 62:257–92.

Sambunaris, G. (1981) "Strategic Minerals and the Third World." *Agenda* 4:11–16.

Schneider, S. H., and S. L. Thompson. (1986) "Future Changes in the Global Atmosphere." In *The Global Possible: Resources, Development, and the New Century*. Robert Reppetto (ed.) New Haven, CT: Yale University Press (in press).

Simon, J. L. (1981) *The Ultimate Resource*. Princeton, NJ: Princeton University Press.

Simon, J. L., and H. Kahn (eds.) (1984) *The Resourceful Earth: A Response to 'Global 2000.'* New York: Basil Blackwell.

Sorokin, P. A. (1964) *Sociocultural Causality, Space, Time*. New York: Russell & Russell.

Sprout, H., and M. Sprout. (1962) *Foundations of International Politics*. Princeton, NJ: Van Nostrand.

Thompson, R. L. (1978) "Water as a Source of Confict." *Strategic Review* 6:62–72.

Tilton, J. E., and H. H. Landsberg. (1983) "Non-Fuel Minerals—The Fear of Shortages and the Search for Policies." In E. N. Castle and K. A. Price (eds.), *U.S. Interests and Global Natural Resources: Energy, Minerals, Food*, pp. 48–80. Washington, D.C.: Resources for the Future.

Turco, R. P., et al. (1983) "Nuclear Winter: Global Consequences of Multiple Nuclear Explosions." *Science* 222:1283–92.

United Nations. (1980) *Patterns of Urban and Rural Population Growth*. New York: United Nations.

U.S. Congress. (1981a) *A Congressional Handbook on U.S. Materials Import Dependency/Vulnerability*. 97th Congress, 1st Session.

———. (1981b) *The Possibility of a Resource War in Southern Africa*. 97th Congress, 1st Session, July 8.

———. (1980) *Nonfuel Minerals Policy Review*. 96th Congress, 2nd Session, September 18.

Waltz, K. N. (1979) *Theory of International Politics*. Reading, MA: Addison-Wesley.

Wilcox, J. G. (1981) "Military Implications of the Global 2000 Report." *Military Review* 61:30–39.

World Bank. (1984) *World Development Report, 1984*. New York: Oxford University Press, for the World Bank.

Wright, Q. (1942) *A Study of War*. Chicago: University of Chicago Press.

Zerubavel, E. (1982) "The Standardization of Time: A Sociohistorical Perspective." *American Journal of Sociology* 88:1–23.

11
Using GLOBUS to Explore Alternative Taxation and Security Policies in the West
Thomas R. Cusack and Barry B. Hughes

Among the most important political/economic trends of the century has been the regular and considerable growth in the share of national economic product accruing to governments around the world. Political debates have recently intensified in Western industrialized countries with respect to this trend and with respect to specific components of government spending financed with these growing revenues. In this essay we are concerned especially with the potential political and economic impacts of different long-range patterns of taxation and defense spending in major Western industrialized nations. The analysis deals with potential long-term national and international trends that might emanate from the imposition of different options in these policy areas. It is undertaken with the assistance of a large-scale computer simulation model, GLOBUS,[1] that incorporates representations of domestic and international political and economic processes for 25 major nations.

A word of caution needs to be put forward at the outset. The results and interpretations provided here are not meant to be forecasts, even conditional ones, of the future. Our goals are more modest, and we do not intend to suggest that GLOBUS is an instrument for prognostication. Rather, our intent has been to attempt to synthesize in a formal model diverse bodies of knowledge spanning a variety of interconnected social phenomena. In the model development process and through analyses with it, we hope to advance our understanding of the political/economic world.

In the pages that follow, we will first turn to a description of the recently developed global simulation model, GLOBUS, used to carry out this study. Space limitations preclude the possibility of an extensive description of the model, but the more general attributes and characteristics are specified here. The succeeding section then provides some more detailed information on the structure of two model sectors, the national economic module and the government resource allocation module, which play central roles in the simulation analysis undertaken for this study. Following that, we present a description of the scenarios that are to be examined along with a set of detailed questions that guide our analysis. This then leads to an analysis of the alternative scenario results at both the international and the national levels. The chapter concludes with a restatement of both the concerns that have guided our analysis and the principal results that have emanated therefrom.

GLOBUS: GENERATING LONG-TERM OPTIONS BY USING SIMULATION

The simulation model, GLOBUS, employed in this study has been designed, in part, to carry out issue analysis centering on questions dealing with domestic and international political and economic behavior. The utility of the model rests on its capacity to examine stresses and strains governments might confront in coping with the complex political and economic environments surrounding them. The model includes representations of 25 nations and their governments (listed in Appendix A). Together these 25 countries produce 85 percent of the global product and contain 75 percent of global population.

Included in the model are basic political and economic interactions both within and among nations. Each of the submodels or modules within GLOBUS represents policy and response functions of government in a specific substantive area or mixtures of such functions and the environmental processes endogenous to the area. An overview of the substantive problems and government policy processes is provided in Figure 11.1.

On the international side, the foreign policy module represents the formation and execution of the policy orientations that each state develops toward others in the multistate system (lower right-hand quadrant of Figure 11.1). Based on an action/reaction model, with political and economic considerations at a variety of levels changing the state's reactivity functions, the module generates hostile and cooperative flows in a dyadic and directional manner among the 25 states represented in the GLOBUS system.

Included as well on the international side is the representation of major international economic flows (lower left-hand quadrant of Figure 11.1). The principal concern here is with the levels and directions of

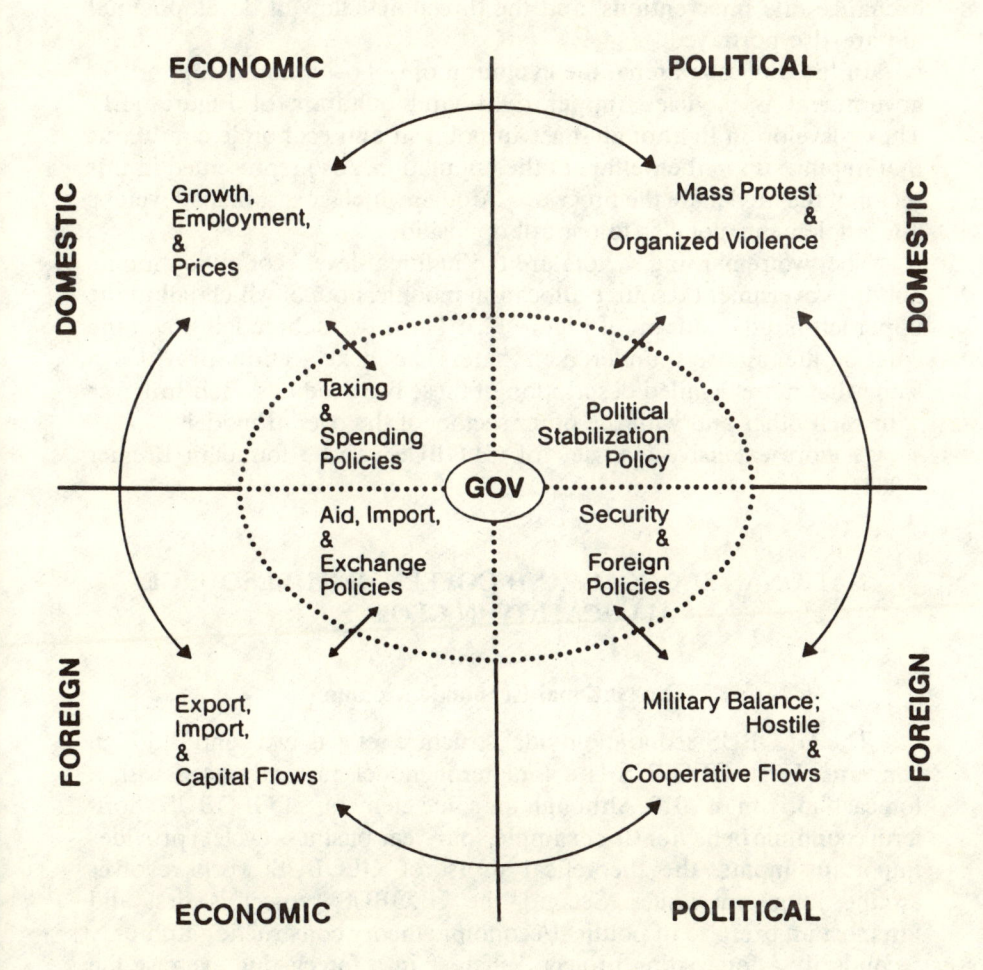

FIGURE 11.1. The role of government in relation to its environment.

trade in six major commodity groupings among the 25 GLOBUS states and a residual "rest of world." Represented are those purely economic factors and processes as well as government policy interventions that introduce bias into what otherwise would be an economically rational exchange pattern in a large and varied market. Borrowing and lending, exchange rate interventions, and the directional flow of developmental aid are also portrayed.

In the domestic arena, the evolution of opposition and support for government is modeled (upper right-hand quadrant of Figure 11.1). These develop in light of changes in political and economic conditions that impinge upon the welfare of the population. Also represented in this sector of the model are the processes through which government develops and implements policies to control opposition.

The two remaining sectors are the national-level economic module and the government resource allocation module, both of which fall in the upper left-hand quadrant of Figure 11.1. These two submodels are at the core of the analysis undertaken here. The next section provides a somewhat more detailed description of these two modules, their linkages with each other and with the other sectors of the overall model.

A more extensive overview of GLOBUS can be found in Bremer (1984).

NATIONAL ECONOMY AND GOVERNMENT RESOURCE ALLOCATION IN GLOBUS

The National Economic Module

The GLOBUS economic model structure reflects two central design concerns. First, GLOBUS is a long-term model currently used with a forecast horizon of 2010. Although for some elements of GLOBUS short-term economic behavior (for example, four-year business cycles) provides important inputs, the theoretical thrust of GLOBUS work revolves around long-term issues. Second, the GLOBUS project is first and foremost an exercise in political/economic theory construction and only secondarily a forecasting project. Whereas in a forecasting exercise the model should be carefully tailored to the issue(s) addressed, issue identification is much less rigorous and fixed in GLOBUS. The GLOBUS economic model must interact with not only the government resource allocation module described below, but with the international trade structure, the international conflict/cooperation module, and the domestic political module. Some issues to be investigated with GLOBUS require supply-side attention—the impact on capital formation of government activities, the implications for labor force size of alternative demographic futures, or the effect on economic growth of alternative technological progress patterns. Others force concern with demand—governmental taxing and spending levels, disposable income growth patterns, or alternative personal consumption/savings trade-offs. Still others direct attention to trade—pricing patterns in other countries or relative currency values.

In response to these design concerns, the GLOBUS economic module is a dynamic, general economic equilibrium-seeking model. It is dynamic because of the long-term, dynamic character of GLOBUS generally. It is general economic (that is, multiple sector and representing the complete economy) because the representation of long-term structural change requires a multiple-sector model, and a partial representation of the economy would be inadequate. Specifically, the sectors are agriculture, nonenergy raw materials, energy, manufactures (other than armaments), armaments, and nonfactor services. These are fairly standard except for armaments, which enter GLOBUS for obvious reasons. The model is equilibrium seeking because it represents both the demand and supply sides of national economies and the continual search, whether by market or nonmarket mechanisms, for an equilibrium condition that is itself continually changing.

In fact, the balance between supply and demand side representation and the reliance on explicit equilibrating mechanisms are greater in GLOBUS than in most prior global models. For instance, the Meadows/Forrester (Meadows et al. 1974) and Mesarovic/Pestel (1974) models were dominated by the supply side, while Leontief et al.'s UN model (1977) heavily emphasized the demand side.

The concerns of many more strictly economic global models (see Gupta and Paula 1978; Gunning et al. n.d.; Tims and Waelbroeck 1982; Hickman 1983) have been more specific than those of GLOBUS: an interest in the effects of developed country growth rates on less-developed countries (LDCs) (the first World Bank model), of foreign exchange constraints on LDCs (the second), of the oil shocks, of protectionism, etc. The charge to the GLOBUS economic model of treating a large number of issues strongly influenced the decision to structure an equilibrium-seeking model with explicit demand and supply sides.

The GLOBUS economic model equilibrium-seeking structure contains three levels, represented in Figure 11.2: the "physical" economy of production and demand by sector (modeled in value terms), the domestic financial economy centering on savings and capital formation, and the international financial economy built around trade and capital flows. Each of these levels has a principal equilibrating variable: price, interest rate, and exchange rate, respectively. The degree to which these equil-

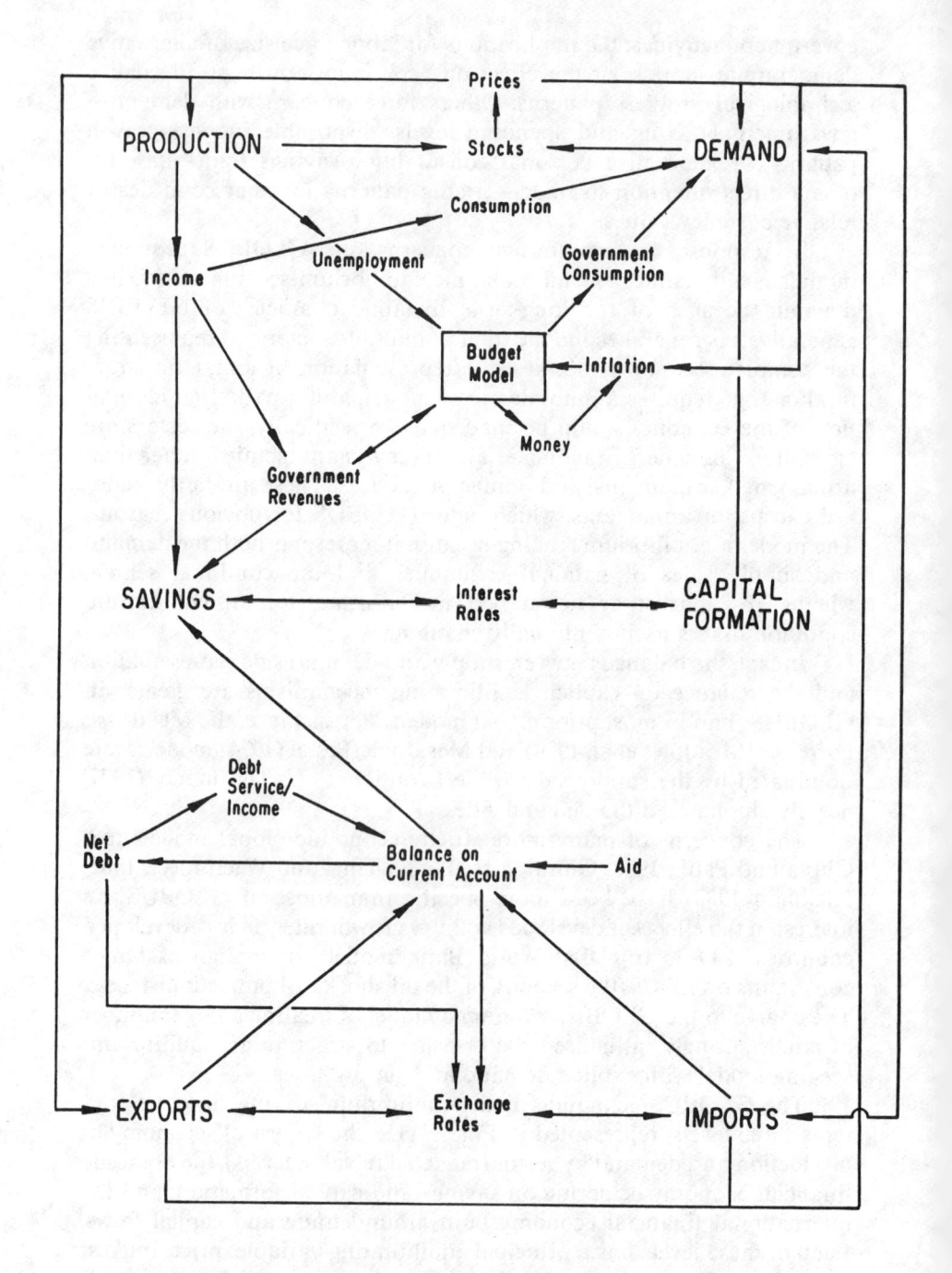

FIGURE 11. 2. The three economy levels elaborated.

ibrating variables are allowed to work in a market varies, of course, dramatically across countries.

These three levels interact in a large number of ways. The income generated by production provides private consumption demand and contributes to savings. The prices that clear demand and supply do so by affecting trade patterns and investment decisions, as well as domestic consumption patterns and production levels. The difference between savings and investment has its equal in the balance on current account. Figure 11.2 sketches only the skeleton of the three levels and the interactions among them.

Figure 11.3 fleshes out, as an example, the core of the physical economic level. It shows a production function based on capital, labor, and technological inputs. This model level makes a sectoral distinction between gross output, value added, and production available for final demand (with consistency maintained by an input/output matrix that changes endogenously in response to economic development level). On the demand side, the model distinguishes expenditure components (private consumption, governmental consumption, capital formation, exports and imports), also by sector. Sectoral stocks serve as buffers between supply and demand, and their levels signal relative price changes.

More detail on all three levels of the economic module is available in Hughes (1985a).

The Government Resource Allocation Module

The model within this sector represents the development of a government budget. It portrays the decision-making processes involved in setting expenditure levels and altering rates of revenue raising. Budgeting is depicted as a set of interrelated activities wherein forces at different levels of government seek to satisfy their interests. As structured in the model, this activity is represented in part by a process whereby the political leadership and those responsible for the financial activities of the government develop and attempt to impose their preference with respect to the overall sum of budgetary outlays. Standing in opposition to this preference as well as in competition with each other are the different sectors of government responsible for its major functions and programs. These competitors attempt to advance their interests and perform their responsibilities in part by acquiring the budgetary resources they calculate as necessary or minimally required. On the revenue side, decisions are depicted as a combination of intention and drift. Their form is seen as following from the leadership's (and other financial authorities') desires for maintaining the fiscal solvency of the government

FIGURE 11.3. Core economic model.

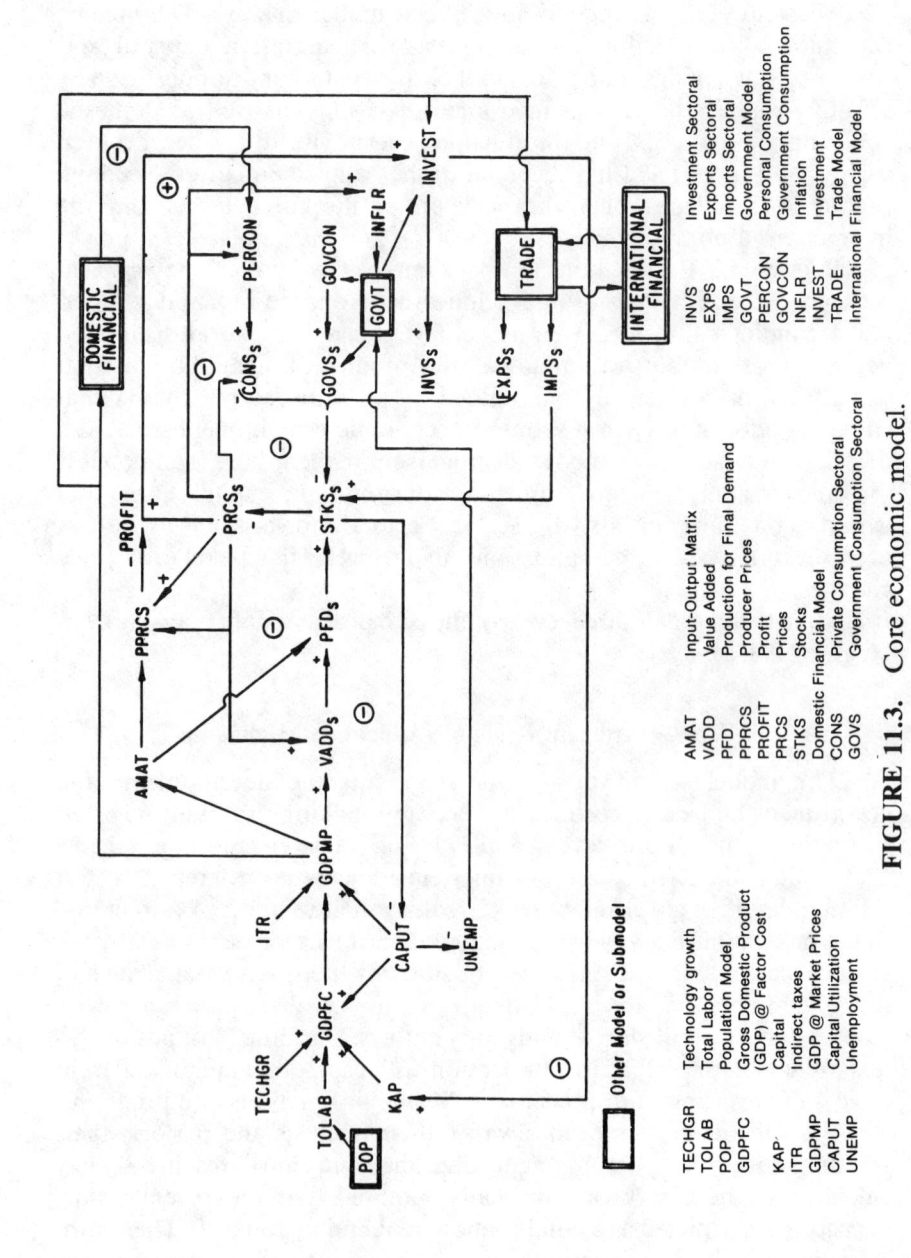

TECHGR	Technology growth
TOLAB	Total Labor
POP	Population Model
GDPFC	Gross Domestic Product (GDP) @ Factor Cost
KAP	Capital
ITR	Indirect taxes
GDPMP	GDP @ Market Prices
CAPUT	Capital Utilization
UNEMP	Unemployment

AMAT	Input-Output Matrix
VADD	Value Added
PFD	Production for Final Demand
PPRCS	Producer Prices
PROFIT	Profit
PRCS	Prices
STKS	Stocks
Domestic Financial Model	
CONS	Private Consumption Sectoral
GOVS	Government Consumption Sectoral

INVS	Investment Sectoral
EXPS	Exports Sectoral
IMPS	Imports Sectoral
GOVT	Government Model
PERCON	Personal Consumption
GOVCON	Government Consumption
INFLR	Inflation
INVEST	Investment
TRADE	Trade Model
International Financial Model	

☐ Other Model or Submodel

and implementing policies in accordance with the leadership's stabilization policy concerns. Figure 11.4 provides an overview of the budgetary model. A generally similar approach can be found in Fischer and Kamlet (1984).

The simulation model of the budgetary decision-making process is divided into four major parts or blocks. This division is intended to capture some of the very distinctive features of the budgetary process. It has as well been heavily influenced by the desire to structure the model in such a way as to enhance our ability to provide an empirical basis for important decision-making parameters.

The four blocks with the module include the following. Block 1 deals with the development of desired spending levels both at the most aggregate level, that is, total spending, and at more disaggregated levels, that is, spending for programs and program components within the civilian and defense areas. The first block also deals with the politically tinged reconciliation of the potentially inconsistent aspirations for the broader categories of spending, viz., total, defense, exhaustive civilian, and capital expenditures, as well as debt management payments. The second and third blocks deal with the disaggregation of defense and civilian expenditures among the different program components within these broad areas. For example, defense appropriations are allocated toward the purchase of capital and labor in the conventional area and for the purpose of maintaining and acquiring strategic nuclear capabilities. On the civilian side in the exhaustive area, appropriations are allocated across social welfare programs, education, etc. The fourth block includes processes for altering four tax rates in light of fiscal and stabilization policy concerns.

Within the first block, desired total spending is represented as being a function of the degree to which authorities wish to adhere to a balanced budget given the level of expected revenues and a stabilization policy response. The latter's formulation hinges upon the type of system being represented, with unemployment motivating response in Western developed economies and foreign sector imbalances stimulating action within centrally planned and developing economies.

The defense and civilian bureaucracies are portrayed as independently formulating desired levels of spending for their areas. In the defense sector, two major programs are represented: The first deals with conventional military capabilities and the second with strategic nuclear systems. In each of these programs, perceived security requirements and pressures for maintaining or expanding previous operational levels generate desires that are aggregated to produce a total for the desired level of defense spending. For both areas as well, security requirements come to be defined on the basis of expected levels of threats, one's own

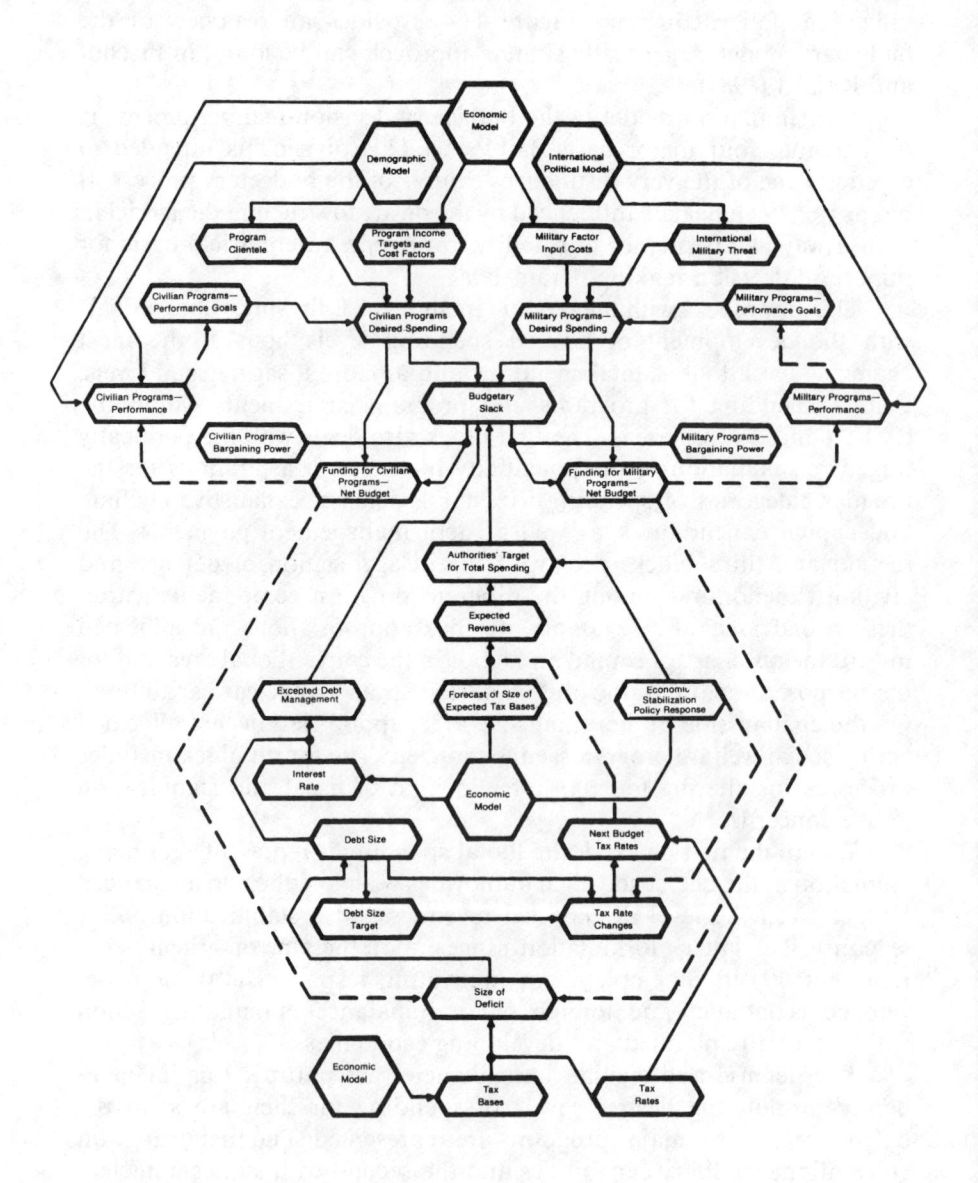

FIGURE 11.4. Major linkages in the budgetary model.

capabilities, expected levels of assistance from other states, a goal with respect to security, and direct cost calculations. Along with capability depreciation considerations, these cost calculations also enter in the determination of spending level aspirations with respect to maintaining previous levels of performance.

The civilian sector includes a number of programs. Two main streams are represented—the first on the exhaustive side and the second on the capital side. With respect to the first, two parallel sets of processes are included. The first is a representation of the development of a desired spending level at an aggregate level for all of the programs within the area. Demographic and economic conditions along with pressure to maintain or expand previous levels of performance in the whole sector generate a desired level of spending. Concurrent with this, but at a very disaggregated level, individual program requests are formulated, based on cost, clientele, and performance considerations, for later use in the allocation block (no. 3). On the capital side, economic growth considerations and a factor representing the tendency for government to assume responsibility for capital formation enter into the determination of a desired level of spending.

The desired aggregate spending levels are principal elements in the reconciliation and finalization of the expenditure side of the budget. However, one other expenditure category also comes into play. Debt management payments are also calculated and are treated in the reconciliation of the different desired spending levels. In that phase, they are normally dealt with as mandatory and have the potential for crowding out one or more of the other spending categories.

Following the generation of these competing levels of aspiration for spending, a reconciliation process is invoked. The degree to which a particular desire is realized hinges critically on the bargaining strength of the sector and the relative presence or absence of slack in the entire system.

Having finalized major expenditure levels for the planning period, specific programs are then allocated funds. In the defense sector, distribution occurs principally between conventional and (where appropriate) strategic components (block 2). Further distribution then occurs on the conventional side, with the appropriated funds being divided between capital (demand is transferred to the arms sector of the economic model) and labor (demand on the service sector). The latter division derives directly from the desired capital-to-labor ratio and expected existing capital stock in the planning period.

In the civilian sector, allocations are made among the various programs and subprograms up to the planned total for nondefense expenditures (block 3). These allocations hinge upon existing program expenditures, requested program expenditures, and the aggregate of existing, requested, and finalized expenditures.

Resource extraction decisions by government are effectively concentrated in the alteration of taxation rates (block 4). These are represented as following from governmental authorities' basic tendency to alter previous levels of extraction in light of overall performance within the economy, concern for restricting the expansion of the size of the public debt relative to the capacity of the economy, and, in the case of both centrally planned and developing economies, untoward developments within the external sector. For more detail on this model, see Cusack (1985).

FOCUS AND IMPLEMENTATION OF SIMULATION ANALYSIS

The central focus of this essay is on alternative patterns of government revenue raising and spending and the impact of those patterns on the broader political economy. There are two eternal debates focusing on these issues, which, in large part because of sputtering economic performance in the last decade, have intensified for industrial countries. These are the size and nature of defense efforts and, even more fundamentally, the overall size of the public sector.

There is no real debate that defense spending has always been and remains an essential aspect of state policy—in fact, it is based directly on the territorial responsibilities and sovereignty of statehood. As Rose (1976, p. 249) puts it, external defense and internal security are the sine qua non activities, those that appeared with the state system and preceded all subsequent expansion of state roles. The debate, of course, rages over the magnitude of the defense effort, specifically the budget size.

In the late 1970's the debate took new life. As a reaction to what was seen as a diminution in the relative conventional force capabilities of the Western Alliance, a proposal was put forward and accepted that the member states of the NATO alliance should adopt and implement a policy of regularly increasing their real defense outlays. The operational aim of the proposal was to elevate this spending at a rate of 3 percent per annum, and in so doing to enhance the conventional force capabilities of the alliance, which in turn would improve the alliance's power relative to the Eastern bloc. As a consequence this was expected to reduce the potential for hostile behavior on the part of the Eastern bloc. While adopted as a guideline, acceptance was not universal. Indeed, opposition to what came to be called the "3 percent solution" arose. On the one side, many argued that such a policy was counterproductive with respect to its purposes and costly beyond the means of those who would bear it. On the other side, opposition was founded on the argument that the "solution" was no solution at all in that it was unsufficient to redress the imbalance that confronted the West, and thus would only increase aggressive behavior on the part of the East, thereby elevating both the level of international tensions and the threat to the West.

For a variety of reasons, the pattern of implementation among the alliance members has been divergent. Economic stagnation, competing resource claims, and shifts in national policy stances have produced different performances. Still, across the alliance the goal has been slightly surpassed. To a great extent this achievement was the product of the largest member, the United States, going well beyong the guideline figure because of the Reagan administration's efforts to create a "rearmed America."

Simultaneously, debate has flared on the second eternal issue. Sometimes this takes the form of disagreement over the size of other (nondefense) governmental activities. Historically most modern industrial countries gradually added resource development (the state's own and those of the supporting economy) and social benefits to its expenditure patterns (Rose 1976). For some critics, the latter or even both of these activities remain illegitimate arenas for governmental effort. Most often it is the extent of resources directed by public authorities to these secondary targets that occasions ire.

In reality the second debate normally takes the form of attention to the total size of the public budget. Scholars have devoted considerable effort to explaining the steady growth of the governmental role during the industrial era, which has come to be known as Wagner's law of expanding state activity. Wagner [1883; see also Kelley (1977)] identified three primary bases for the phenomenon. First, and related again to the fundamental defense activity of a state, Wagner saw the need for regulative and protective activity by the state increasing with industrialization, in part because of growing strains on individuals. Second, certain income-elastic consumption activities, such as education, health, and cultural activity, are best provided collectively. Third, market imperfections such as monopolies, exacerbated with industrial growth, require public action. Since Wagner, the hypotheses have proliferated: Tarschys (1975) explores nine categories of factors that might help explain the growth of the Swedish public sector in the 1960s, and Cameron (1978) tests five clusters of hypotheses for 18 developed capitalist nations.

Obviously related to the preferred explanation(s) for growth, the debate on government size extends to the consequences of growth. Some see the government as a generally benign, if not always effective, economic finetuner; the apparent failures of many fiscal and monetary policies during the 1970s and 1980s, however, have shaken significant numbers of these, and have helped birth the rational expectations school. Others portray an active state economic role as a partial bulwark, especially for small and open economies, against the vicissitudes of the global economy [this argument is reviewed in Cameron (1978, pp. 1249-51)]. While still others argue that government economic meddling decreases the efficiency of the economy in direct relationship to the size of its spending (Brunner 1978), the contrasting argument is that the inherent drop in efficiency requires increased government size (O'Connor 1973; Gough 1979).

Industrial countries as a whole are still a long way from full economic recovery after the deepest recession since the 1930s. Unemployment in 1984 for major industrial countries remained over 7 percent, more than double that of 1973 (Hughes 1985b, p. 19). In this context the old debate has taken new urgency. It pits those who argue the necessity of governmental social spending to help the unemployed and, through fiscal stimulation, to aid the recovery against those who see the roots of current economic weakness in the Organization for Economic Cooperation and Development (OECD) precisely within an overextended governmental role.

In the case of the United States, the opponents of governmental spending have focused in large part on revenues. Major tax cuts were enacted with the intention of reducing the burden of government so as to improve private incentive structures. Some also saw the cuts as traditional fiscal policy in the face of an ailing economy. This focus on taxes as the ultimate determinant of the government role remains in the tradition of Schumpeter [1954; reviewed in Bell (1974)]. In our analysis here we selected this variable as the key one.

SCENARIO ANALYSIS

On the average, the portion of their economic output that industrial countries have directed to the military has quite steadily declined over the last two decades. In 1980 industrial countries spent 4.6 percent of their gross domestic products (GDPs) on defense, down from 7.5 percent in 1960 (Sivard 1983, p. 32). The "3 percent solution" would maintain military spending growth at roughly that of the economy, if postwar economic growth rates prevailed, and thereby largely stop the decline.

Here we look at three alternative future defense-spending paths: 0, 3, and 6 percent growth (the last being least likely, given historical trends, except in the United States). We impose the defense-spending growth rate on all seven major industrial market economy countries: the United States, Canada, Britain, France, the Federal Republic of Germany, Italy, and Japan. The scenarios take effect in 1980; between 1970 and 1980 spending levels are determined endogenously in the model. Our overall time horizon is 1970 through 2010.

At the aggregate level, the total public expenditure-to-GDP ratio for major industrial countries has climbed steadily—from 29.3 percent in 1961 to 40.9 percent in 1980 (World Bank 1984, p. 17). In terms of total government, the average for the seven countries in our study grew from 29 percent to nearly 37 percent during the same period. This includes transfer payments, and their growth was especially rapid. In fact, Beck (1979) found that between the early 1950s and the early 1970s real public consumption declined as a percentage of GDP in 7 of 13 industrial countries. More recently, Beck (1982, p. 163) has pointed out that between 1969 and 1979 transfer payments rose from 8 to 12 percent of the gross national product while governmental purchases fell from 24 to 19 percent. With the exception of the United States, however, Gould (1983) has contradicted Beck's contention of governmental consumption decline in an analysis of the same 13 countries. He attributes the U.S. exception to the reduction of Vietnam-related defense spending in the 1970s.

Although total public expenditure (upon which we focus here) is a broader concept than central government expenditure, the latter grew at about the same rate—from 18.6 percent of GDP in 1960 to 24.4 percent in 1980 [data from International Monetary Fund (IMF) (1983)]. For industrial countries as a whole, central government spending has grown a little slower than state and local government outlays in the 1960-79 period (Gould 1983, p. 59). Revenues have climbed a bit less rapidly, especially in recent years. For central governments they rose from 18.4 percent in 1960 to 24.4 percent in 1980. Whereas revenues and expenditures were nearly in balance on average in 1960, the unweighted average of central government deficits in industrial countries reached 3.5 percent of GDP in 1980. It continued to climb to 7 percent in 1983 (Hughes 1985b, based on IMF sources).

Short-term issues and contemporary political debate thus now focus heavily on deficits. Our longer-term perspective will center primarily on the issue of government size as ultimately shaped by revenues (which obviously does have important implications for deficits). Specifically we examine two scenarios for revenue growth. The first scenario is continued revenue growth, as determined endogenously in the model through the interaction of demands for spending and revenue options. The second imposes a freeze on taxes so as to keep the share of GDP extracted through taxes constant after 1980. A scenario of tax decrease was not included for purposes of eliminating the proliferation of model output and thus enhancing our ability to interpret it.

The interaction of these two sets of scenarios produces six cases for analysis—revenue change and no revenue change, each with 0, 3, and 6 percent defense growth options.

Debate concerning the consequences (beneficial or detrimental) of defense spending and government tax levels draws our attention to four categories of potential impact. The first is the level of governmental control over GDP itself. This is of interest not simply because of its secondary impact on a broad range of social performance measures, but in and of itself. For some in the public debate, the issue is a stark trade-off between larger government and greater individual liberty. In addition, the size of government is held by some to be one of the most critical elements in the performance of the political system—indeed, in its ability to survive congenital opposition or opposition that through its own policies and programs it has helped foster (Deutsch 1961). On the one side, there are those who see that government growth in resource control is almost an unblemished asset as it enhances the survival capacity of the state in a dangerous international environment even while profoundly reshaping the lives of the mass of its citizenry (Organski et al. 1984). On the other hand, this same capacity for coping is held to be jeopardized through growth, which causes government to lose organizational effectiveness because of overcomplexity and inefficiency and to lose popular authority as it places greater claims on citizens (Rose 1984b).

The second category of policy impact is national defense position. Choice among the 0, 3, and 6 percent options effectively determines the absolute level of defense spending. As with governmental spending, that level can be important in and of itself. More often debate focuses on the relative expenditures of East and West and their security implications. Realizing that there will be a response by Warsaw Pact countries to Western spending patterns (both real world and in the model), we want to look at the relative spending implications of our scenarios. Both absolute and relative spending levels also help determine the climate or environment of hostility and cooperation between East and West, as well as the security implications in terms of the threats these groupings might perceive from the international environment. GLOBUS can suggest possible scenario impact in this area as well.

Economic performance constitutes the third category of policy impact. In particular, we want to focus on the consumer. Private and social consumption levels, both individually and together, provide indications as to how policies affect the average citizen. These indicators lie at the heart of the debate between those who view larger government spending (and/or military outlays) as debilitating for the economy, and those who view this as on average beneficial or neutral [for an extensive review, see Lindgren (1984)].

Averages, particularly when it comes to incomes or consumption levels, can conceal widespread inequity. Our fourth category of indicators for evaluation of the scenarios contains measures of social impact. Here we are concerned with the degree to which government will influence the income levels of the population. While the overall scope of its direct activities (through taxation and transfers) does not hold a one-to-one correspondence with the generation of equality, studies do suggest that concerted activity in this area is likely to produce a more egalitarian income distribution [see, for example, OECD (1976), Thurow (1981), and Saunders (1984)]. Specifically, in the light of alternative policy choices, we want to examine the transfers between households and the governmental sector and social welfare transfers as a portion of national disposable income. Since distributional issues do not stop at national borders, international transfers (foreign aid) also merit our attention and presumably will respond to such significant differences in policy direction.

RESULTS

Fiscal Dimension of Government

Few surprises should appear in our scenarios with respect to the size of government (as measured by revenues), which is largely determined by our scenario inputs. Table 11.1 reports the initial conditions (1970) and final values (2010) for government revenues as a percentage of GDP under each of the six different assumption combinations. Results are reported both for the seven largest OECD countries and for the Soviet Union (which was subject to no policy change and is listed in all tables primarily because of its centrality to the defense concerns).

In fact, no real surprises do appear. In the three cases where tax rates are frozen in 1980, final 2010 values are consistently larger than 1970 levels only because the 1980 values proved larger (as expected) than 1970 ones. In all cases except Japan and to a lesser extent the Federal Republic of Gemany, ending values prove significantly higher still when endogenous revenue change continues. The two exceptions are consistent with the historical trends, because central government revenues as a percentage of GDP actually dropped in Japan from 1960 to 1980, while they increased only marginally in Germany. It is actually a bit surprising to see the sharp climb in the French revenue percentage, because it is the third of the seven countries for which the ratio of revenue to GDP was quite stable over the last 20 years.

TABLE 11.1
Government sector revenues expressed as a percentage of gross domestic product

Nation 1970 Value	0% Def Rev Ch	3% Def Rev Ch	6% Def Rev Ch	0% Def Rev 0	3% Def Rev 0	6% Def Rev 0
USA 27.5	45.5	45.4	45.1	32.0	32.0	32.0
CAN 33.1	62.8	62.8	61.5	43.0	43.0	43.0
UKG 34.6	61.0	61.0	60.8	40.3	40.3	40.2
FRN 34.9	61.2	61.2	61.1	40.5	40.5	40.4
FRG 34.2	44.1	44.0	42.9	39.7	39.7	39.6
ITA 29.1	51.5	51.5	51.4	34.0	34.0	34.0
JPN 18.8	20.3	20.3	20.3	20.3	20.3	20.3
USR 40.2	40.3	40.2	40.2	40.3	40.2	40.2

See Appendix A for country abbreviations. Def—Defense spending, annual increase rate; Rev—Revenue; Ch—Change; Rev 0—No revenue.

Wildavsky (1975, pp. 232–35) has put forward what Cameron (1978, p. 1245) called a "counter-Wagner" law, arguing that the rate of public sector expansion varies inversely with economic growth rate. Rapid growth obviates the need for some expenditures and simultaneously generates rapidly increasing revenues even at constant tax rates. This argument has been used to explain the absence of pressure for increased government economic share in Japan and to a lesser extent France. The causality for this possible inverse relationship has also been reversed by those who argue that faster governmental growth slows economic growth. Whatever the explanation, Gould (1983) did find an inverse correlation between economic rate and growth in governmental share over 1960–79 for 13 industrial countries. In general, however, this principle receives very mixed support from our analysis. As we shall see below, the most rapid economic growth appears in Japan and Italy, followed by France.

Yet Table 11.1 places both France and Italy among the countries with the most rapid government revenue share growth. The historical stability of government revenue share in Japan and the rapid expansion of it in Italy appear better able to explain GLOBUS results.

Two results that might be somewhat surprising do appear in Table 11.1. First, in the three endogenous revenue change cases, four countries greet 2010 with 50 percent or more of their GDP passing through the government. For three countries (Britain, France, and Canada), the level actually exceeds 60 percent. In light of widespread concerns throughout the OECD that government taxing is already too high, this result may seem unrealistic to some. On the other hand, general government expenditures alone in Italy and Britain reached 47.5 and 53.7 percent, respectively, in 1982 (OECD 1984), and the trend is still upward (as it is for Sweden at 62.1 percent. Clearly the model is behaving in a largely extrapolative manner here (as models normally do); the tax freeze scenario is directed at those who doubt the trend's continuation.

The second, and actually more surprising, result lies in the effective absence of variation within the two revenue assumption scenario sets. Specifically, the 0, 3, and 6 percent options seem to have no implications for the overall size of government, even when revenue change is endogenous. The basis for this in the model appears to be a very effective (probably too much so) crowding out of civilian expenditures by increased defense. It is an area of model structure and parameterization that calls for more attention.

Tables 11.2 and 11.3 portray government expenditures and government debt. As noted earlier, the rule in recent years, not the exception, has been that expenditures exceed revenues in these countries, with the average central government annual deficit reaching 7 percent in 1983 (5.1 percent for general government in 1982). By those standards the deficits implied in Table 11.2 and the growth in debt shown in Table 11.3 are moderate. In reality, of course, cumulative government debt levels that reach 1.5 times GDP (as in Canada and Germany) imply debt service levels of perhaps 15 percent of GDP. Although Britain already has a debt level greater than GDP and the United States is trying hard to catch up, such possibilities help clarify what some have called the crisis of the welfare state: expanding pressure for government spending in the face of constrained revenue raising and borrowing ability.

Defense Position

Just as the government size responded primarily to assumptions about revenue, the differences in defense position respond overwhelmingly to the choice of the 0, 3, or 6 percent options. In Table 11.4 we can

TABLE 11.2
Government sector total spending expressed as a percentage of gross domestic product

Final (2010) Values for Scenario

Nation 1970 Value	0% Def Rev Ch	3% Def Rev Ch	6% Def Rev Ch	0% Def Rev 0	3% Def Rev 0	6% Def Rev 0
USA 32.2	48.3	48.0	47.2	34.7	34.7	34.4
CAN 29.8	51.4	51.4	51.7	33.9	33.9	34.2
UKG 33.8	64.4	64.3	66.5	44.0	44.0	45.8
FRN 35.2	70.6	69.5	69.1	47.8	46.7	46.6
FRG 34.7	49.5	49.6	49.5	45.1	45.2	46.1
ITA 32.9	53.8	53.6	54.0	36.5	36.3	36.8
JPN 19.7	22.8	22.9	23.1	22.8	22.8	23.1
USR 40.7	41.3	41.5	41.9	41.4	41.6	41.9

See Appendix A for country abbreviations. Def—Defense spending, annual increase rate; Rev—Revenue; Ch—Change; Rev 0—No revenue.

see how strikingly different the portion of the GDP devoted to defense would be were the respective options pursued consistently over the 1980–2010 period. In most cases the 3 percent option results in a relatively stable share of defense in GDP. The slow economic growth of Britain and the more rapid growth of Canada make them exceptions. In Table 11.4 also note how sensitive Soviet levels are to those of the OECD countries. This results partly from the inclusion of a threat stimulus in the budgetary process.

In fact, the Soviet Union and other Warsaw Pact countries are "underresponding," as shown in Table 11.5, to either the 0 or 6 percent options. Because of inertia and, in the case of the 6 percent solution, economic constraints, the East's share of the GLOBUS system conventional capabilities varies in 2010 only from 28.2 to 39.1 percent in the

TABLE 11.3
Government sector debt as a percentage of gross domestic product

Nation 1970 Value	0% Def Rev Ch	3% Def Rev Ch	6% Def Rev Ch	0% Def Rev 0	3% Def Rev 0	6% Def Rev 0
USA 50.3	84.0	81.4	76.6	91.0	88.9	85.1
CAN 45.0	158.1	158.5	146.2	150.1	150.3	139.9
UKG 106.8	99.2	102.8	122.9	114.1	118.6	137.9
FRN 126.1	118.4	112.2	106.5	112.3	106.7	102.4
FRG 12.2	160.3	162.8	172.4	163.7	166.1	174.4
ITA 16.2	92.2	90.8	93.6	99.0	98.0	101.3
JPN 41.4	54.1	54.9	56.9	53.8	54.5	56.5
USR 0.0	19.4	22.5	27.0	20.2	23.2	27.4

See Appendix A for country abbreviations. Def—Defense spending, annual increase rate; Rev—Revenue; Ch—Change; Rev 0—No revenue.

three cases. In the 0 percent defense-spending growth case, however, Western capabilities drop from 41.7 percent of the total in 1970 to 18.9 percent. And in the 6 percent case they climb to 56.1 percent. This is a generally surprise-free pattern for these capabilities, which are determined in the GLOBUS governmental budget model on the basis of defense spending. We would not expect the East to want to reduce spending over GDP as fast as the West does with the 0 percent option, nor to be capable of increasing it sufficiently fast to match the 6 percent option. The relative capabilities should and do reflect this.

Table 11.6 contains other indicators of the East/West environment when the three options are compared. The first row shows Western capabilities as a percentage of Eastern (considering, of course, only those members of the two groups that are represented in GLOBUS). In 1970

TABLE 11.4
Defense expenditures expressed as a percentage of gross domestic product

Final (2010) Values for Scenario

Nation 1970 Value	0% Def Rev Ch	3% Def Rev Ch	6% Def Rev Ch	0% Def Rev 0	3% Def Rev 0	6% Def Rev 0
USA 8.0	3.3	7.9	19.2	3.4	8.3	19.9
CAN 2.5	0.5	1.2	3.0	0.6	1.4	3.3
UKG 4.8	3.2	7.9	20.0	3.5	8.8	22.2
FRN 4.2	2.2	5.3	12.7	2.4	5.8	14.0
FRG 3.3	1.7	4.1	10.2	1.7	4.2	10.4
ITA 2.7	1.0	2.6	6.3	1.1	2.8	6.8
JPN 0.8	0.3	0.8	2.0	0.3	0.8	2.0
USR 12.0	12.1	14.3	17.8	12.2	14.3	17.7

See Appendix A for country abbreviations. Def—Defense spending, annual increase rate; Rev—Revenue; Ch—Change; Rev 0—No revenue.

that ratio was 132 percent. The 3 percent option is the only one that comes close to maintaining parity—both of the others result in one side or the other having an advantage of two to one.

On the other hand, the East/West climate (the sum of East/West hostility flows over the sum of East/West cooperation) improves (marginally) only under the 0 percent option. Even in the 3 percent case it deteriorates significantly.

A threat measure is also calculated in GLOBUS, integrating hostility and cooperation levels determined in the international political submodel with the conventional capabilities of the governmental model. Threat varies directly with hostility received and the capabilities of senders, but inversely with cooperation received, in a formulation (Cusack 1984a) with roots in an earlier one of Singer (1958). Capabilities

TABLE 11.5
Distribution of conventional military capabilities

Final (2010) Values for Scenario
(Figures in parentheses represent percentage share of system total)

Regional Grouping 1970 Value	0% Def	3% Def	6% Def
West 750.5 (41.7%)	265.4 (18.9%)	676.7 (37.4%)	1647.7 (56.1%)
East 568.1 (31.6%)	548.1 (39.1%)	656.5 (36.3%)	827.6 (28.2%)
South 438.9 (24.4%)	453.0 (32.3%)	346.7 (19.2%)	334.7 (11.4%)
OPEC 41.1 (2.3%)	134.6 (9.6%)	128.8 (7.1%)	126.6 (4.3%)
GLOBUS System Total: 1,798.7	1,401.1	1,808.6	2,936.6

OPEC, Organization of Petroleum-Exporting Countries.

over threat is a useful indicator of the ability of a country to meet threat. The last two rows of Table 11.6 show the inverse relationship between that measure for the West and the East. Obviously the West is better situated with greater spending. In the 3 percent case the two adversaries are most closely balanced on the indicator.

These results together suggest a dilemma for the West—while the balance of capabilities is most even in the 3 percent case, the East/West climate is best in the 0 percent case, and the Western capabilities-to-threat ratio is superior in the 6 percent case. Among other things this indicates the difficulty of unilaterally trying to improve the overall defensive position. For a more extensive analysis of the trade-offs and consequences associated with the three options, see Cusack (1984b).

Economic Performance

Considering the economic impact of the scenarios analyzed here takes us very quickly into the heart of contemporary economic debate, much of which focuses precisely on the macroeconomic impact of

TABLE 11.6
East/West environment

Variable 1970 Value	Final (2010) Values for Scenario		
	0% Def	3% Def	6% Def
West Caps. as % East 132.1%	48.4	103.1	199.1
East/West Climate 1.24	1.10	2.56	3.71
West: Caps./Threat 1.10	0.50	0.80	1.74
East: Caps./Threat 1.09	1.45	1.06	0.71

government taxing and spending levels and patterns [for an excellent survey, see the first chapter of Bosworth (1984)].

To simplify somewhat an exceedingly complex question of possible policy effects, let us consider first the possible implications of our taxing scenarios, and then return to the role of military spending. Our two taxing scenarios are actually two taxing/spending scenarios, because total spending varies in close proportion to taxing (remember the relative similarities in government debt growth in both cases).

In a traditional Keynesian analysis, this covariation of spending and taxing and relatively unchanged net fiscal stimulus suggests that aggregate economic performance would not be affected significantly. Increased taxation would depress private income and private spending, while increased governmental spending would offset the declines. If the higher spending in the revenue change case were to significantly "lead" revenues, there might be at least a small net stimulus and this could actually result in somewhat faster growth. This Keynesian outcome would be especially possible in a situation where surplus labor or capital existed and the actual growth path of the economy was falling below its potential. Keynesians worry relatively little about the potential crowding out of investment by government when production factors are in surplus. Many would also point to the important investment role of government itself, in both physical and human capital.

A neoclassical perspective draws our attention more sharply to the potential supply-side impact of the scenarios by emphasizing rate of return considerations. Higher business taxes could reduce the rate of return and thus dampen investment. The perspective also points to the importance of relative prices in the economy. A shift of spending from private consumers to the government might increase demand and at least temporarily prices for services relative to manufactures. If productivity levels in the production of the former are growing less quickly, the shift could weaken growth. On the other hand, if the government spending actually consists of transfer payments (not direct consumption) and the incomes and demand of lower-income individuals are increased, total spending on food and manufactures might increase.

The even purer supply-side orientation of economists who have adopted that label would draw attention also to the change in effective wages and therefore in the incentive to work implied by higher marginal tax rates. In this unambiguous view, the high-revenue scenario should drive down growth.

In reality, the GLOBUS economic submodel, because it is global and longer term rather than national and shorter term, is not sufficiently disaggregated to allow a clear-cut representation of any of these perspectives with their contradictory expectations for the results of our scenarios. In fact, the GDP of the seven industrial countries (not shown here) is scarcely affected by the alternative assumptions about taxing/spending.

There is another important level for this analysis, however. Even if the aggregate performance of the economy is little affected by the combined shift of taxing and spending, we would expect that the shift, plus the significant variations in defense spending, would considerably affect levels of consumption, private and public. Specifically, the higher taxing and spending case should shift consumption from the household to government, and the higher defense-spending cases should reduce social consumption overall.

These expectations are generally borne out in Tables 11.7 to 11.9. The consistency is greatest in Table 11.7, reporting per capita social consumption (health and education). Per capita social consumption is in nearly every instance larger in the higher tax/spending cases and in the lower defense-spending cases. Only in Japan does the pattern break, simply because there is no real difference for Japan between the tax freeze and revenue change scenarios.

In contrast, in Table 11.8 per capita personal consumption is higher (as expected) in the tax freeze case for the United States, Canada, and Britain. Personal consumption is reduced considerably by higher defense spending, as is social consumption. The surprise in Table 11.8 is that for France and Italy the revenue change (increase) cases coincide with higher personal consumption, and that for the Federal Republic of Germany no relationship appears.

The explanation can be found, at least in part, in Table 11.9, where we see combined consumption and investment. In the revenue change cases, it is down for the United States, Canada, and Britain, as is consumption alone. It is also down for Italy (marginally) and unchanged

TABLE 11.7
Per capita social consumption
(in constant price, local currency units)

	Final (2010) Values for Scenario (figures in parentheses are final values expressed as percentages of initial values)					
Nation 1970 Value	0% Def Rev Ch	3% Def Rev Ch	6% Def Rev Ch	0% Def Rev 0	3% Def Rev 0	6% Def Rev 0
USA 245	837 (341%)	806 (329%)	643 (262%)	595 (243%)	531 (217%)	267 (109%)
CAN 472	2,094 (444%)	2,073 (439%)	2,043 (432%)	1,281 (271%)	1,195 (253%)	1,144 (243%)
UKG 67	451 (673%)	419 (625%)	334 (499%)	238 (355%)	207 (309%)	120 (179%)
FRN 1118	5,827 (521%)	5,708 (510%)	5,395 (483%)	3,535 (316%)	3,335 (298%)	2,819 (252%)
FRG 578	1,691 (292%)	1,640 (284%)	1,435 (248%)	1,489 (258%)	1,435 (248%)	1,250 (216%)
ITA[a] 51	230 (451%)	229 (449%)	223 (437%)	138 (270%)	131 (257%)	116 (227%)
JPN[a] 30	108 (360%)	106 (353%)	101 (337%)	108 (360%)	106 (353%)	101 (337%)
USR 120	292 (243%)	266 (222%)	222 (185%)	293 (244%)	267 (222%)	223 (186%)

See Appendix A for country abbreviations.

[a] Note that Italian and Japanese figures are given in thousands of local currency units.

for France. Clearly what has happened in these last two countries is that consumption was maintained in the revenue change case at the expense of domestic investment. Continued growth in the economy in this situation would require positive net investment from abroad and would not be indefinitely sustainable.

Welfare Implications

Even when analysts believe that a policy like higher taxes and spending levels might reduce aggregate economic performance, or at least

TABLE 11.8
Per capita personal consumption
(in constant price, local currency units)

Final (2010) Values for Scenario
(figures in parentheses are final values
expressed as percentages of initial values)

Nation 1970 Value	0% Def Rev Ch	3% Def Rev Ch	6% Def Rev Ch	0% Def Rev 0	3% Def Rev 0	6% Def Rev 0
USA 3,020	6,355 (210%)	6,196 (205%)	5,742 (190%)	6,525 (216%)	6,385 (211%)	6,029 (199%)
CAN 2,324	4,204 (180%)	4,165 (172%)	4,219 (182%)	4,532 (195%)	4,500 (194%)	4,568 (197%)
UKG 566	1,228 (217%)	1,177 (208%)	1,021 (180%)	1,312 (231%)	1,260 (223%)	1,105 (195%)
FRN 9,263	26,676 (288%)	26,025 (281%)	24,035 (259%)	24,552 (265%)	23,941 (258%)	22,413 (242%)
FRG 6,055	13,556 (244%)	13,288 (219%)	12,444 (206%)	13,570 (224%)	13,308 (220%)	12,488 (206%)
ITA[a] 688	2,039 (296%)	2,018 (293%)	1,947 (282%)	1,963 (285%)	1,944 (282%)	1,877 (273%)
JPN[a] 370	1,041 (281%)	1,036 (280%)	1,023 (276%)	1,042 (281%)	1,037 (280%)	1,025 (277%)
USR 777	2,326 (299%)	2,319 (298%)	2,294 (295%)	2,327 (299%)	2,316 (298%)	2,294 (295%)

See Appendix A for country abbreviations.

[a]Note that Italian and Japanese figures are given in thousands of local currency units.

average consumption level, many would continue to support such policies for welfare reasons, particularly income distribution. Here expectations are reasonably noncontroversial—a greater governmental role should support greater transfers among income categories, and lower defense spending should reinforce that tendency. The only dissent would come from those who foresaw as a result of that role a longer-term diminution of the pie, which would be so great as to ultimately lower governmental capabilities.

Table 11.10 supports the more common expectation. In all countries but Japan, with its lack of differentiation between the tax policy cases,

TABLE 11.9
Per capita personal consumption and investment, combined
(in constant price, 1970, local currency units)

Final (2010) Values for Scenario
(figures in parentheses are final values
expressed as percentages of initial values)

Nation 1970 Value	0% Def Rev Ch	3% Def Rev Ch	6% Def Rev Ch	0% Def Rev 0	3% Def Rev 0	6% Def Rev 0
USA 3,721	7,725 (208%)	7,559 (203%)	7,141 (192%)	8,078 (217%)	7,948 (214%)	7,642 (205%)
CAN 3,024	5,458 (180%)	5,418 (179%)	5,503 (182%)	6,026 (199%)	5,994 (198%)	6,102 (202%)
UKG 702	1,486 (212%)	1,433 (204%)	1,268 (181%)	1,639 (233%)	1,586 (226%)	1,421 (202%)
FRN 12,697	33,806 (266%)	33,299 (262%)	31,701 (250%)	33,407 (263%)	32,949 (260%)	31,587 (249%)
FRG 8,665	18,821 (217%)	18,577 (214%)	17,701 (204%)	19,021 (220%)	18,781 (217%)	17,898 (207%)
ITA[a] 901	2,593 (288%)	2,576 (286%)	2,504 (278%)	2,604 (289%)	2,990 (287%)	2,520 (280%)
JPN[a] 598	1,849 (309%)	1,839 (308%)	1,818 (304%)	1,848 (309%)	1,841 (308%)	1,821 (305%)
USR[b] 1,257	3,841 (306%)	3,818 (304%)	3,776 (300%)	3,842 (306%)	3,819 (304%)	3,777 (300%)

See Appendix A for country abbreviations.

[a]Note that Italian and Japanese figures are given in thousands of local currency units.

[b]Includes total investment.

higher taxing/spending does support a greater role for social welfare transfers as a portion of disposable personal income. Moreover, the lower the rate of defense-spending increase, the higher the transfer percentage.

Although higher transfers over disposable income clearly imply that some will benefit, it bears emphasizing that it does not mean that consumers as a whole will. In Table 11.11 we see the net per capita transfers from the government to the household sector (welfare benefits minus contributions and personal taxes). In general, these figures are

TABLE 11.10
Social welfare program transfers to the household sector expressed as a percentage of disposable personal income

Nation 1970 Value	0% Def Rev Ch	3% Def Rev Ch	6% Def Rev Ch	0% Def Rev 0	3% Def Rev 0	6% Def Rev 0
USA 11.7	29.6	26.5	17.8	17.2	14.3	7.0
CAN 13.2	35.1	34.6	33.3	20.6	20.1	18.8
UKG 14.4	40.0	37.2	30.8	21.5	18.4	11.1
FRN 24.5	59.5	57.4	52.8	36.3	33.2	26.7
FRG 20.8	33.1	31.5	26.5	28.6	27.0	22.9
ITA 20.2	41.9	40.8	38.6	24.7	23.5	20.9
JPN 7.4	9.6	9.3	8.6	9.6	9.3	8.5
USR 10.5	13.2	12.1	10.2	13.2	12.1	10.2

Final (2010) Values for Scenario

See Appendix A for country abbreviations.

negative, implying an average household loss to government. The exception is France. The implication of the exception is that French transfers to the household are heavily subsidized in 2010 by revenues generated elsewhere—such as business taxes. That explanation, which merits further investigation, would be consistent with the significantly lower investment noted above in France under the revenue change case.

Except again for France and Italy (leaving aside Japan), the industrial countries exhibit greater net transfers away from households in the revenue change case. For all countries the average household does less well the greater the rate of defense-spending increase.

Earlier we suggested that international transfer implications of policy ought to be considered as well as domestic ones. We would expect capabilities for transfers to increase with government revenues and to

TABLE 11.11
Per capita net transfers from government to household sector
(in constant price, 1970, local currency units)

	Final (2010) Values for Scenario					
Nation 1970 Value	0% Def Rev Ch	3% Def Rev Ch	6% Def Rev Ch	0% Def Rev 0	3% Def Rev 0	6% Def Rev 0
USA −396	−934	−1,153	−1,689	−825	−1,010	−1,417
CAN −195	−684	−712	−862	−572	−597	−711
UKG −82	−301	−341	−407	−222	−258	−324
FRN −377	+4,359	+3,463	+1,659	+1,109	+305	−1,228
FRG −877	−1,678	−1,910	−2,361	−1,628	−1,855	−2,307
ITA[a] −27	−36	−60	−104	−105	−124	−159
JPN[a] −25	−137	−138	−142	−137	−139	−143
USR +1	+75	+46	−3	+76	+47	−2

See Appendix A for country abbreviations.

[a]Note that Italian and Japanese figures are given in thousands of local currency units.

decrease with defense spending. That pattern appears quite consistently in Table 11.12. The one exception is that British foreign aid as a percentage of GDP is lower in the 0 percent defense-spending case than in the 3 percent case. While difficult to disentangle the roots of this, the international political orientation of potential aid recipients does influence aid decisions in the model. Thus, the more activist foreign policy role that might result from the 3 percent option could engender a situation where Britain would be marginally more prepared to allocate resources to aid.

TABLE 11.12
Foreign economic aid as a percentage
of gross domestic product

Nation 1970 Value	0% Def Rev Ch	3% Def Rev Ch	6% Def Rev Ch	0% Def Rev 0	3% Def Rev 0	6% Def Rev 0
USA 0.31	0.55	0.23	0.19	0.48	0.20	0.14
CAN 0.42	0.22	0.22	0.20	0.20	0.20	0.18
UKG 0.39	0.28	0.32	0.31	0.24	0.29	0.23
FRN 0.68	0.56	0.55	0.51	0.52	0.49	0.43
FRG 0.32	0.54	0.52	0.47	0.51	0.50	0.45
ITA 0.16	0.22	0.22	0.20	0.20	0.19	0.18
JPN 0.22	0.26	0.17	0.16	0.27	0.17	0.16

See Appendix A for country abbreviations.

CONCLUSIONS

This essay has had as its purpose the investigation of broad sets of implications for industrial countries of alternative policies with respect to the rate of increase in defense spending and taxation. Although there have been few surprises in the results of the six scenarios, there have nonetheless been interesting results. And in view of the widely competing theory that characterizes this field, almost any result contradicts at least some expectations. We should summarize a few of the findings.

When overall taxing and spending levels are left endogenous to the model, the portion of the economy going to or through the government by 2010 exceeds 60 percent in three countries, in large part because of the inertial growth of demands upon government. This pattern is clearly an indicator of the seriousness with which alternative scenarios, such as the tax freeze examined here, should be taken. The pattern of continued expenditure growth in the face of constrained revenues has been called "fiscal overload" (Rose 1984a). One of its results is persistent deficit spending. In our scenarios the movement of government debt to over 100 percent of GDP for four countries in 2010 suggests the reality of the so-called "crisis of the welfare state."

Our analysis of defense options suggests important trade-offs. Policies best suited to improve the relative balance of East/West capabilities (from the perspective of the West) are not the ones that improve East/West climate or provide the best capabilities-to-threat ratio.

Trade-offs can equally well be the theme of our analysis of economic performance. Defense spending and both social and private consumption are inversely related. Although the guns and butter quandary is hardly unexpected, the absence of a consistent relationship across all countries to develop between personal consumption and government size is more interesting. It should be the basis for further investigation.

Finally, we sketched the impact of different policies on domestic and international transfers. Both are generally greater when government size is larger and when defense expenditures are lower—not a surprising result, but by no means a certain one.

It must be emphasized again that our purpose has not been to forecast. None of the six scenarios constitutes a very probable future; far too many policy decisions in far too many countries over far too long an analysis horizon (30 years) will shape the future for us to reasonably suggest a highly probable scenario rooted in only two aspects of policy.

Expression of caution must go one large step further. GLOBUS is a very complex model. Analysis, as opposed to development, has received high priority only recently. Much more "exercise" of the model and the further development work that always follows model analysis efforts will be needed before much confidence exists in even conditional if/then statements.

GLOBUS will remain a theoretical statement about the nature of the global political/economic system. In a field of incomplete and competing theory, GLOBUS will always be more a theory-building effort than a forecasting project.

Nevertheless, an examination of model results under different scenarios, like that that we have undertaken here, is of great importance. GLOBUS already constitutes perhaps the most extensive, highly integrated theoretical representation of the global political/economic system now extant. Results produced by it certainly will serve as tests of the model and aids to further development; in particular, a number of the more unexpected findings obtained here must be investigated further. But as work on the model continues, its results will also increasingly serve as tests of theory and should in fact be more and more suggestive with respect to the real world impact of policy.

APPENDIX A   COUNTRIES IN THE GLOBUS SYSTEM

Alphabetical   *Russett/Singer/Small**

Alphabetical	Russett/Singer/Small*
ARG—Argentina	002—USA 1
BRA—Brazil	020—CAN 2
CAN—Canada	070—MEX 3
CHN—China	101—VEN 4
CZE—Czechoslovakia	140—BRA 5
EGY—Egypt	160—ARG 6
FRG—Federal Republic of Germany	200—UKG 7
FRN—France	220—FRA 8
GDR—German Democratic Republic	260—FRG 9
IND—India	265—GDR 10
INS—Indonesia	290—POL 11
IRN—Iran	315—CZE 12
ITA—Italy	325—ITA 13
JPN—Japan	365—USR 14
MEX—Mexico	475—NIG 15
NIG—Nigeria	560—SAF 16
PAK—Pakistan	630—IRN 17
POL—Poland	640—TUR 18
SAF—South Africa	651—EGY 19
SAU—Saudi Arabia	670—SAU 20
TUR—Turkey	710—CHN 21
UKG—United Kingdom	740—JPN 22
USA—United States	750—IND 23
USR—Soviet Union	770—PAK 24
VEN—Venezuela	850—INS 25

NOTE

1. GLOBUS is a team effort under the leadership of Dr. Stuart Bremer. The authors wish to express appreciation to all team members for their contributions to the work reported here.

---

*From Bruce M. Russett, J. David Singer, and Melvin Small. 1968. "National Political Units in the Twentieth Century: A Standardized List," *American Political Science Review* 62:932-51.

REFERENCES

Beck, Morris. 1979a. "Public Sector Growth: A Real Perspective." *Public Finance* 34: 313–55.

⸺.1982. "Towards a Theory of Public Sector Growth." *Public Finance* 37:163–77.

Bell, Daniel. 1974. "The Public Household—On 'Fiscal Sociology' and the Liberal Society." *Public Interest* 37:29–68.

Bosworth, Barry P. 1984. *Tax Incentives and Economic Growth*. Washington, D.C.: Brookings Institution.

Bremer, Stuart A. 1984. "The GLOBUS Model: History, Structure and Illustrative Results." Science Center Berlin. Paper delivered at the Second International Congress of Arts and Sciences, June 4–15, Rotterdam, the Netherlands.

Brunner, Karl. 1978. "Reflections on the Political Economy of Government: The Persistent Growth of Government." *Zeitschrift fuer Volkswirtschaft und Statistik* 3:649–79.

Cameron, David R. 1978. "The Expansion of the Public Economy: A Comparative Analysis." *American Political Science Review* 72:1243–61.

Cusack, Thomas R. 1985. "Contention and Compromise: A Comparative Analysis of Budgeting Politics." Science Center Berlin, unpublished.

⸺.1984a. "The Evolution of Power, Threat, and Security: Past and Potential Developments." Science Center Berlin, IIVG/dp 84/103. Paper presented to the General Systems Theory and Analysis of Political Systems Section, AAAS Annual Meeting, May 1984, New York. Forthcoming in *International Transactions*.

⸺.1984b. "One Problem, Three Solutions: A Simulation Analysis of Alternative Western Defense Policy Options." Science Center Berlin, IIVG/dp 84-109.

Deutsch, Karl W. 1961. "Social Mobilization and Political Development." *American Political Science Review* 55:493–514.

Fischer, G. W., and M. S. Kamlet. 1984. "Exploring Presidential Priorities: The Competing Aspiration Levels Model of Macrobudgetary Decision-Making." *American Political Science Review* 78:356–71.

Gough, Ian. 1979. *The Political Economy of the Welfare State*. London: Macmillan.

Gould, Frank. 1983. "The Development of Public Expenditures in Western, Industrialized Countries: A Comparative Analysis." *Public Finance* 38:38–69.

Gunning, J. W., G. Carrin, J. Waelbroeck, and associates. n.d. "Growth and Trade of Developing Countries: A General Equilibrium Analysis." Discussion Paper 8210, Centre d'Economie Mathematique et d'Econometrie, Universite Libre de Bruxelles.

Gupta, S., and R. Paula. 1978. "A Global Model for Interregional, Intertemporal Analysis of Trade, Capital Flows and Development." Washington, D.C.: World Bank. Paper contributed to the Sixth IIASA Global Modeling Conference, October 17–20.

Hickman, Bert G. 1983. *Global International Economic Models*. Amsterdam: North-Holland.
Hughes, Barry B. 1985a. "GLOBUS Project: Natmod 6 Economic Model." Science Center Berlin, unpublished.
_____.1985b. "The First Two Oil Shocks: Energy Crisis Continued." University of Denver, unpublished.
International Monetary Fund. 1983. *International Monetary Statistics Yearbook*. Washington, D.C.: International Monetary Fund.
Kelley, Allen C. 1977. "Demographic Change and the Size of the Government Sector." *Southern Journal of Economics* 43:1056–66.
Leontief, Wassily, et al. 1977. *The Future of the World Economy*. New York: Oxford University Press.
Levy, Susan. 1984. "The Un-managed Economy." *Forbes 135* (December 17): 147–58.
Lindgren, Goeran. 1984. "Armaments and Economic Performance in Industrialized Market Economies." *Journal of Peace Research* 21:375–87.
Meadows, Dennis L., William W. Behrens III, Donella H. Meadows, Roger F. Naill, Jorgen Randers, and Erich K. O. Zahn. 1974. *Dynamics of Growth in a Finite World*. Cambridge, MA: Wright-Allen Press.
Mesarovic, Mihajlo D., and Eduard Pestel. 1974. *Mankind at the Turning Point*. New York: E. P. Dutton.
O'Connor, James. 1973. *The Fiscal Crisis of the State*. New York: St. Martin's Press.
Organization for Economic Cooperation and Development. 1984. *Historical Statistics: 1960–1982*. Paris: Organization for Economic Cooperation and Development.
_____.1976. *Public Expenditures on Income Maintenance Programs*. Paris: Organization for Economic Cooperation and Development.
Organski, A. F. K., Jacek Kugler, J. Timothy Johnson, and Youssef Cohen, 1984. *Birth, Death and Taxes: The Demographic and Political Transitions*. Chicago: University of Chicago Press.
Rose, Richard. 1984a. "Meta-Policies for Mega-Government." *Public Interest* No. 75:99–110.
_____.1984b. *Understanding Big Government: The Programme Approach*. London: Sage.
_____.1976. "On the Priorities of Government: A Development Analysis of Public Policies." *European Journal of Political Research* 4:247–89.
Saunders, Peter. 1984. *Evidence on Income Redistribution by Governments*. Working Paper No. 11. Paris: Organization for Economic Cooperation and Development.
Schumpeter, Joseph. 1954. "The Crisis of the Tax State." *International Economic Papers* No. 4:5–38.
Singer, J. David. 1958. "Threat Perception and the Armament-Tension Dilemma." *Journal of Conflict Resolution* 2:90–105.
Sivard, Ruth Leger. 1983. *World Military and Social Expenditures 1983*. Washington, D.C.: World Priorities.

Tarschys, Daniel. 1975. "The Growth of Public Expenditures: Nine Modes of Explanation." *Scandinavian Political Studies* 10:9–31.
Thurow, Lester C. 1981. "Equity, Efficiency, Social Justice and Redistribution," in Organization for Economic Cooperation and Development. *The Welfare State in Crisis*. Paris: Organization for Economic Cooperation and Development.
Tims, Wouter, and Jean Waelbroeck. 1982. *Global Modeling in the World Bank, 1973-76*. World Bank Staff Working Paper No. 544. Washington, D.C.: World Bank.
Wagner, Adolph. 1893. *Grundlagen der Politischen Oekonomie*, 3rd ed. Leipzig: C. F. Winter.
Wildavsky, Aaron. 1975. *Budgeting: A Comparative Theory of Budgeting Process*. Boston: Little, Brown.
World Bank. 1984. *World Development Report 1984*. Washington, D.C.: World Bank.

12
Multiple Thresholds and Fertility Declines in Third World Populations: Paths to Low Fertility by the Years 2000 and 2010

Phillips Cutright and Herbert L. Smith

INTRODUCTION

The persistence of high fertility among many less-developed countries (LDCs) despite widespread understanding of the damaging impact of high rates of population growth on efforts to upgrade education, labor force participation, health, and economic development (McNicoll 1984) has distressed officials in many countries. Awareness of the negative effects of rapid growth has resulted in widespread adoption of policies aimed at depressing fertility and thus population growth. But in many LDCs fertility rates have not responded to the pleas of national leaders, and the continuation of high fertility and rapid population growth has led some to despair.

This chapter reviews recent empirical research on the determinants of fertility among LDCs and then develops a new method of forecasting birth rates. The results indicate reason for optimism in some large LDCs, but also suggest that population growth rates in the year 2010 will remain high (2 percent a year or greater) in 15 of the 33 largest less-developed nations.

The Threshold Hypothesis

As formulated by U.N. researchers (1965), the threshold hypothesis states that gains in social or economic development will have no impact on fertility until a certain "threshold" is surpassed. After this threshold is achieved, fertility "is likely to enter a decided decline and to continue downward until it is again stabilized on a much lower plane" (p. 143).

Following the bold but neglected paper by Berelson (1978), we explore the hypothesis that multiple developmental thresholds will provide better forecasts of fertility levels in 83 LDCs over the next 25 years than will standard projection methods. Unlike most previous forecasts {for example, United Nations (1981); World Bank (1984) [as discussed by Demeny (1984)]}, our fertility projections are based on empirical analyses of the linkage of life expectancy and the fertility experience of LDCs in the post-World War II era.

Previous research on threshold effects (United Nations 1965; Beaver 1975; Srikantan 1982; Bulatao and Elwan 1983; Cutright and Hargens 1984) attempted to locate a single tipping point in the level of some measure of social or economic development that, when exceeded, would, after some time lag, eventually result in a significant decrease from traditional levels of high fertility [see Bulatao and Elwan (1983, Table 4) for a detailed report on lag times]. An implicit assumption has been that once fertility begins to drop, it will automatically continue until it reaches replacement levels (Kirk 1971). But some recent observers (Gallager 1980; Beaujot 1984) have noted that fertility declines in countries such as Costa Rica and Tunisia have "stalled"—an observation that might extend to Sri Lanka as well. This suggests that for really low fertility to occur, levels of development in LDCs will have to be much higher than the threshold required to trigger an initial drop in fertility from its traditional high rate. This hypothesis is examined in this chapter, and its utility demonstrated in the context of forecasts of the crude birth rate (CBR) in LDCs through the year 2010.

REVIEW OF THE LITERATURE

Threshold Hypothesis Research

Following a methodological critique of earlier threshold research, Cutright and Hargens (1984) conducted a multivariate regression analysis of pooled observations of fertility and different measures of development for 20 Latin American LDCs for 1950, 1960, 1970, and 1980. They found robust empirical support for an initial threshold to the effects of literacy and life expectancy on fertility.

Perhaps the most comprehensive attempt to apply threshold levels of developmental indicators to future fertility levels was reported by Berelson (1978). His methodology employed so-called "correspondence points" on several measures of social and economic development, garnered from U.N. studies that included both developed and less-developed countries (McGranahan et al. 1972). Levels of life expectancy, infant mortality, adult literacy, school enrollment, economic development (per capita gross national product), and other development indicators common to populations with CBRs of 35 and 20 per 1,000 population were estimated. Rather than relying on a continuation of past trends in fertility to predict future fertility trends, Berelson estimated the expected future level of fertility for each population from its expected future levels of development. His method resulted in projected levels of CBRs for the year 2000 higher than the then-current U.N. projections. Berelson's great insight was that for fertility to drop to really low rates, literacy, life expectancy, and possibly other measures would necessarily exceed levels well beyond those needed to trigger the initial decline in fertility. Other forecasters assumed that once fertility began to decline, the trend would continue (United Nations 1965; Kirk 1971). Whether these researchers assumed that measures of health and education would continue to improve or whether this thought was seen as irrelevant is not known, but Berelson openly groped with the problem.

We prefer Berelson's conceptual approach to projecting fertility rates, but not his method of testing his ideas. Among the possible flaws is the implicit assumption that the threshold levels needed to start a fertility decline, or the level needed to reach a still lower level, are constant over time. The literature on the impact of diffusion over time suggests that this assumption is worth testing. Second, the U.N. team headed by McGranahan et al. (1972) that developed the "correspondence points" used by Berelson (1978) included both more- and less-developed countries in their analyses, a procedure that may bias estimates of threshold effects among LDCs, few of which have reached low levels of fertility. Third, this model is a linear one, thus ignoring the possibility that declines in fertility may be slow after the initial threshold is reached, but then increase after higher developmental thresholds are surpassed. Fourth, Berelson banked on the use of multiple-indicators development to protect him from the risk of measurement error. This procedure makes sense only if all measures of development are equally important in determining fertility declines, a hypothesis rejected by Cutright (1983—see also supporting literature cited therein).

Selecting Predictors of Fertility Decline

A recent review of the literature on socioeconomic determinants of fertility levels and fertility change among LDCs (Cutright 1983) reports that a consensus may be emerging that social rather than economic factors are probably the key ingredients behind recent fertility declines. This view is supported by Cutright's empirical tests (1983) and more recently by other researchers (World Bank 1984). Improved education and health, buttressed by vigorous family-planning programs, are believed to offer the quickest route to lower fertility rates.

We selected life expectancy as our major predictor of future fertility declines for theoretical, empirical, and practical reasons. As a practical matter, we note that, assuming a ten-year lag, a prediction of fertility in the year 2010 requires an estimate of the predictor around the year 2000. An alternative predictor to life expectancy would be a measure of education such as adult literacy, but projected adult literacy rates are available only to the year 1990. Also, there are questions about the comparability of adult literacy rates, the educational standards used to assess literacy, and the operative linkage between educational content and fertility (LeVine 1980). In contrast, the meaning of life expectancy is comparable across time, geographic areas, and cultural contexts (Preston 1978).

While life expectancy as a concept that is comparable across countries is a strength, it is also true that the data used to estimate life expectancy in many of the poorer LDCs are either nonexistent or out of date by a decade or more. Existing estimates are often based on sample surveys or censuses, rather than on complete or nearly complete annual vital registration of mortality. For example, the U.S. Census (Table 6) notes that of the 1983 population of 516 million Africans, only 50 percent were in countries with good 1970-79 life expectancy statistics, while 18 percent were in countries with no reliable data at any time. In Asia 44 percent of these populations lived in countries with good data at some time after 1970, but 44 percent were in countries with no reliable data at any time. This latter statistic, however, was just 9 percent in Latin American countries. Thus, the 1950, 1960, and 1970 life expectancy data we use to develop a model to project future levels of CBRs are subject to some degree of measurement error, the level of which may vary by region. This should tend to depress the association between life expectancy and CBR. There is, however, no evidence of bias in these data, and our use of projected life expectancy for the years 1990 and 2000 accords with our belief that these figures come as close to capturing the actual state of affairs—past, present, and future—as can reasonably be anticipated.

Figure 12.1 gives some sense of the likelihood that U.N. projections of life expectancy to the years 1990 and 2000 are reasonable. Nations with 10 million or more inhabitants in 1975 are grouped within regions, by high or low 1950 and 1960 life expectancy, to increase homogeneity within each category. The three Latin American and seven Asian countries classified as "high" on 1950 and 1960 life expectancy are represented by the top two lines, with the three Latin American countries with lower life expectancies on the third trajectory. Next are three North African and Middle Eastern countries (the one high country in this group was Turkey, and it is omitted from the graph). Next are the means for Kenya and Uganda (high African) with low Asian and low African countries at the bottom of the chart. Based on the advances in life expectancy between 1950 and 1980 in countries that vary greatly by the level of life expectancy in 1950 and 1960, we conclude that the projected increases in life expectancy to the year 2000 seem reasonable, and even, in the case of low life expectancy Latin American countries, conservative.

There are three lines of demographic theory that suggest why life expectancy should be an important predictor of fertility. First, the adjustment model of the European demographic transition states that high fertility is a response to high mortality, and low fertility is an adjustment to low mortality. This model is followed by Notestein (1953), Davis (1963), Goldscheider (1971), and Freedman (1982). See also Oechsli and Kirk (1975, Figure 2) for an application of this idea to Latin America.

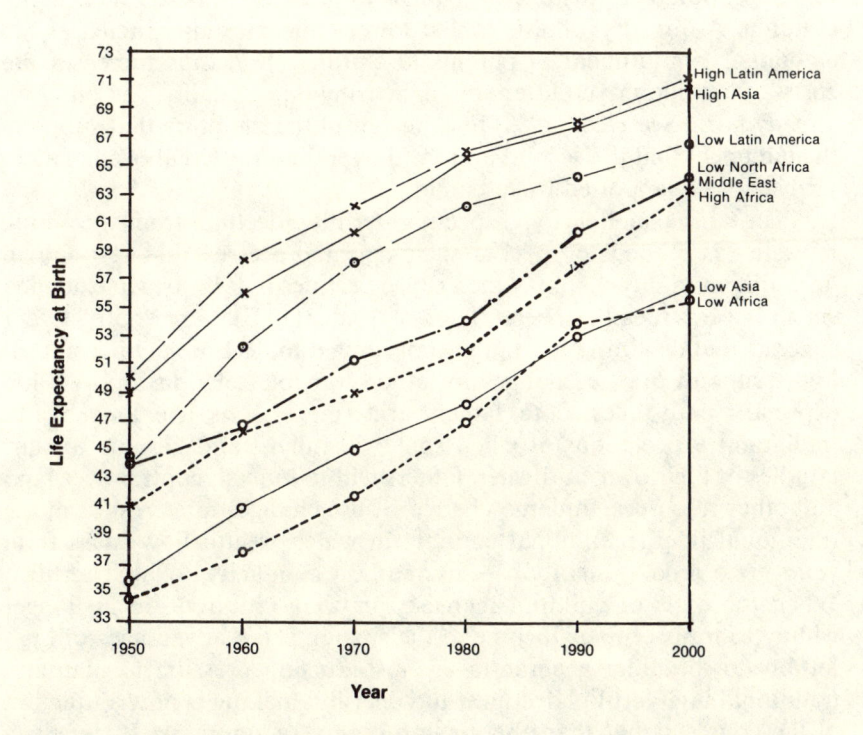

FIGURE 12.1. Estimated and projected life expectancy 1950–2000, for selected less-developed countries grouped by region and 1950–1960 life expectancy. (Data from Table 12A.2.)

Coale (1974), Dumond (1975), Hassan (1980), and Handwerker (1983) have argued a similar case for periods long before the transition from high fertility and mortality to low fertility and mortality in European populations. These authors report that birth rates increased during the agricultural revolution, and remained high in agricultural populations because death rates also went up as population density grew.

A second set of hypotheses predicting lower fertility with lower mortality focuses on infant and child mortality. Bulatao and Elwan (1983) summarize this perspective. First, and well supported by research, is the view that lower infant mortality lengthens the time between births, because an infant death causes an end to breastfeeding and postpartum infecundability. There is a physiological link between child mortality and fertility. On more speculative grounds, a second hypothesis states that longer child survival will reduce the demand or need for parents to have additional births, or, in another variant of this idea, longer child survival will reduce the need of parents to hoard children—they will not have "extra" children as insurance against eventual deaths of their living children. A third hypothesis is that lower child mortality increases the emotional commitment of parents to children, and thus increases the costs of additional children by increasing the "quality" of children already born. See Heer (1983) for a review of the literature that supports the judgment that the second and third hypotheses listed above have not yet been well supported by research.

The third model for expecting fertility decline from declining mortality is related to specific sociological processes that respond to declining mortality that may then cause declines in fertility. An extended version of this idea has been offered by Ryder (1983). Very briefly, Ryder suggests that declining mortality—not limited to declining child mortality—results in drastic changes in father-son role relationships. As life expectancy advances, both fathers and (more) sons live longer, and traditional expectations of when sons will inherit and be able to start families of their own, and when fathers will relinquish control over land and other resources, undergo change. These changes force a shift in the traditional intergenerational contract in which wealth flows pass from younger to older generations—a condition conducive to high fertility. When the costs of children increase, or when children are no longer willing to transfer their income to their parents, the advantages of high fertility to the older generation are lost, kinship pressure to maintain traditional high fertility declines, and decision making is now a function of the couple rather than the kinship group. In summary, Ryder links processes related to mortality decline to change in the intergenerational flow of resources in much the same way that Caldwell (1980) relates changes in mass education to changes in the intergenerational flow of resources and thus fertility change.

METHODOLOGY

Our model for predicting CBRs as a function of life expectancy involves the specification of the correct relationship between the two variables across three periods of time (1950-60, 1960-70, 1970-80) for the 83 LDCs for which data were available. In particular, we sought to model CBR in 1960 as a function of life expectancy at birth—and other variables—as of 1950, CBR in 1970 as a function of life expectancy, etc., in 1960, and so on. Three special problems presented themselves: First, a scatter plot of 1960, 1970, and 1980 CBRs against, respectively, 1950, 1960, and 1970 life expectancies reveals that the relationship between the two variables is a decidedly nonlinear one. There is virtually no relationship between the two variables through life expectancies of approximately 46 years—roughly the mean life expectancy among our 249 (83 countries multiplied by 3 years) observations. After 46 years a strong negative relationship begins, which then intensifies at about 56 years of life expectancy, or at roughly one standard deviation above the mean. This regularity—that is, the presence of two "thresholds" for the effect of life expectancy on CBR—obtains even after adjusting for the effects of other variables, such as family-planning program effort (FPPE). To model these thresholds, we have considered spline functions, with the aforementioned "cut points" of 46 and 56 years defining the three piece-wise slopes for a regression of CBR on life expectancy at birth.

Second, the design of these data—they constitute a pooled cross-sectional time series [for example, Dielman (1983)]—suggests the potential for statistical misspecification due to correlated disturbances attendant to the basic design: that is, within countries over time and/or across countries within given time periods. To compensate for this possibility, we have considered analysis of covariance specifications featuring the introduction of sets of dummy variables corresponding to country-specific and/or period-specific effects (Pindyck and Rubinfeld 1976, pp. 203-6).

Third, in pooling cross-sectional data from three separate time periods, we are assuming that the process linking CBR with the various regressors, especially the life expectancy spline, is static. In other words, this is a "fixed effects" model. We have experimented with alternative models that allow coefficients to vary over time; and while there are occasional instances of time-specific variation in slopes, there is no evidence of any systematic changes in the key relationship between CBR and life expectancy. Note that in addition to providing a statistical rationale for the pooling of cross-sectional data, these results represent (1) evidence against the hypothesis of shifts in thresholds over time and (2) reassurance for the implicit assumption embodied in the use of these equations for forecasting, namely, that the process generating the forecasts is not itself changing over time.

The preferred specification from column 4b of Table 12A.1 is as follows:

$$CBR_{i(t+10)} = \mu_0 + \mu_1 + \mu_2 + (\gamma_0 + \gamma_1 + \gamma_2)EXP_{it} + \sigma FPPE_{i(1970)} + \alpha_{t+10}$$

$$+ \beta_i + e_{i(t+10)},$$

where, for $i = 1$ to 83 countries and $t = 1950, 1960$, and 1970,

$CBR_{i(t+10)}$ is the CBR in country i at time $t + 10$;
μ_0 is the y-intercept when $EXP_{it} < 46$,
$\mu_0 + \mu_1$ is the y-intercept when $46 \leq EXP_{it} < 56$,
$\mu_0 + \mu_1 + \mu_2$ is the y-intercept when $EXP_{it} \geq 56$,
EXP_{it} is the life expectancy at birth in country i at time t,
γ_0 is the slope for the regression of CBR on EXP when $EXP_{it} < 46$,
$\gamma_0 + \gamma_1$ is the slope for the regression of CBR on EXP when $46 \leq EXP_{it} < 56$,
$\gamma_0 + \gamma_1 + \gamma_2$ is the slope for the regression of CBR on EXP when $EXP_{it} \geq 56$,
$FPPE_{i(1970)}$ is the FPPE score for country i circa 1970 (for $t = 1950, 1960$, $FPPE_{it} = 0$),
α_{t+10} is the effect associated with the $t + $ 10th time period, $\Sigma_t \alpha_{t+10} = 0$,
β_i is the effect associated with the ith country, $\Sigma_i \beta_i = 0$, and
$e_{i(t+10)}$ is the normally distributed residual for the ith country at the time $t + 10$, $\Sigma_i \Sigma_t e_{i(t+10)} = 0$.

Predicted CBRs for the years 1990, 2000, and 2010 were then generated from the parameter estimates of this equation via the prediction equation

$$C\hat{B}R_{i(t'+10)} = \hat{\mu}_0 + \hat{\mu}_1 + \hat{\mu}_2 + (\hat{\gamma}_0 + \hat{\gamma}_1 + \hat{\gamma}_2) EXP_{it'} + (\hat{\delta}/4)FPPE_{i(1980)}$$

$$+ \hat{\alpha}_{t'+10} + \hat{\beta}_i$$

where for $i = 1$ to 83 countries and $t' = 1980, 1990$, and 2000,
$CBR_{i(t'+10)}$ is the predicted CBR in country i at time $t' + 10$,

$\hat{\mu}_0 = 43.5$ is the y-intercept when $\text{EXP}_{it'} < 46$,
$\hat{\mu}_0 + \hat{\mu}_1 = 63.0$ is the y-intercent when $46 \leq \text{EXP}_{it'} < 56$,
$\hat{\mu}_0 + \hat{\mu}_1 + \hat{\mu}_2 = 83.5$ is the y-intercept when $\text{EXP}_{it} \geq 56$,
$\text{EXP}_{it'}$ is the life expectancy at birth in country i at time t', as estimated or forecasted by the United Nations (1981),
$\hat{\gamma}_0 = 0.06$ is the estimated weight of EXP when $\text{EXP}_{it'} < 46$,
$\hat{\gamma}_0 + \hat{\gamma}_1 = -0.38$ is the estimated weight of EXP when $46 \leq \text{EXP}_{it'} < 56$,
$\hat{\gamma}_0 + \hat{\gamma}_1 + \hat{\gamma}_2 = -0.78$ is the estimated weight of EXP when $\text{EXP}_{it} \geq 56$,
$\hat{\delta} = -0.22$ is the estimated weight of FPPE, scaled in units of FPPE $_{1970}$;
$\text{FPPE}_{i(1980)}$ is the FPPE score for country i circa 1980,
$\hat{\alpha}_{t'+10}$ is the estimated "period effect" ($\hat{\alpha}_{1990} = -1.48$, $\hat{\alpha}_{2000} = -2.33$, $\hat{\alpha}_{2010} = -3.18$; $\hat{\alpha}_{t'+10} = [\hat{\alpha}_{1980} - (-\hat{\alpha}_{1970} - \hat{\alpha}_{1980})]/2$), and is the estimated country-specific deviation.
$\hat{\beta}_i$

To see how this equation is used to generate predictions of CBRs, consider the example of forecasting the CBR in Pakistan as of 1990. The relevant inputs for Pakistan include

- An estimated 1980 life expectancy of 52
- A 1982 FPPE score of 49
- An estimated country-specific deviation (β) of 0.89; that is, according to the first equation, the CBR of Pakistan—net of all other included variables—was 0.89 point lower than the average fertility of the total of 83 LDCs observed in 1960, 1970, and 1980.

Substituting these values into the prediction equation yields

$$43.50 + 19.53 + (0.059 - 0.440)52 + (-0.220/4)49 - 1.48 + 0.89 = 39.9,$$

which corresponds to the predicted CBR in Table 12A.3.

FINDINGS

The uses and interpretations of fertility forecasts can differ. Such forecasts can be used to project population size and age-sex composition, a task we do not undertake. Rather, we use one model to test the consistency between alternative methods of predicting national fertility rates in the future. By examining projected rates developed by different methods, we may find systematic differences in projected fertility rates that may also be evaluated.

Table 12A.2 reports the life expectancy values used in the pooled multiple-regression analysis of 1960, 1970, and 1980 CBRs, and the U.N. projected values for life expectancy for years 1980, 1990, and 2000, which were used to project CBRs in 1990, 2000, and 2010. Only countries with populations of 10 million or more around 1975 are listed because our analysis of specific countries is limited to these large LDCs.

Table 12A.3 shows U.N. projected CBRs and crude death rates (CDRs) and the resulting rates of natural increase (RNIs) for the years 1990, 2000, and 2010 for all 33 LDCs in our study with 10 million or more inhabitants around 1975. (Subtracting the CDR from the CBR yields the RNI—see Table 12A.3). Our projected CBRs (using U.N. estimates of life expectancy for 1980, 1990, and 2000) for these nations are also shown. Our examination of specific countries is limited to large LDCs to facilitate the presentation. Also, as Berelson (1978) commented, the 35 LDCs with the largest populations contained some 90 percent of all the world's LDC population. Because of data problems, we omit Vietnam and North Korea from this list.

Using these 33 large LDCs, we first examine Berelson's estimates of which nations would achieve CBRs of 20 or less by the year 2000. We then discuss the difference between our projected CBRs and those of the United Nations (1981), plus the effect of differences between the two methods of projecting CBRs on the expected rate of natural increase for each large LDC in the year 2010.

Comparison with Berelson's Estimates of Nations That Would Achieve Crude Birth Rates of 20 or Less by Year 2000

Based on his analyses of developmental thresholds required for CBRs of 20 or less, and the likelihood that a country would surpass one or more of those thresholds, Berelson divided LDCs with 10 million or more inhabitants into four categories: countries he was "certain" would achieve CBRs below 20, those he thought were "probable," those that were "possible," and those that were "unlikely" to achieve low fertility by the year 2000. These categories and our projected CBRs for the years 2000 and 2010 are displayed in Table 12.1.

Table 12.1 finds projected CBRs well below 20 in the three countries deemed by Berelson to be "certain" to reach low fertility by the turn of the century, although none of the three had actually achieved this level by 1982 (World Bank 1984, Table 20).

TABLE 12.1
Comparisons of Berelson's projected less-developed countries with crude birth rates equal to or less than 20 by the year 2000 with Smith–Cutright projected year 2000 and 2010 crude birth rates

Berelson's Category and Country[a,b]	Smith–Cutright Projected Crude Birth Rates 2000	2010
The Certain		
South Korea	15.7	13.0[c]
Taiwan	15.2	13.6
Chile	14.1	13.0[c]
The Probable		
China	13.0	13.0[c]
Brazil	22.7	20.3
Mexico	25.5	22.3
Philippines	24.7	21.5
Thailand	21.7	18.5
Turkey	24.2	20.3
Colombia	24.7	22.3
Sri Lanka	18.7	16.3
Venezuela	26.9	24.5
Malaysia	23.4	21.0
The Possible		
India	30.5	23.8
Indonesia	33.0	27.4
Egypt	26.3	22.3
Peru	27.0	23.9

The Unlikely
Sixteen nations, none of which has a Smith–Cutright projected year 2000 crude birth rate of 30 or less.

[a]Berelson's (1978, p. 597) correspondence point for crude birth rate = 20 was E_0 of 69 years. See Table 12A.2 for projected life expectancy values used in this essay.
[b]Countries are ordered by 1970 population size within categories.
[c]Estimated values below 13.0 set to equal 13.0.

Of the ten countries thought "probable" to reach a CBR of 20 or below, only two (China and Sri Lanka) have a predicted CBR below 20, although Thailand is projected to be very close—at 22. All remaining seven countries are 3 to 8 points above a CBR of 20 in the year 2000, but seven of the ten are projected to reach 21.5 or below by the year 2010.

The four nations thought by Berelson to be "possible" are not likely to fulfill that wish—India and Indonesia are both above 30, and Egypt and Peru remain in the high twenties. An additional ten years finds only one of the four with a CBR below 23.

Berelson placed the remaining 16 large LDCs in the "unlikely" group, and our projections support that view: None of the 16 has a projected CBR of 30 or below by the year 2000.

It is, of course, quite likely that measurement errors in past CBRs or life expectancy and/or incorrect projections of the life expectancy values used will result in some of these forecasts being in serious error. Also, civil war in Sri Lanka and ethnic or religious strife in Malaysia, Lebanon, or elsewhere might maintain lower levels of life expectancy than expected, or otherwise promote higher fertility that is predicted here. On the other hand, improvements in contraceptive technology (for example, the five-year contraceptive female implant) and/or more rapid diffusion of smaller family size goals as being economically rational and morally acceptable (Coale 1973; Freedman 1982), coupled with major improvements in delivery of family-planning services, could result in more rapid declines in fertility than those projected by our model.

Comparing U.N. and Smith-Cutright Projected Crude Birth Rates and Rates of Natural Increase

The comparisons of U.N. and our projected CBRs and the resulting projected rates of natural increase reported in Table 12A.3 are summarized in Table 12.2. In the first three columns, the difference found when our projection is subtracted from the U.N. projection for 1990, 2000, and 2010 is reported. In the upper row, for example, we report that the U.N. estimate for Ethiopia in 1990 was −1.2 points below our estimate, and the discrepancy grows rapidly to −10.2 by the year 2010. Because we use the same projected CDRs as does the United Nations, the difference between the U.N. and our projected RNIs is equal to the difference in the two estimates of CBRs. In the case of Ethiopia, the U.N. estimate of an RNI of 22.7 in 2010 is just 69 percent of our estimated rate of 32.9. Our higher CBRs for Ethiopia result in large part from our assumption that continuing low levels of life expectancy below the threshold for initial fertility declines, as projected by the United Nations, make substantial fertility declines unlikely. In virtually all the remaining countries in this table in which the differences between projected CBRs are substantial and negative, a similar explanation applies.

Among the first group of seven countries in sub-Saharan Africa, our CBR projections for Ethiopia, Nigeria, and the Sudan are much higher than those of the United Nations. On the other hand, we project lower fertility for both Kenya and Uganda than does the United Nations. Both sets of projections agree in the case of Tanzania, and are close for Zaire as well.

In the six large LDCs in the Middle East–North African region, U.N. CBRs are lower than ours in Algeria, Iran, Iraq, and Morocco; we agree with U.N. estimates for Egypt and Turkey.

Among the 14 Asian countries, U.N. estimates of CBRs are generally much lower than ours in Afghanistan, Bangladesh, India, Indonesia, Nepal, and Pakistan. The two projections generally agree on Burma, China, South Korea, Malaysia, Sri Lanka, and Thailand. No comparison is possible for Taiwan, but that is not a problematic country so far as high CBRs are concerned.

For Latin American countries, U.N. projections are somewhat higher than ours in Brazil, Chile, and Peru, while the difference is generally small in Columbia, Mexico, and Venezuela.

Mean values of RNIs resulting from the two sets of projected CBRs for the year 2010 are shown in Table 12.2 for each regional block. In the sub-Saharan group our mean RNI is 3.5 per 1,000 population higher than that of the United Nations, while in the Middle East and North African cluster the difference is 2.2. The difference rises to 4.0 among Asian LDCs, while it declines to −2.2 among the Latin American LDCs—a result consistent with our predictions of generally lower CBRs than those of the United Nations in Latin America. These mean regional differences may be judged as "small" by some analysts. In our view, estimates of possible underestimation of future CBRs on population growth rates should focus on individual countries for the purpose of planning population-related programs. Thus, population planners in Nepal need to be concerned with the issue of how to avoid facing a 2010 RNI of 26.4 in their country and can take little comfort from the likelihood that the mean RNI in Asia generally will be much lower. On the other hand, the relatively small mean differences in RNI from U.N. or our projected CBRs among regions (other than Asia and sub-Saharan Africa) suggest that the U.N. projections of regional population size in other regions may not be seriously underestimated, an observation that accords with Stoto's finding (1983) of a diminishing bias in U.N. population projections for LDCs.

A Validity Test

To test the likely validity of the two sets of projected CBRs, we assume that, other things being equal, a country with a high level of literacy is more likely than a country with a low level of literacy to have declining fertility. By comparing the level of projected future literacy (1)

TABLE 12.2
Differences in Smith–Cutright and U.N. projected crude birth rates and rates of natural increase among large less-developed countries by region, 1990–2010

	Difference in Projected Rates[a]			Year 2010 Rate of Natural Increase	
Country	1990	2000	2010	U.N.	Smith–Cutright
Sub-Saharan Africa					
Ethiopia	−1.2	−6.4	−10.2	22.7	32.9
Kenya	6.5	7.3	4.0	33.7	29.7
Nigeria	−3.5	−6.8	−10.8	27.4	38.2
Sudan	−4.1	−6.8	−8.0	21.9	29.9
Tanzania	0.5	0.7	−1.2	26.5	27.7
Uganda	3.5	5.2	5.5	29.7	24.2
Zaire	−0.7	−2.4	−3.3	23.8	27.1
Mean				26.5	30.0
Middle East–North Africa					
Algeria	−0.9	−1.3	−4.9	22.2	27.1
Egypt	−0.6	0.9	1.4	16.5	15.1
Iraq	−1.0	−2.1	−4.5	21.8	26.4
Morocco	0.8	−2.4	−3.7	20.5	24.2
Turkey	1.8	0.2	0.6	14.5	13.9
Mean				19.1	21.3
Asia					
Afghanistan	−3.5	−9.5	−14.0	20.0	34.0

Bangladesh	−4.2	−9.1	−12.0	27.0	39.0
Burma	−3.8	−2.3	−2.8	16.6	19.4
China	5.5	3.8	1.0	6.5	5.5
India	−3.9	−7.0	−4.6	10.5	15.1
Indonesia	−8.2	−10.7	−9.0	9.0	18.0
Iran	−4.2	−5.7	−5.6	18.1	23.7
Korea (South)	2.1	1.6	2.9	8.3	5.4
Malaysia	−0.2	−1.8	−2.5	12.8	15.3
Nepal	−2.7	−6.0	−9.6	16.8	26.4
Pakistan	−4.9	−9.4	−8.1	16.4	24.5
Philippines	0.5	−1.0	−1.5	14.3	15.8
Sri Lanka	2.7	0.3	0.5	10.1	9.6
Taiwan		United Nations Omits Taiwan		11.4	12.2
Thailand	0.2	−0.9	−0.8	14.1	18.1
Mean					
Latin America					
Brazil	3.7	3.6	4.5	17.9	13.4
Chile	5.2	5.4	4.8	9.9	5.1
Colombia	0.8	−1.4	−2.0	13.5	15.5
Mexico	3.3	0.8	0.5	17.6	17.1
Peru	5.8	6.5	6.9	24.6	17.9
Venezuela	1.6	−0.8	−1.3	18.2	19.5
Mean				16.9	14.7

[a] A negative difference means that the U.N. projection was lower than that of Smith and Cutright in Table 12A.3. Positive signs indicate that U.N. projected birth rates are high than Smith–Cutright projections.

in countries in which U.N. estimates of future CBRs are much lower than ours with (2) countries in which the two estimates are similar and (3) countries where U.N. estimates are much higher than ours, we can provide a partial test of the face validity of the two methods.

Results are presented in Table 12.3. In the upper panel, we show the projected literacy rates in 1990 in the three countries where U.N. fertility projections were much lower than ours, and contrast literacy rates in this set of three countries with those in which the two methods produced little difference or U.N. estimates were higher than ours. In the upper panel of the table, we find that the difference in literacy levels is striking—all three sub-Saharan countries with U.N. CBR projections much lower than ours are low literacy countries, while the four sub-Saharan countries with substantial agreement between both projections, or where U.N. projections were higher than ours, are all high literacy populations. This pattern lends support to our projections over those of the United Nations in cases where either large positive or negative differences exist.

A similar pattern holds for the four Mediterranean countries, although the size of the difference in projected CBRs is generally small, and we have no instance in which the United Nations projects CBRs five or more points above ours.

Among Asian countries five of the seven countries with much lower U.N. projections than ours are low literacy countries, while the remaining seven countries are all high literacy countries among which differences in projected CBRs generated by the two methods are small.

The results among Latin American countries are also interesting. In this region the U.N. projects three substantially higher CBRs than do we. But there may be little reason to accept the higher U.N. projected CBRs since the level of literacy in all three of these populations is very high by 1990 and should, in the case of Brazil and Peru, continue to even higher levels by the year 2000.

DISCUSSION

The first goal of this research was to test the hypothesis that more than one threshold level exists for the effect of life expectancy on CBRs, and that additional years of life expectancy beyond the second and higher threshold will have greater effects on fertility than will life expectancy increases beginning at lower levels. Results indicate that after the initial threshold required to trigger a fertility decline is reached, it is necessary to reach and surpass a still higher threshold for the rate of

TABLE 12.3
Differences in crude birth rates using U.N. and Smith–Cutright projected years 2000 and 2010 crude birth rates, and levels of adult literacy estimated for 1990, by region

Country	Adult Literacy[a] 1990	Difference in U.N. Minus Smith–Cutright Crude Birth Rates 2000	2010
Sub-Saharan Africa			
Nigeria	43	−6.8	−10.8
Sudan	33	−6.8	−8.0
Ethiopia	12	−6.4	−10.2
Zaire	70	−2.4	−3.3
Tanzania	63	0.7	−1.2
Uganda	57	5.2	5.5
Kenya	69	7.3	4.0
North Africa and Near East			
Algeria	56	−1.3	−4.9
Morocco	36	−2.4	−3.7
Iraq	58	−2.1	−4.5
Egypt	62	0.9	1.4
Turkey	76	0.2	−0.6
Asia			
Afghanistan	16	−9.5	−14.0
Bangladesh	54	−9.1	−12.0
Nepal	26	−6.0	−9.6
India	46	−7.0	−9.6
Pakistan	45	−9.4	−8.1
Iran	64	−5.7	−5.6
Indonesia	77	−10.7	−9.0
Malaysia	83	−1.8	−2.5
Burma	77	−2.3	−2.8
Philippines	93	−1.0	−1.5
Sri Lanka	88[b]	0.3	0.5
Thailand	91	−0.9	−0.8
S. Korea	95	1.6	2.9
China	78–84[b]	3.8	1.0
Latin America			
Colombia	93	−1.7	−2.7
Venezuela	88	−0.8	−1.3
Mexico	91	0.8	0.5
Brazil	84	3.6	4.5
Chile	95	5.4	4.8
Peru	89	6.5	6.9

[a] From UN Educational, Scientific, and Cultural Organization (1978, Table 3).
[b] Estimated by the authors.

fertility decline to accelerate further. In particular, life expectancy of at least 46 years is required for any fertility decline, and a threshold of 56 years must be passed for the decline in fertility to increase sharply. These results were robust and held in the face of introducing measures of FPPE, period, urbanization, literacy, and dummy variables for each country.

The second goal was to project CBRs for each of our 83 LDCs in 1990, 2000, and 2010. This was accomplished by including in the prediction equation projected values of life expectancy in 1980, 1990, and 2000, that is, lagged ten years behind the respective projected CBRs.

We first compared our projections with Berelson's for the year 2000 (1978). Berelson appears to have been overly optimistic in many instances, mainly because he relied on many indicators of thresholds, some of which were redundant and/or empirically irrelevant.

We then compared our projected CBRs with recent U.N. projections. Discrepancies and similarities were discussed, and their impact on the RNI in 2010 among two of the largest LDCs was reported. A test for the probable validity of the U.N. projections compared with ours was conducted, and the results were interpreted as supporting our projections both in cases where U.N. projections were lower than ours and when their projections were higher.

Our introduction noted that the demographic measure of greatest concern is the rate of population growth, rather than birth or death rates alone. Because death rates in LDCs were generally reduced rapidly after 1950, while birth rates generally remained stable, the RNI—our measure of annual population growth—leaped upward and created the "population explosion." Even countries with substantial reductions in fertility between 1960 and 1980 (for example, India) often showed no decline in population growth because declining death rates kept pace with the lowering birth rates. However, for many LDCs the fall in mortality is nearly over, and future diminution of fertility should have substantial impact on growth rates. The extent to which various regions and countries will have much lower growth rates in 2010 than they had in 1980 can be addressed by comparing the RNI around 1980 (Population Reference Bureau 1984) with our year 2010 projections from Table 12.2.

The mean projected RNI in 2010 among Latin American nations is 63 percent of the 1980 rate, and all six countries are expected to experience a drop of at least 25 percent. Latin America has the largest average decline of any region. Next are the five North African and Middle Eastern populations with a mean RNI in 2010 that is 74 percent of the 1980 rate, and all five may experience a decline of at least 17 percent. Close behind are the 15 Asian nations—their mean RNI in 2010 is projected to be 78 percent of the 1980 level. But the 2010 rate is actually over 25 percent higher in both Afghanistan and Bangladesh than it was in 1980, while Nepal's rate is 4 percent greater. In contrast, the 2010 growth rates in China, South Korea, and Taiwan are all 40 percent or more below their 1980 rates. Finally, the mean RNI for the seven countries in sub-Saharan Africa is 95 percent of the 1980 rate, with only Kenya and Uganda expected to have growth rates as much as 23 percent below the 1980 rates.

Our results support the view that low rates of population growth among LDCs are not likely by the year 2010. Only 4 of the 33 large LDCs in this study are expected to have 2010 growth rates below 1 percent annually—Chile, China, South Korea, and Taiwan. (These four nations are also the only large LDCs with RNIs under 2 percent in 1980.) Fourteen of the 29 LDCs with 1980 RNIs above 2 percent may move down to the 1.0 to 1.9 percent range by 2010, but the remaining 15 are expected to remain above 2 percent, and 6 of these 15 are likely to have growth rates above 3 percent. A growth rate of 2 percent, if maintained over time, results in a doubling of the population in just 35 years. If a doubling time of 35 years is judged as "high," then we expect that nearly half of all large LDCs will still be experiencing rapid growth in the year 2010.

Keyfitz (1982) has observed that in spite of decades of advances in our understanding of population processes, our most reliable methods of making forecasts are still self-contained projections or extrapolations—those based only on past patterns of a demographic variable, without reference to factors known to explain or otherwise impinge upon the variable's behavior. The reasons for this are many and varied, but most relate to the fact that the complexity inherent in explanation involves too much "conditioning" of outcomes to create serviceable forecasts. Yet extrapolated projections themselves make unsatisfactory forecasts, since the underlying assumptions are typically implicit and/or insufficiently articulated. By linking the CBR to a fairly static function of levels and thresholds of life expectancy, we have sought to generate forecasts via a mechanism that is at once explicit and open to criticism and amendment, yet not so involved as to make the outcomes debatable only after a myriad of a priori judgments and assumptions. Whether these forecasts themselves represent an improvement over those currently extant will, of course, be resolved only with the passage of time. In the interim, however, we submit that their face validity appears high, and hope that our formulation of the underlying mechanism by which such forecasts can be obtained will itself be of use to researchers in this area.

APPENDIX
TABLE 12A.1

Models for the regression of crude birth rates on life expectancy, for pooled cross-sectional data from 83 less-developed countries: 1960, 1970, and 1980[a]

Parameters[c] (Standard Errors)	(1a)	(1b)	(2a)	(2b)	(3a)	(3b)	(4a)	(4b)	(5a)	(5b)
μ_0	72.60	54.64	68.11	54.20	68.73	51.95	64.08	43.50	67.61	46.11
	(1.42)	(3.61)	(1.47)	(3.48)	(1.50)	(3.71)	(5.41)	(6.09)	(5.46)	(6.49)
μ_1		17.69		19.16		19.57		19.53		17.24
		(10.35)		(9.98)		(10.03)		(7.76)		(7.94)
μ_2		29.65		13.40		9.38		20.47		21.84
		(13.07)		(13.10)		(13.19)		(10.22)		(10.31)
γ_0	−0.648	−0.189	−0.532	−0.176	−0.542	−0.218	−0.444	0.059	−0.402	0.051
	(0.03)	(0.09)	(0.03)	(0.09)	(0.03)	(0.10)	(0.12)	(0.14)	(0.12)	(0.14)
γ_1		−0.404		−0.429		−0.428		−0.440		−0.389
		(0.22)		(0.21)		(0.21)		(0.16)		(0.17)
γ_2		−0.568		−0.274		−0.198		−0.395		−0.421
		(0.24)		(0.24)		(0.24)		(0.19)		(0.19)
δ			−0.416	−0.281	−0.513	−0.352	−0.416	−0.220	−0.393	−0.214
			(0.06)	(0.06)	(0.07)	(0.07)	(0.05)	(0.06)	(0.05)	(0.06)
α_{1960}[d]					−0.69	−0.20	−0.04	1.07	−0.89	0.63
α_{1970}					−0.82	−0.66	−0.64	−0.44	−0.64	−0.45
					(0.40)	(0.38)	(0.28)	(0.26)	(0.28)	(0.26)

α_{1980}	1.51		0.86		0.68		1.53		−0.18	
	(0.44)		(0.44)		(0.62)		(0.68)		(0.68)	
β_i					−0.63		−0.130		−0.019	
					(0.58)		(0.06)		(0.06)	
			Included						Included	
τ_1							−0.071		−0.060	
							(0.05)		(0.04)	
τ_2										
R^2	0.648	0.729	0.702	0.750	0.715	0.754	0.908	0.929	0.912	0.930
df	247	243	246	242	244	240	162	158	160	156
SEE	4.67	4.13	4.31	3.98	4.23	3.96	2.96	2.63	2.90	2.63

[a] Years refer to crude birth rates; life expectancy and other covariates (family planning program effort, urbanization, literacy) are as measured approximately ten years earlier.

[b] There are five general models: Model (1) includes only the life expectancy variable as a predictor; Model (2) adds in the 1972 measure of family planning effort; Model (3) allows for intercept differences across the three periods (1960, 1970, and 1980); Model (4) allows for 83 country-specific differences in intercepts; and Model (5) incorporates the variables urbanization and literacy. Version (a) of each model assumes a single slope across the entire range of the independent variable life expectancy, while Version (b) allows for different slopes in the intervals below 46 years, from 46 through 56 years, and above 56 years.

[c] μ_0 is the basic intercept; μ_1 is the offset to that intercept when life expectancy is between 46 and 56 years, while μ_2 is the additional offset when life expectancy is 56 years or greater. Similarly, γ_0 is the basic slope for the regression of crude birth rate on life expectancy; γ_1 is the change in this slope when life expectancy is between 46 and 56 years, while γ_2 is the additional change in slope when life expectancy is 56 years or greater. δ is the slope for the regression of crude birth rate on family-planning program effort circa 1972. The α values are offsets to the basic intercept for each of the three years 1960, 1970, and 1980; the β values are the 83 country-specific offsets to the intercept. τ_1 is the slope for the regression of crude birth rate on percent urban; τ_2 is the slope for the regression of crude birth rate on percent literate. R^2 is the basic measure of goodness of fit (variance explained); df refers to degrees of freedom (249 minus the number of independently estimated parameters); and SEE is the standard error of the estimate—that is, the standard deviation of the difference between predicted and observed crude birth rates.

[d] This parameter is not estimated independently, but is instead derived from $-(\alpha_{1970} + \alpha_{1980})$; hence, no standard error is shown.

TABLE 12A.2
Observed and expected life expectancy (e_0) among large less-developed countries, by region: 1950-2000

	Life Expectancy					
Country	1950	1960	1970	1980	1990	2000
Asia						
Afghanistan	30	33	39	40	44	49
Bangladesh	36	40	40	46	51	56
Burma	40	44	49	54	59	63
China	46	53	60	69	71	73
India	38	43	48	50	53	60
Indonesia	35	41	46	49	54	59
Iran	42	45	50	54	59	64
Korea (S.)	47	54	59	64	67	70
Malaysia	48	53	58	64	68	70
Nepal	27	36	41	44	49	54
Pakistan	43	47	49	52	55	60
Philippines	46	53	57	62	66	69
Sri Lanka	55	62	67	66	69	71
Taiwan	57	64	68	72	74	75
Thailand	45	52	57	61	65	68
Sub-Saharan Africa						
Ethiopia	33	36	38	40	44	50
Kenya	44	47	49	55	59	63
Nigeria	36	39	44	49	54	59
Sudan	35	39	46	45	53	58
Tanzania	34	38	43	52	57	61
Uganda	39	44	49	54	58	63
Zaire	37	40	43	47	52	57
North Africa-Middle East						
Algeria	41	47	52	55	61	65
Egypt	42	46	51	56	60	64
Iraq	41	46	51	56	61	65
Morocco	43	47	52	57	61	65
Turkey	47	51	56	61	65	69
Latin America						
Brazil	43	57	61	63	66	68
Chile	48	57	62	66	69	71
Colombia	48	53	60	63	65	67
Mexico	48	58	62	65	68	71
Peru	40	48	55	58	62	65
Venezuela	53	59	64	67	69	71

TABLE 12A.3
Comparisons of Smith-Cutright and U.N. projected crude birth rate and rate of national increase among less-developed countries with 10 million or more inhabitants around 1970, by region

Nation	Statistics	1990	2000	2010
Sub-Saharan Africa				
Ethiopia	CBR—U.N.	47.5	41.7	34.9
	CDR	20.0	15.7	12.2
	RNI	27.5	26.0	22.7
	CBR—S.C.	48.7	48.1	45.1
Kenya	CBR—U.N.	51.1	46.6	39.4
	CDR	10.3	7.6	5.7
	RNI	40.8	39.0	33.7
	CBR—S.C.	44.6	39.3	35.4
Nigeria	CBR—U.N.	46.7	41.6	35.2
	CDR	13.2	10.1	7.8
	RNI	33.5	31.5	27.4
	CBR—S.C.	50.2	48.4	46.0
Sudan	CBR—U.N.	42.3	36.9	30.4
	CDR	13.8	10.7	8.5
	RNI	28.5	26.2	21.9
	CBR—S.C.	46.4	43.7	38.4
Tanzania	CBR—U.N.	44.1	39.5	33.6
	CDR	11.7	9.1	7.1
	RNI	32.4	30.4	26.5
	CBR—S.C.	43.6	38.8	34.8
Uganda	CBR—U.N.	43.8	40.7	36.3
	CDR	10.7	8.4	6.6
	RNI	33.1	32.3	29.7
	CBR—S.C.	40.3	35.5	30.8
Zaire	CBR—U.N.	42.7	38.2	32.5
	CDR	14.1	11.0	8.7
	RNI	28.6	27.2	23.8
	CBR—S.C.	43.4	40.6	35.8
North Africa–Middle East				
Algeria	CBR—U.N.	44.3	35.3	27.8
	CDR	10.0	7.2	5.6
	RNI	34.3	28.1	22.2
	CBR—S.C.	43.4	36.6	32.7
Egypt	CBR—U.N.	30.8	27.2	23.7
	CDR	9.6	8.1	7.2
	RNI	21.2	19.1	16.5
	CBR—S.C.	30.2	26.3	22.3

TABLE 12A.3 *(continued)*

Nation	Statistics	1990	2000	2010
Iraq	CBR—U.N.	40.0	34.1	27.8
	CDR	9.3	7.3	5.9
	RNI	30.7	26.8	21.9
	CBR—S.C.	41.0	36.2	32.3
Morocco	CBR—U.N.	38.9	31.7	26.5
	CDR	9.4	7.1	6.0
	RNI	29.5	24.6	20.5
	CBR—S.C.	38.1	34.1	30.2
Turkey	CBR—U.N.	30.0	24.4	20.9
	CDR	7.9	6.6	6.4
	RNI	22.1	17.8	14.5
	CBR—S.C.	28.2	24.2	20.3
Asia				
Afghanistan	CBR—U.N.	45.5	38.8	31.7
	CDR	19.5	15.2	11.7
	RNI	26.0	23.6	20.0
	CBR—S.C.	49.0	48.3	45.7
Bangladesh	CBR—U.N.	40.5	32.9	25.5
	CDR	14.2	10.7	8.5
	RNI	26.3	22.2	27.0
	CBR—S.C.	44.7	42.0	37.5
Burma	CBR—U.N.	33.0	28.2	23.8
	CDR	10.7	8.6	7.2
	RNI	22.3	19.6	16.6
	CBR—S.C.	36.2	30.5	26.6
China	CBR—U.N.	18.5	16.8	14.0
	CDR	7.0	6.7	6.9
	RNI	11.8	9.9	6.5
	CBR—S.C.	13.0	13.0[a]	13.0[a]
India	CBR—U.N.	28.6	23.5	19.2
	CDR	11.7	9.7	8.7
	RNI	16.9	13.8	10.5
	CBR—S.C.	32.5	30.5	23.8
Indonesia	CBR—U.N.	27.5	22.3	18.4
	CDR	12.5	10.5	9.4
	RNI	15.0	11.8	9.0
	CBR—S.C.	35.7	33.0	27.4
Iran	CBR—U.N.	36.0	28.9	24.2
	CDR	9.4	7.2	6.1
	RNI	26.6	21.7	18.1
	CBR—S.C.	40.2	34.6	29.8

TABLE 12A.3 *(continued)*

Nation	Statistics	1990	2000	2010
Korea (South)	CBR—U.N.	21.0	17.3	15.9
	CDR	7.1	7.0	7.6
	RNI	13.9	10.3	8.3
	CBR—S.C.	18.9	15.7	13.0[a]
Malaysia	CBR—U.N.	27.1	21.6	18.5
	CDR	6.1	5.5	5.7
	RNI	21.0	16.1	12.8
	CBR—S.C.	27.3	23.4	21.0
Nepal	CBR—U.N.	39.1	33.2	26.8
	CDR	16.0	12.6	10.0
	RNI	23.1	20.6	16.8
	CBR—S.C.	41.8	39.2	36.4
Pakistan	CBR—U.N.	35.0	28.5	23.8
	CDR	11.4	8.9	7.4
	RNI	23.7	19.6	16.4
	CBR—S.C.	39.9	37.9	31.9
Philippines	CBR—U.N.	29.1	23.7	20.0
	CDR	6.5	5.8	5.7
	RNI	22.6	17.9	14.3
	CBR—S.C.	28.6	24.7	21.5
Sri Lanka	CBR—U.N.	24.5	19.0	16.8
	CDR	6.5	6.2	6.7
	RNI	18.0	12.8	10.1
	CBR—S.C.	21.8	18.7	16.3
Taiwan		United Nations omits Taiwan		
	CBR—S.C.	17.6	15.2	13.6
Thailand	CBR—U.N.	25.9	20.8	17.7
	CDR	6.9	6.2	6.3
	RNI	19.0	14.6	11.4
	CBR—S.C.	25.7	21.7	18.5
Latin America				
Brazil	CBR—U.N.	29.6	26.3	24.8
	CDR	7.7	7.1	6.9
	RNI	21.3	19.2	17.9
	CBR—S.C.	25.9	22.7	20.3
Chile	CBR—U.N.	22.5	19.5	17.8
	CDR	7.4	7.2	7.9
	RNI	15.1	12.3	9.9
	CBR—S.C.	17.3	14.1	13.0[a]
Colombia	CBR—U.N.	27.9	23.3	20.3
	CDR	7.2	6.8	6.8

TABLE 12A.3 (continued)

Nation	Statistics	1990	2000	2010
Mexico	RNI	20.7	16.5	13.5
	CBR—S.C.	27.1	24.7	22.3
	CBR—U.N.	31.9	26.3	22.8
	CDR	5.9	5.2	5.2
Peru	RNI	26.0	21.1	17.6
	CBR—S.C.	28.6	25.5	22.3
	CBR—U.N.	36.8	33.5	30.8
	CDR	8.8	7.2	6.2
Venezuela	RNI	28.0	26.3	24.6
	CBR—S.C.	31.0	27.0	23.9
	CBR—U.N.	30.9	26.1	23.2
	CDR	5.0	4.8	5.0
	RNI	25.9	21.3	18.2
	CBR—S.C.	29.3	26.9	24.5

CBR, crude birth rate; CDR, crude death rate; RNI, rate of natural increase; S.C., Smith-Cutright estimate. Both CBR—U.N. and CDR are from United Nations (1981, Tables A-6 and A-9). Both rates are median rather than low or high projections.

[a]Estimated values below 13.0 set to 13.0.

TABLE 12A.4
Sources and data

Source		Data
United Nations (1981)	Table A-15	Life Expectancy: 1950, 1980–2000
	Table A-6	Crude Birth Rate 1990–2010 (median variant)
	Table A-9	Crude Death Rate, 1980–2010 (median variant)
Mauldin and Berelson (1978)	Table 8	1970–1972 Family-Planning Program Effort
	Table 6	1970 Life Expectancy
	Table D	1960 Life Expectancy
Lapham and Mauldin (1984)	Table 1	Family-Planning Program Effort, 1982
Mauldin (1978, p. 75)		Crude Birth Rates, 1950, 1960
U.N. Educational, Scientific, and Cultural Organization (1978)	Table 3	Adult Literacy, 1990
U.S. Bureau of the Census (1974)	Table 1	Crude Birth Rates, 1970–72
World Bank (1984)	Table 20	Crude Birth Rates, 1980–82

REFERENCES

Beaujot, Rodric. 1984. "How LDC Fertility Declines Stall—The Case of Tunisia." *Population Today* 12:6-7.

Beaver, Steven E. 1975. *Demographic Transition Theory Reinterpreted*. Lexington, MA: Lexington Books.

Berelson, Bernard. 1978. "Prospects and Programs for Fertility Reduction: What? Where?" *Population and Development Review* 4:579-616.

Bulatao, Rodolfo A., and Ann Elwan. 1983. "Mortality Thresholds for Fertility Transition in Developing Countries." Background paper for the 1984 World Development Report, World Bank.

Caldwell, John. 1980. "Mass Education as a Determinant of the Timing of Fertility Decline." *Population and Development Review* 6:225-55.

Coale, Ansley. 1974. "The History of the Human Population." *Scientific American* 231:41-51.

———. 1973. "The Demographic Transition Reconsidered." Pp. 53-73 in *International Population Conference, 1973, Vol. I*. Liege, Begium: International Union for the Scientific Study of Population.

Cutright, Phillips. 1983. "The Ingredients of Recent Fertility Decline in Developing Countries." *International Family Planning Perspectives* 9:101-9.

Cutright, Phillips, and Lowell Hargens. 1984. "The Threshold Hypothesis: Latin America 1950-1980." *Demography* 21:435-58.

Davis, Kingsley. 1963. "The Theory of Change and Response in Modern Demographic History." *Population Index* 29:345-66.

Demeny, Paul. 1984. "A Perspective on Long-Term Population Growth." *Population and Development Review* 10:103-26.

Dielman, Terry E. 1983. "Pooled Cross-Sectional and Time Series Data: A Survey of Current Statistical Methodology." *American Statistician* 37:116-22.

Dumond, Don E. 1975. "The Limitation of Human Population: A Natural Science." *Science* 187:713-21.

Freedman, Ronald. 1982. "Fertility Decline: Theories." Pp. 258-66 in J. A. Ross (ed.), *International Encyclopedia of Population, Vol. 1*. New York: Free Press.

Gallager, Charles F. 1980. "Demography and Development, The Lessons of Costa Rica." American Universities Field Staff Reports, No. 16.

Goldscheider, Calvin. 1971. *Population, Modernization, and Social Structure*. Boston: Little, Brown.

Handwerker, W. Penn. 1983. "The First Demographic Transition: An Analysis of Subsistence Choices and Reproductive Consequences." *American Anthropologist* 85:5-27.

Hassan, Fekri A. 1980. "The Growth and Regulation of Human Populations in Prehistoric Times." Pp. 305-320 in M. N. Cohen, R. S. Malpas, and H. G. Klein (eds.), *Biosocial Mechanisms of Population Regulation*. New Haven, CT: Yale University Press.

Heer, David M. 1983. "Infant and Child Mortality and the Demand for Children." Pp. 369-87 in Rodolfo A. Bulatao and Ronald D. Lee (eds),

Determinants of Fertility in Developing Countries, Vol. 1, New York: Academic Press.
Keyfitz, Nathan. 1982. "Can Knowledge Improve Forecasts?" *Population and Development Review* 8:729-51.
Kirk, Dudley. 1971. "A New Demographic Transition?" Pp. 123-47 in *Rapid Population Growth*. Study Committee of the Office of the Foreign Secretary, National Academy of Sciences. Baltimore: Johns Hopkins University Press.
Lapham, Robert J., and W. Parker Mauldin. 1984. "Family Planning Program Effort and Birthrate Decline in Developing Countries." *International Family Planning Perspectives* 10:109-18.
LeVine, Robert. 1980. "Influences of Women's Schooling on Maternal Behavior in the Third World." *Comparative Education Review* 24:S78-105.
Mauldin, W. Parker. 1978. "Patterns of Fertility Decline in Developing Countries, 1950-75." *Studies on Family Planning* 9:75-84.
Mauldin, W. Parker, and B. Berelson. 1978. "Conditions of Fertility Decline in Developing Countries 1965-75." *Studies on Family Planning* 9:89-147.
McGranahan, O. V., C. Richard-Provst, N. V. Sovani, and M. Subramanian. 1972. *Contents and Measurement of Socioeconomic Development*. New York: Praeger.
McNicoll, Geoffrey. 1984. "Consequences of Rapid Population Growth: Overview and Assessment." *Population and Development Review* 10:177-240.
Notestein, Frank W. 1953. "Economic Problems of Population Change." Pp. 13-31 in *International Conference of Agricultural Economists, 1953*. London: Oxford University Press.
Oechsli, Frank W., and Dudley Kirk. 1975. "Modernization and the Demographic Transition in Latin America and the Caribbean." *Economic Development and Cultural Change* 23:391-419.
Pindyck, Robert, and Daniel Rubinfeld. 1976. *Econometric Models and Economic Forecasts*. New York: McGraw-Hill.
Population Reference Bureau. 1984. *1984 World Population Data Sheet of the Population Reference Bureau*. Washington, D.C.: Population Reference Bureau.
Preston, Samuel H. 1978. "Mortality Trends." *Annual Review of Sociology* 4:163-78.
Retherford, Robert D., and James A. Palmore. 1983. "Diffusion Processes Affecting Fertility Regulation." Pp. 295-339 in Rodolfo A. Bulatao and Ronald D. Lee (eds.), *Determinants of Fertility in Developing Countries, Vol. 2*. New York: Academic Press.
Ryder, Norman B. 1983. "Fertility and Family Structure." Pp. 15-34 in *Population Bulletin of the United Nations, No. 15*. New York: United Nations.
Srikantan, K. S. 1982. "The Threshold Hypothesis." Pp. 261-67 in J. A. Ross (ed.), *International Encyclopedia of Population, Vol. 1*. New York: Free Press.
Stoto, Michael A. 1983. "The Accuracy of Population Projections." *Journal of the American Statistical Association* 78:13-20.
U.N. Educational, Scientific, and Cultural Organization. 1978. *Estimates and Projections of Illiteracy Age 15 and Over*. CSR/E/29. Paris: U.N. Educational, Scientific, and Cultural Organization.

United Nations. 1981. *World Population Prospects as Assessed in 1980. Population Studies, No. 78.* New York: United Nations.

———. 1965. *Population Bulletin No. 7-1963, with Special References to Conditions and Trends of Fertility in the World.* New York: United Nations.

U.S. Bureau of the Census. 1983. *World Population, 1983: Recent Demographic Estimates for the Countries and Regions of the World.* Washington, D.C.: U.S. Government Printing Office.

———. 1974. *World Population: 1973 Recent Demographic Estimates for the Countries and Regions of the World.* Washington, D.C.: U.S. Government Printing Office.

World Bank. 1984. *World Development Report, 1984.* New York: Oxford University Press.

Index

Adler, Kenneth P. 104
Afghanistan 105, 285, 291
Africa 22, 79, 178, 219, 227, 288, 294; subsaharan 285, 291; horn of, 220; southern, 233
Algeria 289
Allende, Salvador 175
Allison, Graham T. 106
Almond, Gabriel A. 47
Anti-Ballistic Missile (ABM) Treaty 203, 206
Aristotle 48-49
arms control, definition and interpretation 197-199; goal of 5; agenda for 201-202, 204-206; and stability 5, 201-204
arms race 5
Arad, R. W. 219, 220n
Arad, U. B. 219, 220n
Ashby 39, 46-47
Asia 79, 277, 285, 290
Austria 46, 47, 82, 138
Austria-Hungary 82
Australia 180, 219
Aron, Raymond 47, 48

Balance of Power Politics 27-28, 47, 60, 78
Baldwin, David 230n
Baltzly, Alexander 133
Bangladesh 220, 285, 291
Bardes, Barbara 100, 103
Barnet, Richard J. 17
Barraclough, Geoffrey 63
Beaujot, Rodric 224n
Beaver Steven E. 224n
Beck, Morris 251n
Bell, Daniel 250
Bentham, Jeremy 28
Berelson, Bernard 274, 275, 283, 284
Barney, G. O. 211, 223
Bennet, J. W. 217n

Bergsen, A. 84
"bias shift" in decision making 231-232
biological resource bases 224-226
bionumber See conservational variables
Black, C.E. 47, 56
Blalock, H. M. 85
Bolsheviks 160
Braudel, F. 221
Brazil 285, 288
Bremer, Stuart A. 131, 144
Bretton Woods 104
Brezhnev, Leonid 178
Brinkley, David 18
Brito, Dagobert 5
Brodie, Bernard 17
Bronowski, Jacob 13, 24
Brunner, Karl 250n
Bryson, R. A. 214n
Buddha, Gautama 181
Buddhism, 45
Bueno de Mesquita, Bruce 76
Bulatao, Rodolfo A. 274, 279
Bull, Hedley 227n
bureaucratic politics 19
Burma 285
Bykov, O. N. 173

Caldwell, John 279
Callaghy, T. M. 227n
Cambodia 175
Cameron, David R. 249, 250n, 254
Canada 180, 219, 251, 254, 255, 256
Cannon, Walter B. 58-59
Cardon, S. 57, 60, 65
Carr, E. H. 12
Carroll, Lewis 60n
carrying capacity 217, 223; social, of cities 226; of countries 227; of state systems 217, 223, 226, 227; of the environment 227-229

303

Cascade Spectrum 54-55, 64
Catholic 182
Chatterjee, P. 78
Chavez, Cesar 180
Chicago Council on Foreign
    Relations 105, 114
Chile 157, 175, 178, 285, 291
China 23, 50, 82, 158, 160, 177-178,
    182, 221, 283, 285, 291
Chomsky, Noam 99-100
Choucri, Nazli 48, 55, 78, 218, 252
Claude, Inis, Jr. 60, 77
Coale, Ansley 278, 284
Cobden, Richard 16, 28
coercion, general theory and
    definition of 152-157, 158, 161,
    162-165; state coercion 150-151,
    153, 159-160, 163, 173, 175;
    political coercion 152, 154,
    155-157, 160; violent
    coercion 154, 157, 163; nonviolent
    coercion 155; and
    socio economic cleavages 159,
    165; syndrome of 4, 161
Cold War 15, 28, 29, 76, 104
Coleman, James S. 51
colonial frontier 78-81, 84-86, 93
Colombia 281
command-control processes 49, 58, 61
communism, threat of 114, 117, 122
competitive conflict process,
    characteristics of 188-89
competitiveness/community See
    normative dimensions
Comte, Auguste 47, 66
Confucius 49, 57
Congo 219
Congress of Vienna 141
Converse, Philip E. 102
consensus, foreign policy 100, 104,
    123; breakdown of 3, 29, 100, 121
conservational variables 38-41, 42,
    44, 60
Costa Rica 278
contagion, war 126-127, 129-144;
    systemic-level 3, 126, 143-144
containment, policy of 104, 113

crude birth rates, (CBR) 274-275,
    283-285, 288, 290-291; model for
    predicting 279-282; and life
    expectancy 276, 279-282
crude death rate (CDR) 283-285
Cuban missile crisis 198-199
cultural conditioning zone 176
Cultural Revolution 57
Cusack, Thomas 130, 144, 248, 258,
    259
Cutright, Phillips 274, 275, 277, 284
cybernetics 46-47, 57

Dahlberg, K. 213n
Darwin 25
Davis, Kingsley 278
Davis, William W. 130
de Cuellar, J. P. 227n
defense spending, and foreign policy
    beliefs 112-113, 121-122
Demeny, Paul 274n
demographic momentum 216,
    221-224, 226
demographic transition 278
Dehio, L. 77n
Denton, Frank H. 53
de Tocqueville, Alexis 27, 190
Dewey, Edward R. 53
Deutsch, Karl W. 57, 76, 252
Deutsch, Morton 5
Dielman, Terry E. 280
Diesing, P. 76n
disarmament, definition and
    interpretation 197-198, 199-200;
    goal of 201-202
Disraeli, Benjamin 16
dissonance reduction 191
domestic political-module 240
Doyle, Sir Arthur Conan 58
Dumond, Don E. 278
Dupuy, R. Ernest 133n
Dupuy, Trevor N. 133n
Durham, W. H. 218
Durkheim, E. 214, 233
Duvall, Raymond 151, 153, 154, 163

Eckes, A. E. 219

Eckholm, E. 228
economic aid, and foreign policy beliefs 112-113, 117, 121-122
Egypt 285
Ehrlich, P. R. 217, 227
Einstein, Albert 11
Eisenstadt, S. N. 101
elitist/non-elitist See normative dimensions
El Salvador 222
Elwan, Ann 274, 279
Emory, F. E. 215, 233
Enloe, C. H. 218n
Engels, Friedrich 49, 56, 66
Ethiopia 160, 284
Etzioni, Amitai 194
Europe 20-22, 23, 76, 77, 158, 190, 218
expansionist activity, outlets for 3; See also colonial frontier

fan of expanding nonviolent alternatives 176-177
Faraday I. 11
Ferguson, Yale 2, 4
Ferree, G. David 103
fertility, determinants of 273, 275-279; decline in rates 273-274, 275, 279, 284; forecasts of 273-275, 282-283, 284-285, 288, 290
Fischer, G. W. 245
folie a deux 185; definition of 185; and arms race 192-193
Forrester, Jay 48, 55
fossil fuels 224, 226, 228
France 22, 24, 46, 47, 79, 82, 126, 138, 157, 158, 251, 254-255, 261-262, 265
Freedman, Ronald 278, 284
Freud, Sigmund 20, 40
functionalism 4, 30
funnel of violent causality 175-176

Gallager, Charles F. 274n
Galtung, Johan 150
Gamson 162

Gandhiism 171, 178-180
Gandhi, Mohandas 171, 181
Garnham, David 126, 130, 131, 144
Gastil, Raymond 150
Geertz, C. 214n
generation and foreign policy beliefs 3, 100-103, 105-123, 127-128; pre-world war II 105-106, 112, 114, 117, 121; World War II: 100, 105-107, 117, 121; Vietnam 3, 100, 103, 105-107, 112-123; Post-Vietnam 3, 105-113, 115-120, 122-123
generational succession 121
genocide 151, 175
Germany, 22, 46, 49-50, 82, 106, 128, 175, 180; Federal Republic of 82, 157, 162, 251, 253, 255
Gilpin, S. 220n
Gladstone 16
global issue agenda 22, 29
global resource base, 28; issues regarding, 213
Global 2000 Report 211-212
GLOBUS 374-403; description of 6, 237-269; [description] 238-240
Goldschneider, Calvin 278
Gough, Ian 250n
Gould, Frank 251, 254
Gouldner, Alvin W. 160
government resource allocation module 240-241, 243, 245-248
graduated reciprocation in tension reduction (GRIT) process 194
Grathwol, Robert P. 128n
Great Britain (England) 22, 24, 46, 48, 49, 126, 138, 139, 158, 255, 259, 260, 265, 270
Great Depression 22, 105
great power wars 3-4, 75-77, 81-84, 93-94, 131-133, 135-141
Greece 21, 33
Greens 171, 180
Gunning, J. W. 241
Guppy, N. 225
Gupta, S. 241
Gurr, Erika 163

Gurr, Ted Robert 4, 150, 151, 152, 153, 159, 160, 163, 164, 165

Haas, Michael 76
Hamilton, Alexander 16
Handberg, Roger B. 102
Handwerker, W. Penn 278
Hanssan, Fekri A. 278
Hapsburgs 82, 138
Harff, Barbara 151, 154n
Hargens, Lowell 274n
Harris, Marvin 40
Harrod, J. 223
Hawley, A. H. 217, 227
Heer, David M. 279
hegemony 20, 42, 50, 77, 83
Heilbroner, Robert 25
Henige, D. 84
Heritage Foundation 211, 212
Herman, Edward S. 100
Hibbs, Douglas 150, 163, 164
Hickman, Bert G. 241
Hill, David Jayne 133
Hindu 182
Hitler, Adolf 16
Hoffman, Stanley H. 47, 49, 78
Holsti, Ole R. 100, 103, 106, 121, 126
homeokinesis 59–60, 62
homeostasis 58–60, 62
Honduras 222
Hopkins, Terence K. 48
Hord, John 48, 49, 53
Howard, Michael 140n
Hughes, Barry B. 6, 243, 250, 251
Huntington, Elsworth 53

Iberall, Arthur S. 2, 3, 39, 57, 59, 60, 64, 65, 66
idealism 14–15; vs. realism 14–30
Ikle, F. C. 94
imperial wars 83
India 23, 178, 182, 220, 283, 285, 290
Indian Ocean 224
Indonesia 182, 283, 285
interdependence 20, 25, 36

International Atomic Energy Agency (IAEA) 207
international conflict/cooperation module 207, 240, 258
International Monetary Fund (IMF) 251
international (world) systems, types of 46–50
internationalism 100, 104, 105, 107, 121
Intriligator, Michael 5
Iraq 285
Italy 24, 82, 106, 157, 251, 254, 255, 261, 265
Iran 105, 160, 161, 285
Ireland, Northern 157
Irish Republican Army (IRA) 162
isolationism 3, 100, 102, 104, 105, 107, 121–122

Jackson, Steven 152, 153, 164
Jackson, William D. 76n
Japan 50, 82, 106, 182, 251, 253, 254, 261, 263
Jeffries, Vincent 102
Jodice, David A. 39, 150, 162, 164
Johnson, D. G. 221

Kahn, Herman 46, 48, 212, 225
Kamlet, M. S. 245
Kaplan, Morton A. 39, 46, 49, 56, 59
Karyakin, Yu. F. 177
Kegley, Charles W., Jr. 48
Kelley, Allen C. 226, 249
Kelman, Herbert 159n
Kennan, George 28
Kennedy, Donald 214
Kennedy, John 18, 193
Kenya 221, 223, 227, 284, 291
Keohane, Robert 29, 30, 131
Keyes, Gene 171
Keyfitz, Nathan 291
Keynesian economics 260
killing zone 175, 176
King, Joel 130
King, Martin Luther, Jr. 180, 181

Kirk, Dudley 275, 278
Kissinger, Henry A. 99
Klein, Ross 103
Kleinman, D. S. 218, 222
Klingberg, Frank L. 102
Koehl, Robert Lewis 160
Kondratieff, Nikolai 38, 46, 49, 55
Korea (North) 283
Korea (South) 182, 285, 291
Krasner, S. D. 227
Kriesberg, Louis, 103
Kugler, Jacek 47, 50n
Kuhn, Thomas 11–13, 15, 16, 19, 30, 31
Kutscher G. 218

LaFeber, Walter 99
LaMettrie 66
Landsberg, H. H. 221, 224
Langer, William L. 133
Latin America 274, 276, 278, 285, 288, 290
League of Nations 23
Lebanon 288
LeGoff, Jacques 214, 217
Lenin, Vladimir Ilych 55, 78
Leontief, Wassily 241
lethal socialization zone 175–176
level of analysis problem 3–4, 28, 37–38, 75–76, 95, 131, 143, 144, 150, 162, 164
LeVine, Robert 280
Levy, Jack S. 3, 6, 75, 76, 77, 82, 83, 84, 85, 95, 126, 130, 131, 132, 133, 134, 140, 144
Li, R. P. Y. 76n
Lichbach, Mark I. 152, 153, 157, 163, 164
life expectancy, and fertility rates 6, 273–280, 282–284, 288, 290; threshold of 291
limits to growth, 25n
Lindgren, Goeran 253n
linkage 29
Linn, J. 226
Lippmann, Walter 31

literacy level, and fertility rates 274–278, 276, 285, 288
London Suppliers Group 203
long cycles 38–39, 46, 48–49, 50–51, 54–56
Lopez, George A. 155
Lucretius 60
Lunch, William L. 102

Machiavelli, Niccolo 14, 17, 28, 175
macropolitical theory 45–51, 55–57
"mad dictator," problem of 175–178
Maggiotto, Michael A. 100, 103
Malaysia 284, 285
malignant social process 5, 6; characteristics of 186–193; reversal of 193–196
Malthus, Thomas 42
Mannheim, Karl 101
Mansbach, Richard W. 2, 4
Mao Tse-Tung (Zedong) 57
Markus, Gregory B. 150
Martin, Anthony D. 47
Marx, Karl 40, 42, 49, 56, 66
Marxism/Leninism 15, 23, 45, 48, 56, 178, 182
Maxwell, 60
McCarthy, John D. 162
McCulloch, W. 39, 60n
McEvedy, Colin 63
McGowan, Pat 48
McGranahan, O. V. 270, 271
McLuhan, Marshall 232
McNamara, R. S. 223
McNicholl, Geoffrey 273
Meadows, Donella 48
Meadows, Dennis L. 241
Mediterranean 288
Melko, Mathew 48, 49, 53
Mencius 49
Mesarovic, Mihajlo D. 241
Mexico 233, 289
Michels, Robert 41
Middle East 276, 285, 290
military aid, and foreign policy beliefs 107, 112, 117, 121; consequences of 112, 114

military power, utility of 3, 117, 121-122
Miller J. A. 219n
Modelski, George 38, 47, 49, 50, 55, 82, 132
moods, in foreign policy 102
Mongolia 182
Morgan, T. Clifton 3, 6, 75, 83, 95
Morgenthau, Hans J. 15, 17, 23, 26, 28, 77, 78
Morocco 285
Mosca, Gaetano 41
Most, Benjamin A. 130
Mowat R. B. 133
Mueller, John E. 102
Muller, Edward N. 162, 163
Munich 99
Murray, T. J. 214n
Mussolini, Benito 218
mutability/immutability, See normative dimensions
mutual deterrence 202, 203; stability of 202-204, 206

Nardin, Terry 150, 152, 153
national economic module 238-241, 243
national interest 18, 26
NATO 193, 195, 248
neo-functionalists 4, 10, 30
neo-Marxists 14
Nepal 285, 291
Nesvold, Betty A. 150
Netherlands (Holland) 46, 48, 50, 82
Newtonian doctrine 11, 36, 58
Niebuhr, Reinhold 23, 42
Nigeria 221, 284
Nogee, J. L. 76n
non-fuel minerals 224, 226
nonkilling society 172-174, 182-183; economic basis of 179-180
Nonproliferation Treaty (NPT) 203
non-rational decision factors 4, 153, 187
nonstate actors 24
nonviolence 1, 172, 179-181; causes of 172, 182; alternatives of, 5, 176, 181; knowledge of 180-183, 279-83
nonviolent revolution 177-178
normative dimensions 21, 29
North, Robert C. 48, 55, 78, 222
Notestein, Frank W. 278
nuclear war, threat of 5; fears of 20; deterrence of 21
nuclear winter 227-228, 229

Odum, Howard T. 40
Oechsli, Frank W. 278
O'Connor, James 250n
Oldendick, Robert 100, 103
Opp, Karl-Dieter 162
optimism/pessimism. See Normative Dimension
Organization of Economic Cooperation and Development (OECD) 219, 250, 253, 255, 256
Organization of Petroleum Exporting Countries (OPEC) 220
Organski, A. F. K. 47, 50, 55, 252
Orwell, George 41
Osgood, Charles 193
Osgood, Robert 140
Ottoman Empire 82; See also Turkey

Paige, Glenn H. 4-5
Pakistan 282, 285
Pareto, Vilfredo 41
partisan groups 4, 149-150, 155, 157-159, 161, 162, 165; violence of 150, 164
pathological social processes 5, 185, 192; mechanisms of 192-193
Peckinpah, Sam 173
Persian Gulf 219
Peru 285, 288
Pastel, Eduard 241
physical reductionism 35-38, 45, 58, 60
physicalist biology 39, 58
Pindyck, Robert 280n
Plato 14, 48, 49
Plimak, E. G. 177
Podhoretz, Norman 99

polarity 3, 26–27, 46, 49, 75–81, 84–89, 93
political economy 29
population/resource issue types 218–229
population, size and attributes 218–219; rate of growth 290–291; forecasts of 291; See also fertility
Portugal 48, 50
post-realism 29
power transition theory 47
pragmatism 13, 16, 17
Preston, Samuel H. 276n
"Prisoners Dilemma," game of 186–187
Prussia 82, 138

Quigley, Carroll 47, 49, 50, 53, 56

Rabb, T. K. 214n
Rapkin, D. P. 76
rate of natural increase (RNI) 283, 284, 285, 290
rational decision factors 4, 153, 158, 165, 186
Reagan, Ronald 249
realism vs. idealism 14–31
realist paradigm 2, 14–19
regimes, international 1, 29, 227
repression 4, 149, 151, 155, 165; structures of 4, 150, 160–161, 167, 168; policy of 154, 164
resource bases, sustainability of 224–226, 230
resource distribution and access 219–221
resource growth scenarios 251
"resource wars" 219–220
Ricardo, David 38
Richardson, Lewis Fry 39, 47, 62, 65, 83, 126, 127, 130, 133, 144
Ridker, R. G. 224n
Rose, Richard 248, 249, 252, 268
Rosecrance, Richard N. 47, 49n, 59n, 76

Rosenau, James 12, 100, 103, 106, 121, 126
Roskin, Michael 102, 106
Rotberg, R. I. 218
Rubinfield, Daniel 280
Ruggie, John Gerard 12, 233
Rummel, R. J. 13, 39
Russell, M. 224
Russett, Bruce 220n
Russia 46, 49, 50, 79, 82, 138, 158, 160; See also Soviet Union
Ryder, Norman B. 279

Sagan, Carl 227n
Saint-Simon, Claude-Henri 66
SALT I 198
SALT II 198
SALT/START process 199
Sambunaris G. 220n
Saunders, Peter 253
Schmid, Alex P. 154n
Schneider, S. H. 228
Schoenberg, R. 84
Schuman, Howard 102
Schumpeter, Joseph 250
Sharp, Gene 171, 178
Simon J. L. 216, 223, 225
Singer, J. David 53, 76, 77, 83, 84, 126, 130, 131, 132, 133, 144, 258
Sivard, Ruth Leger 250n
Small, Melvin 53, 77, 83, 84, 126, 130, 132, 133, 144
Smith, Adam 25, 42, 60
Smith, Herbert L. 284
Smoke, R. 94
Snyder, G. P. 76n
Social Darwinism 25
social thermodynamics 40, 43, 53
socioeconomic cleavages and coercion 159–160; and violent conflict 218
sociophysics 38
Socrates 14
Solidarity 171
Solzhenitsyn, Alexander 160
Soodak, H. 38, 60

Sophists 21
Sorokin, Pitirim I. 46, 48, 49, 53, 84, 127, 133, 214n
Soule, George 24
South Africa 159, 223, 224
Soviet Union 82, 104, 105, 106, 112, 117, 173, 178, 180, 182, 185–196, 197, 198, 199, 201, 203, 204, 205, 218, 219, 253, 256; See also Russia
Snow, C. P. 35
Snyder, David 150, 157, 162
Spain 46, 49, 82, 138, 139
spectroscopy 52–54
Spencer, Herbert 49, 66
Spengler, Oswald 46, 48, 49, 53
Sperlich, Peter 102
Sprout, H. 216, 218, 222
Sprout, M. 216, 218, 222
Srikantan, K. S. 274n
Sri Lanka, 182, 274, 284, 285
Stalin, Josef 23, 175
Starr, Harvey 130
state terrorism 151
Stohl, Michael 151, 153, 154, 155, 164n
Stoto, Michael A. 285
Strinkowski, Nicholas 162
structural realism 14, 29–30
structural violence 150
supply-side economics 150
Sweden 46, 49, 82, 249, 255

Taiwan 285, 291
Tanzania 285
Tarchys, Daniel 249
Taylor, Charles Lewis 39, 162, 164
terrorism 153, 155, 158–159, 161; definition of 159, 244
Thailand 289
Third World 3, 4, 99, 134, 149, 152, 165, 171, 226; growth in urban populations of 223
Thirty Years' War 21
Thompson, D. 78, 79
Thompson, R. L. 220n
Thompson, S. L. 228n
Thompson, William R. 76, 82

Thrasymachus 14
Thucydides 3, 14
Thurow, Lester C. 253
Tilton, J. E. 220, 221, 224
time frames 6, 51–52; and issue types 213–217, 233; and appropriate policy response 213; conjunctural 215, 216, 221, 226, 229, 230; incremenal 215, 216, 221, 226, 229, 230; secular 215, 217, 229
time scalings 51, 53, 63
Tims, Wouter 241
Tilly, Charles 150, 151, 162, 164
Tojo 191
Toynbee, Arnold 46, 48, 49, 129
transnationalism 1, 4, 20, 26, 29
Trist, E. L. 219, 233
Turco, R. P. 227
Turkey 138, 277, 280; See also Ottoman Empire
Tunisia 270

Uganda 277, 280, 291
United Nations 198, 223, 231, 241, 273, 274, 275, 276, 282, 283, 284, 285, 288, 290
United States 14, 17, 18, 20, 23, 24, 29, 46, 48, 49, 50, 53, 82, 99–123, 126, 133, 163, 174, 178, 179, 180, 181, 182, 185–196, 197, 198, 199, 201, 202, 203, 216, 218, 219, 220, 229, 230, 249, 251, 255, 261
United States Arms Control and Disarmament Agency 198
United States Congress 223

value-in-trade, See conservational variables
Venezuela 285
verifiability 201
Vico, Giambattista 53
Vietnam 20, 99–123, 251, 283; legacy of 6, 99–101, 113, 122, 122–123, 126, 132; lessons of 99, 107, 112
violence, by states and opposition groups 171–175, 179, 181, 182; See also coercion

violent conflict, cycles of 5, 6; patterns of, 6
von Treitschke, Heinrich 13

Wagner, Adolph 249, 254
Walbroeck, Jean 241n
Wallerstein, Immanuel 39, 42, 48, 49, 56, 82
Waltz, Kenneth N. 27, 28, 30-31, 34, 41, 43, 80, 135, 227
war 13, 25, 27, 50, 51, 54, 68, 69; seriousness of 3; related to frequency of 3, 79-99; prevention of measures 52; war-weariness, concept of 3, 6, 132-134, 135; hypothesis 130-132, 134-135, 136, 137, 138, 139-140, 145, 148
Warsaw Pact 193, 195, 252, 256
Washington Naval Agreement 198, 199
Wayman, F. W. 76n
Weber, Max 44
Wells, Robert A. 3, 6
Wesson, Robert G. 48, 49, 54, 56

Wight, Martin 46, 48, 49, 50, 54
Wilcox, J. G. 218n
Wildavsky, Aaron 254
Wilkinson, David 2, 3, 39, 42, 43, 49, 50, 56, 64, 66
Williamson, J. G. 226n
Wilson, Woodrow 27
Wilsonians 16, 27
Wittkopf, Eugene R. 100, 103
Wolfers, Arnold 18
Woods, Frederick Adams 133
World Bank 210, 219, 221, 226, 227, 241, 251, 274, 275, 283
world system analysis 48
World War I 16, 126, 128, 200
World War II 15, 16, 22, 56, 100, 102, 104, 122, 181, 198
Wright, Quincy 77, 133, 222

Zald, Mayer N. 162
Zaire 285; See also Congo
Zerubavel, E. 214
Zhang Yiping 178
Zimmerman, Ekkart 163

About the Editor and Contributors

DAGOBERT L. BRITO is Peterkin Professor of Economics at Rice University. He is the coeditor of *Strategies for Managing Nuclear Proliferation—Economic and Political Issues* (1983).

THOMAS P. CUSACK is affiliated with the Science Center in Berlin, West Germany.

PHILLIPS CUTRIGHT is Professor of Sociology at Indiana University, Bloomington. He is the author of numerous works on demography.

MORTON DEUTSCH is Edward Lee Thorndike Professor of Psychology and Education at Teachers College, Columbia University, and the author of numerous books including *The Resolution of Conflict* and *Distributive Justice: A Social-Psychological Perspective* (1985).

YALE FERGUSON, Professor of Political Science at Rutgers University—Newark, is the coauthor of *The Web of World Politics: Nonstate Actors in the Global System* (1976), the coeditor of *Continuing Issues in International Politics* (1973), the editor of *Contemporary Inter-American Relations* (1972), and the author of numerous articles and essays dealing with Latin America. He is currently working on a book, *The Elusive Quest: Theory and International Relations*, with Richard W. Mansbach.

TED ROBERT GURR is Professor of Political Science and Director of the Center for Comparative Politics at the University of Colorado (Boulder). The author/editor of a dozen books and monographs on polilitical conflict, governmental authority and performance, and criminal justice, he has recently completed (with Desmond S. King) a book on *The State and the City*.

BARRY B. HUGHES holds the rank of Professor at the Graduate School of International Studies, University of Denver. He has consulted for the governments of West Germany, Iran, and Egypt, as well as for agencies in the U.S. government, and is the author of *The Domestic Context of American Foreign Policy* (1978), *World Modeling* (1980), *World Futures* (1985), as well as numerous articles.

ARTHUR S. IBERALL has had an extensive career in research and development in government at the National Bureau at Standards; in industry, directing research; in his own research and development company; and finally in academia. These components have been assembled to attempt to create a general physical science for all complex systems.

MICHAEL D. INTRILIGATOR is Professor of Economics and Political Science and Director of the Center for International and Strategic Affairs at the University of California, Los Angeles. He is the author of *Strategy in a Missile War* (1967) and coeditor of *National Security and International Stability* (1983) and *Strategies for Managing Nuclear Proliferation—Economic and Political Issues* (1983).

MARGARET P. KARNS is Associate Professor of Political Science and Director of the Center for International Studies at the University of Dayton. She is currently working on a book on *The United States and International Organizations: Changing Patterns of Instrumentality and Influence* with Karen A. Mingst.

JACK S. LEVY is Associate Professor of Government at the University of Texas at Austin. He is the author of *War in the Modern Great Power system, 1495-1975*, as well as numerous articles.

RICHARD W. MANSBACH is Chair and Professor of the Department of Political Science at Rutgers University. His recent publications include *Structure and Process of International Politics* (1973), *The Web of World Politics* (1976), and *In Search of Theory: A New Paradigm for Global Politics* (1981). He is currently writing a book on the decline of U.S.-European relations and, with Yale Ferguson, is completing a manuscript entitled *The Elusive Quest: Theory and International Relations*.

T. CLIFTON MORGAN is Assistant Professor of Political Science at Florida State University. He has authored or coauthored articles dealing with the application of spatial modeling to the study of bargaining in international crises and the empirical analysis of the causes of war.

GLENN D. PAIGE is Professor of Political Science, University of Hawaii at Manoa. He is author of *The Korean Decision: June 24-30, 1950* (1968), *Political Leadership* (1972), *The Scientific Study of Political Leadership* (1977), and "On Values and Science: *The Korean Decision* Reconsidered." *American Political Science Review*, 71 (1977).

JOHN GERARD RUGGIE is Professor of Political Science and a member of the Institute of War and Peace Studies as well as of the International Economics Research Center at Columbia University. He has published widely on various theoretical and empirical aspects of change and continuity in the world political economy, and consults frequently on the policy implications of these issues for U.S. and U.N. agencies.

HERBERT L. SMITH is Assistant Professor of Sociology at Indiana University, Bloomington. Prior to joining the faculty at Indiana, he served as a Visiting Research Fellow in the Population Sciences Division of the Rockefeller Foundation.

ROBERT A. WELLS is Visiting Assistant Professor at the University of New Orleans.

DAVID WILKINSON is Professor of Political Science at the University of California, Los Angeles. His books include *MALRAUX: An Essay in Political Criticism* (1967), *Comparative Foreign Relations: Framework and Methods* (1969), *Revolutionary Civil War: The Elements of Victory and Defeat*, and *Deadly Quarrels* (1980).

has published widely on various theoretical and empirical aspects of change and continuity in the world political economy, and consults frequently on the policy implications of these issues for U.S. and U.N. agencies.

HERBERT L. SMITH is Assistant Professor of Sociology at Indiana University, Bloomington. Prior to joining the faculty at Indiana, he served as a Visiting Research Fellow in the Population Sciences Division of the Rockefeller Foundation.

ROBERT A. WELLS is Visiting Assistant Professor at the University of New Orleans.

DAVID WILKINSON is Professor of Political Science at the University of California, Los Angeles. His books include *MALRAUX: An Essay in Political Criticism* (1967), *Comparative Foreign Relations: Framework and Methods* (1969), *Revolutionary Civil War: The Elements of Victory and Defeat*, and *Deadly Quarrels* (1980).